DYKES AND SUNDRY OTHER CARBON-BASED LIFE-FORMS TO WATCH OUT FOR

Also by Alison Bechdel

Dykes To Watch Out For
More Dykes To Watch Out For
New, Improved Dykes To Watch Out For
Dykes To Watch Out For: The Sequel
Spawn of Dykes To Watch Out For
Unnatural Dykes To Watch Out For
Hot, Throbbing Dykes To Watch Out For
Split-Level Dykes To Watch Out For
The Indelible Alison Bechdel
Post-Dykes To Watch Out For

DYKES AND SUNDRY OTHER CARBON-BASED LIFE-FORMS TO WATCH OUT FOR

ALISON BECHDEL

alyson books
los angeles

Manufactured in Canada.

This trade paperback original is published by Alyson Publications,
P.O. Box 4371, Los Angeles, California 90078-4371.
Distribution in the United Kingdom by Turnaround Publisher Services Ltd.,
Unit 3, Olympia Trading Estate, Coburg Road, Wood Green,
London N22 6TZ England.

First edition: October 2003

03 04 05 06 07 **a** 10 9 8 7 6 5 4 3 2 1

ISBN 1-55583-828-6

Library of Congress Cataloging-in-Publication Data
Bechdel, Alison, 1960–
   Dykes and sundry other carbon-based
life-forms to watch out for / Alison Bechdel.
   ISBN 1-55583-828-6 (alk. paper)
   I. Title.
PN6728.D94B46 2003
741.5'973—DC21   2003052254

INTRODUCTION

ON THE OCCASION OF THE TWENTIETH ANNIVERSARY OF "DYKES TO WATCH OUT FOR"

PERHAPS IT'S TRITE OF ME TO OBSERVE THAT IT SEEMS LIKE JUST YESTERDAY WHEN I DREW MY FIRST DYKE TO WATCH OUT FOR. BUT 1983 DOES INDEED SEEM LIKE JUST YESTERDAY, IF ONLY BECAUSE TODAY SEEMS SO MUCH LIKE "1984," AS I WRITE THIS IN THE ORWELLIAN FOG OF BUSH'S SECOND GULF WAR.

I'LL TRY TO PUT THE "SHOCK AND AWE" BOMBING CAMPAIGN AND THE LATEST NEWSPEAK FROM THE HOMELAND SECURITY DEPARTMENT OUT OF MY MIND FOR A MOMENT, AND TURN MY ATTENTION BACK TWENTY YEARS TO WHAT'S STARTING TO LOOK LIKE THE HALCYON DAYS OF THE REAGAN ADMINISTRATION.

IT WAS A TRANSITIONAL PERIOD, AFTER ANITA BRYANT AND BEFORE "ON OUR BACKS." I WAS TWO YEARS OUT OF COLLEGE, WITH NO VISIBLE AMBITIONS IN LIFE BEYOND BEING A FULL-TIME LESBIAN -- A HIGHLY

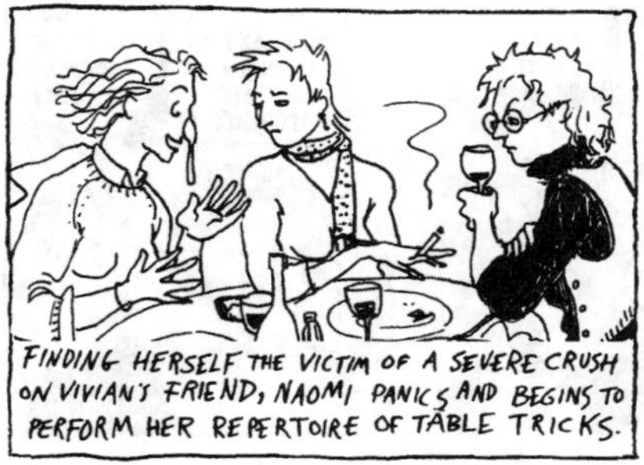
FINDING HERSELF THE VICTIM OF A SEVERE CRUSH ON VIVIAN'S FRIEND, NAOMI PANICS AND BEGINS TO PERFORM HER REPERTOIRE OF TABLE TRICKS.

1983

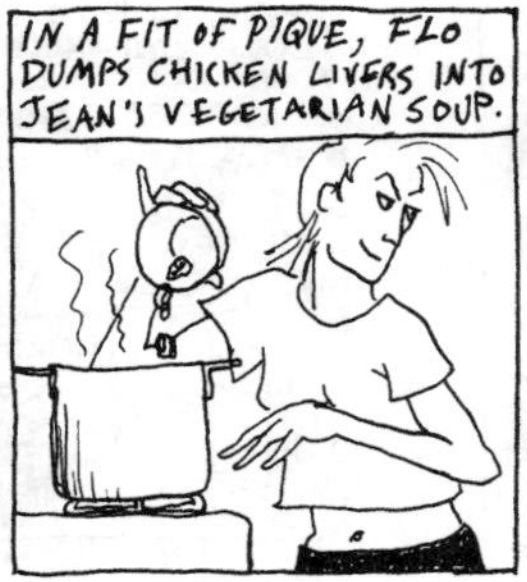
IN A FIT OF PIQUE, FLO DUMPS CHICKEN LIVERS INTO JEAN'S VEGETARIAN SOUP.

1984

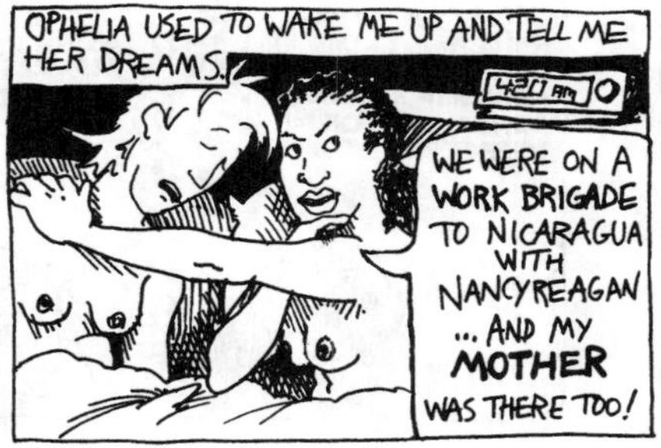
OPHELIA USED TO WAKE ME UP AND TELL ME HER DREAMS.
4:20 AM
WE WERE ON A WORK BRIGADE TO NICARAGUA WITH NANCY REAGAN ... AND MY MOTHER WAS THERE TOO!

1985

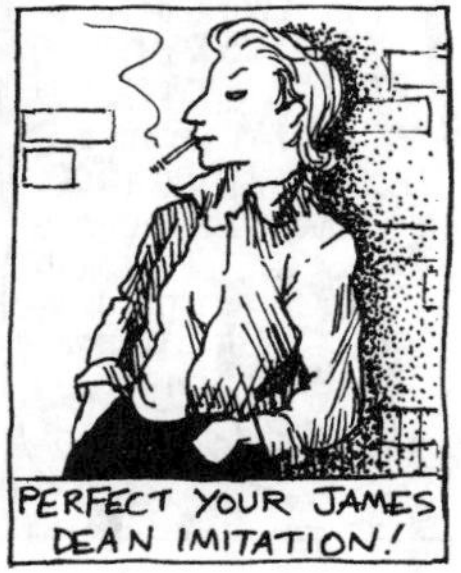
PERFECT YOUR JAMES DEAN IMITATION!

1986

GRATIFYING, IF NOT PARTICULARLY LUCRATIVE, OCCUPATION. BUT I FELT RICH WITH REVOLUTIONARY RESOLVE.

AT FIRST, I ADMIT, WHAT ATTRACTED ME ABOUT LESBIANISM WAS THE SEX. BUT I HAPPENED TO FALL IN WITH A ROUGH CROWD -- WOMEN WHO WERE ALWAYS THROWING BLOOD ON THE PENTAGON, OR BLOCKADING WALL STREET, OR GOING OFF TO NICARAGUA TO HELP THE SANDINISTAS WITH THE COFFEE HARVEST. WHILE I STOOD ON THE SIDELINES GAPING WITH AWE, IT BECAME CLEAR TO ME THAT SEX WAS MERELY THE TIP OF THE LESBIAN ICEBERG.

WHAT LURKED BENEATH WAS A WORLDVIEW, AN ENTIRE LOGICAL SYSTEM IN WHICH HOMOPHOBIA WAS INEXTRICABLY LINKED TO SEXISM AND RACISM AND MILITARISM AND CLASSISM AND IMPERIALISM. AND A FEW OTHER THINGS. AND THE BEAUTY OF IT WAS THIS: THAT IN ORDER TO ADDRESS ANY ONE OF THESE PROBLEMS, WE NEEDED TO ADDRESS THEM ALL. IT WAS A COMPELLING SCHEMA, AND IF IN MY EXCITEMENT I CONFUSED THE PERSONAL WITH THE POLITICAL, WELL, THAT WAS PART OF THE IDEA.

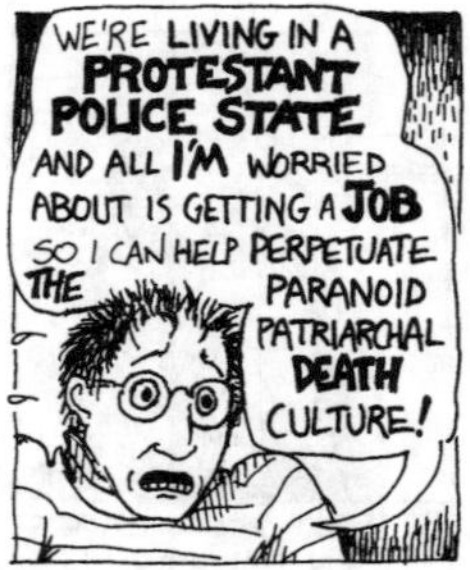
WE'RE LIVING IN A **PROTESTANT POLICE STATE** AND ALL **I'M** WORRIED ABOUT IS GETTING A **JOB** SO I CAN HELP PERPETUATE **THE** PARANOID PATRIARCHAL **DEATH** CULTURE!

1987

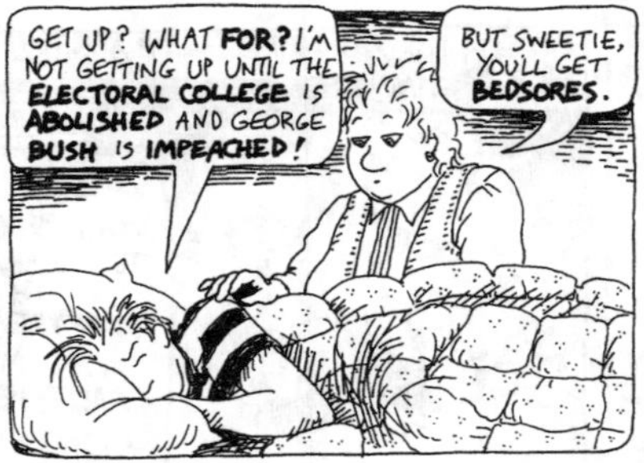
GET UP? WHAT **FOR?** I'M NOT GETTING UP UNTIL THE **ELECTORAL COLLEGE** IS **ABOLISHED** AND GEORGE **BUSH** IS **IMPEACHED**!
BUT SWEETIE, YOU'LL GET **BEDSORES**.

1988

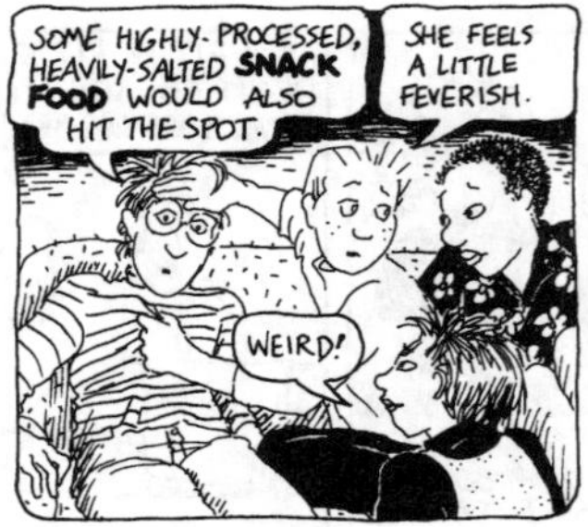
SOME HIGHLY-PROCESSED, HEAVILY-SALTED **SNACK FOOD** WOULD ALSO HIT THE SPOT.
SHE FEELS A LITTLE FEVERISH.
WEIRD!

1989

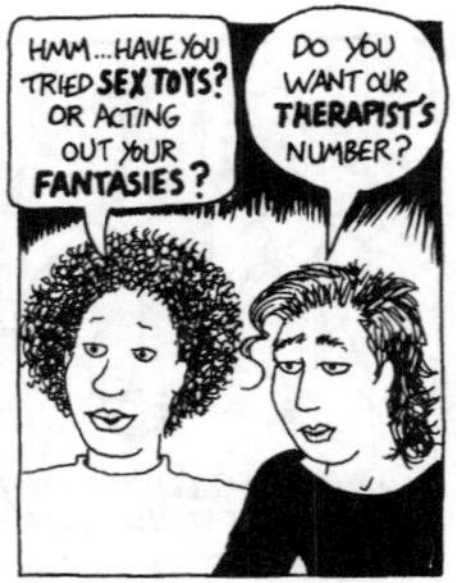
HMM... HAVE YOU TRIED **SEX TOYS?** OR ACTING OUT YOUR **FANTASIES?**
DO YOU WANT OUR **THERAPIST'S** NUMBER?

1990

IMAGINE MY SENSE OF PURPOSE WHEN ONE DAY IT OCCURRED TO ME TO HARNESS THE CENTRAL ORGANIZING PRINCIPLE OF MY EXISTENCE -- MY LESBIANISM -- TO MY SOLE OTHER INTEREST -- DRAWING SILLY PICTURES. THROUGH MY CARTOONS, I WOULD PROVE TO THE WORLD, OR AT LEAST OTHER LESBIANS -- OR, FAILING THAT, MYSELF -- THAT DYKES WERE HUMAN.

WHEN I WAS JUST GETTING STARTED, SOME STRAIGHT CARTOONISTS SAID TO ME, "YOUR STUFF ISN'T BAD. HAVE YOU EVER THOUGHT ABOUT DOING COMICS FOR A GENERAL AUDIENCE?" THIS IRKED ME, BECAUSE I THOUGHT I WAS DOING COMICS FOR A GENERAL AUDIENCE. PERHAPS IT WAS THE TITLE, BUT I'VE NEVER INTENDED MY CARTOONS TO BE ONLY FOR DYKES. YES, THEY'RE ABOUT DYKES. SO? SURELY IF I COULD SIT THROUGH A BRUCE WILLIS MOVIE, JOE BLOW COULD READ A LESBIAN COMIC STRIP.

JOE BLOW, HOWEVER, WAS SLOWER TO EMBRACE MY OEUVRE THAN I'D ANTICIPATED, IN MY YOUTHFUL NAÏVETÉ. (PERHAPS IF I DIDN'T USE SO MUCH FRENCH.) BUT I REMAINED UNCOMPROMISING IN MY

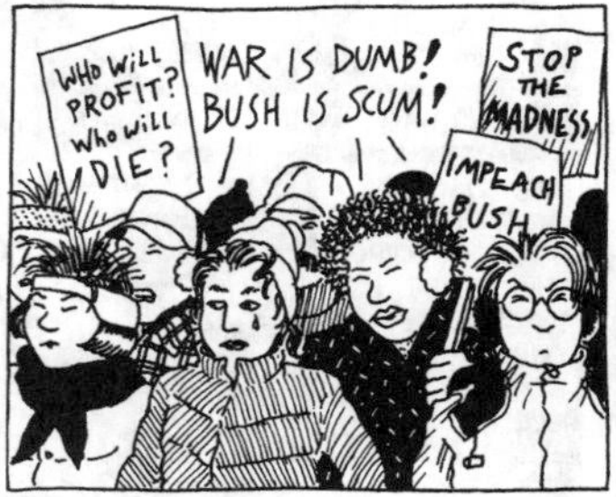
Who will PROFIT? Who will DIE?
WAR IS DUMB! BUSH IS SCUM!
STOP THE MADNESS
IMPEACH BUSH

1991

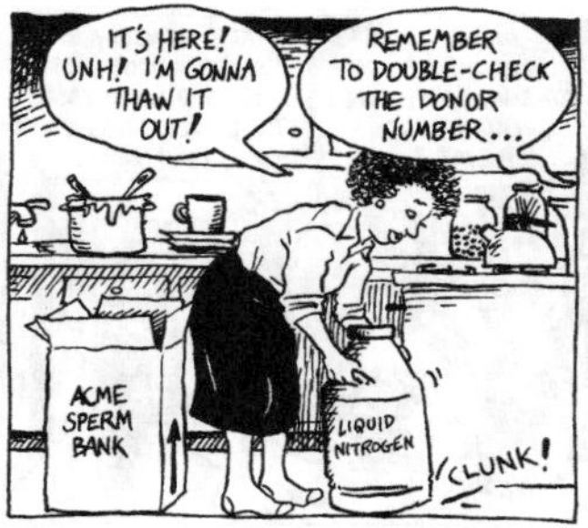
IT'S HERE! UNH! I'M GONNA THAW IT OUT!
REMEMBER TO DOUBLE-CHECK THE DONOR NUMBER...
ACME SPERM BANK
LIQUID NITROGEN
CLUNK!

1992

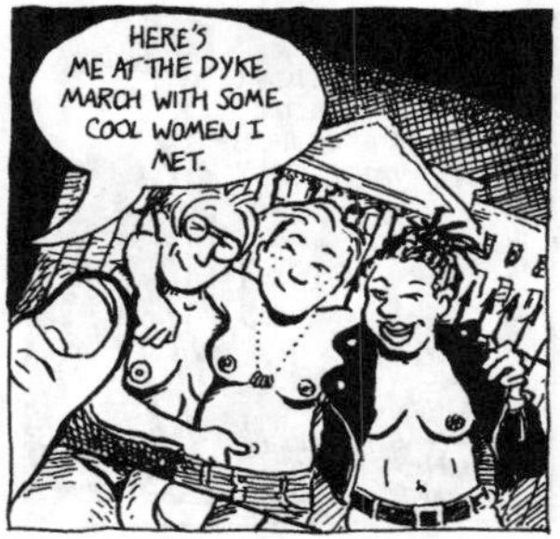
HERE'S ME AT THE DYKE MARCH WITH SOME COOL WOMEN I MET.

1993

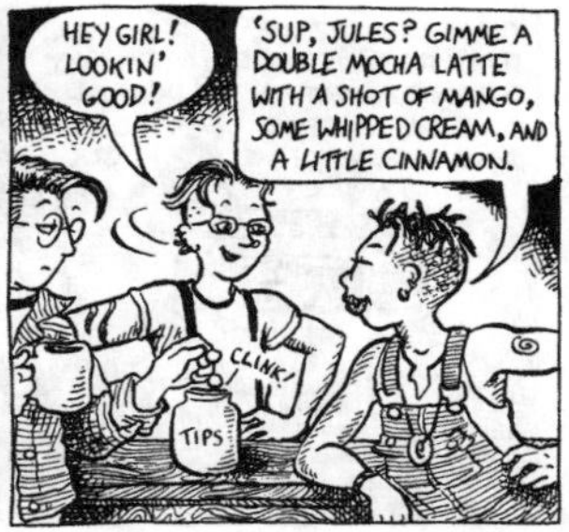
HEY GIRL! LOOKIN' GOOD!
'SUP, JULES? GIMME A DOUBLE MOCHA LATTE WITH A SHOT OF MANGO, SOME WHIPPED CREAM, AND A LITTLE CINNAMON.
CLINK!
TIPS

1994

INSISTENCE THAT LESBIAN STORIES WERE HUMAN STORIES, AND IF PEOPLE DIDN'T LIKE IT THEY COULD JUST READ "THE FAMILY CIRCUS."

THROUGH THE SHIFTING SANDS OF TIME -- AS I WATCHED OUR LIBERATION MOVEMENT FLOWER INTO FIRST A NICHE MARKET, THEN A SITCOM PUNCHLINE, THEN A FULL-BLOWN SITCOM PREMISE, BEFORE WITHERING OUT OF FASHION LIKE A PIERCED SEPTUM -- MY NEED TO BE REASSURED THAT I WAS HUMAN LESSENED CONSIDERABLY. THIS WAS APPARENTLY TRUE FOR OTHERS, TOO, AS THE LOCUS OF QUEER ACTIVISM MOVED FROM THE UNIVERSITIES TO THE HIGH SCHOOLS AND THEN TO THE MIDDLE SCHOOLS.

LATELY, THE YOUNG ACTIVISTS I MEET SEEM TO HAVE CUT THEIR TEETH ORGANIZING GAY-STRAIGHT ALLIANCES IN THEIR DAY-CARE CENTERS. AND MANY OF THEM HAVE MOVED BEYOND THE NEED FOR EVEN THE CATEGORIES "GAY" AND "STRAIGHT." I'VE RELUCTANTLY COME TO ACCEPT THAT THE WHOLE POINT OF A LIBERATION MOVEMENT, AFTER ALL, IS TO RENDER ITSELF OBSOLETE. BUT I WAS RESISTANT AT FIRST.

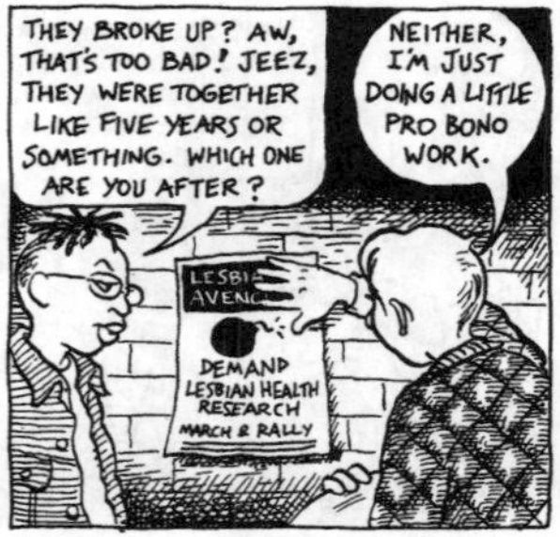
THEY BROKE UP? AW, THAT'S TOO BAD! JEEZ, THEY WERE TOGETHER LIKE FIVE YEARS OR SOMETHING. WHICH ONE ARE YOU AFTER?
NEITHER, I'M JUST DOING A LITTLE PRO BONO WORK.
DEMAND LESBIAN HEALTH RESEARCH
MARCH & RALLY

1995

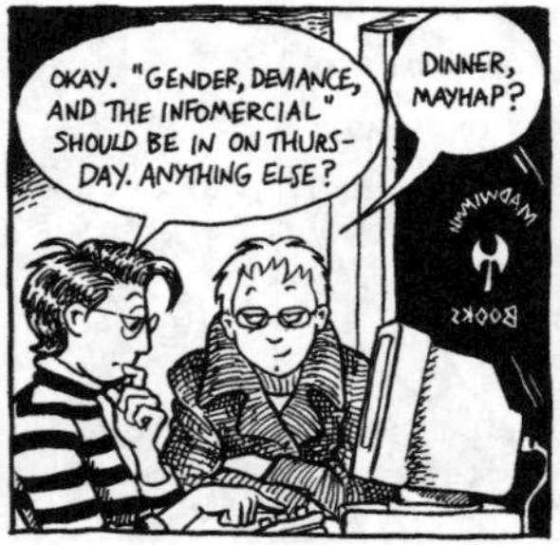
OKAY. "GENDER, DEVIANCE, AND THE INFOMERCIAL" SHOULD BE IN ON THURSDAY. ANYTHING ELSE?
DINNER, MAYHAP?

1996

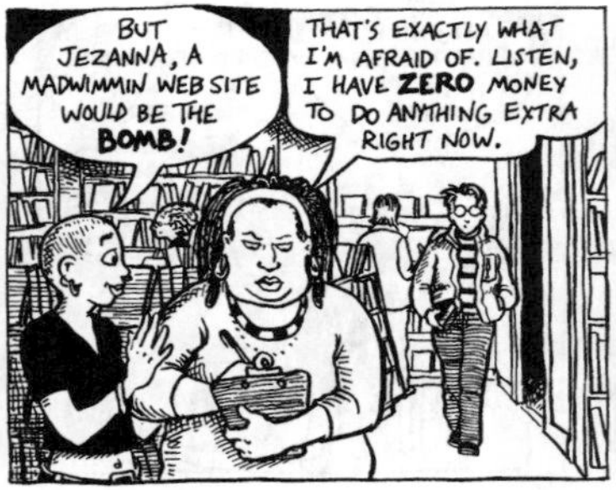
BUT JEZANNA, A MADWIMMIN WEB SITE WOULD BE THE BOMB!
THAT'S EXACTLY WHAT I'M AFRAID OF. LISTEN, I HAVE ZERO MONEY TO DO ANYTHING EXTRA RIGHT NOW.

1997

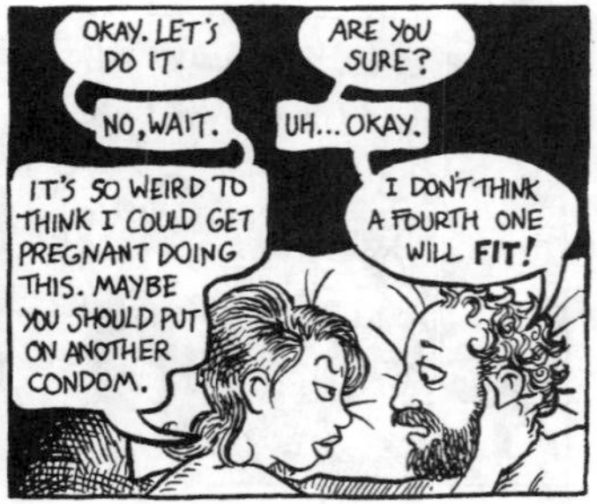
OKAY. LET'S DO IT.
ARE YOU SURE?
NO, WAIT.
UH... OKAY.
IT'S SO WEIRD TO THINK I COULD GET PREGNANT DOING THIS. MAYBE YOU SHOULD PUT ON ANOTHER CONDOM.
I DON'T THINK A FOURTH ONE WILL FIT!

1998

IF MY MISSION WAS TO DRAW A COMIC STRIP ABOUT A SUBCULTURE, AND THAT SUBCULTURE WAS DISINTEGRATING AROUND MY EARS, WAS I GOING TO HAVE TO GET A REAL JOB?

FORTUNATELY, NOT YET. AND WHATEVER HAPPENS TO THE SUBCULTURE, I FEEL AS STRONGLY AS I EVER DID THAT MY CARTOONS ADDRESS "GENERAL" ISSUES. RACISM, SEXISM, MILITARISM, CLASSISM, IMPERIALISM, AND HOMOPHOBIA ARE ALIVE AND WELL, MORE SO THAN THEY WERE UNDER REAGAN, TWENTY LONG RIP VAN WINKLE YEARS AGO. BUT I KNOW NOW THAT YOU DON'T HAVE TO BE A LESBIAN, IN THE TECHNICAL SENSE, TO WANT TO DO SOMETHING ABOUT THEM. YOU JUST HAVE TO BE A HUMAN. OR AT THE VERY LEAST, A CARBON-BASED LIFE-FORM.

ALISON BECHDEL
MARCH 2003

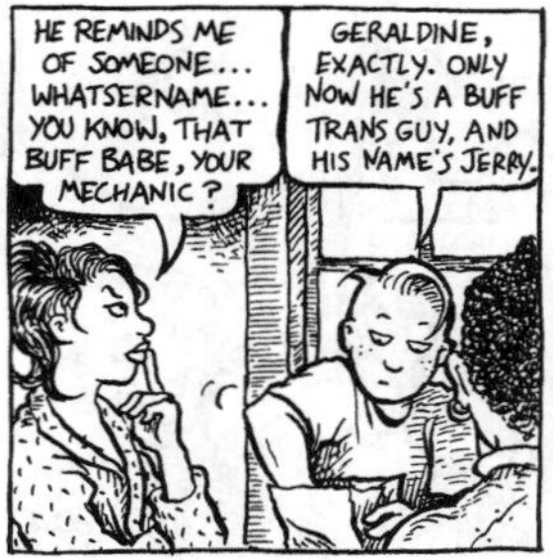
HE REMINDS ME OF SOMEONE... WHATSERNAME... YOU KNOW, THAT BUFF BABE, YOUR MECHANIC?
GERALDINE, EXACTLY. ONLY NOW HE'S A BUFF TRANS GUY, AND HIS NAME'S JERRY.

1999

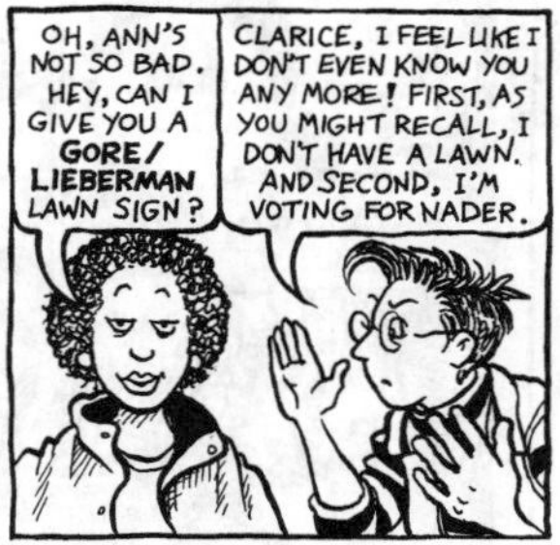
OH, ANN'S NOT SO BAD. HEY, CAN I GIVE YOU A **GORE/LIEBERMAN** LAWN SIGN?
CLARICE, I FEEL LIKE I DON'T EVEN KNOW YOU ANY MORE! FIRST, AS YOU MIGHT RECALL, I DON'T HAVE A LAWN. AND SECOND, I'M VOTING FOR NADER.

2000

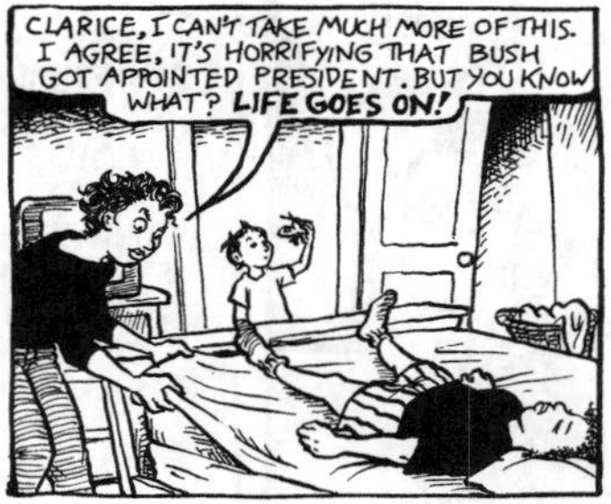
CLARICE, I CAN'T TAKE MUCH MORE OF THIS.
I AGREE, IT'S HORRIFYING THAT BUSH GOT APPOINTED PRESIDENT. BUT YOU KNOW WHAT? **LIFE GOES ON!**

2001

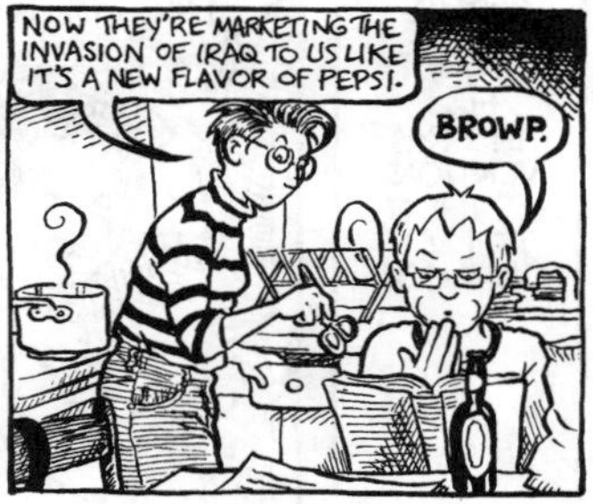
NOW THEY'RE MARKETING THE INVASION OF IRAQ TO US LIKE IT'S A NEW FLAVOR OF PEPSI.
BROWP.

2002

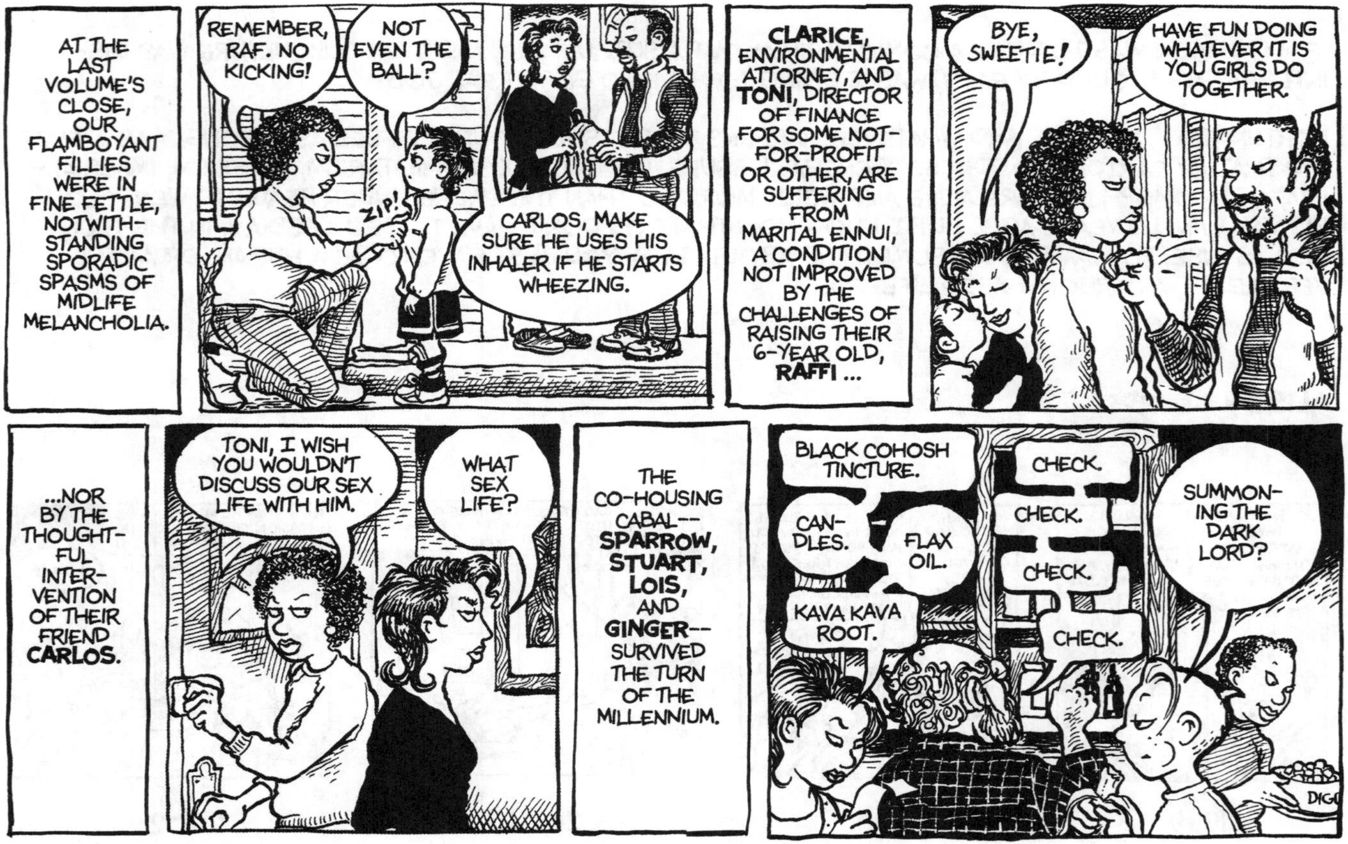
AT THE LAST VOLUME'S CLOSE, OUR FLAMBOYANT FILLIES WERE IN FINE FETTLE, NOTWITHSTANDING SPORADIC SPASMS OF MIDLIFE MELANCHOLIA.
REMEMBER, RAF. NO KICKING!
NOT EVEN THE BALL?
ZIP!
CARLOS, MAKE SURE HE USES HIS INHALER IF HE STARTS WHEEZING.
CLARICE, ENVIRONMENTAL ATTORNEY, AND TONI, DIRECTOR OF FINANCE FOR SOME NOT-FOR-PROFIT OR OTHER, ARE SUFFERING FROM MARITAL ENNUI, A CONDITION NOT IMPROVED BY THE CHALLENGES OF RAISING THEIR 6-YEAR OLD, RAFFI ...
BYE, SWEETIE!
HAVE FUN DOING WHATEVER IT IS YOU GIRLS DO TOGETHER.
...NOR BY THE THOUGHTFUL INTERVENTION OF THEIR FRIEND CARLOS.
TONI, I WISH YOU WOULDN'T DISCUSS OUR SEX LIFE WITH HIM.
WHAT SEX LIFE?
THE CO-HOUSING CABAL--SPARROW, STUART, LOIS, AND GINGER--SURVIVED THE TURN OF THE MILLENNIUM.
BLACK COHOSH TINCTURE.
CHECK.
CANDLES.
FLAX OIL.
CHECK.
CHECK.
KAVA KAVA ROOT.
CHECK.
SUMMONING THE DARK LORD?

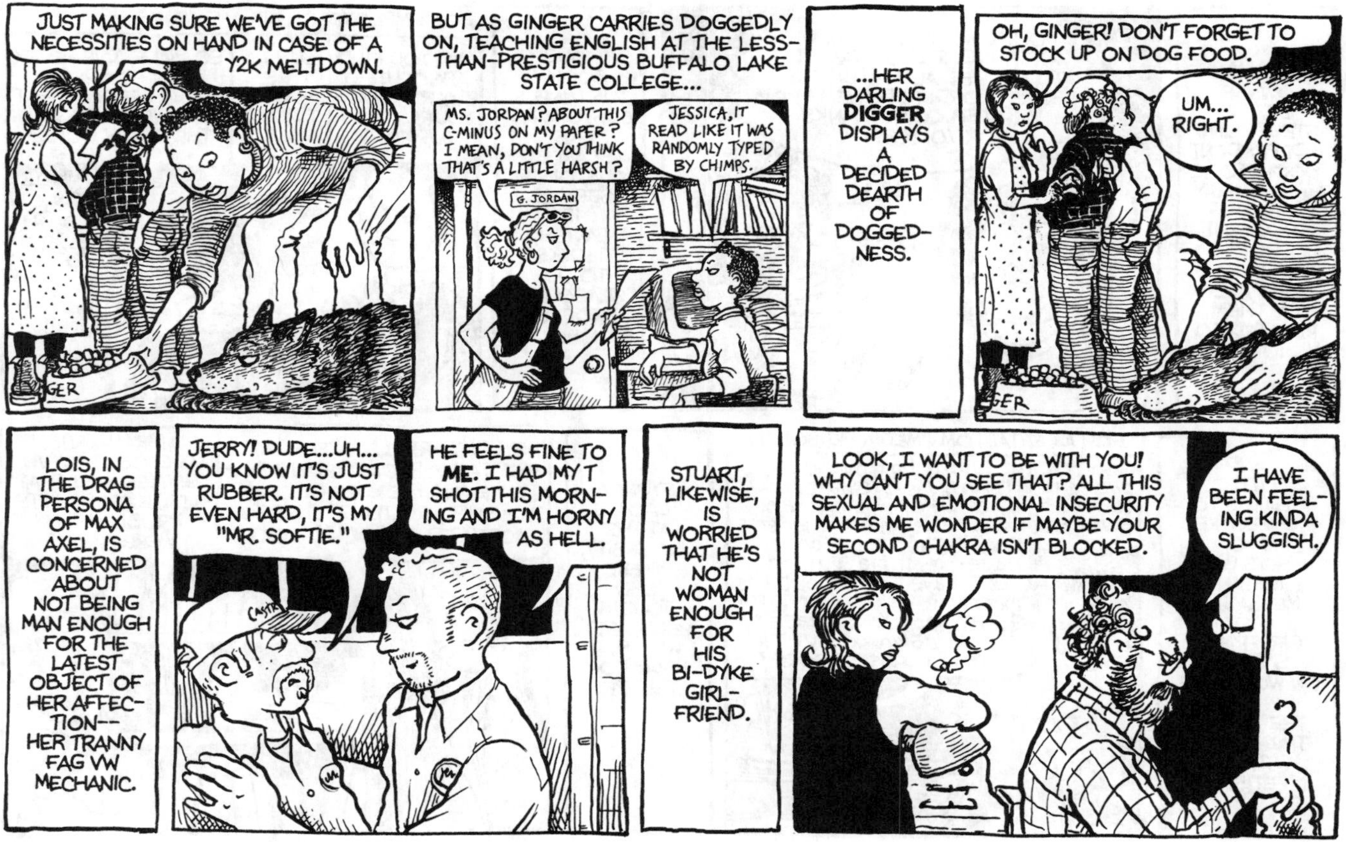

JUST MAKING SURE WE'VE GOT THE NECESSITIES ON HAND IN CASE OF A Y2K MELTDOWN.
BUT AS GINGER CARRIES DOGGEDLY ON, TEACHING ENGLISH AT THE LESS-THAN-PRESTIGIOUS BUFFALO LAKE STATE COLLEGE...
MS. JORDAN? ABOUT THIS C-MINUS ON MY PAPER? I MEAN, DON'T YOU THINK THAT'S A LITTLE HARSH?
JESSICA, IT READ LIKE IT WAS RANDOMLY TYPED BY CHIMPS.
G. JORDAN
...HER DARLING DIGGER DISPLAYS A DECIDED DEARTH OF DOGGEDNESS.
OH, GINGER! DON'T FORGET TO STOCK UP ON DOG FOOD.
UM... RIGHT.
LOIS, IN THE DRAG PERSONA OF MAX AXEL, IS CONCERNED ABOUT NOT BEING MAN ENOUGH FOR THE LATEST OBJECT OF HER AFFECTION-- HER TRANNY FAG VW MECHANIC.
JERRY! DUDE...UH... YOU KNOW IT'S JUST RUBBER. IT'S NOT EVEN HARD, IT'S MY "MR. SOFTIE."
HE FEELS FINE TO ME. I HAD MY T SHOT THIS MORNING AND I'M HORNY AS HELL.
STUART, LIKEWISE, IS WORRIED THAT HE'S NOT WOMAN ENOUGH FOR HIS BI-DYKE GIRLFRIEND.
LOOK, I WANT TO BE WITH YOU! WHY CAN'T YOU SEE THAT? ALL THIS SEXUAL AND EMOTIONAL INSECURITY MAKES ME WONDER IF MAYBE YOUR SECOND CHAKRA ISN'T BLOCKED.
I HAVE BEEN FEELING KINDA SLUGGISH.

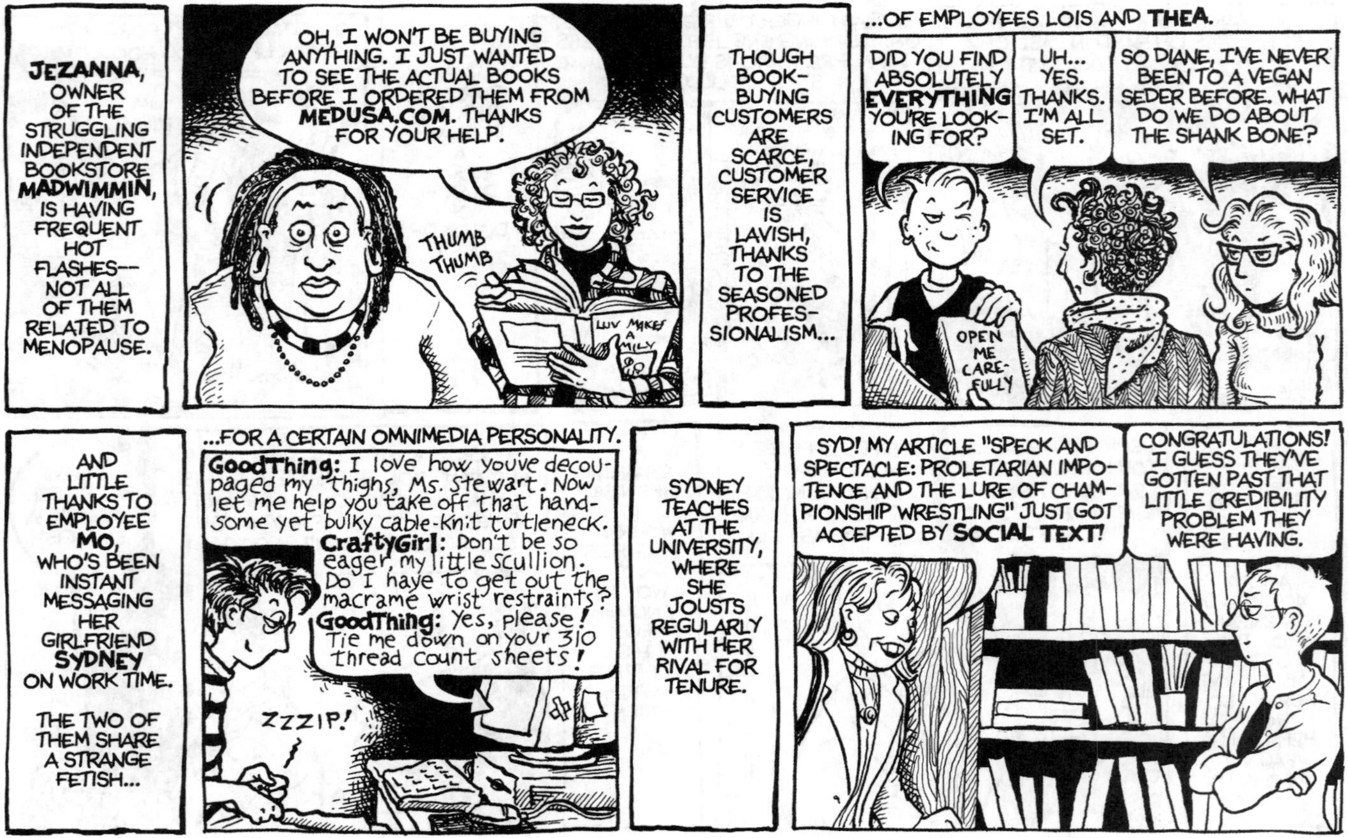

JEZANNA, OWNER OF THE STRUGGLING INDEPENDENT BOOKSTORE MADWIMMIN, IS HAVING FREQUENT HOT FLASHES-- NOT ALL OF THEM RELATED TO MENOPAUSE.
OH, I WON'T BE BUYING ANYTHING. I JUST WANTED TO SEE THE ACTUAL BOOKS BEFORE I ORDERED THEM FROM MEDUSA.COM. THANKS FOR YOUR HELP.
THUMB THUMB
LUV MAKES A MILY
THOUGH BOOK-BUYING CUSTOMERS ARE SCARCE, CUSTOMER SERVICE IS LAVISH, THANKS TO THE SEASONED PROFESSIONALISM...
...OF EMPLOYEES LOIS AND THEA.
DID YOU FIND ABSOLUTELY EVERYTHING YOU'RE LOOKING FOR?
UH... YES. THANKS. I'M ALL SET.
SO DIANE, I'VE NEVER BEEN TO A VEGAN SEDER BEFORE. WHAT DO WE DO ABOUT THE SHANK BONE?
OPEN ME CAREFULLY
AND LITTLE THANKS TO EMPLOYEE MO, WHO'S BEEN INSTANT MESSAGING HER GIRLFRIEND SYDNEY ON WORK TIME.
THE TWO OF THEM SHARE A STRANGE FETISH...
...FOR A CERTAIN OMNIMEDIA PERSONALITY.
GoodThing: I love how you've decoupaged my thighs, Ms. Stewart. Now let me help you take off that handsome yet bulky cable-knit turtleneck.
CraftyGirl: Don't be so eager, my little scullion. Do I have to get out the macrame wrist restraints?
GoodThing: Yes, please! Tie me down on your 310 thread count sheets!
ZZZIP!
SYDNEY TEACHES AT THE UNIVERSITY, WHERE SHE JOUSTS REGULARLY WITH HER RIVAL FOR TENURE.
SYD! MY ARTICLE "SPECK AND SPECTACLE: PROLETARIAN IMPOTENCE AND THE LURE OF CHAMPIONSHIP WRESTLING" JUST GOT ACCEPTED BY SOCIAL TEXT!
CONGRATULATIONS! I GUESS THEY'VE GOTTEN PAST THAT LITTLE CREDIBILITY PROBLEM THEY WERE HAVING.

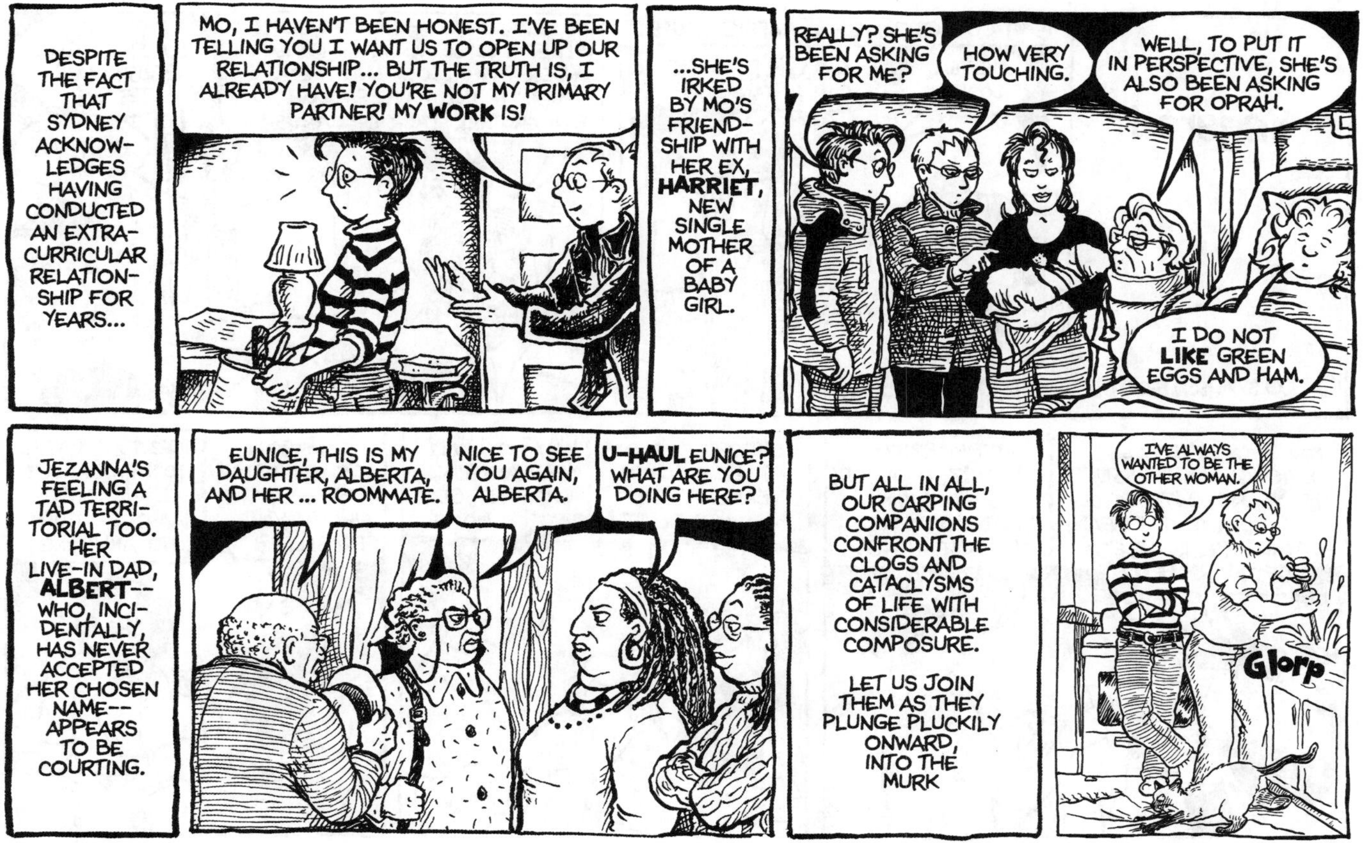
DESPITE THE FACT THAT SYDNEY ACKNOWLEDGES HAVING CONDUCTED AN EXTRA-CURRICULAR RELATIONSHIP FOR YEARS...
MO, I HAVEN'T BEEN HONEST. I'VE BEEN TELLING YOU I WANT US TO OPEN UP OUR RELATIONSHIP... BUT THE TRUTH IS, I ALREADY HAVE! YOU'RE NOT MY PRIMARY PARTNER! MY **WORK** IS!
...SHE'S IRKED BY MO'S FRIENDSHIP WITH HER EX, **HARRIET**, NEW SINGLE MOTHER OF A BABY GIRL.
REALLY? SHE'S BEEN ASKING FOR ME?
HOW VERY TOUCHING.
WELL, TO PUT IT IN PERSPECTIVE, SHE'S ALSO BEEN ASKING FOR OPRAH.
I DO NOT **LIKE** GREEN EGGS AND HAM.
JEZANNA'S FEELING A TAD TERRITORIAL TOO. HER LIVE-IN DAD, **ALBERT**-- WHO, INCIDENTALLY, HAS NEVER ACCEPTED HER CHOSEN NAME-- APPEARS TO BE COURTING.
EUNICE, THIS IS MY DAUGHTER, ALBERTA, AND HER ... ROOMMATE.
NICE TO SEE YOU AGAIN, ALBERTA.
U-HAUL EUNICE? WHAT ARE YOU DOING HERE?
BUT ALL IN ALL, OUR CARPING COMPANIONS CONFRONT THE CLOGS AND CATACLYSMS OF LIFE WITH CONSIDERABLE COMPOSURE.
LET US JOIN THEM AS THEY PLUNGE PLUCKILY ONWARD, INTO THE MURK
I'VE ALWAYS WANTED TO BE THE OTHER WOMAN.
Glorp

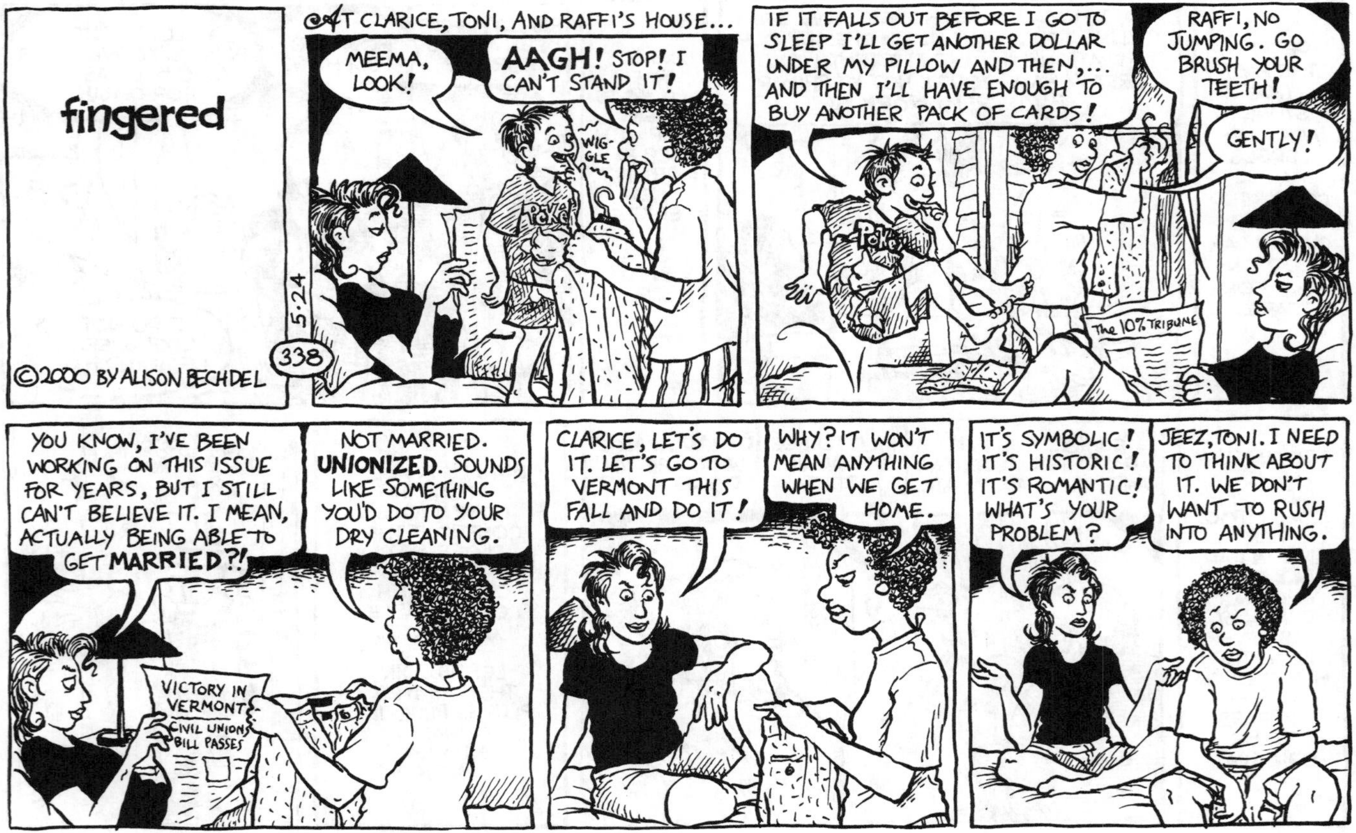
fingered
©2000 BY ALISON BECHDEL
338
5·24
AT CLARICE, TONI, AND RAFFI'S HOUSE...
MEEMA, LOOK!
AAGH! STOP! I CAN'T STAND IT!
WIG-GLE
IF IT FALLS OUT BEFORE I GO TO SLEEP I'LL GET ANOTHER DOLLAR UNDER MY PILLOW AND THEN,... AND THEN I'LL HAVE ENOUGH TO BUY ANOTHER PACK OF CARDS!
RAFFI, NO JUMPING. GO BRUSH YOUR TEETH!
GENTLY!
The 10% TRIBUNE
YOU KNOW, I'VE BEEN WORKING ON THIS ISSUE FOR YEARS, BUT I STILL CAN'T BELIEVE IT. I MEAN, ACTUALLY BEING ABLE TO GET MARRIED?!
NOT MARRIED. UNIONIZED. SOUNDS LIKE SOMETHING YOU'D DO TO YOUR DRY CLEANING.
VICTORY IN VERMONT
CIVIL UNIONS BILL PASSES
CLARICE, LET'S DO IT. LET'S GO TO VERMONT THIS FALL AND DO IT!
WHY? IT WON'T MEAN ANYTHING WHEN WE GET HOME.
IT'S SYMBOLIC! IT'S HISTORIC! IT'S ROMANTIC! WHAT'S YOUR PROBLEM?
JEEZ, TONI. I NEED TO THINK ABOUT IT. WE DON'T WANT TO RUSH INTO ANYTHING.

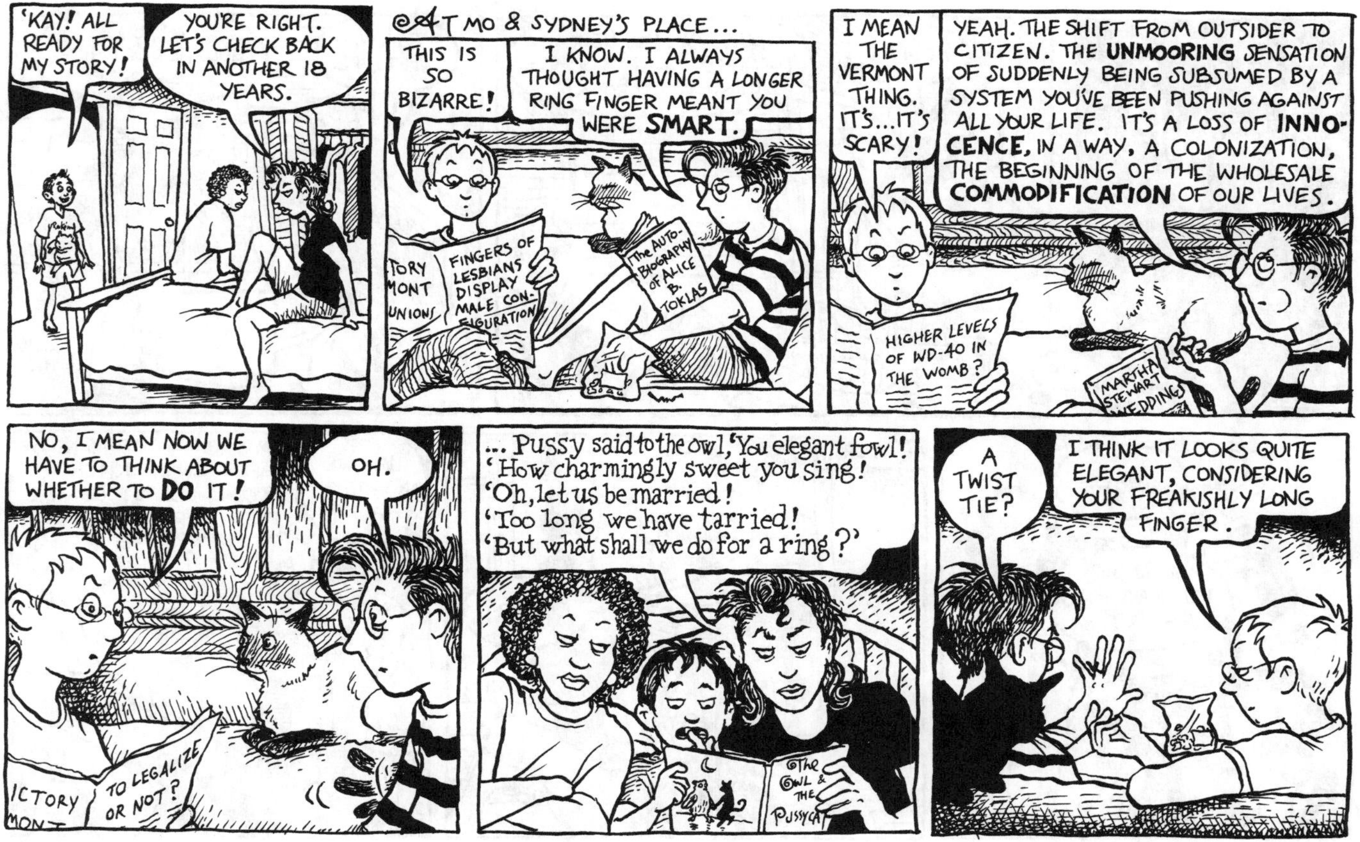
'KAY! ALL READY FOR MY STORY!
YOU'RE RIGHT. LET'S CHECK BACK IN ANOTHER 18 YEARS.
AT MO & SYDNEY'S PLACE...
THIS IS SO BIZARRE!
I KNOW. I ALWAYS THOUGHT HAVING A LONGER RING FINGER MEANT YOU WERE SMART.
FINGERS OF LESBIANS DISPLAY MALE CON-FIGURATION
The AUTO-BIOGRAPHY OF ALICE B. TOKLAS
I MEAN THE VERMONT THING. IT'S...IT'S SCARY!
YEAH. THE SHIFT FROM OUTSIDER TO CITIZEN. THE UNMOORING SENSATION OF SUDDENLY BEING SUBSUMED BY A SYSTEM YOU'VE BEEN PUSHING AGAINST ALL YOUR LIFE. IT'S A LOSS OF INNO-CENCE, IN A WAY, A COLONIZATION, THE BEGINNING OF THE WHOLESALE COMMODIFICATION OF OUR LIVES.
HIGHER LEVELS OF WD-40 IN THE WOMB?
MARTHA STEWART WEDDINGS
NO, I MEAN NOW WE HAVE TO THINK ABOUT WHETHER TO DO IT!
OH.
TO LEGALIZE OR NOT?
... Pussy said to the owl, 'You elegant fowl!
'How charmingly sweet you sing!
'Oh, let us be married!
'Too long we have tarried!
'But what shall we do for a ring?'
The OWL & THE PUSSYCAT
A TWIST TIE?
I THINK IT LOOKS QUITE ELEGANT, CONSIDERING YOUR FREAKISHLY LONG FINGER.

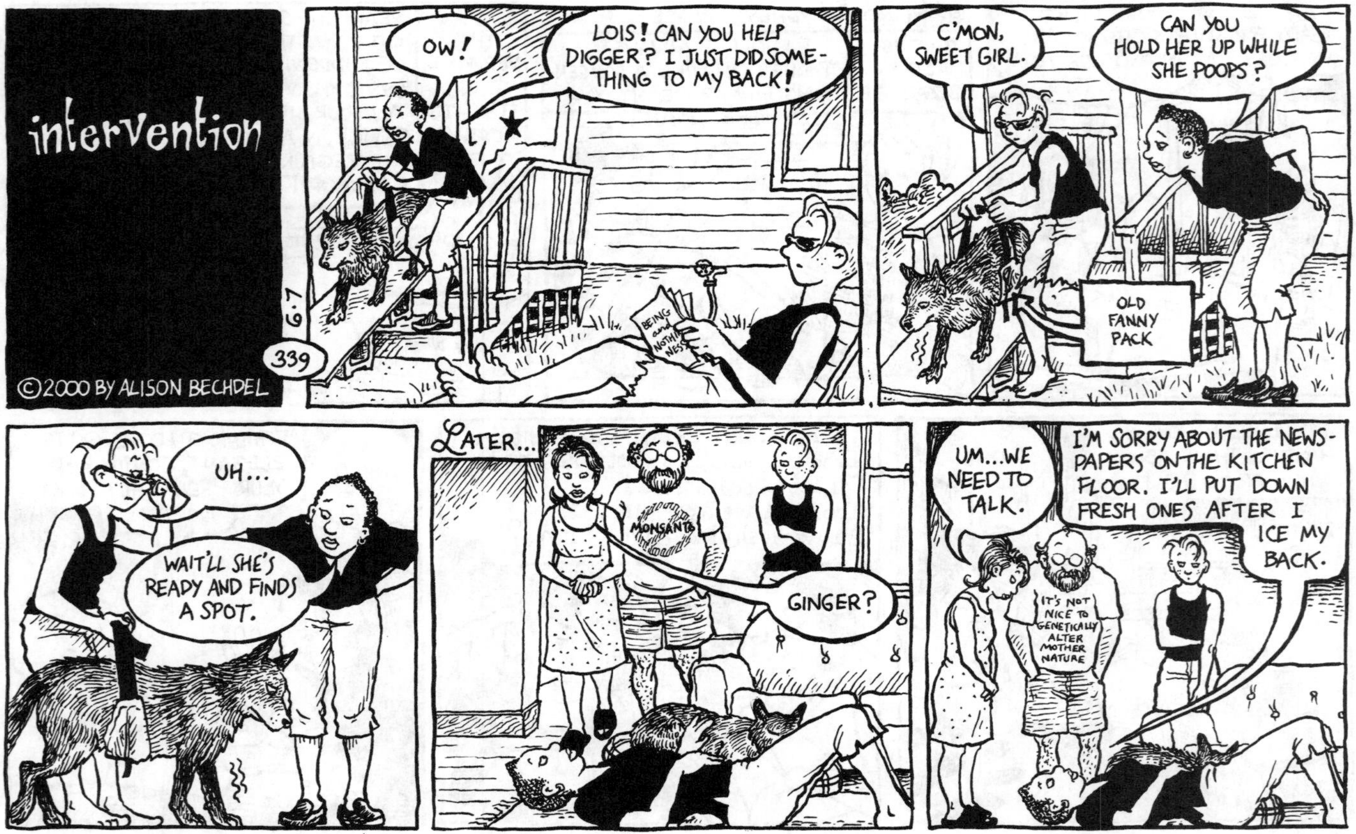
intervention
©2000 BY ALISON BECHDEL
339
6.7
OW!
LOIS! CAN YOU HELP DIGGER? I JUST DID SOMETHING TO MY BACK!
BEING and NOTHINGNESS
C'MON, SWEET GIRL.
CAN YOU HOLD HER UP WHILE SHE POOPS?
OLD FANNY PACK
UH...
WAIT'LL SHE'S READY AND FINDS A SPOT.
LATER...
MONSANTO
GINGER?
UM...WE NEED TO TALK.
I'M SORRY ABOUT THE NEWSPAPERS ON THE KITCHEN FLOOR. I'LL PUT DOWN FRESH ONES AFTER I ICE MY BACK.
IT'S NOT NICE TO GENETICALLY ALTER MOTHER NATURE

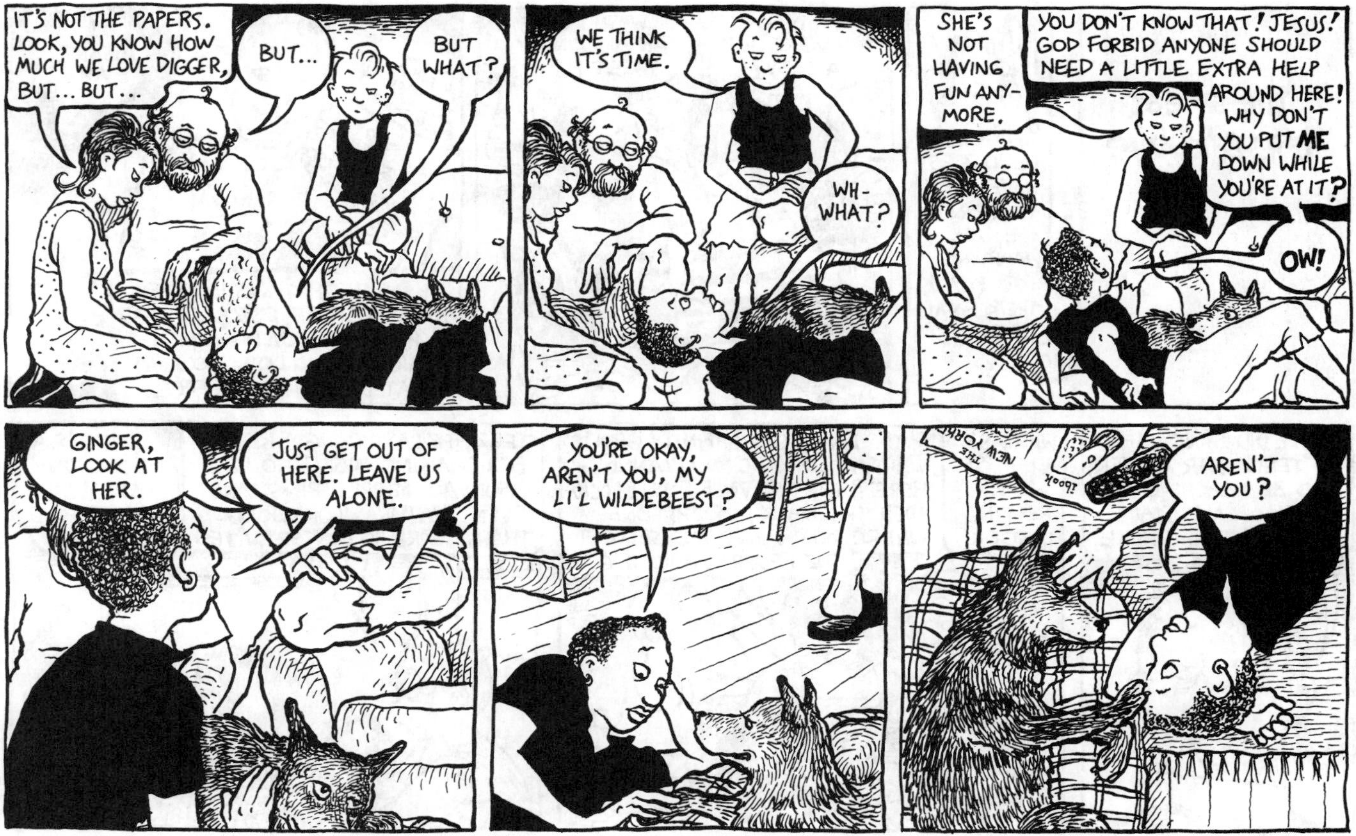
IT'S NOT THE PAPERS. LOOK, YOU KNOW HOW MUCH WE LOVE DIGGER, BUT... BUT...
BUT...
BUT WHAT?
WE THINK IT'S TIME.
WH-WHAT?
SHE'S NOT HAVING FUN ANY-MORE.
YOU DON'T KNOW THAT! JESUS! GOD FORBID ANYONE SHOULD NEED A LITTLE EXTRA HELP AROUND HERE! WHY DON'T YOU PUT **ME** DOWN WHILE YOU'RE AT IT?
OW!
GINGER, LOOK AT HER.
JUST GET OUT OF HERE. LEAVE US ALONE.
YOU'RE OKAY, AREN'T YOU, MY LI'L WILDEBEEST?
THE NEW YORK
iBook
AREN'T YOU?

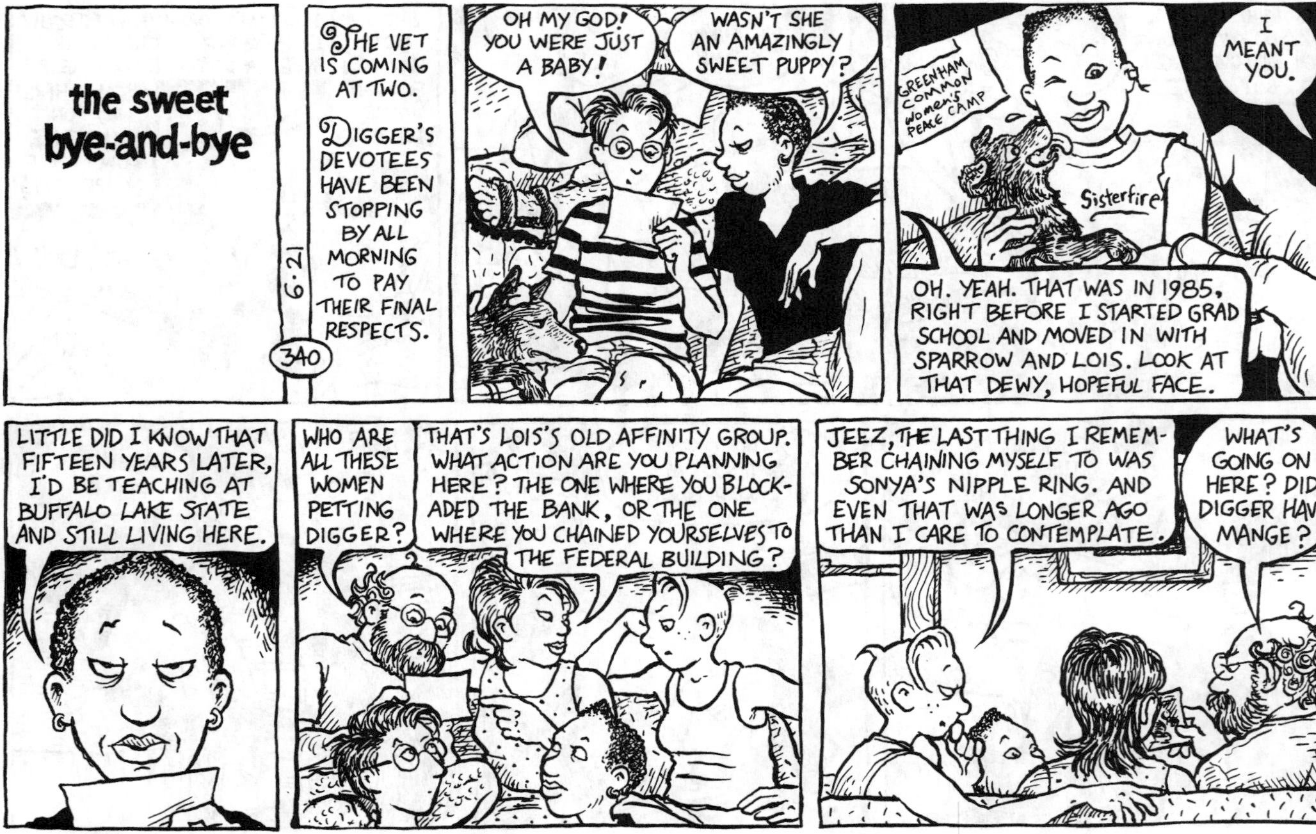
the sweet bye-and-bye
6·21
340
THE VET IS COMING AT TWO.
DIGGER'S DEVOTEES HAVE BEEN STOPPING BY ALL MORNING TO PAY THEIR FINAL RESPECTS.
OH MY GOD! YOU WERE JUST A BABY!
WASN'T SHE AN AMAZINGLY SWEET PUPPY?
GREENHAM COMMON women's PEACE CAMP
Sisterfire
I MEANT YOU.
OH. YEAH. THAT WAS IN 1985, RIGHT BEFORE I STARTED GRAD SCHOOL AND MOVED IN WITH SPARROW AND LOIS. LOOK AT THAT DEWY, HOPEFUL FACE.
LITTLE DID I KNOW THAT FIFTEEN YEARS LATER, I'D BE TEACHING AT BUFFALO LAKE STATE AND STILL LIVING HERE.
WHO ARE ALL THESE WOMEN PETTING DIGGER?
THAT'S LOIS'S OLD AFFINITY GROUP. WHAT ACTION ARE YOU PLANNING HERE? THE ONE WHERE YOU BLOCKADED THE BANK, OR THE ONE WHERE YOU CHAINED YOURSELVES TO THE FEDERAL BUILDING?
JEEZ, THE LAST THING I REMEMBER CHAINING MYSELF TO WAS SONYA'S NIPPLE RING. AND EVEN THAT WAS LONGER AGO THAN I CARE TO CONTEMPLATE.
WHAT'S GOING ON HERE? DID DIGGER HAVE MANGE?

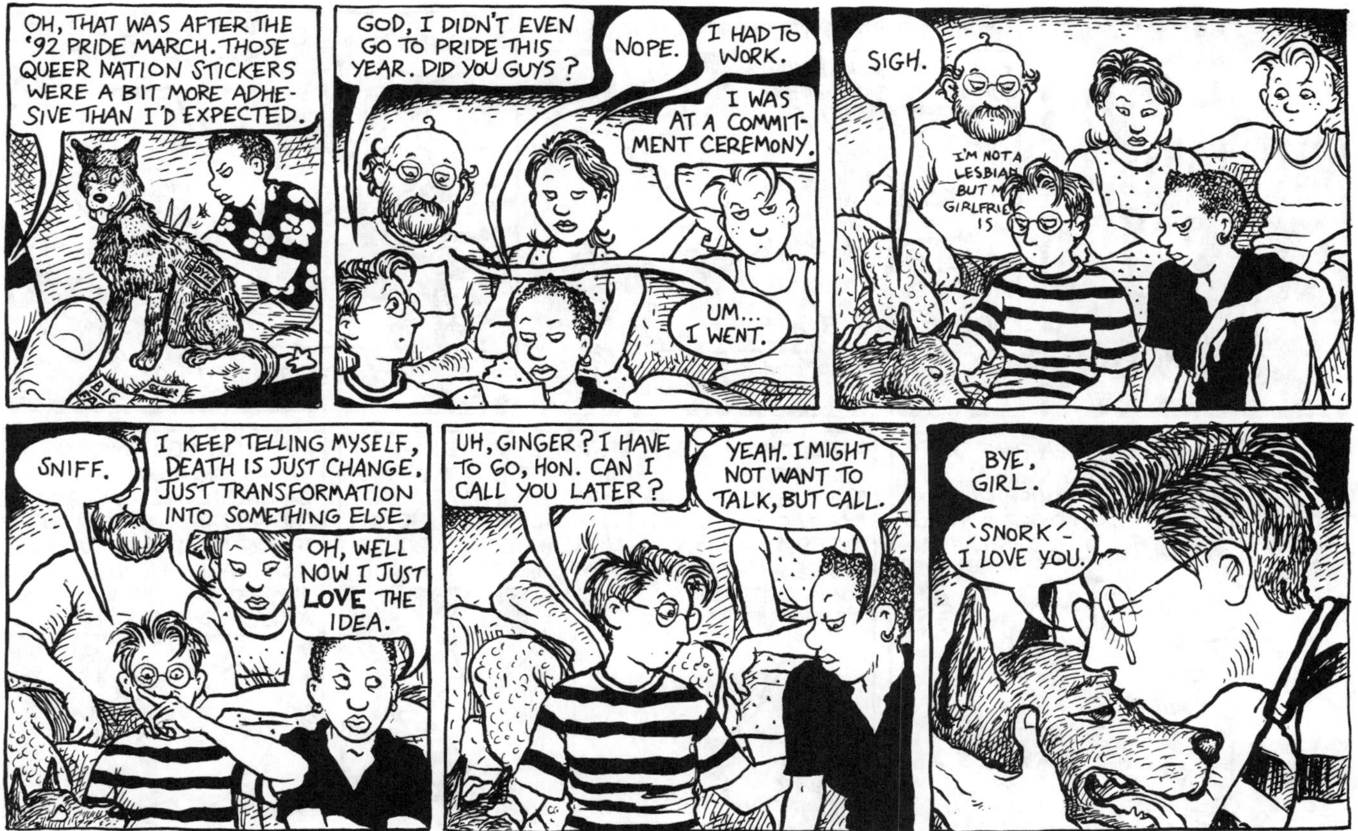
OH, THAT WAS AFTER THE '92 PRIDE MARCH. THOSE QUEER NATION STICKERS WERE A BIT MORE ADHESIVE THAN I'D EXPECTED.
GOD, I DIDN'T EVEN GO TO PRIDE THIS YEAR. DID YOU GUYS ?
NOPE.
I HAD TO WORK.
I WAS AT A COMMITMENT CEREMONY.
UM... I WENT.
SIGH.
SNIFF.
I KEEP TELLING MYSELF, DEATH IS JUST CHANGE. JUST TRANSFORMATION INTO SOMETHING ELSE.
OH, WELL NOW I JUST **LOVE** THE IDEA.
UH, GINGER? I HAVE TO GO, HON. CAN I CALL YOU LATER?
YEAH. I MIGHT NOT WANT TO TALK, BUT CALL.
BYE, GIRL.
SNORK
I LOVE YOU.

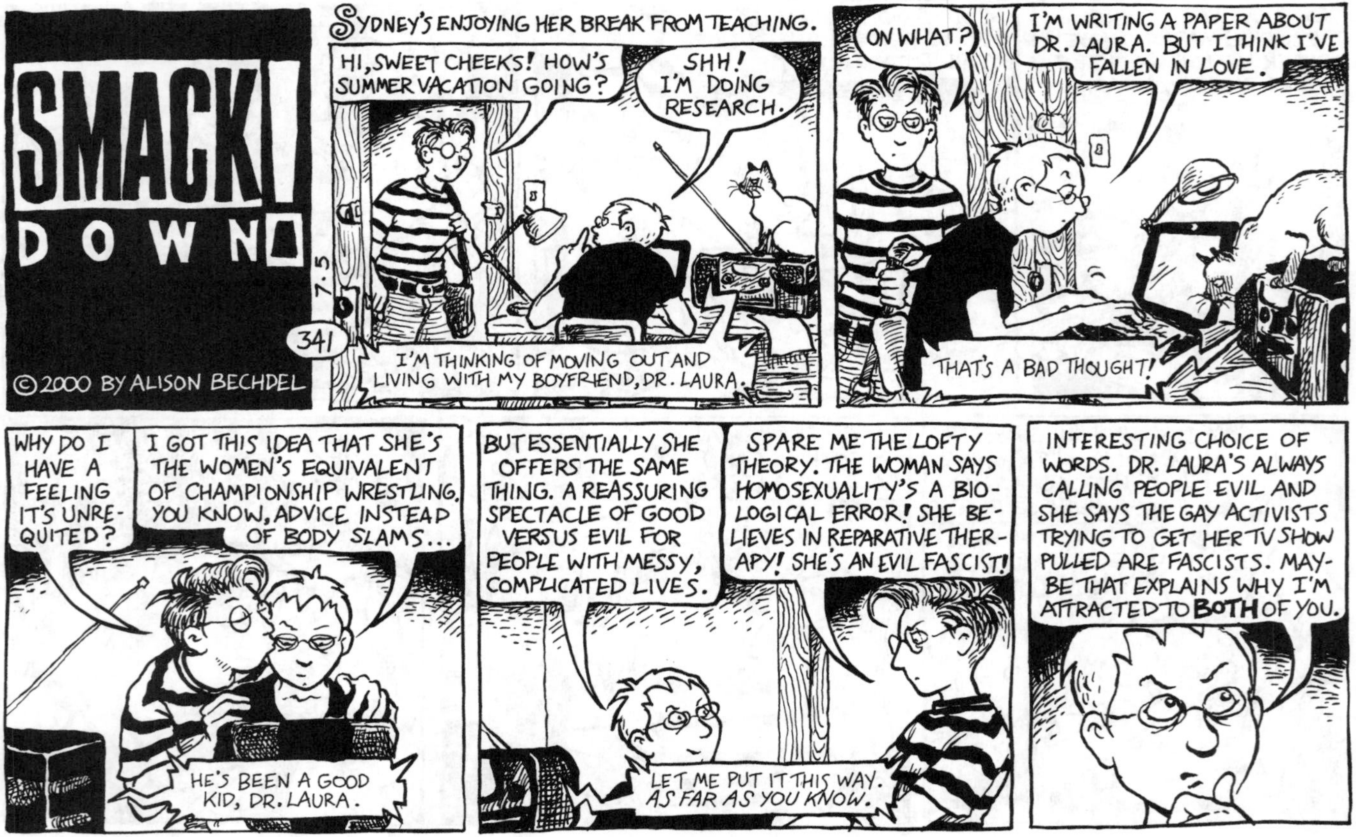
SMACK DOWN
7.5
341
©2000 BY ALISON BECHDEL
SYDNEY'S ENJOYING HER BREAK FROM TEACHING.
HI, SWEET CHEEKS! HOW'S SUMMER VACATION GOING?
SHH! I'M DOING RESEARCH.
I'M THINKING OF MOVING OUT AND LIVING WITH MY BOYFRIEND, DR. LAURA.
ON WHAT?
I'M WRITING A PAPER ABOUT DR. LAURA. BUT I THINK I'VE FALLEN IN LOVE.
THAT'S A BAD THOUGHT!
WHY DO I HAVE A FEELING IT'S UNREQUITED?
I GOT THIS IDEA THAT SHE'S THE WOMEN'S EQUIVALENT OF CHAMPIONSHIP WRESTLING. YOU KNOW, ADVICE INSTEAD OF BODY SLAMS...
HE'S BEEN A GOOD KID, DR. LAURA.
BUT ESSENTIALLY SHE OFFERS THE SAME THING. A REASSURING SPECTACLE OF GOOD VERSUS EVIL FOR PEOPLE WITH MESSY, COMPLICATED LIVES.
SPARE ME THE LOFTY THEORY. THE WOMAN SAYS HOMOSEXUALITY'S A BIOLOGICAL ERROR! SHE BELIEVES IN REPARATIVE THERAPY! SHE'S AN EVIL FASCIST!
LET ME PUT IT THIS WAY. AS FAR AS YOU KNOW.
INTERESTING CHOICE OF WORDS. DR. LAURA'S ALWAYS CALLING PEOPLE EVIL AND SHE SAYS THE GAY ACTIVISTS TRYING TO GET HER TV SHOW PULLED ARE FASCISTS. MAYBE THAT EXPLAINS WHY I'M ATTRACTED TO BOTH OF YOU.

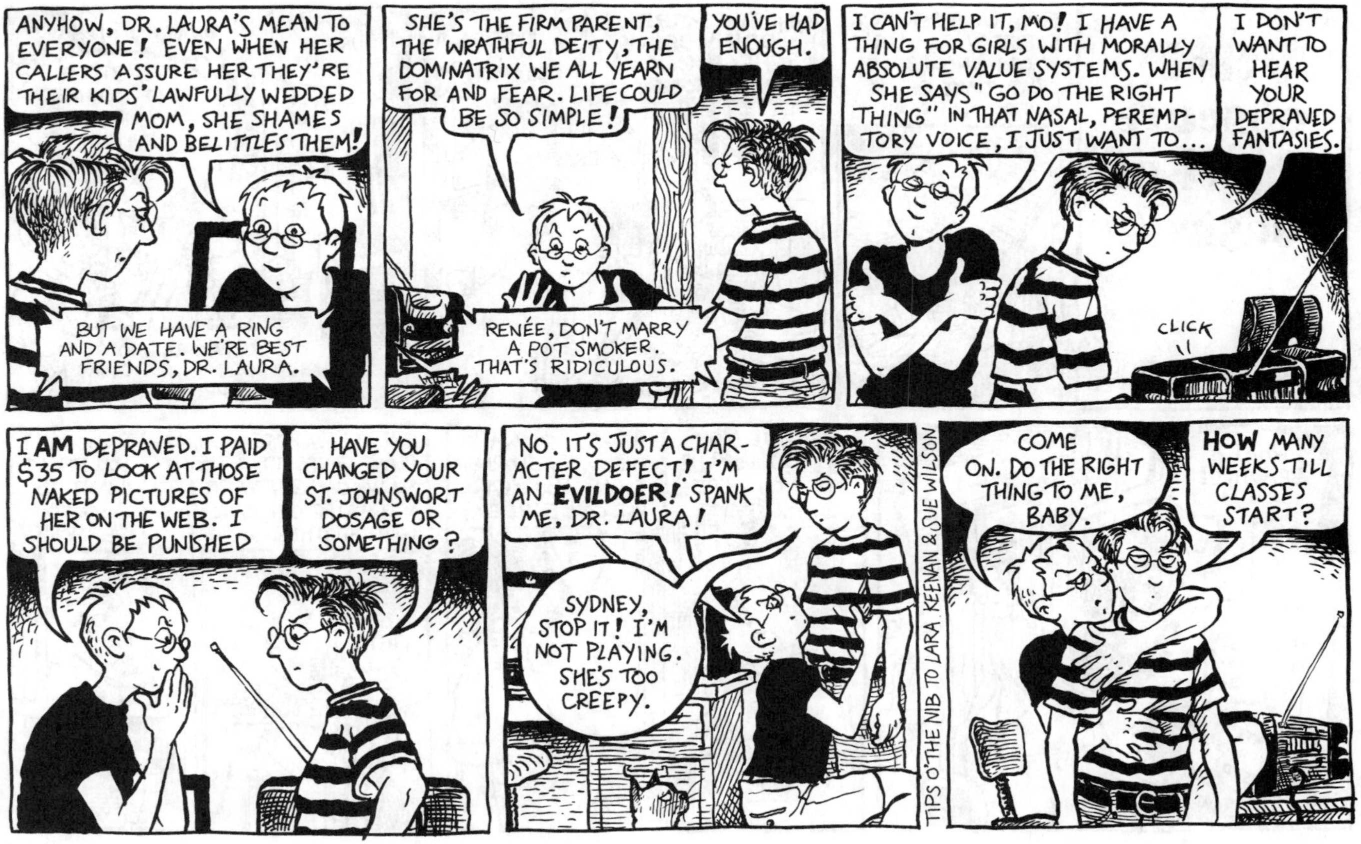

ANYHOW, DR. LAURA'S MEAN TO EVERYONE! EVEN WHEN HER CALLERS ASSURE HER THEY'RE THEIR KIDS' LAWFULLY WEDDED MOM, SHE SHAMES AND BELITTLES THEM!
BUT WE HAVE A RING AND A DATE. WE'RE BEST FRIENDS, DR. LAURA.
SHE'S THE FIRM PARENT, THE WRATHFUL DEITY, THE DOMINATRIX WE ALL YEARN FOR AND FEAR. LIFE COULD BE SO SIMPLE!
YOU'VE HAD ENOUGH.
RENÉE, DON'T MARRY A POT SMOKER. THAT'S RIDICULOUS.
I CAN'T HELP IT, MO! I HAVE A THING FOR GIRLS WITH MORALLY ABSOLUTE VALUE SYSTEMS. WHEN SHE SAYS "GO DO THE RIGHT THING" IN THAT NASAL, PEREMPTORY VOICE, I JUST WANT TO...
I DON'T WANT TO HEAR YOUR DEPRAVED FANTASIES.
CLICK
I AM DEPRAVED. I PAID $35 TO LOOK AT THOSE NAKED PICTURES OF HER ON THE WEB. I SHOULD BE PUNISHED
HAVE YOU CHANGED YOUR ST. JOHNSWORT DOSAGE OR SOMETHING?
NO. IT'S JUST A CHARACTER DEFECT! I'M AN EVILDOER! SPANK ME, DR. LAURA!
SYDNEY, STOP IT! I'M NOT PLAYING. SHE'S TOO CREEPY.
TIPS O' THE NIB TO LARA KEENAN & SUE WILSON
COME ON. DO THE RIGHT THING TO ME, BABY.
HOW MANY WEEKS TILL CLASSES START?

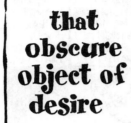

that obscure object of desire

© 2000 BY ALISON BECHDEL

342

Ahh... a perfect Saturday summer's morn. How best to partake of its ambrosial promise?

♪ Phoe-be

WHEEEE SKRRRR! DOINK DOINK SCHSCHXXX! WEL-COME!

WHO'S THAT POKÉMON?!

A.O. HELL

SCIENTISTS CRACK GENETIC CODE... BOOK OF LIFE... GOD... PINNACLE HISTORY OF MANKIND ETC. ETC.

RAFFI! TURN IT DOWN!

WHAT?

THIS BITES. DON'T YOU HAVE ANY FROSTED FRUITBATS?

GRANOLA

IT'S INSIPACHU, WHO ANESTHETIZES ITS VICTIMS WITH SHODDY ANIMATION.

WHAT A BEAUTIFUL DAY!

FARE FINDER

DISEASE WILL BE ERADICATED! AGING PROCESS REVERSED! STATIC CLING BANISHED!

WHERE'VE YOU BEEN? I WOKE UP AND YOU WERE GONE.

I WAS FAST WALKING WITH GLORIA. DIDN'T YOU HEAR HER CALL EARLIER?

FOR SALE: CLEAN CHEAP SAFE NUCLEAR POWER PLANT

SHIK

GREAT. I'M RESEARCHING PLANE FARES TO VERMONT SO WE CAN GET MARRIED AND YOU'RE OFF CAVORTING WITH ANOTHER WOMAN.

I THOUGHT YOU DIDN'T WANT TO GO TO VERMONT!

TORONTO WOMEN'S BOOK STORE

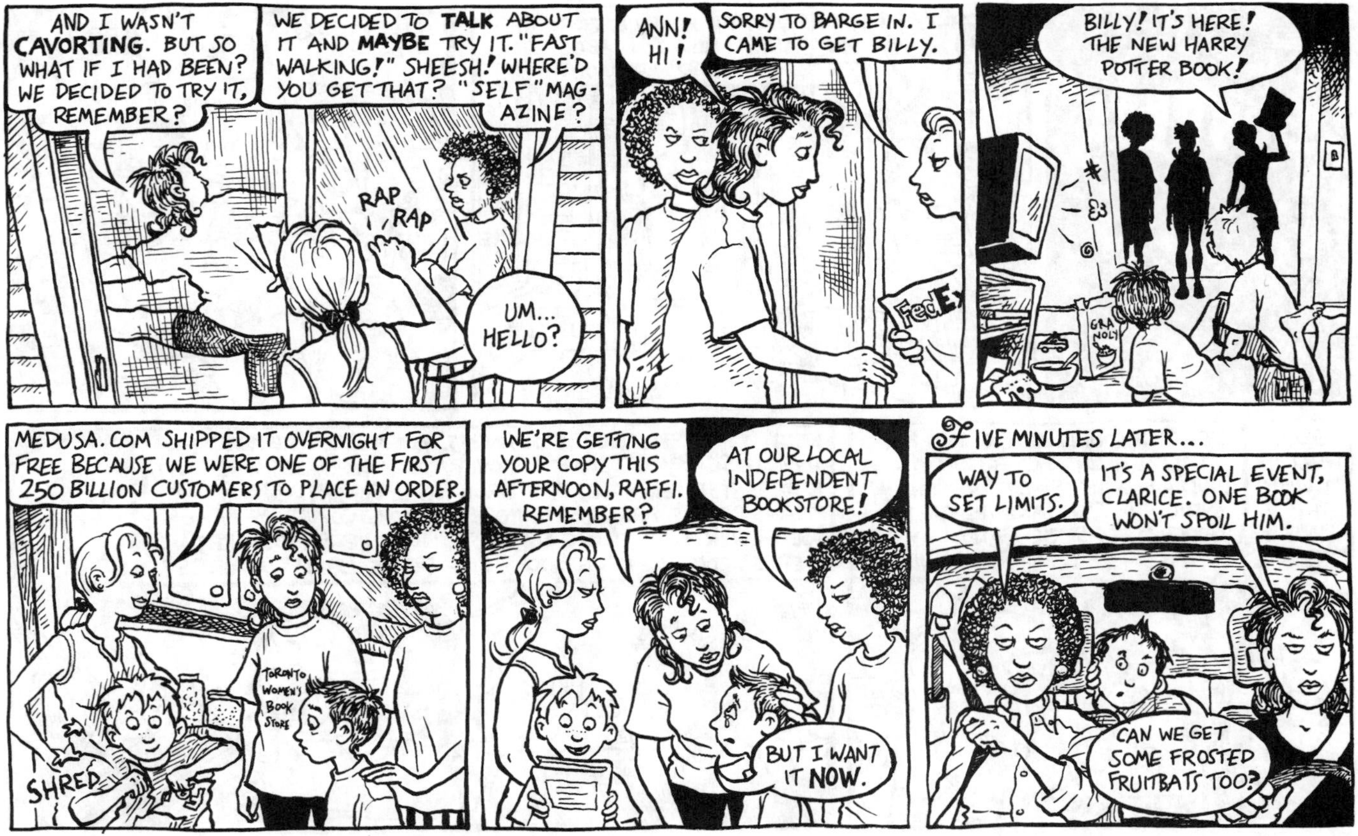
AND I WASN'T CAVORTING. BUT SO WHAT IF I HAD BEEN? WE DECIDED TO TRY IT, REMEMBER?
WE DECIDED TO TALK ABOUT IT AND MAYBE TRY IT. "FAST WALKING!" SHEESH! WHERE'D YOU GET THAT? "SELF" MAGAZINE?
RAP RAP
UM... HELLO?
ANN! HI!
SORRY TO BARGE IN. I CAME TO GET BILLY.
FedEx
BILLY! IT'S HERE! THE NEW HARRY POTTER BOOK!
GRA NOLY
MEDUSA.COM SHIPPED IT OVERNIGHT FOR FREE BECAUSE WE WERE ONE OF THE FIRST 250 BILLION CUSTOMERS TO PLACE AN ORDER.
TORONTO WOMEN'S BOOK STORE
SHRED
WE'RE GETTING YOUR COPY THIS AFTERNOON, RAFFI. REMEMBER?
AT OUR LOCAL INDEPENDENT BOOKSTORE!
BUT I WANT IT NOW.
FIVE MINUTES LATER...
WAY TO SET LIMITS.
IT'S A SPECIAL EVENT, CLARICE. ONE BOOK WON'T SPOIL HIM.
CAN WE GET SOME FROSTED FRUITBATS TOO?

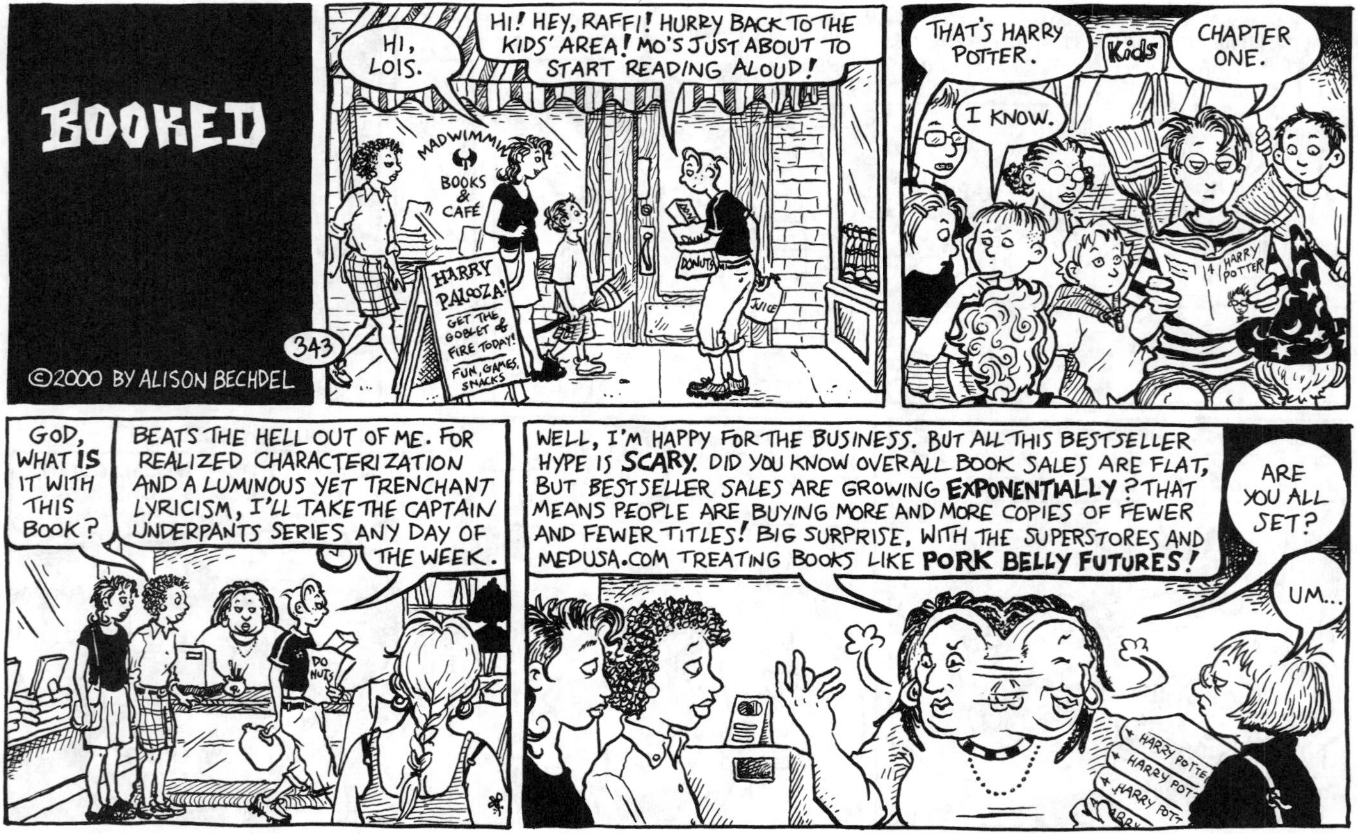
BOOKED
©2000 BY ALISON BECHDEL
343
HI, LOIS.
HI! HEY, RAFFI! HURRY BACK TO THE KIDS' AREA! MO'S JUST ABOUT TO START READING ALOUD!
MADWIMMIN BOOKS & CAFÉ
HARRY PALOOZA! GET THE GOBLET of FIRE TODAY! FUN, GAMES, SNACKS
DONUTS
JUICE
THAT'S HARRY POTTER.
Kids
CHAPTER ONE.
I KNOW.
HARRY POTTER
GOD, WHAT IS IT WITH THIS BOOK?
BEATS THE HELL OUT OF ME. FOR REALIZED CHARACTERIZATION AND A LUMINOUS YET TRENCHANT LYRICISM, I'LL TAKE THE CAPTAIN UNDERPANTS SERIES ANY DAY OF THE WEEK.
DO NUTS
WELL, I'M HAPPY FOR THE BUSINESS. BUT ALL THIS BESTSELLER HYPE IS SCARY. DID YOU KNOW OVERALL BOOK SALES ARE FLAT, BUT BESTSELLER SALES ARE GROWING EXPONENTIALLY? THAT MEANS PEOPLE ARE BUYING MORE AND MORE COPIES OF FEWER AND FEWER TITLES! BIG SURPRISE, WITH THE SUPERSTORES AND MEDUSA.COM TREATING BOOKS LIKE PORK BELLY FUTURES!
ARE YOU ALL SET?
UM...

MEANWHILE... WHERE'S YOUR SCAR IF YOU'RE HARRY POTTER?

LOOK, I'M **NOT HARRY POTTER**, OKAY? NOW SIT DOWN AND LISTEN!

JEEZ, WE SHOULD BUY SOME NON-BLOCKBUSTERS WHILE WE STILL CAN!

LIKE THIS ONE?

The ETHICAL SLUT INFINITE SEXUAL POSSIBILITIES

WELL, IF WE'RE SERIOUS ABOUT TRYING TO OPEN UP OUR RELATIONSHIP, A BOOK MIGHT HELP.

RELATIONSHIPS

EBB & FLOW

YAK

BILL & HILL

POLYAMORY THE NEW LOVE WITHOUT LIMITS

HI, GIRLS! TONI, I THOUGHT YOU WEREN'T COMING TILL THIS AFTERNOON!

GLORIA! I...UH, WE...

JANE AUSTEN'S INVESTMENT GUIDE

WOMAN: AN INTIMATE TRIPTIK

TIPPING THE VELVEETA

SOME MYSTERY

WE HAD A LITTLE POWER STRUGGLE AND LOST.

TELL ME ABOUT IT. GOD, I'VE BEEN READING HARRY POTTER TO STELLA FOR MONTHS ON END. I'M DYING FOR A GROWN-UP BOOK. GOT ANY RECOMMENDATIONS?

RELATIONSHIPS

THE RELATIONSHIP **WORK** BOOK

THIS IS AN ABSOLUTELY **TERRIFIC** READ. CHANGED MY LIFE.

HUH.

WHAT A LAME-O HARRY POTTER COSTUME.

PATHETIC MUGGLE.

RELATIONSHIPS

STRIFE

MONOGAMY A PRECIOUS FLOWER

21

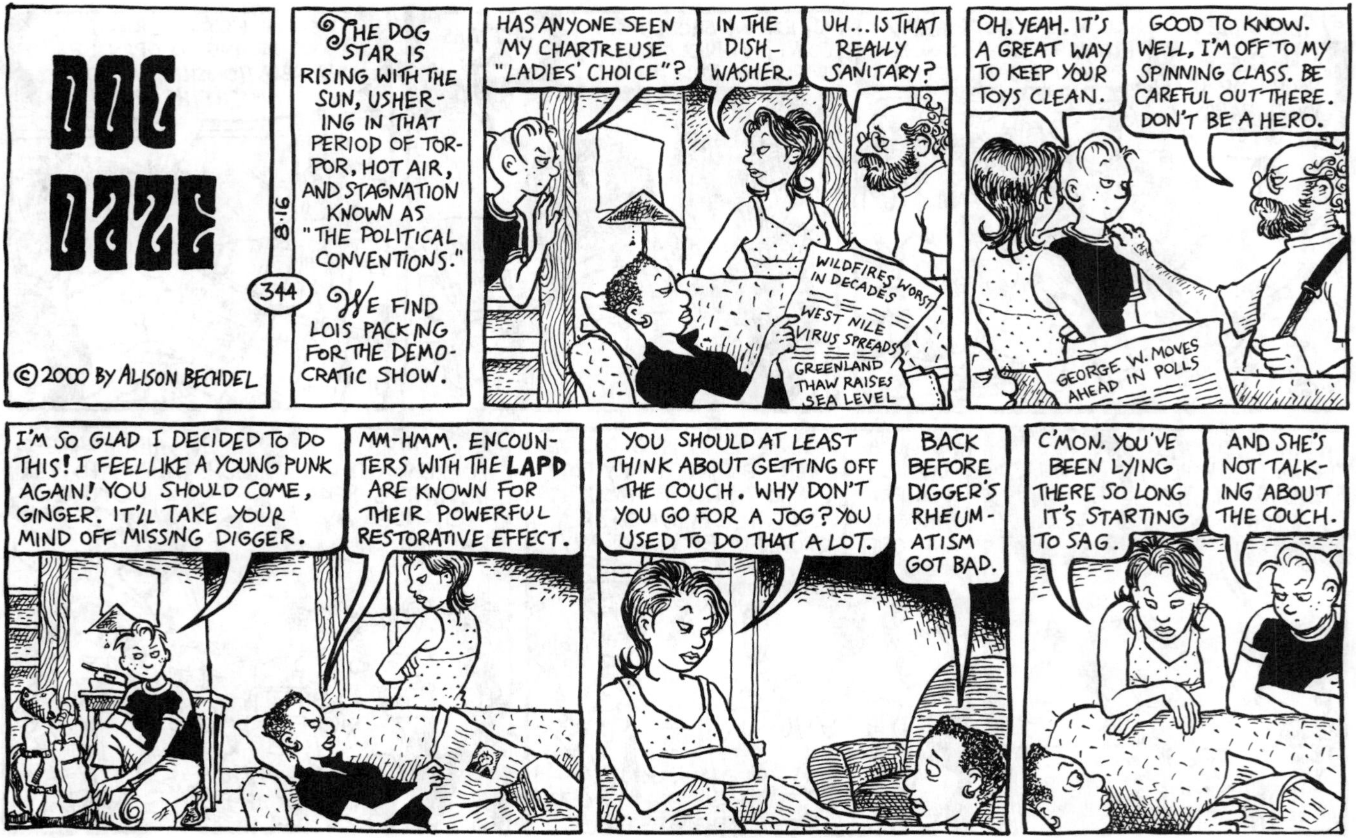
DOG DAZE
© 2000 BY ALISON BECHDEL
344
8·16
THE DOG STAR IS RISING WITH THE SUN, USHERING IN THAT PERIOD OF TORPOR, HOT AIR, AND STAGNATION KNOWN AS "THE POLITICAL CONVENTIONS."
WE FIND LOIS PACKING FOR THE DEMOCRATIC SHOW.
HAS ANYONE SEEN MY CHARTREUSE "LADIES' CHOICE"?
IN THE DISHWASHER.
UH... IS THAT REALLY SANITARY?
WILDFIRES WORST IN DECADES
WEST NILE VIRUS SPREADS
GREENLAND THAW RAISES SEA LEVEL
OH, YEAH. IT'S A GREAT WAY TO KEEP YOUR TOYS CLEAN.
GOOD TO KNOW. WELL, I'M OFF TO MY SPINNING CLASS. BE CAREFUL OUT THERE. DON'T BE A HERO.
GEORGE W. MOVES AHEAD IN POLLS
I'M SO GLAD I DECIDED TO DO THIS! I FEEL LIKE A YOUNG PUNK AGAIN! YOU SHOULD COME, GINGER. IT'LL TAKE YOUR MIND OFF MISSING DIGGER.
MM-HMM. ENCOUNTERS WITH THE LAPD ARE KNOWN FOR THEIR POWERFUL RESTORATIVE EFFECT.
YOU SHOULD AT LEAST THINK ABOUT GETTING OFF THE COUCH. WHY DON'T YOU GO FOR A JOG? YOU USED TO DO THAT A LOT.
BACK BEFORE DIGGER'S RHEUMATISM GOT BAD.
C'MON. YOU'VE BEEN LYING THERE SO LONG IT'S STARTING TO SAG.
AND SHE'S NOT TALKING ABOUT THE COUCH.

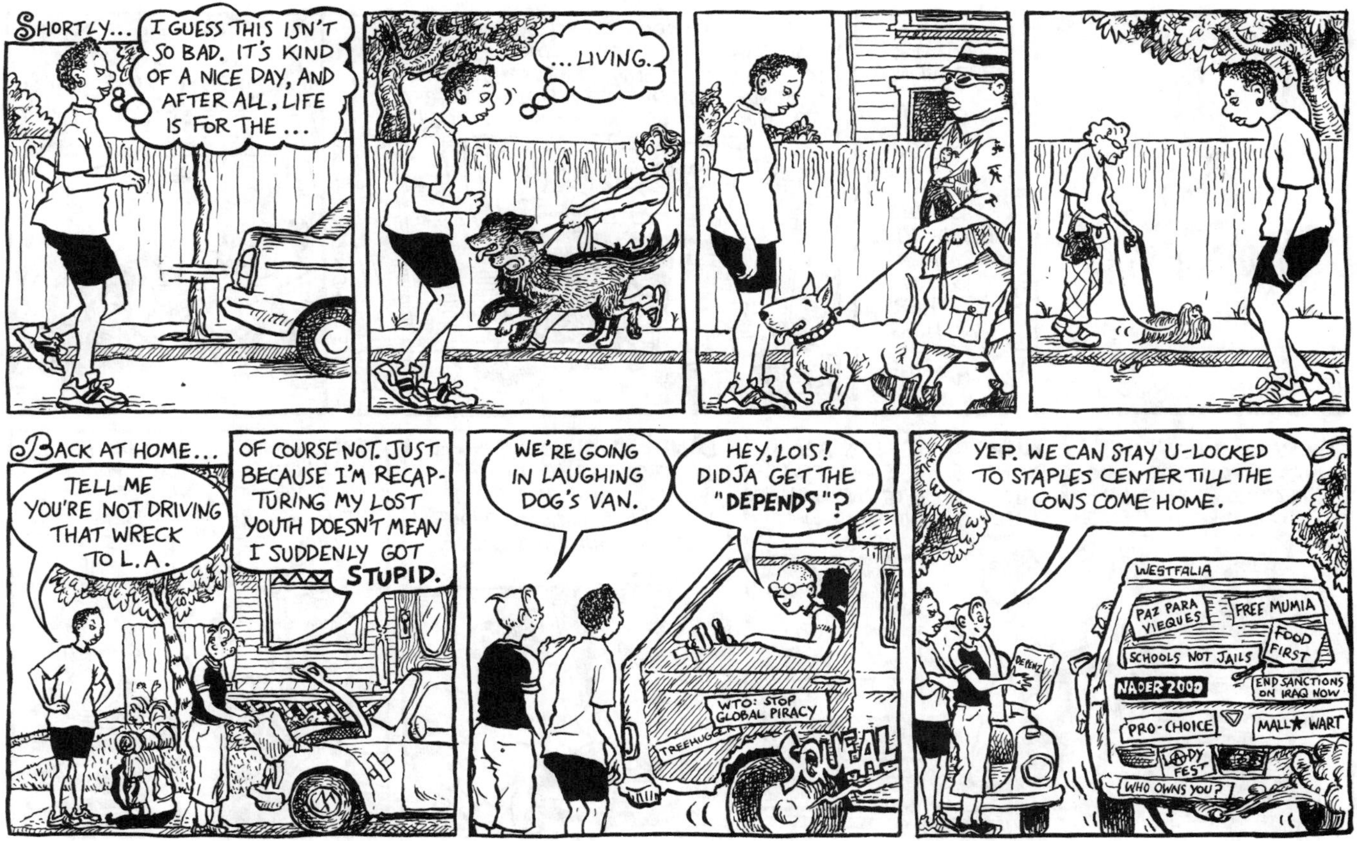
SHORTLY...
I GUESS THIS ISN'T SO BAD. IT'S KIND OF A NICE DAY, AND AFTER ALL, LIFE IS FOR THE ...
... LIVING.
BACK AT HOME...
TELL ME YOU'RE NOT DRIVING THAT WRECK TO L.A.
OF COURSE NOT. JUST BECAUSE I'M RECAPTURING MY LOST YOUTH DOESN'T MEAN I SUDDENLY GOT STUPID.
WE'RE GOING IN LAUGHING DOG'S VAN.
HEY, LOIS! DIDJA GET THE "DEPENDS"?
WTO: STOP GLOBAL PIRACY
TREEHUGGER
SQUEAL
YEP. WE CAN STAY U-LOCKED TO STAPLES CENTER TILL THE COWS COME HOME.
WESTFALIA
PAZ PARA VIEQUES
FREE MUMIA
FOOD FIRST
SCHOOLS NOT JAILS
NADER 2000
END SANCTIONS ON IRAQ NOW
PRO-CHOICE
MALL★WART
LADY FEST
WHO OWNS YOU?

Getting & Spending

© 2000 BY ALISON BECHDEL

8/30
345

@After prevailing upon Mo to accompany her on a shopping excursion, Sydney is now rather wishing she hadn't.

WELL, NO **WONDER** I FEEL SO INCOMPLETE, SO AWASH WITH FREE-FLOATING ANXIETY, SO... SO SPIRITUALLY **STARVED**! I DON'T HAVE A HUNDRED-AND-THIRTY-DOLLAR LEVER-ARM WINE BOTTLE UNCORKING DEVICE!

BED BATH & BITE ME*

* A BITE O' THE NIB TO AMY RUBIN

HEY, THOSE THINGS ARE GREAT! MY DAD HAS ONE.

$129.99

UNCORKR UNCORKR UNCORKR UNCORKR UNCORKR UNCORKR

KITCHEN

GOD! ALL THIS **STUFF**! WHAT A PORNOGRAPHIC SPECTACLE OF OVER-CONSUMPTION!

YOU'RE RIGHT. LET'S ABANDON THIS FALSE, MATERIALISTIC EXISTENCE AND GO LIVE SIMPLY OFF THE LAND. WHERE ARE THE TOWELS?

SPINNER | SPINNER
Gas Powered SALAD SPINNER | Gas Powered SALAD SPIN-R
Gas Powered SALIT SPIN-R | Gas Powered SALIT SPINR
Gas Powered SALAD | Diesel SALAD

LAND? WHAT LAND?! WE'VE DESTROYED THE NATURAL WORLD AND REPLACED IT WITH A PRE-PACKAGED ONE WE CAN ONLY AFFORD BY WORKING ALL DAY AT JOBS WE **HATE**!

SHOWER RADIO/ BAGEL SLICER
SHOWER RADIO/ MARTINI MISTER
SHOWER RADIO/ S.U.V.

I THOUGHT YOU LOVED YOUR JOB AT THE BOOKSTORE.

I...I DO. BUT I HATE HAVING NO MONEY AND NO BENEFITS.

BATH

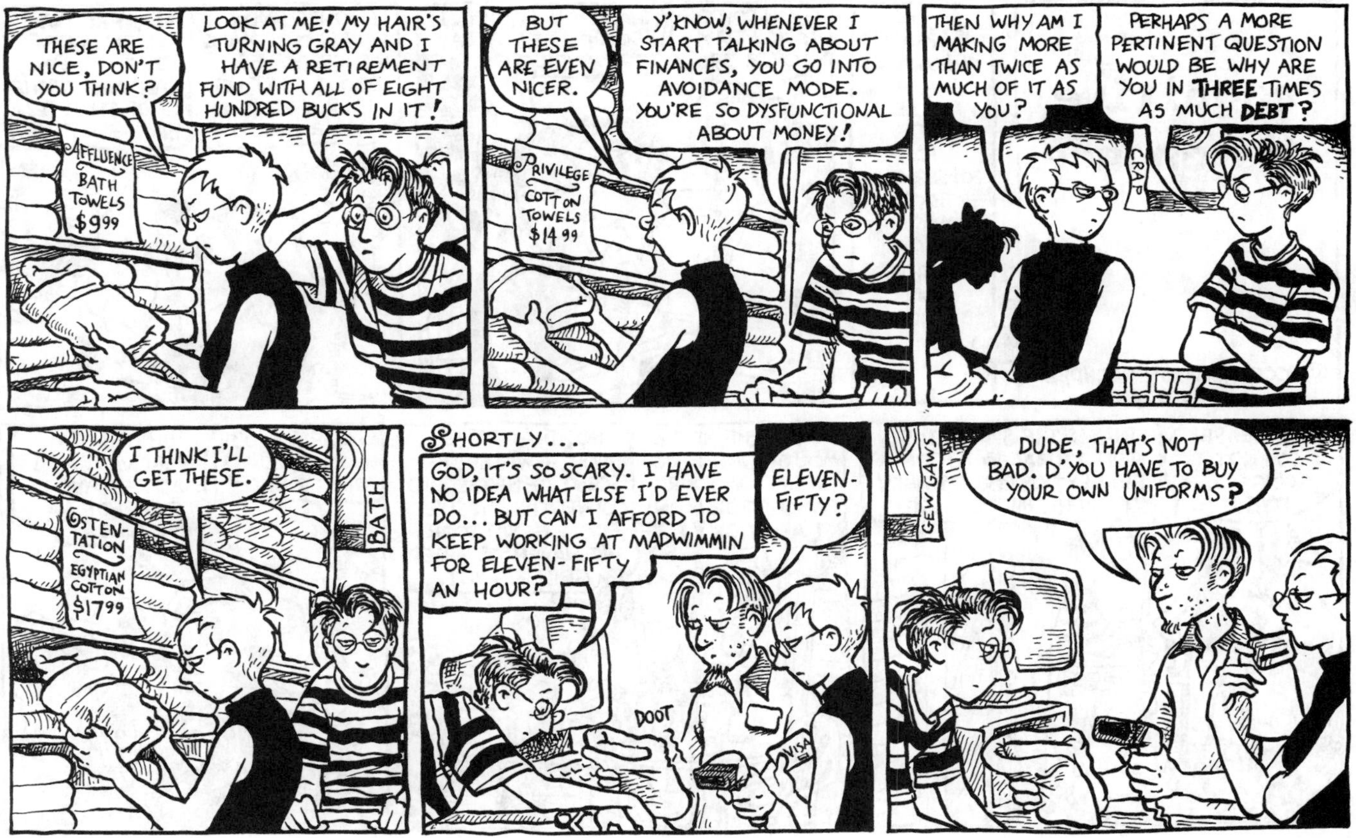
THESE ARE NICE, DON'T YOU THINK?
LOOK AT ME! MY HAIR'S TURNING GRAY AND I HAVE A RETIREMENT FUND WITH ALL OF EIGHT HUNDRED BUCKS IN IT!
AFFLUENCE BATH TOWELS $9.99
BUT THESE ARE EVEN NICER.
Y'KNOW, WHENEVER I START TALKING ABOUT FINANCES, YOU GO INTO AVOIDANCE MODE. YOU'RE SO DYSFUNCTIONAL ABOUT MONEY!
PRIVILEGE COTTON TOWELS $14.99
THEN WHY AM I MAKING MORE THAN TWICE AS MUCH OF IT AS YOU?
PERHAPS A MORE PERTINENT QUESTION WOULD BE WHY ARE YOU IN THREE TIMES AS MUCH DEBT?
CRAP
I THINK I'LL GET THESE.
OSTENTATION EGYPTIAN COTTON $17.99
BATH
SHORTLY...
GOD, IT'S SO SCARY. I HAVE NO IDEA WHAT ELSE I'D EVER DO... BUT CAN I AFFORD TO KEEP WORKING AT MADWIMMIN FOR ELEVEN-FIFTY AN HOUR?
ELEVEN-FIFTY?
DOOT
VISA
GEW GAWS
DUDE, THAT'S NOT BAD. D'YOU HAVE TO BUY YOUR OWN UNIFORMS?

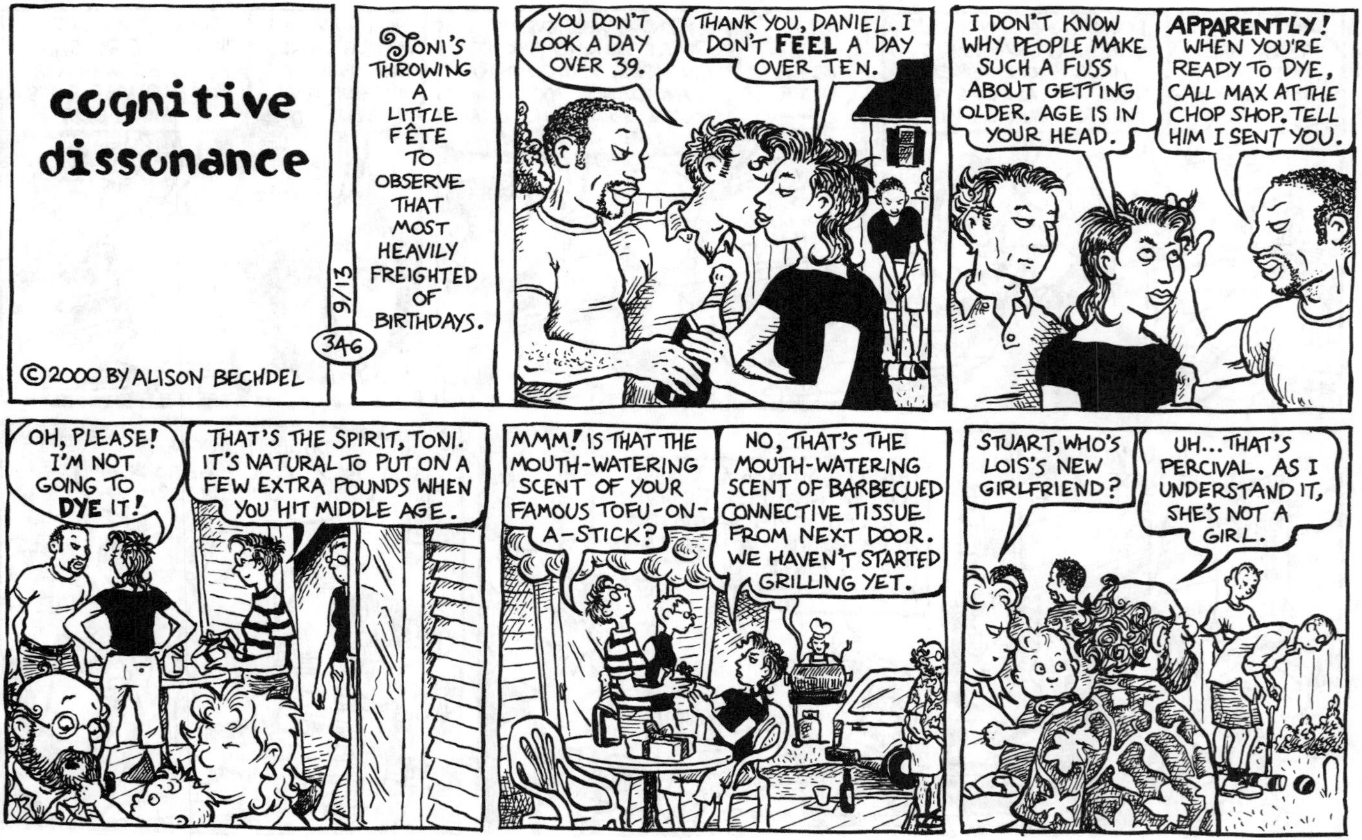
cognitive dissonance
©2000 BY ALISON BECHDEL
9/13
346
TONI'S THROWING A LITTLE FÊTE TO OBSERVE THAT MOST HEAVILY FREIGHTED OF BIRTHDAYS.
YOU DON'T LOOK A DAY OVER 39.
THANK YOU, DANIEL. I DON'T FEEL A DAY OVER TEN.
I DON'T KNOW WHY PEOPLE MAKE SUCH A FUSS ABOUT GETTING OLDER. AGE IS IN YOUR HEAD.
APPARENTLY! WHEN YOU'RE READY TO DYE, CALL MAX AT THE CHOP SHOP. TELL HIM I SENT YOU.
OH, PLEASE! I'M NOT GOING TO DYE IT!
THAT'S THE SPIRIT, TONI. IT'S NATURAL TO PUT ON A FEW EXTRA POUNDS WHEN YOU HIT MIDDLE AGE.
MMM! IS THAT THE MOUTH-WATERING SCENT OF YOUR FAMOUS TOFU-ON-A-STICK?
NO, THAT'S THE MOUTH-WATERING SCENT OF BARBECUED CONNECTIVE TISSUE FROM NEXT DOOR. WE HAVEN'T STARTED GRILLING YET.
STUART, WHO'S LOIS'S NEW GIRLFRIEND?
UH... THAT'S PERCIVAL. AS I UNDERSTAND IT, SHE'S NOT A GIRL.

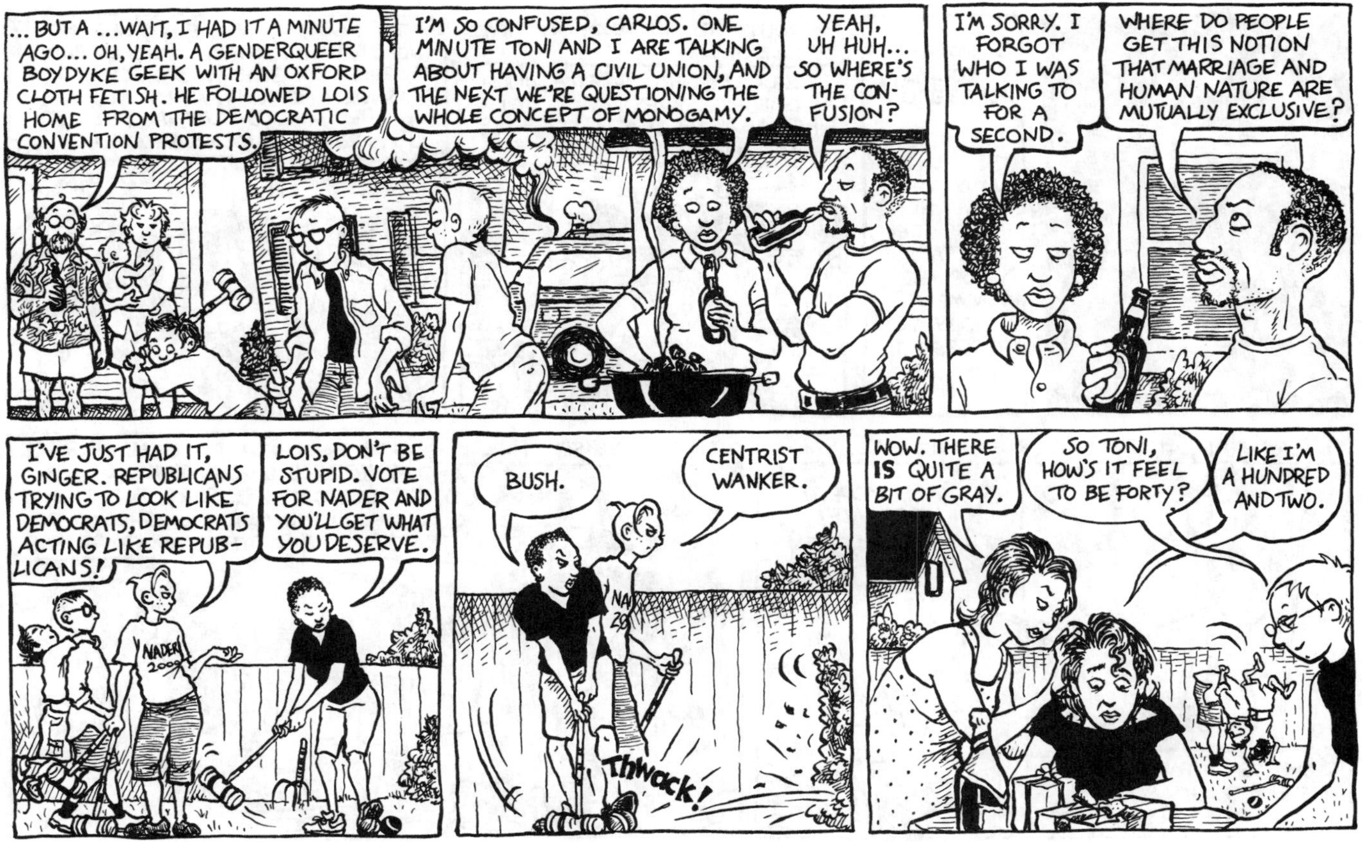

... BUT A ... WAIT, I HAD IT A MINUTE AGO... OH, YEAH. A GENDERQUEER BOYDYKE GEEK WITH AN OXFORD CLOTH FETISH. HE FOLLOWED LOIS HOME FROM THE DEMOCRATIC CONVENTION PROTESTS.
I'M SO CONFUSED, CARLOS. ONE MINUTE TONI AND I ARE TALKING ABOUT HAVING A CIVIL UNION, AND THE NEXT WE'RE QUESTIONING THE WHOLE CONCEPT OF MONOGAMY.
YEAH, UH HUH... SO WHERE'S THE CONFUSION?
I'M SORRY. I FORGOT WHO I WAS TALKING TO FOR A SECOND.
WHERE DO PEOPLE GET THIS NOTION THAT MARRIAGE AND HUMAN NATURE ARE MUTUALLY EXCLUSIVE?
I'VE JUST HAD IT, GINGER. REPUBLICANS TRYING TO LOOK LIKE DEMOCRATS, DEMOCRATS ACTING LIKE REPUBLICANS!
LOIS, DON'T BE STUPID. VOTE FOR NADER AND YOU'LL GET WHAT YOU DESERVE.
NADER 2000
BUSH.
CENTRIST WANKER.
THWACK!
WOW. THERE IS QUITE A BIT OF GRAY.
SO TONI, HOW'S IT FEEL TO BE FORTY?
LIKE I'M A HUNDRED AND TWO.

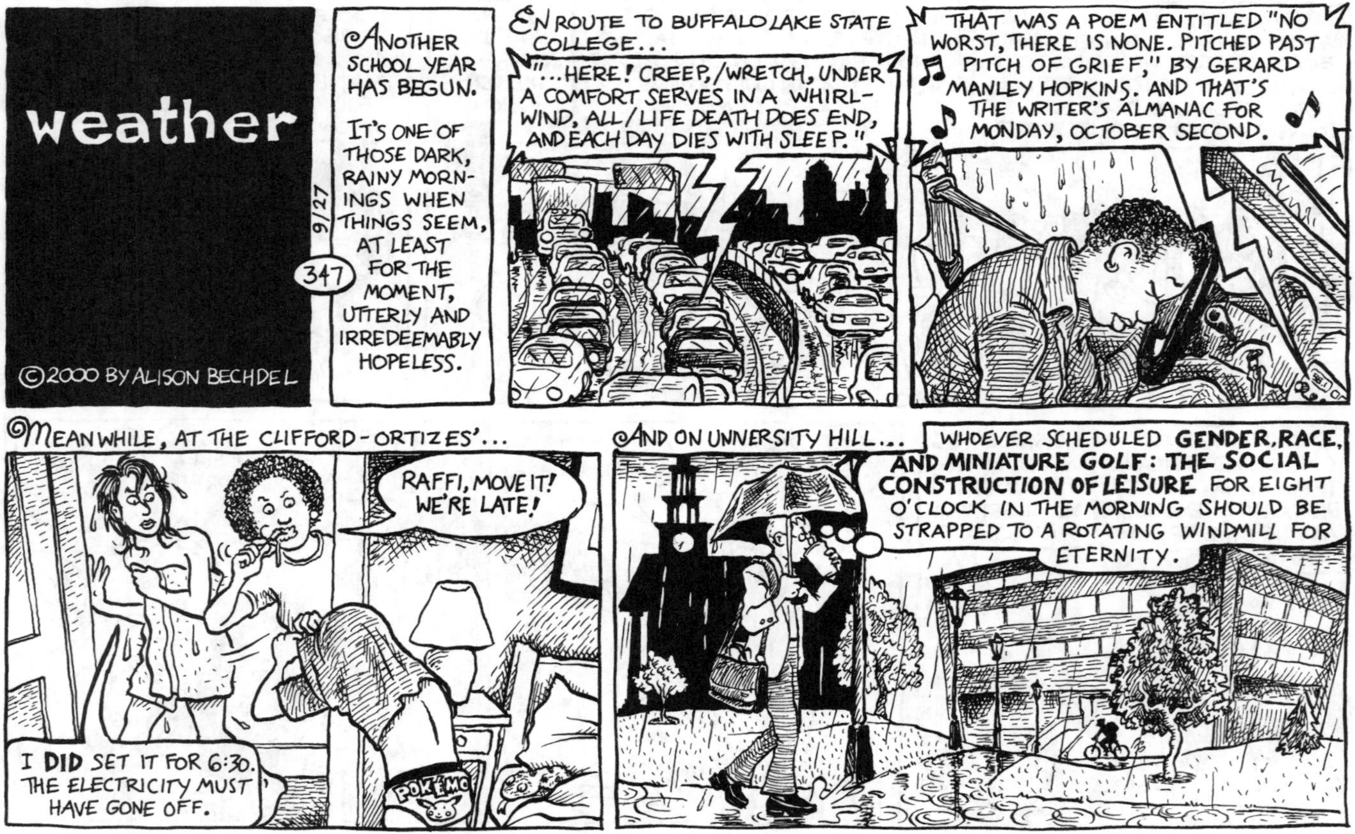
weather
©2000 BY ALISON BECHDEL
9/27
347
ANOTHER SCHOOL YEAR HAS BEGUN.
IT'S ONE OF THOSE DARK, RAINY MORNINGS WHEN THINGS SEEM, AT LEAST FOR THE MOMENT, UTTERLY AND IRREDEEMABLY HOPELESS.
EN ROUTE TO BUFFALO LAKE STATE COLLEGE...
"...HERE! CREEP, / WRETCH, UNDER A COMFORT SERVES IN A WHIRLWIND, ALL / LIFE DEATH DOES END, AND EACH DAY DIES WITH SLEEP."
THAT WAS A POEM ENTITLED "NO WORST, THERE IS NONE. PITCHED PAST PITCH OF GRIEF," BY GERARD MANLEY HOPKINS. AND THAT'S THE WRITER'S ALMANAC FOR MONDAY, OCTOBER SECOND.
MEANWHILE, AT THE CLIFFORD-ORTIZES'...
RAFFI, MOVE IT! WE'RE LATE!
I **DID** SET IT FOR 6:30. THE ELECTRICITY MUST HAVE GONE OFF.
POKÉMO
AND ON UNIVERSITY HILL...
WHOEVER SCHEDULED **GENDER, RACE, AND MINIATURE GOLF: THE SOCIAL CONSTRUCTION OF LEISURE** FOR EIGHT O'CLOCK IN THE MORNING SHOULD BE STRAPPED TO A ROTATING WINDMILL FOR ETERNITY.

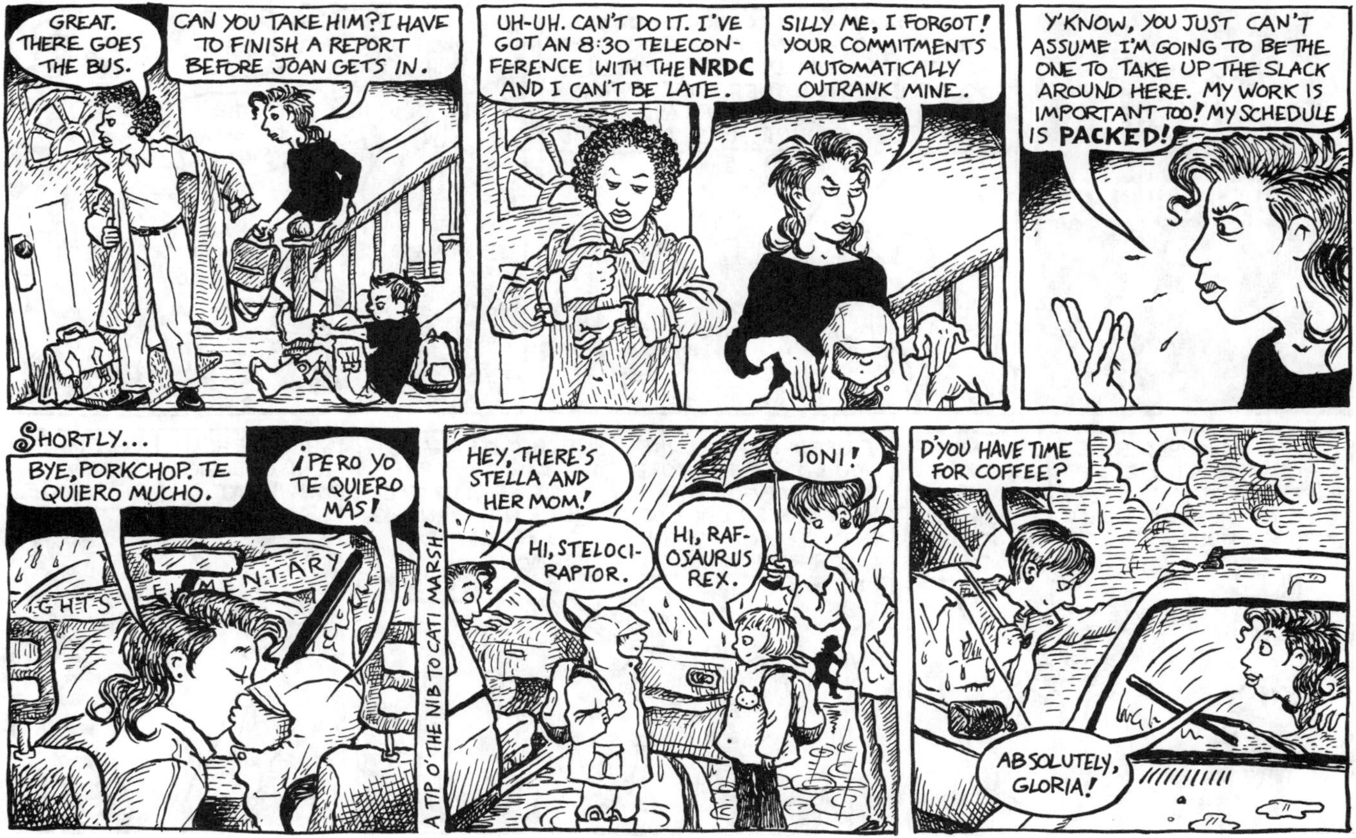
GREAT. THERE GOES THE BUS.
CAN YOU TAKE HIM? I HAVE TO FINISH A REPORT BEFORE JOAN GETS IN.
UH-UH. CAN'T DO IT. I'VE GOT AN 8:30 TELECON-FERENCE WITH THE **NRDC** AND I CAN'T BE LATE.
SILLY ME, I FORGOT! YOUR COMMITMENTS AUTOMATICALLY OUTRANK MINE.
Y'KNOW, YOU JUST CAN'T ASSUME I'M GOING TO BE THE ONE TO TAKE UP THE SLACK AROUND HERE. MY WORK IS IMPORTANT TOO! MY SCHEDULE IS **PACKED!**
SHORTLY...
BYE, PORKCHOP. TE QUIERO MUCHO.
¡PERO YO TE QUIERO MÁS!
A TIP O' THE NIB TO CATI MARSH!
HEY, THERE'S STELLA AND HER MOM!
HI, STELOCI-RAPTOR.
HI, RAF-OSAURUS REX.
TONI!
D'YOU HAVE TIME FOR COFFEE?
ABSOLUTELY, GLORIA!

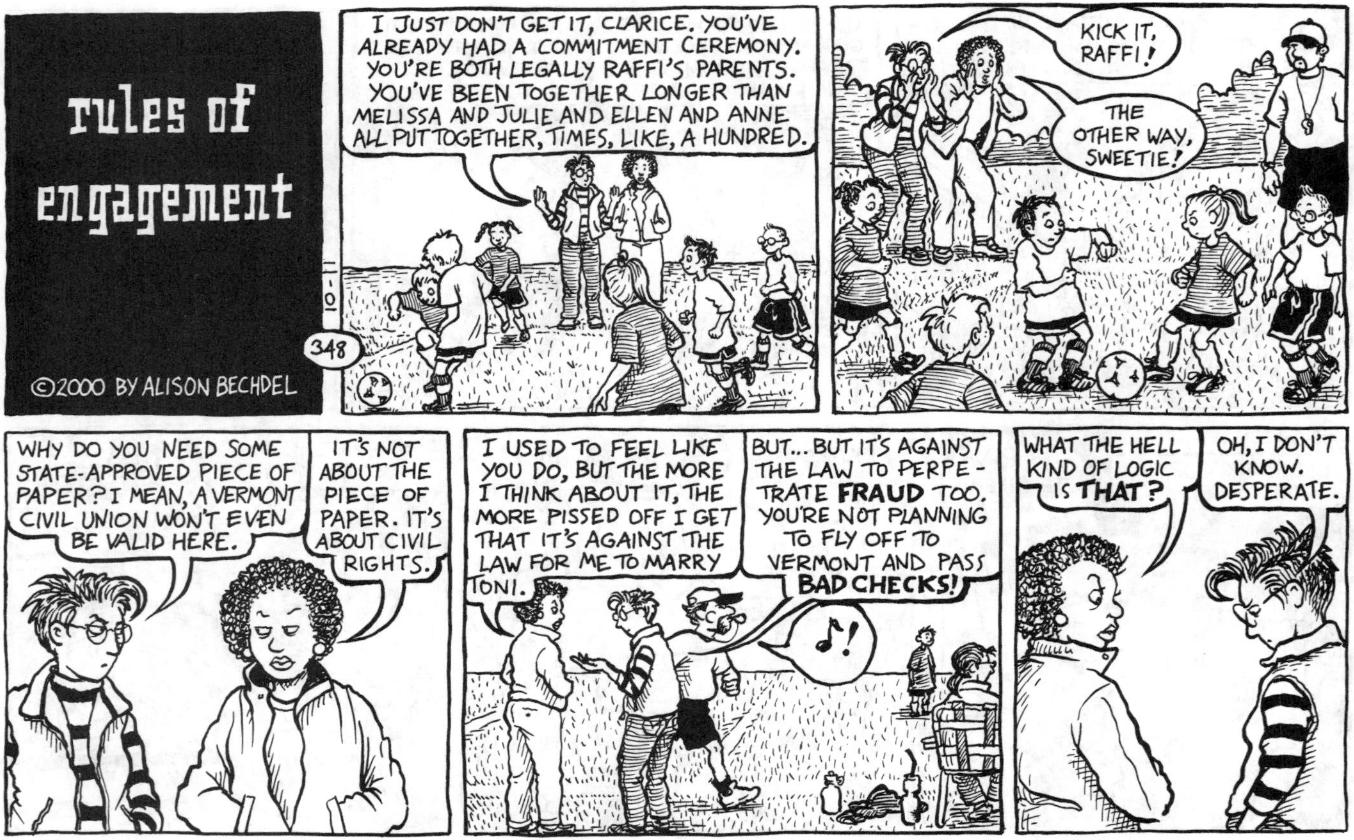
rules of engagement
©2000 BY ALISON BECHDEL
348
I JUST DON'T GET IT, CLARICE. YOU'VE ALREADY HAD A COMMITMENT CEREMONY. YOU'RE BOTH LEGALLY RAFFI'S PARENTS. YOU'VE BEEN TOGETHER LONGER THAN MELISSA AND JULIE AND ELLEN AND ANNE ALL PUT TOGETHER, TIMES, LIKE, A HUNDRED.
KICK IT, RAFFI!
THE OTHER WAY, SWEETIE!
WHY DO YOU NEED SOME STATE-APPROVED PIECE OF PAPER? I MEAN, A VERMONT CIVIL UNION WON'T EVEN BE VALID HERE.
IT'S NOT ABOUT THE PIECE OF PAPER. IT'S ABOUT CIVIL RIGHTS.
I USED TO FEEL LIKE YOU DO, BUT THE MORE I THINK ABOUT IT, THE MORE PISSED OFF I GET THAT IT'S AGAINST THE LAW FOR ME TO MARRY TONI.
BUT... BUT IT'S AGAINST THE LAW TO PERPE-TRATE **FRAUD** TOO. YOU'RE NOT PLANNING TO FLY OFF TO VERMONT AND PASS **BAD CHECKS!**
♪!
WHAT THE HELL KIND OF LOGIC IS **THAT**?
OH, I DON'T KNOW. DESPERATE.

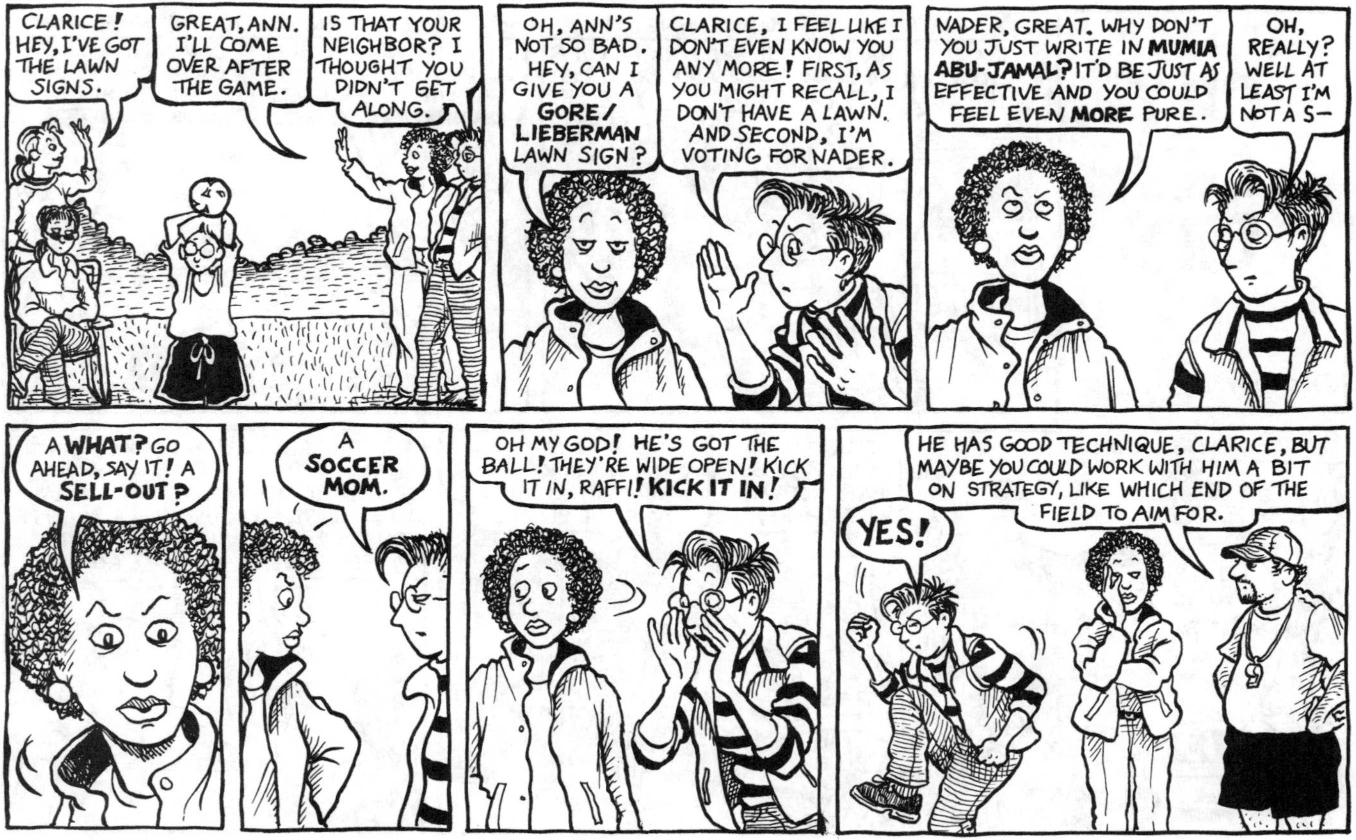

CLARICE! HEY, I'VE GOT THE LAWN SIGNS.
GREAT, ANN. I'LL COME OVER AFTER THE GAME.
IS THAT YOUR NEIGHBOR? I THOUGHT YOU DIDN'T GET ALONG.
OH, ANN'S NOT SO BAD. HEY, CAN I GIVE YOU A GORE/LIEBERMAN LAWN SIGN?
CLARICE, I FEEL LIKE I DON'T EVEN KNOW YOU ANY MORE! FIRST, AS YOU MIGHT RECALL, I DON'T HAVE A LAWN. AND SECOND, I'M VOTING FOR NADER.
NADER, GREAT. WHY DON'T YOU JUST WRITE IN MUMIA ABU-JAMAL? IT'D BE JUST AS EFFECTIVE AND YOU COULD FEEL EVEN MORE PURE.
OH, REALLY? WELL AT LEAST I'M NOT A S—
A WHAT? GO AHEAD, SAY IT! A SELL-OUT?
A SOCCER MOM.
OH MY GOD! HE'S GOT THE BALL! THEY'RE WIDE OPEN! KICK IT IN, RAFFI! KICK IT IN!
YES!
HE HAS GOOD TECHNIQUE, CLARICE, BUT MAYBE YOU COULD WORK WITH HIM A BIT ON STRATEGY, LIKE WHICH END OF THE FIELD TO AIM FOR.

CRY CRY CRY

© 2000 BY ALISON BECHDEL

MO AND SYDNEY ARE BABYSITTING...

THANK YOU, SYDNEEE!

RAFFI, NOT IN THE PARKING LOT! WE'LL GO HOME AND PRACTICE IN THE DRIVEWAY!

TOYS 'R'... TO... 'R' US...

10-25

SUV 24

349

WHILE CLARICE AND TONI ARRIVE IN VERMONT.

HUH. IT'S NOT QUITE AS PICTURESQUE AS I WAS LED TO BELIEVE.

DON'T WORRY. OUR B&B IS WAY OUT IN THE COUNTRY.

THE HOME DEPOT

WAL★MART

OLD NAVY

STAPLES

BUNS & NOODLE

Thrifty CAR RENTAL

MAP O' VERMONT

TWENTY MILES LATER...

SEE? IT IS PRETTY.

PRETTY WHITE.

WELL, IT'S NO SAMBA FEST. BUT THAT'S NOT WHY WE'RE HERE, IS IT?

LOOK. MORE OF THOSE ANTI-CIVIL UNION SIGNS. GOD, THEY'RE ALL OVER THE PLACE.

TAKE BACK VERMONT

TAKE BACK VERMONT

DAMN IT, CLARICE! THIS IS SUPPOSED TO BE A FUN, ROMANTIC ADVENTURE! WILL YOU STOP FOCUSING ON EVERY POSSIBLE NEGATIVE?

I CAN'T HELP IT, TONI. I'M A REALIST, NOT A ROMANTIC.

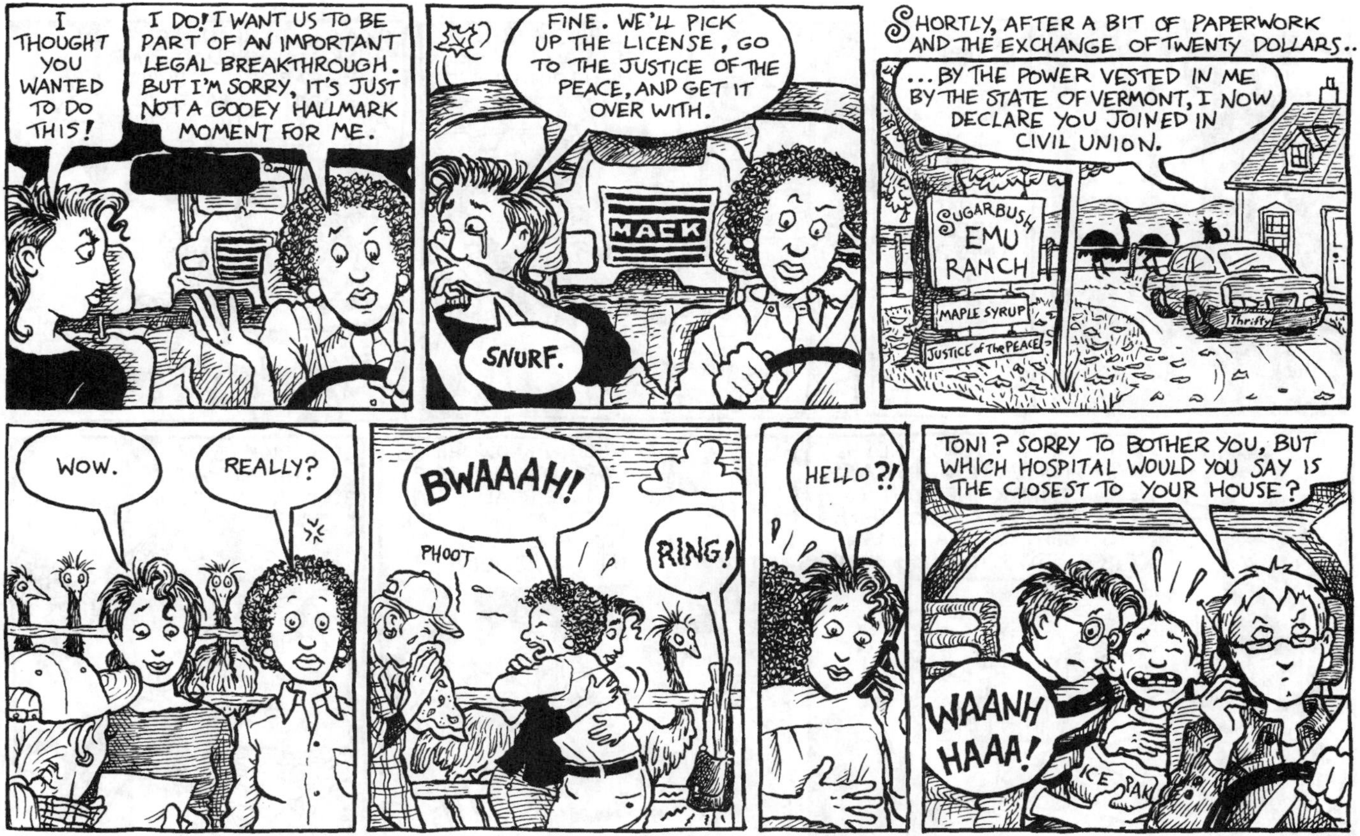
I THOUGHT YOU WANTED TO DO THIS!
I DO! I WANT US TO BE PART OF AN IMPORTANT LEGAL BREAKTHROUGH. BUT I'M SORRY, IT'S JUST NOT A GOOEY HALLMARK MOMENT FOR ME.
FINE. WE'LL PICK UP THE LICENSE, GO TO THE JUSTICE OF THE PEACE, AND GET IT OVER WITH.
MACK
SNURF.
SHORTLY, AFTER A BIT OF PAPERWORK AND THE EXCHANGE OF TWENTY DOLLARS..
...BY THE POWER VESTED IN ME BY THE STATE OF VERMONT, I NOW DECLARE YOU JOINED IN CIVIL UNION.
SUGARBUSH EMU RANCH
MAPLE SYRUP
JUSTICE of The PEACE
Thrifty
WOW.
REALLY?
BWAAAH!
PHOOT
RING!
HELLO?!
TONI? SORRY TO BOTHER YOU, BUT WHICH HOSPITAL WOULD YOU SAY IS THE CLOSEST TO YOUR HOUSE?
WAANH HAAA!
ICE PAK

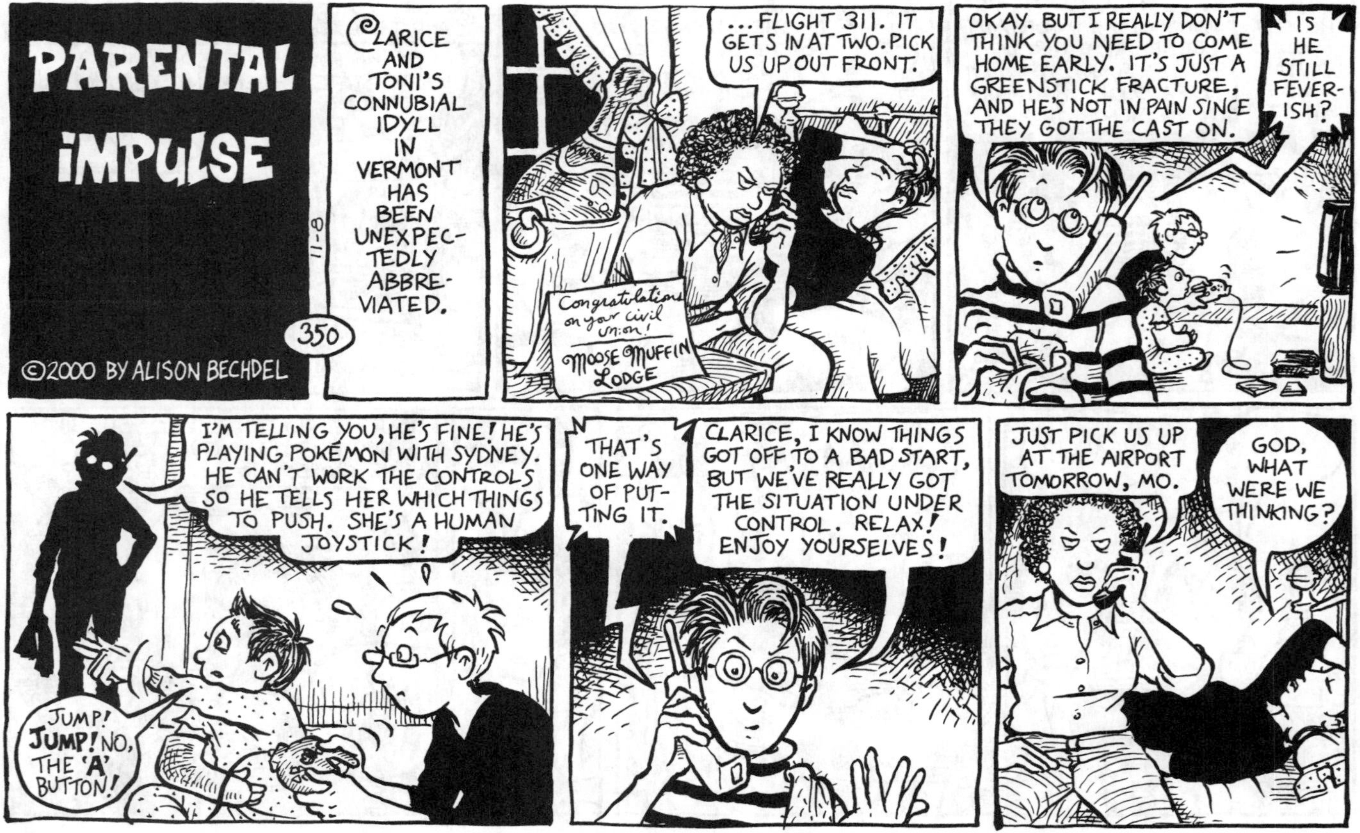

PARENTAL iMPULSE
©2000 BY ALISON BECHDEL
350
11-8
CLARICE AND TONI'S CONNUBIAL IDYLL IN VERMONT HAS BEEN UNEXPECTEDLY ABBREVIATED.
...FLIGHT 311. IT GETS IN AT TWO. PICK US UP OUT FRONT.
Congratulations on your civil union!
MOOSE MUFFIN LODGE
OKAY. BUT I REALLY DON'T THINK YOU NEED TO COME HOME EARLY. IT'S JUST A GREENSTICK FRACTURE, AND HE'S NOT IN PAIN SINCE THEY GOT THE CAST ON.
IS HE STILL FEVERISH?
I'M TELLING YOU, HE'S FINE! HE'S PLAYING POKÉMON WITH SYDNEY. HE CAN'T WORK THE CONTROLS SO HE TELLS HER WHICH THINGS TO PUSH. SHE'S A HUMAN JOYSTICK!
JUMP! JUMP! NO, THE 'A' BUTTON!
THAT'S ONE WAY OF PUTTING IT.
CLARICE, I KNOW THINGS GOT OFF TO A BAD START, BUT WE'VE REALLY GOT THE SITUATION UNDER CONTROL. RELAX! ENJOY YOURSELVES!
JUST PICK US UP AT THE AIRPORT TOMORROW, MO.
GOD, WHAT WERE WE THINKING?

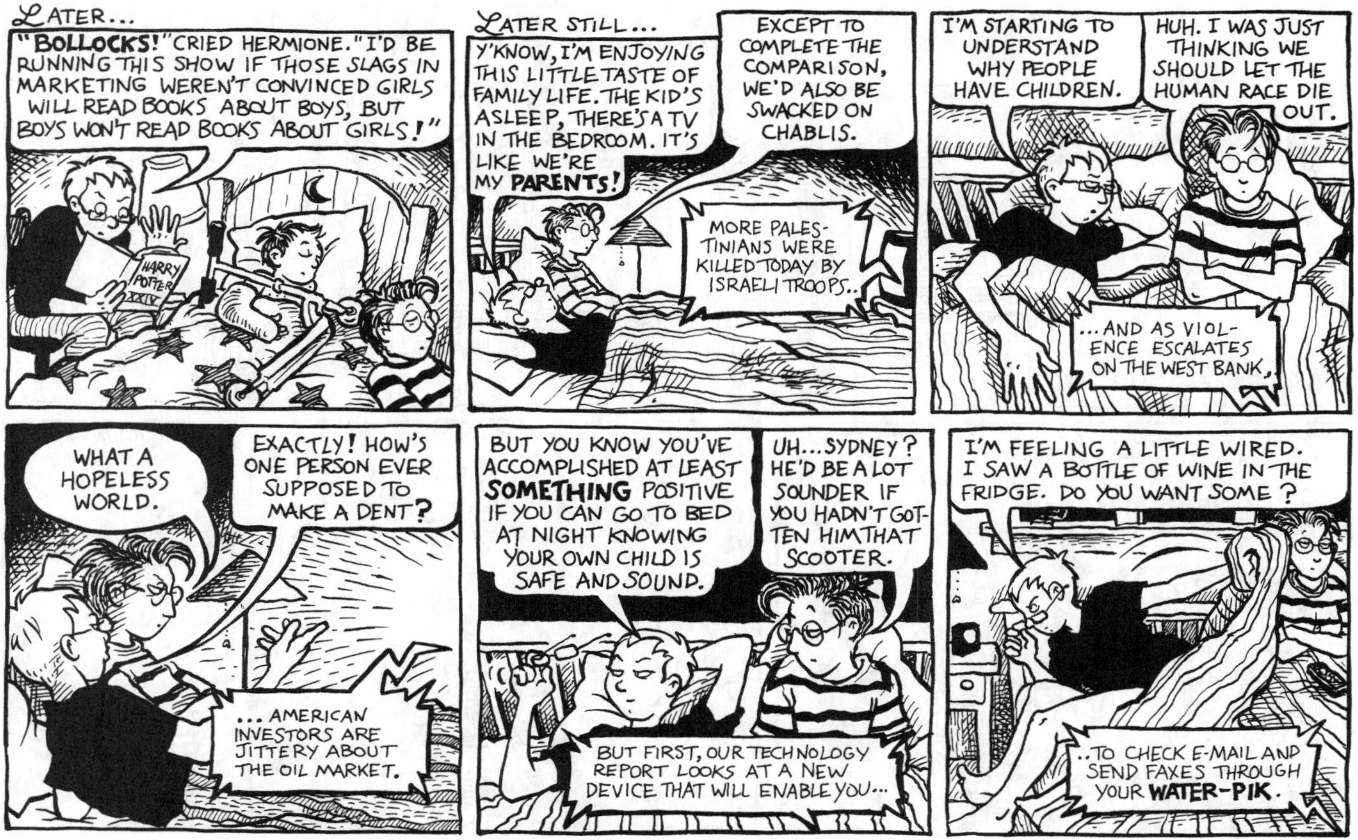

LATER...
"BOLLOCKS!" CRIED HERMIONE. "I'D BE RUNNING THIS SHOW IF THOSE SLAGS IN MARKETING WEREN'T CONVINCED GIRLS WILL READ BOOKS ABOUT BOYS, BUT BOYS WON'T READ BOOKS ABOUT GIRLS!"
HARRY POTTER XXIV
LATER STILL...
Y'KNOW, I'M ENJOYING THIS LITTLE TASTE OF FAMILY LIFE. THE KID'S ASLEEP, THERE'S A TV IN THE BEDROOM. IT'S LIKE WE'RE MY PARENTS!
EXCEPT TO COMPLETE THE COMPARISON, WE'D ALSO BE SWACKED ON CHABLIS.
MORE PALESTINIANS WERE KILLED TODAY BY ISRAELI TROOPS..
I'M STARTING TO UNDERSTAND WHY PEOPLE HAVE CHILDREN.
HUH. I WAS JUST THINKING WE SHOULD LET THE HUMAN RACE DIE OUT.
...AND AS VIOLENCE ESCALATES ON THE WEST BANK,
WHAT A HOPELESS WORLD.
EXACTLY! HOW'S ONE PERSON EVER SUPPOSED TO MAKE A DENT?
...AMERICAN INVESTORS ARE JITTERY ABOUT THE OIL MARKET.
BUT YOU KNOW YOU'VE ACCOMPLISHED AT LEAST SOMETHING POSITIVE IF YOU CAN GO TO BED AT NIGHT KNOWING YOUR OWN CHILD IS SAFE AND SOUND.
UH...SYDNEY? HE'D BE A LOT SOUNDER IF YOU HADN'T GOTTEN HIM THAT SCOOTER.
BUT FIRST, OUR TECHNOLOGY REPORT LOOKS AT A NEW DEVICE THAT WILL ENABLE YOU...
I'M FEELING A LITTLE WIRED. I SAW A BOTTLE OF WINE IN THE FRIDGE. DO YOU WANT SOME?
..TO CHECK E-MAIL AND SEND FAXES THROUGH YOUR WATER-PIK.

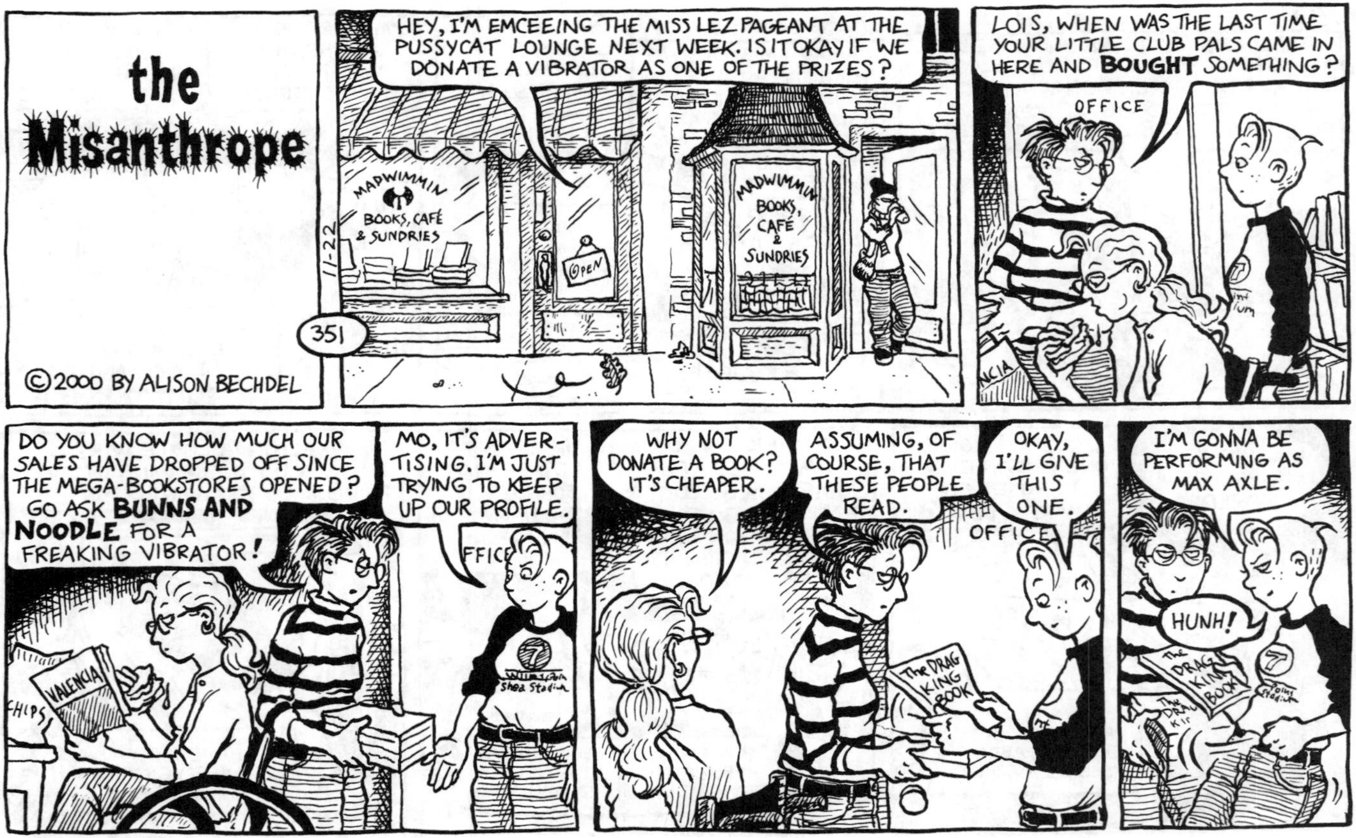
the Misanthrope
©2000 BY ALISON BECHDEL
351
11-22
HEY, I'M EMCEEING THE MISS LEZ PAGEANT AT THE PUSSYCAT LOUNGE NEXT WEEK. IS IT OKAY IF WE DONATE A VIBRATOR AS ONE OF THE PRIZES?
MADWIMMIN BOOKS, CAFÉ & SUNDRIES
OPEN
MADWIMMIN BOOKS, CAFÉ & SUNDRIES
LOIS, WHEN WAS THE LAST TIME YOUR LITTLE CLUB PALS CAME IN HERE AND **BOUGHT** SOMETHING?
OFFICE
DO YOU KNOW HOW MUCH OUR SALES HAVE DROPPED OFF SINCE THE MEGA-BOOKSTORES OPENED? GO ASK **BUNNS AND NOODLE** FOR A FREAKING VIBRATOR!
VALENCIA
CHIPS
MO, IT'S ADVERTISING. I'M JUST TRYING TO KEEP UP OUR PROFILE.
Shea Stadium
WHY NOT DONATE A BOOK? IT'S CHEAPER.
ASSUMING, OF COURSE, THAT THESE PEOPLE READ.
OKAY, I'LL GIVE THIS ONE.
OFFICE
The DRAG KING BOOK
I'M GONNA BE PERFORMING AS MAX AXLE.
HUNH!
The DRAG KING BOOK

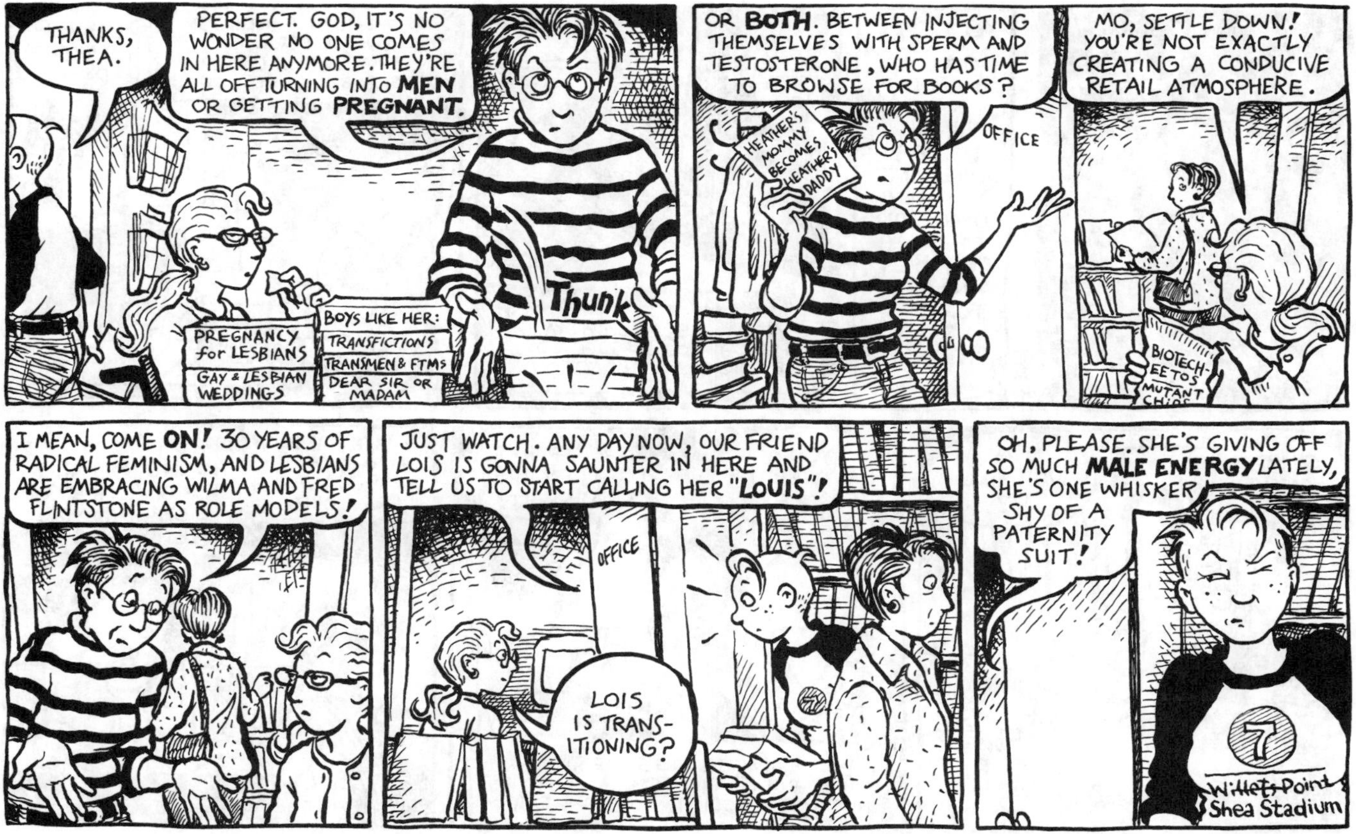
THANKS, THEA.
PERFECT. GOD, IT'S NO WONDER NO ONE COMES IN HERE ANYMORE. THEY'RE ALL OFF TURNING INTO **MEN** OR GETTING **PREGNANT**.
PREGNANCY for LESBIANS
GAY & LESBIAN WEDDINGS
BOYS LIKE HER:
TRANSFICTIONS
TRANSMEN & FTMS
DEAR SIR OR MADAM
Thunk
OR **BOTH**. BETWEEN INJECTING THEMSELVES WITH SPERM AND TESTOSTERONE, WHO HAS TIME TO BROWSE FOR BOOKS?
HEATHER'S MOMMY BECOMES HEATHER'S DADDY
OFFICE
MO, SETTLE DOWN! YOU'RE NOT EXACTLY CREATING A CONDUCIVE RETAIL ATMOSPHERE.
BIOTECH-EETOS
MUTANT CHIPS
I MEAN, COME **ON**! 30 YEARS OF RADICAL FEMINISM, AND LESBIANS ARE EMBRACING WILMA AND FRED FLINTSTONE AS ROLE MODELS!
JUST WATCH. ANY DAY NOW, OUR FRIEND LOIS IS GONNA SAUNTER IN HERE AND TELL US TO START CALLING HER "**LOUIS**"!
OFFICE
LOIS IS TRANSITIONING?
OH, PLEASE. SHE'S GIVING OFF SO MUCH **MALE ENERGY** LATELY, SHE'S ONE WHISKER SHY OF A PATERNITY SUIT!
7
Willets Point
Shea Stadium

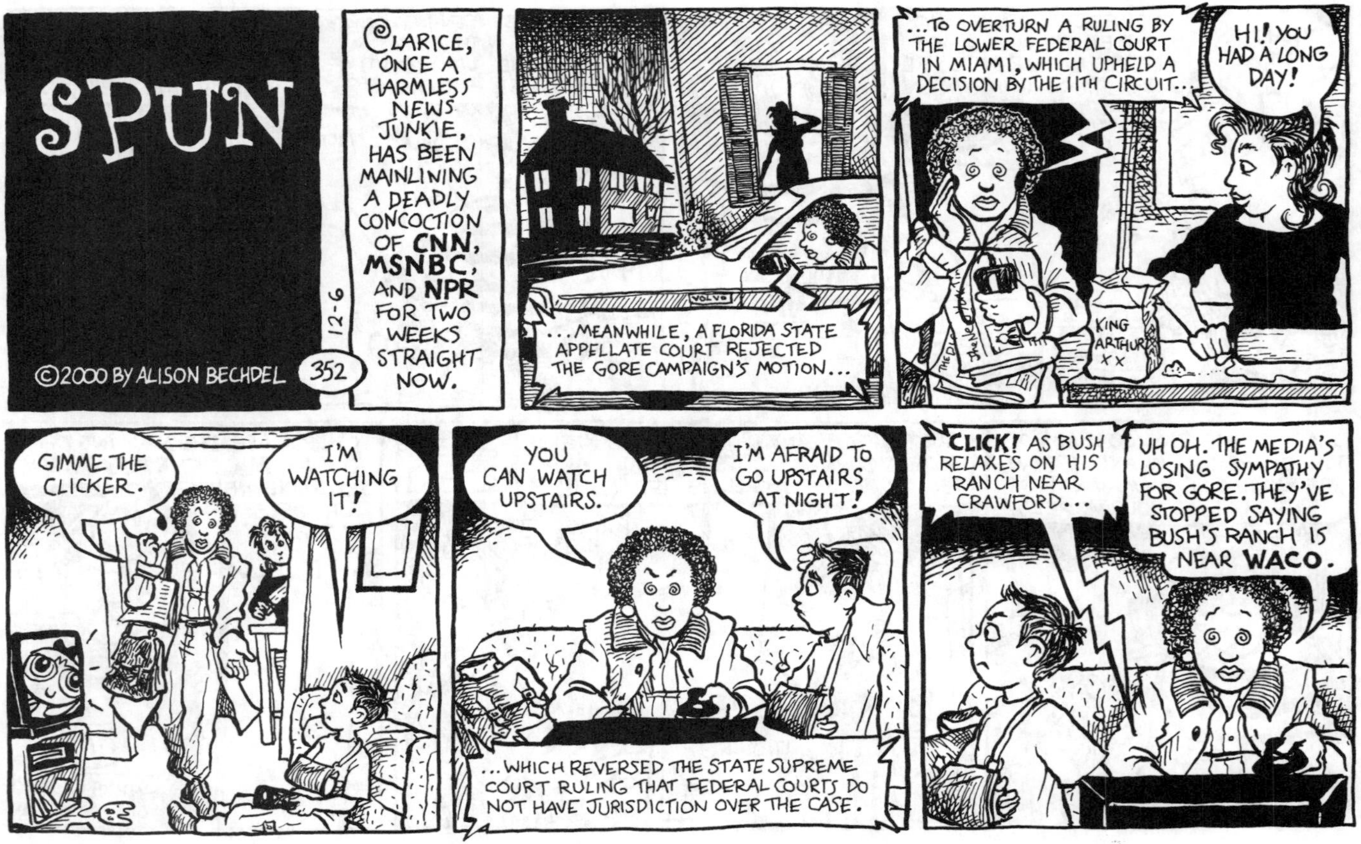
SPUN
©2000 BY ALISON BECHDEL
352
12-6
CLARICE, ONCE A HARMLESS NEWS JUNKIE, HAS BEEN MAINLINING A DEADLY CONCOCTION OF CNN, MSNBC, AND NPR FOR TWO WEEKS STRAIGHT NOW.
VOLVO
...MEANWHILE, A FLORIDA STATE APPELLATE COURT REJECTED THE GORE CAMPAIGN'S MOTION...
...TO OVERTURN A RULING BY THE LOWER FEDERAL COURT IN MIAMI, WHICH UPHELD A DECISION BY THE 11TH CIRCUIT...
HI! YOU HAD A LONG DAY!
KING ARTHUR
XX
GIMME THE CLICKER.
I'M WATCHING IT!
YOU CAN WATCH UPSTAIRS.
I'M AFRAID TO GO UPSTAIRS AT NIGHT!
...WHICH REVERSED THE STATE SUPREME COURT RULING THAT FEDERAL COURTS DO NOT HAVE JURISDICTION OVER THE CASE.
CLICK! AS BUSH RELAXES ON HIS RANCH NEAR CRAWFORD...
UH OH. THE MEDIA'S LOSING SYMPATHY FOR GORE. THEY'VE STOPPED SAYING BUSH'S RANCH IS NEAR WACO.

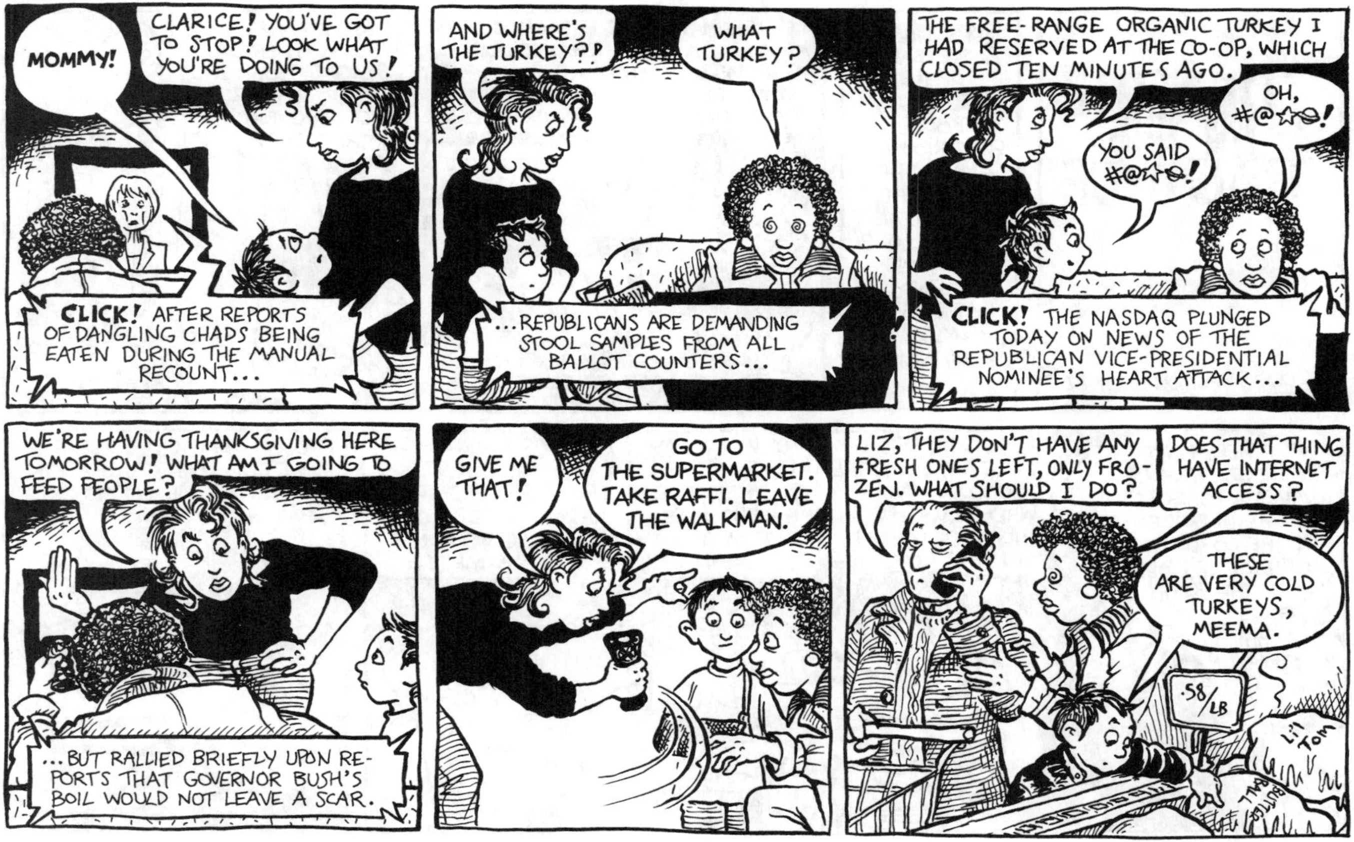
MOMMY!
CLARICE! YOU'VE GOT TO STOP! LOOK WHAT YOU'RE DOING TO US!
CLICK! AFTER REPORTS OF DANGLING CHADS BEING EATEN DURING THE MANUAL RECOUNT...
AND WHERE'S THE TURKEY?!
WHAT TURKEY?
...REPUBLICANS ARE DEMANDING STOOL SAMPLES FROM ALL BALLOT COUNTERS...
THE FREE-RANGE ORGANIC TURKEY I HAD RESERVED AT THE CO-OP, WHICH CLOSED TEN MINUTES AGO.
OH, #@☆☆!
YOU SAID #@☆☆!
CLICK! THE NASDAQ PLUNGED TODAY ON NEWS OF THE REPUBLICAN VICE-PRESIDENTIAL NOMINEE'S HEART ATTACK...
WE'RE HAVING THANKSGIVING HERE TOMORROW! WHAT AM I GOING TO FEED PEOPLE?
...BUT RALLIED BRIEFLY UPON REPORTS THAT GOVERNOR BUSH'S BOIL WOULD NOT LEAVE A SCAR.
GIVE ME THAT!
GO TO THE SUPERMARKET. TAKE RAFFI. LEAVE THE WALKMAN.
LIZ, THEY DON'T HAVE ANY FRESH ONES LEFT, ONLY FROZEN. WHAT SHOULD I DO?
DOES THAT THING HAVE INTERNET ACCESS?
THESE ARE VERY COLD TURKEYS, MEEMA.
.58/LB
LI'L TOM
BUTTERBALL

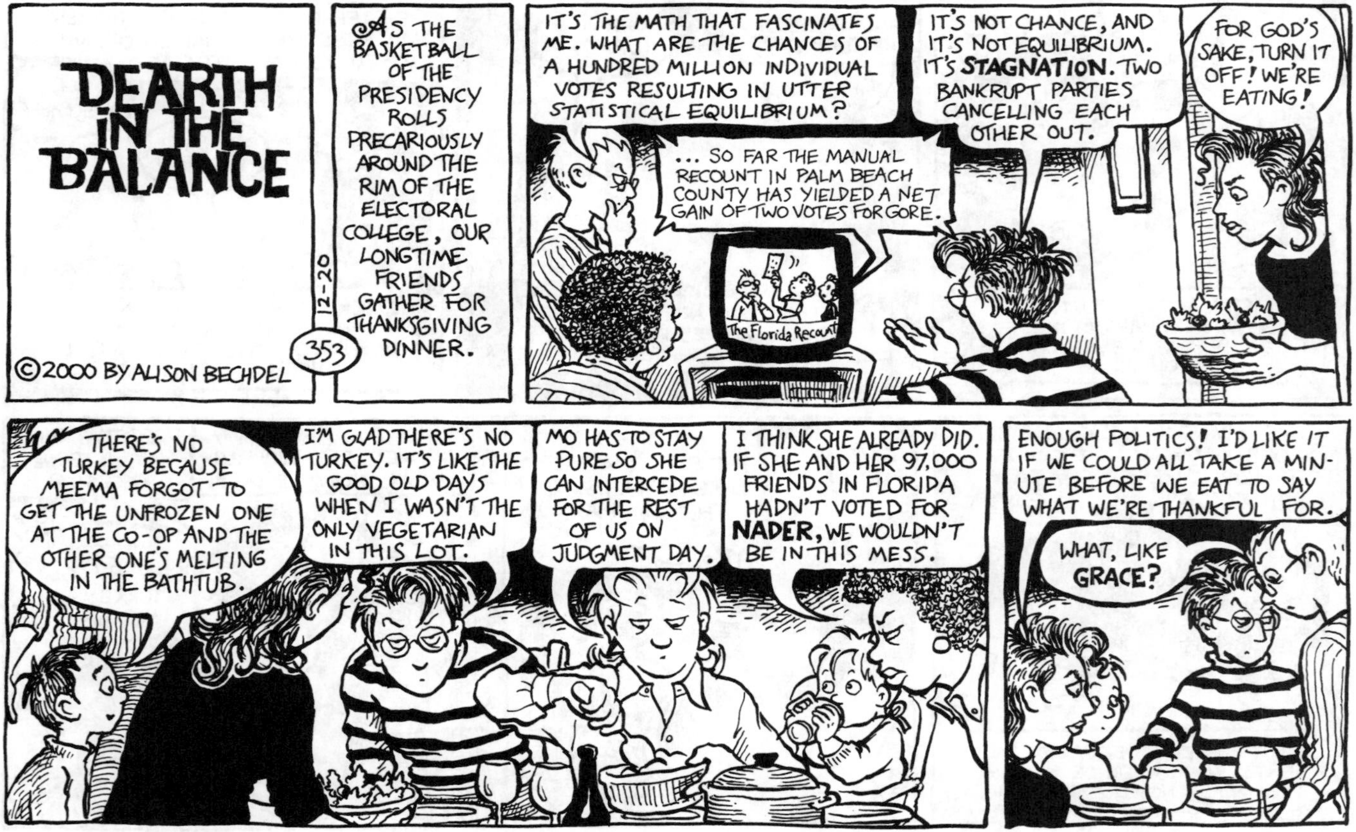
DEARTH IN THE BALANCE
©2000 BY ALISON BECHDEL
353
12-20
AS THE BASKETBALL OF THE PRESIDENCY ROLLS PRECARIOUSLY AROUND THE RIM OF THE ELECTORAL COLLEGE, OUR LONGTIME FRIENDS GATHER FOR THANKSGIVING DINNER.
IT'S THE MATH THAT FASCINATES ME. WHAT ARE THE CHANCES OF A HUNDRED MILLION INDIVIDUAL VOTES RESULTING IN UTTER STATISTICAL EQUILIBRIUM?
... SO FAR THE MANUAL RECOUNT IN PALM BEACH COUNTY HAS YIELDED A NET GAIN OF TWO VOTES FOR GORE.
The Florida Recount
IT'S NOT CHANCE, AND IT'S NOT EQUILIBRIUM. IT'S **STAGNATION**. TWO BANKRUPT PARTIES CANCELLING EACH OTHER OUT.
FOR GOD'S SAKE, TURN IT OFF! WE'RE EATING!
THERE'S NO TURKEY BECAUSE MEEMA FORGOT TO GET THE UNFROZEN ONE AT THE CO-OP AND THE OTHER ONE'S MELTING IN THE BATHTUB.
I'M GLAD THERE'S NO TURKEY. IT'S LIKE THE GOOD OLD DAYS WHEN I WASN'T THE ONLY VEGETARIAN IN THIS LOT.
MO HAS TO STAY PURE SO SHE CAN INTERCEDE FOR THE REST OF US ON JUDGMENT DAY.
I THINK SHE ALREADY DID. IF SHE AND HER 97,000 FRIENDS IN FLORIDA HADN'T VOTED FOR **NADER**, WE WOULDN'T BE IN THIS MESS.
ENOUGH POLITICS! I'D LIKE IT IF WE COULD ALL TAKE A MINUTE BEFORE WE EAT TO SAY WHAT WE'RE THANKFUL FOR.
WHAT, LIKE **GRACE**?

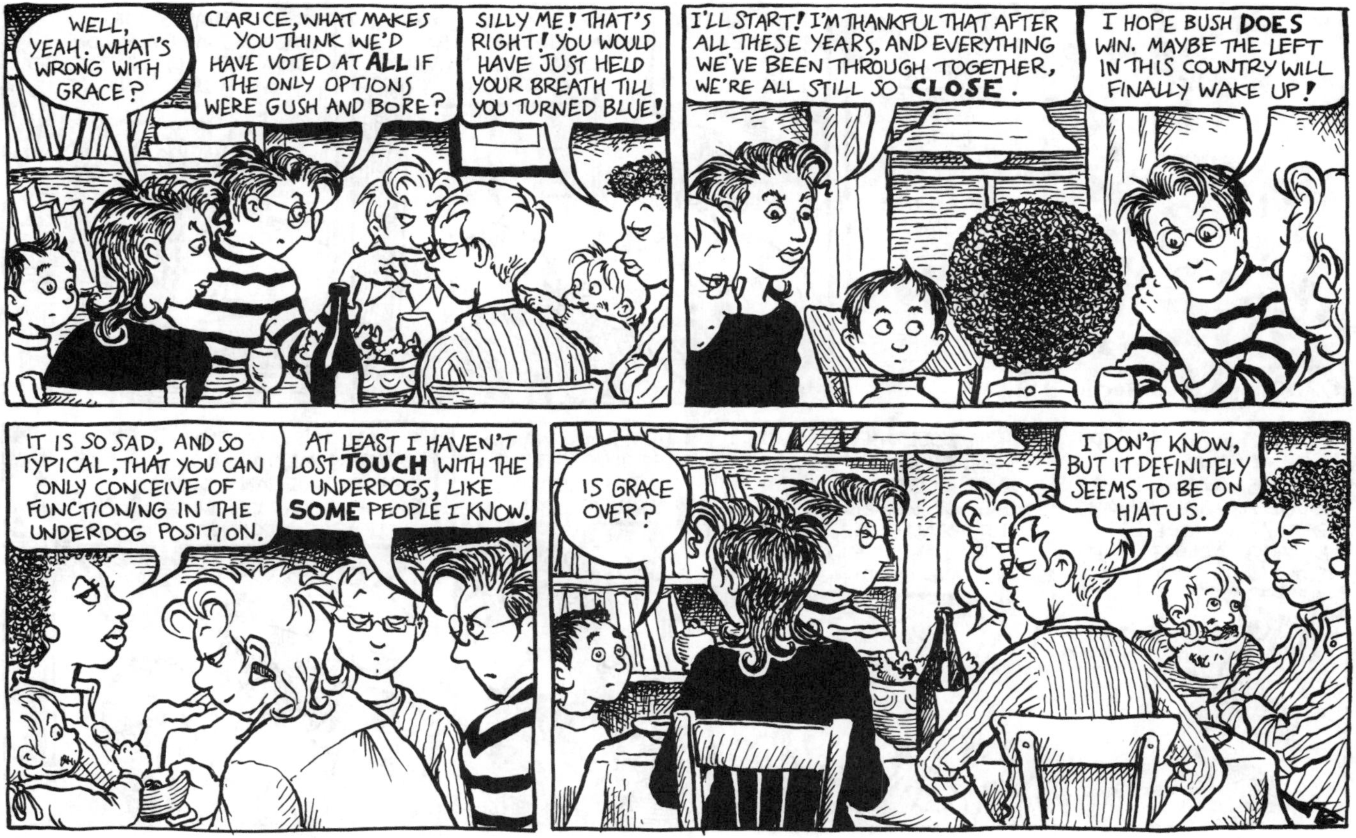
WELL, YEAH. WHAT'S WRONG WITH GRACE?
CLARICE, WHAT MAKES YOU THINK WE'D HAVE VOTED AT ALL IF THE ONLY OPTIONS WERE GUSH AND BORE?
SILLY ME! THAT'S RIGHT! YOU WOULD HAVE JUST HELD YOUR BREATH TILL YOU TURNED BLUE!
I'LL START! I'M THANKFUL THAT AFTER ALL THESE YEARS, AND EVERYTHING WE'VE BEEN THROUGH TOGETHER, WE'RE ALL STILL SO CLOSE.
I HOPE BUSH DOES WIN. MAYBE THE LEFT IN THIS COUNTRY WILL FINALLY WAKE UP!
IT IS SO SAD, AND SO TYPICAL, THAT YOU CAN ONLY CONCEIVE OF FUNCTIONING IN THE UNDERDOG POSITION.
AT LEAST I HAVEN'T LOST TOUCH WITH THE UNDERDOGS, LIKE SOME PEOPLE I KNOW.
IS GRACE OVER?
I DON'T KNOW, BUT IT DEFINITELY SEEMS TO BE ON HIATUS.

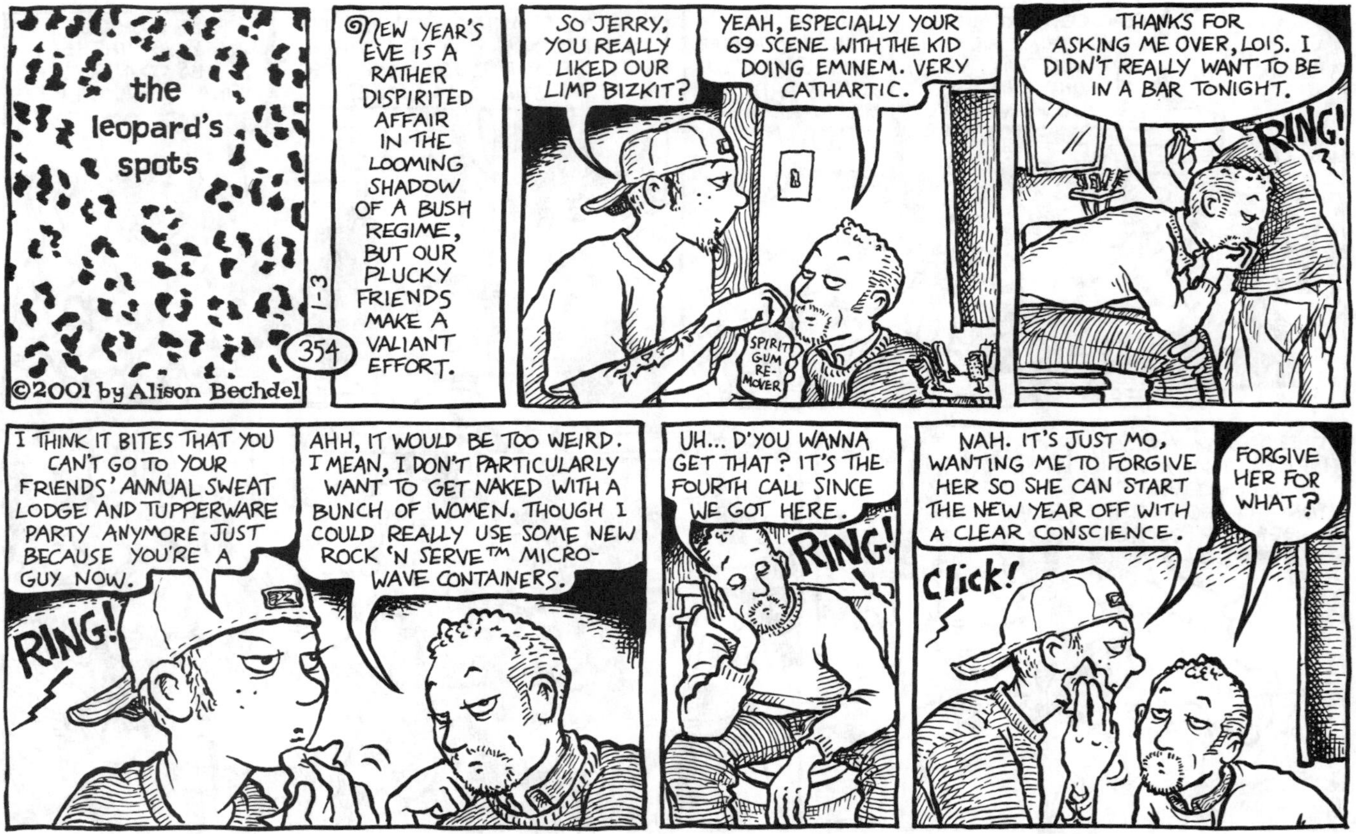

the leopard's spots
©2001 by Alison Bechdel
354
1-3
NEW YEAR'S EVE IS A RATHER DISPIRITED AFFAIR IN THE LOOMING SHADOW OF A BUSH REGIME, BUT OUR PLUCKY FRIENDS MAKE A VALIANT EFFORT.
SO JERRY, YOU REALLY LIKED OUR LIMP BIZKIT?
YEAH, ESPECIALLY YOUR 69 SCENE WITH THE KID DOING EMINEM. VERY CATHARTIC.
SPIRIT GUM RE-MOVER
THANKS FOR ASKING ME OVER, LOIS. I DIDN'T REALLY WANT TO BE IN A BAR TONIGHT.
RING!
I THINK IT BITES THAT YOU CAN'T GO TO YOUR FRIENDS' ANNUAL SWEAT LODGE AND TUPPERWARE PARTY ANYMORE JUST BECAUSE YOU'RE A GUY NOW.
AHH, IT WOULD BE TOO WEIRD. I MEAN, I DON'T PARTICULARLY WANT TO GET NAKED WITH A BUNCH OF WOMEN. THOUGH I COULD REALLY USE SOME NEW ROCK 'N SERVE™ MICRO-WAVE CONTAINERS.
RING!
UH... D'YOU WANNA GET THAT? IT'S THE FOURTH CALL SINCE WE GOT HERE.
RING!
NAH. IT'S JUST MO, WANTING ME TO FORGIVE HER SO SHE CAN START THE NEW YEAR OFF WITH A CLEAR CONSCIENCE.
FORGIVE HER FOR WHAT?
Click!

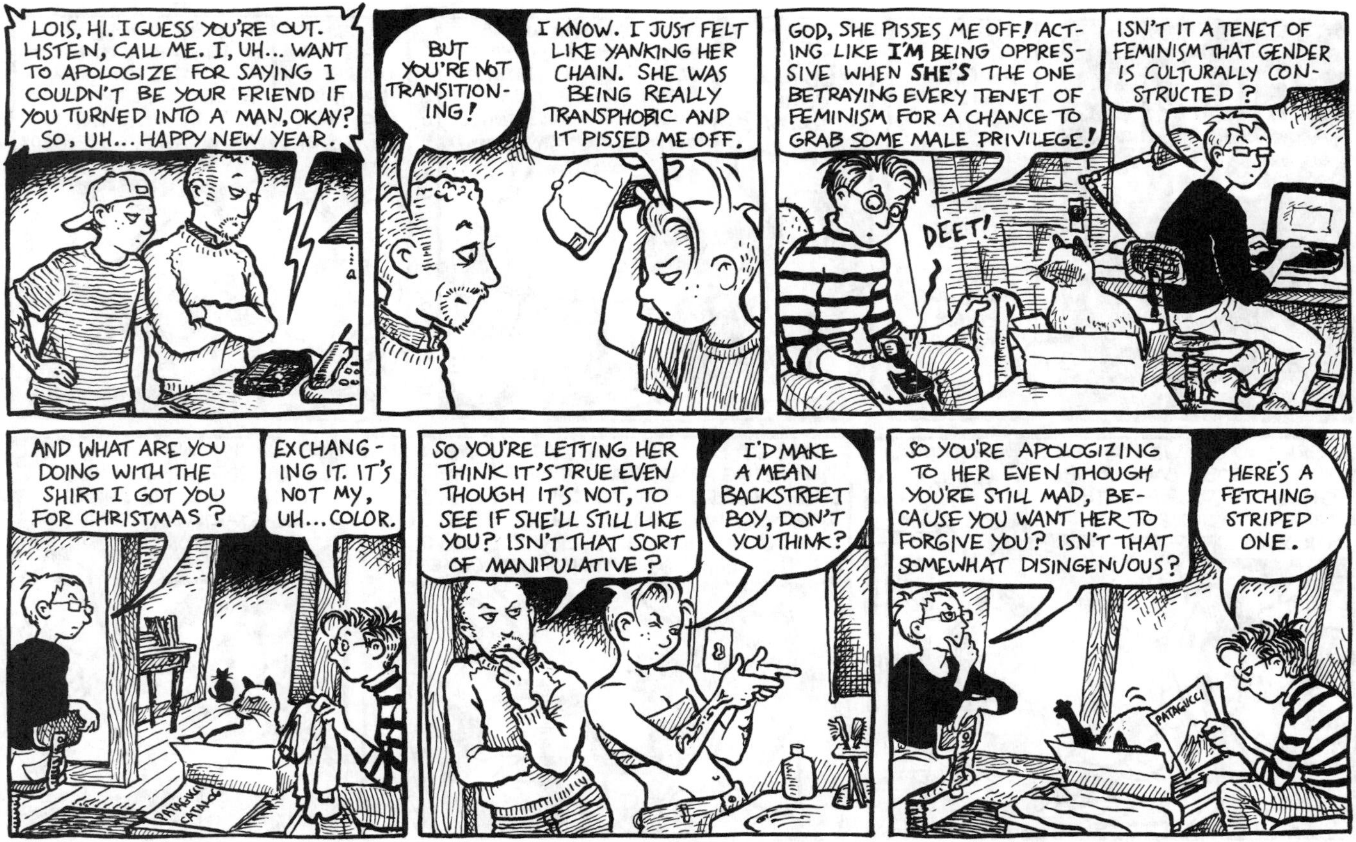
LOIS, HI. I GUESS YOU'RE OUT. LISTEN, CALL ME. I, UH... WANT TO APOLOGIZE FOR SAYING I COULDN'T BE YOUR FRIEND IF YOU TURNED INTO A MAN, OKAY? SO, UH... HAPPY NEW YEAR.
BUT YOU'RE NOT TRANSITIONING!
I KNOW. I JUST FELT LIKE YANKING HER CHAIN. SHE WAS BEING REALLY TRANSPHOBIC AND IT PISSED ME OFF.
GOD, SHE PISSES ME OFF! ACTING LIKE **I'M** BEING OPPRESSIVE WHEN **SHE'S** THE ONE BETRAYING EVERY TENET OF FEMINISM FOR A CHANCE TO GRAB SOME MALE PRIVILEGE!
DEET!
ISN'T IT A TENET OF FEMINISM THAT GENDER IS CULTURALLY CONSTRUCTED?
AND WHAT ARE YOU DOING WITH THE SHIRT I GOT YOU FOR CHRISTMAS?
EXCHANGING IT. IT'S NOT MY, UH... COLOR.
PATAGUCCI CATALOG
SO YOU'RE LETTING HER THINK IT'S TRUE EVEN THOUGH IT'S NOT, TO SEE IF SHE'LL STILL LIKE YOU? ISN'T THAT SORT OF MANIPULATIVE?
I'D MAKE A MEAN BACKSTREET BOY, DON'T YOU THINK?
SO YOU'RE APOLOGIZING TO HER EVEN THOUGH YOU'RE STILL MAD, BECAUSE YOU WANT HER TO FORGIVE YOU? ISN'T THAT SOMEWHAT DISINGENUOUS?
HERE'S A FETCHING STRIPED ONE.
PATAGUCCI

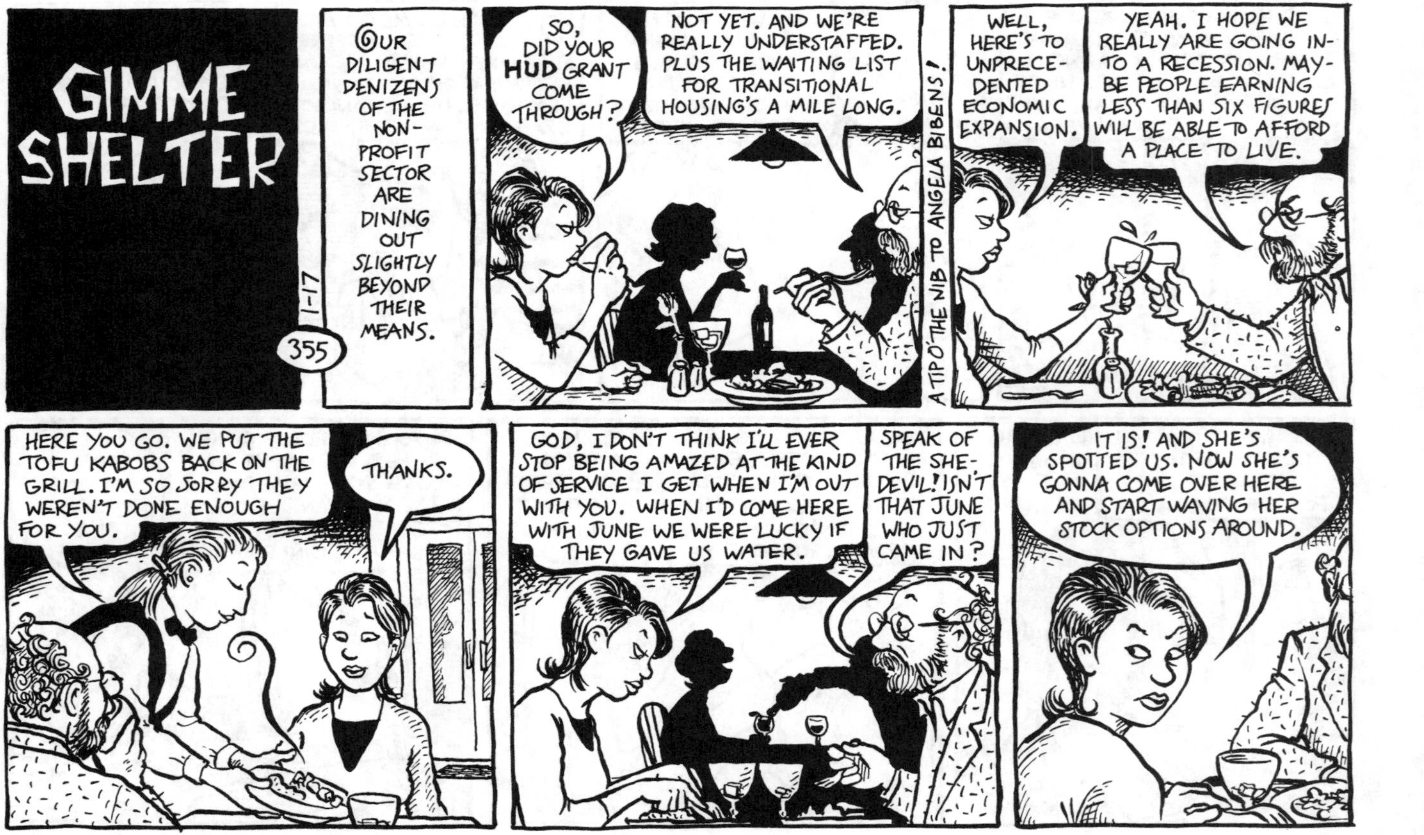
GIMME SHELTER
1-17
355
OUR DILIGENT DENIZENS OF THE NON-PROFIT SECTOR ARE DINING OUT SLIGHTLY BEYOND THEIR MEANS.
SO, DID YOUR HUD GRANT COME THROUGH?
NOT YET. AND WE'RE REALLY UNDERSTAFFED. PLUS THE WAITING LIST FOR TRANSITIONAL HOUSING'S A MILE LONG.
A TIP O' THE NIB TO ANGELA BIBENS!
WELL, HERE'S TO UNPRECE-DENTED ECONOMIC EXPANSION.
YEAH. I HOPE WE REALLY ARE GOING IN-TO A RECESSION. MAY-BE PEOPLE EARNING LESS THAN SIX FIGURES WILL BE ABLE TO AFFORD A PLACE TO LIVE.
HERE YOU GO. WE PUT THE TOFU KABOBS BACK ON THE GRILL. I'M SO SORRY THEY WEREN'T DONE ENOUGH FOR YOU.
THANKS.
GOD, I DON'T THINK I'LL EVER STOP BEING AMAZED AT THE KIND OF SERVICE I GET WHEN I'M OUT WITH YOU. WHEN I'D COME HERE WITH JUNE WE WERE LUCKY IF THEY GAVE US WATER.
SPEAK OF THE SHE-DEVIL! ISN'T THAT JUNE WHO JUST CAME IN?
IT IS! AND SHE'S SPOTTED US. NOW SHE'S GONNA COME OVER HERE AND START WAVING HER STOCK OPTIONS AROUND.

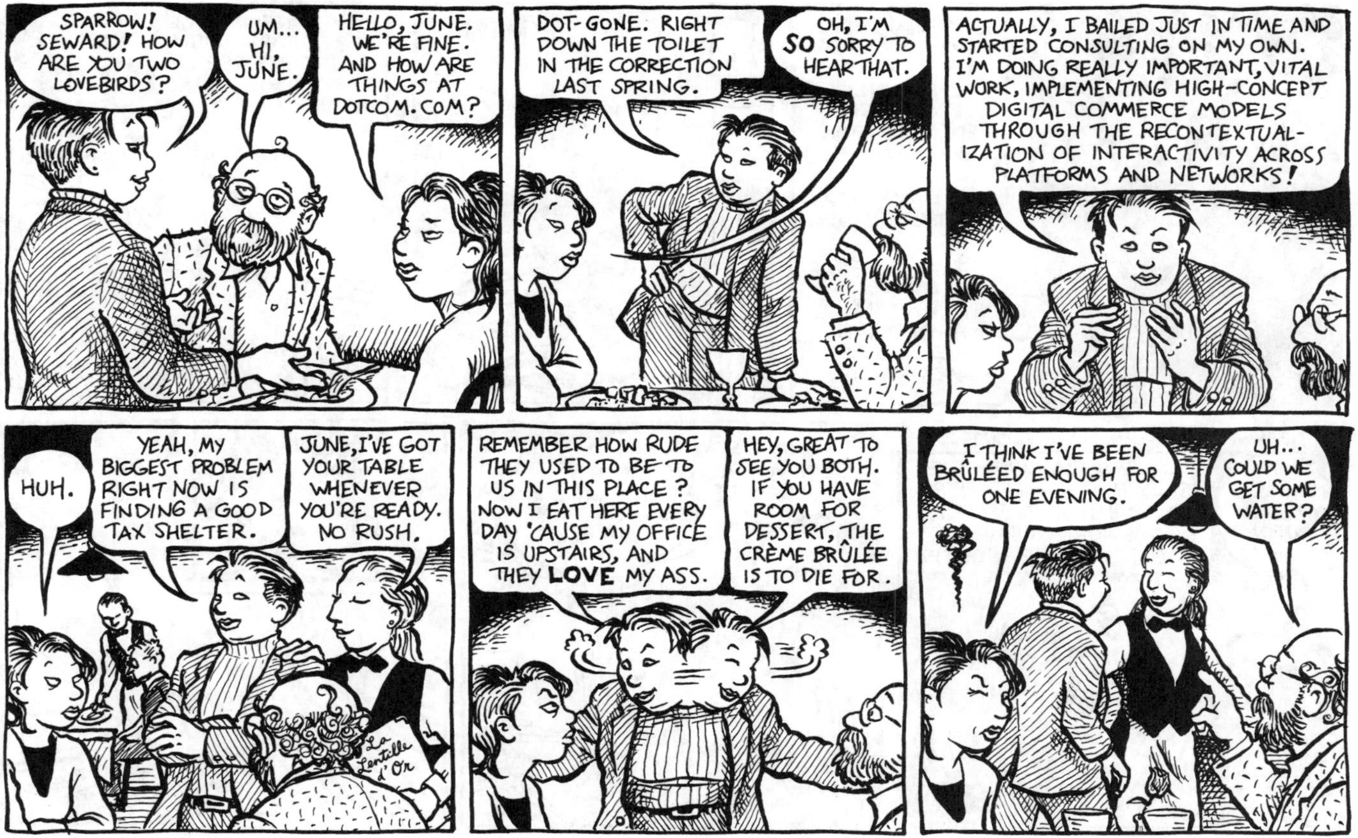
SPARROW! SEWARD! HOW ARE YOU TWO LOVEBIRDS?
UM... HI, JUNE.
HELLO, JUNE. WE'RE FINE. AND HOW ARE THINGS AT DOTCOM.COM?
DOT-GONE. RIGHT DOWN THE TOILET IN THE CORRECTION LAST SPRING.
OH, I'M SO SORRY TO HEAR THAT.
ACTUALLY, I BAILED JUST IN TIME AND STARTED CONSULTING ON MY OWN. I'M DOING REALLY IMPORTANT, VITAL WORK, IMPLEMENTING HIGH-CONCEPT DIGITAL COMMERCE MODELS THROUGH THE RECONTEXTUALIZATION OF INTERACTIVITY ACROSS PLATFORMS AND NETWORKS!
HUH.
YEAH, MY BIGGEST PROBLEM RIGHT NOW IS FINDING A GOOD TAX SHELTER.
JUNE, I'VE GOT YOUR TABLE WHENEVER YOU'RE READY. NO RUSH.
La Lentille d'Or
REMEMBER HOW RUDE THEY USED TO BE TO US IN THIS PLACE? NOW I EAT HERE EVERY DAY 'CAUSE MY OFFICE IS UPSTAIRS, AND THEY LOVE MY ASS.
HEY, GREAT TO SEE YOU BOTH. IF YOU HAVE ROOM FOR DESSERT, THE CRÈME BRÛLÉE IS TO DIE FOR.
I THINK I'VE BEEN BRÛLÉED ENOUGH FOR ONE EVENING.
UH... COULD WE GET SOME WATER?

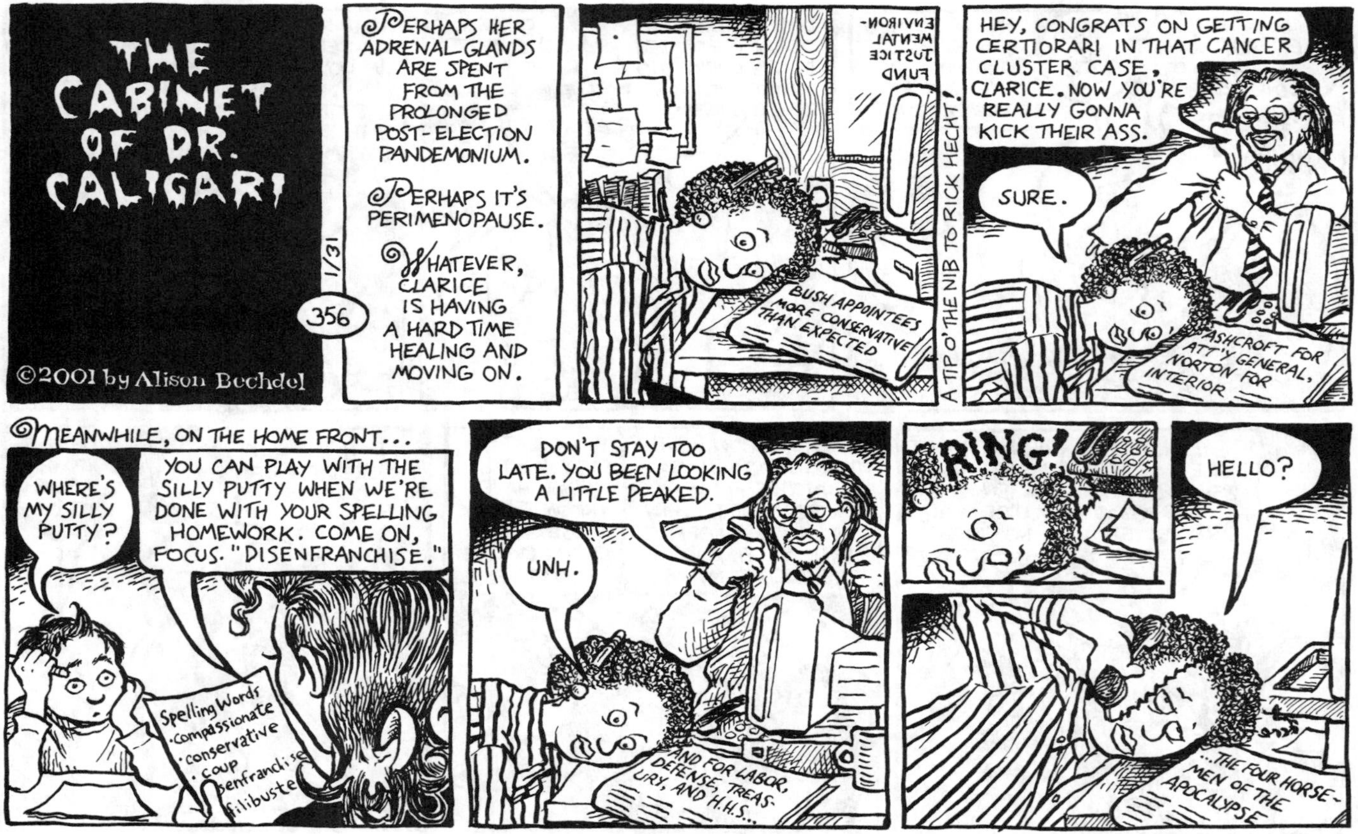
THE CABINET OF DR. CALIGARI
©2001 by Alison Bechdel
356
1/31
PERHAPS HER ADRENAL GLANDS ARE SPENT FROM THE PROLONGED POST-ELECTION PANDEMONIUM.
PERHAPS IT'S PERIMENOPAUSE.
WHATEVER, CLARICE IS HAVING A HARD TIME HEALING AND MOVING ON.
ENVIRON-MENTAL JUSTICE FUND
BUSH APPOINTEES MORE CONSERVATIVE THAN EXPECTED
A TIP O' THE NIB TO RICK HECHT!
HEY, CONGRATS ON GETTING CERTIORARI IN THAT CANCER CLUSTER CASE, CLARICE. NOW YOU'RE REALLY GONNA KICK THEIR ASS.
SURE.
ASHCROFT FOR ATT'Y GENERAL, NORTON FOR INTERIOR
MEANWHILE, ON THE HOME FRONT...
WHERE'S MY SILLY PUTTY?
YOU CAN PLAY WITH THE SILLY PUTTY WHEN WE'RE DONE WITH YOUR SPELLING HOMEWORK. COME ON, FOCUS. "DISENFRANCHISE."
Spelling Words
·compassionate
·conservative
·coup
·disenfranchise
·filibuster
DON'T STAY TOO LATE. YOU BEEN LOOKING A LITTLE PEAKED.
UNH.
AND FOR LABOR, DEFENSE, TREASURY, AND H.H.S...
RING!
HELLO?
...THE FOUR HORSEMEN OF THE APOCALYPSE

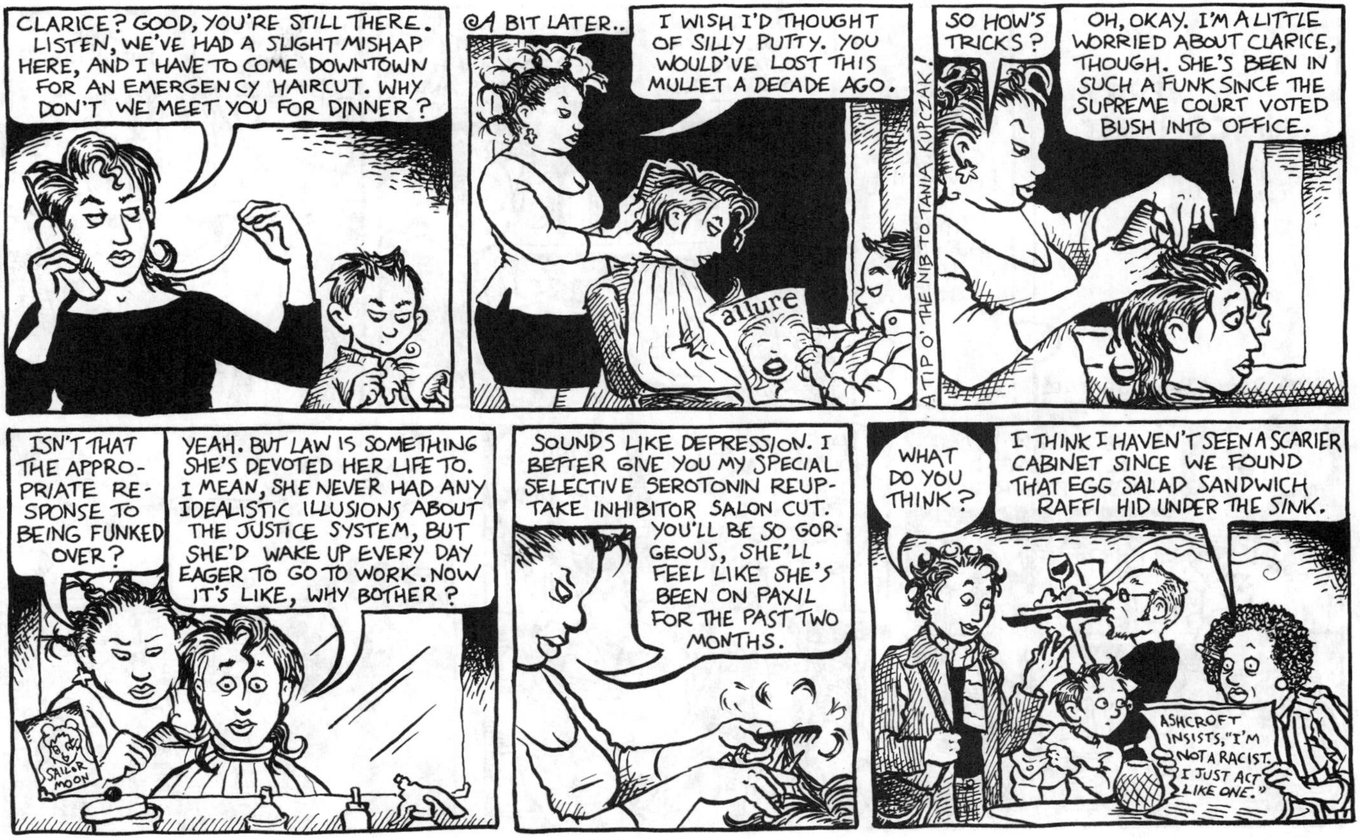

CLARICE? GOOD, YOU'RE STILL THERE. LISTEN, WE'VE HAD A SLIGHT MISHAP HERE, AND I HAVE TO COME DOWNTOWN FOR AN EMERGENCY HAIRCUT. WHY DON'T WE MEET YOU FOR DINNER?
A BIT LATER..
I WISH I'D THOUGHT OF SILLY PUTTY. YOU WOULD'VE LOST THIS MULLET A DECADE AGO.
allure
A TIP O' THE NIB TO TANIA KUPCZAK!
SO HOW'S TRICKS?
OH, OKAY. I'M A LITTLE WORRIED ABOUT CLARICE, THOUGH. SHE'S BEEN IN SUCH A FUNK SINCE THE SUPREME COURT VOTED BUSH INTO OFFICE.
ISN'T THAT THE APPROPRIATE RESPONSE TO BEING FUNKED OVER?
YEAH. BUT LAW IS SOMETHING SHE'S DEVOTED HER LIFE TO. I MEAN, SHE NEVER HAD ANY IDEALISTIC ILLUSIONS ABOUT THE JUSTICE SYSTEM, BUT SHE'D WAKE UP EVERY DAY EAGER TO GO TO WORK. NOW IT'S LIKE, WHY BOTHER?
SAILOR MOON
SOUNDS LIKE DEPRESSION. I BETTER GIVE YOU MY SPECIAL SELECTIVE SEROTONIN REUPTAKE INHIBITOR SALON CUT.
YOU'LL BE SO GORGEOUS, SHE'LL FEEL LIKE SHE'S BEEN ON PAXIL FOR THE PAST TWO MONTHS.
WHAT DO YOU THINK?
I THINK I HAVEN'T SEEN A SCARIER CABINET SINCE WE FOUND THAT EGG SALAD SANDWICH RAFFI HID UNDER THE SINK.
ASHCROFT INSISTS, "I'M NOT A RACIST. I JUST ACT LIKE ONE."

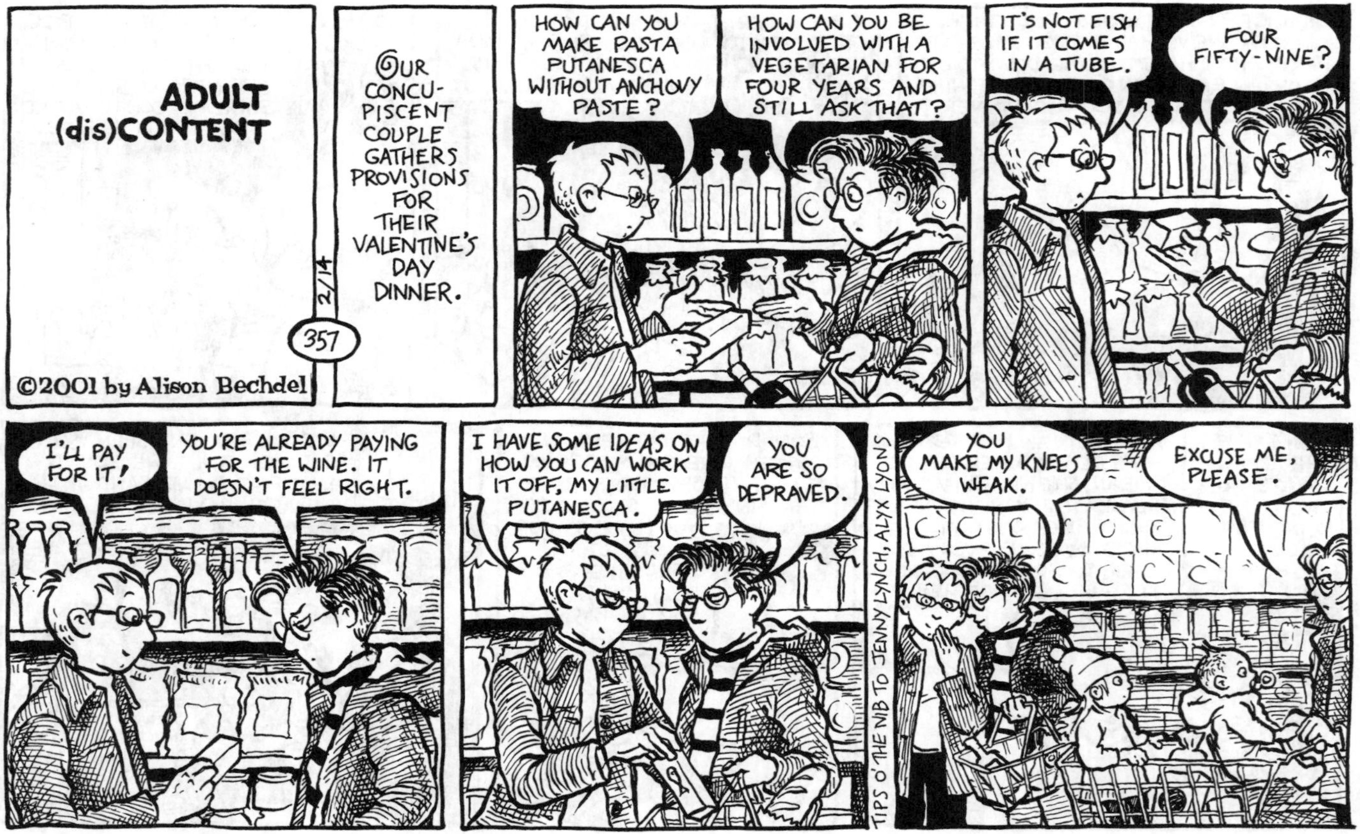
ADULT (dis)CONTENT
©2001 by Alison Bechdel
357
2/14
OUR CONCUPISCENT COUPLE GATHERS PROVISIONS FOR THEIR VALENTINE'S DAY DINNER.
HOW CAN YOU MAKE PASTA PUTANESCA WITHOUT ANCHOVY PASTE?
HOW CAN YOU BE INVOLVED WITH A VEGETARIAN FOR FOUR YEARS AND STILL ASK THAT?
IT'S NOT FISH IF IT COMES IN A TUBE.
FOUR FIFTY-NINE?
I'LL PAY FOR IT!
YOU'RE ALREADY PAYING FOR THE WINE. IT DOESN'T FEEL RIGHT.
I HAVE SOME IDEAS ON HOW YOU CAN WORK IT OFF, MY LITTLE PUTANESCA.
YOU ARE SO DEPRAVED.
TIPS O' THE NIB TO JENNY LYNCH, ALYX LYONS
YOU MAKE MY KNEES WEAK.
EXCUSE ME, PLEASE.

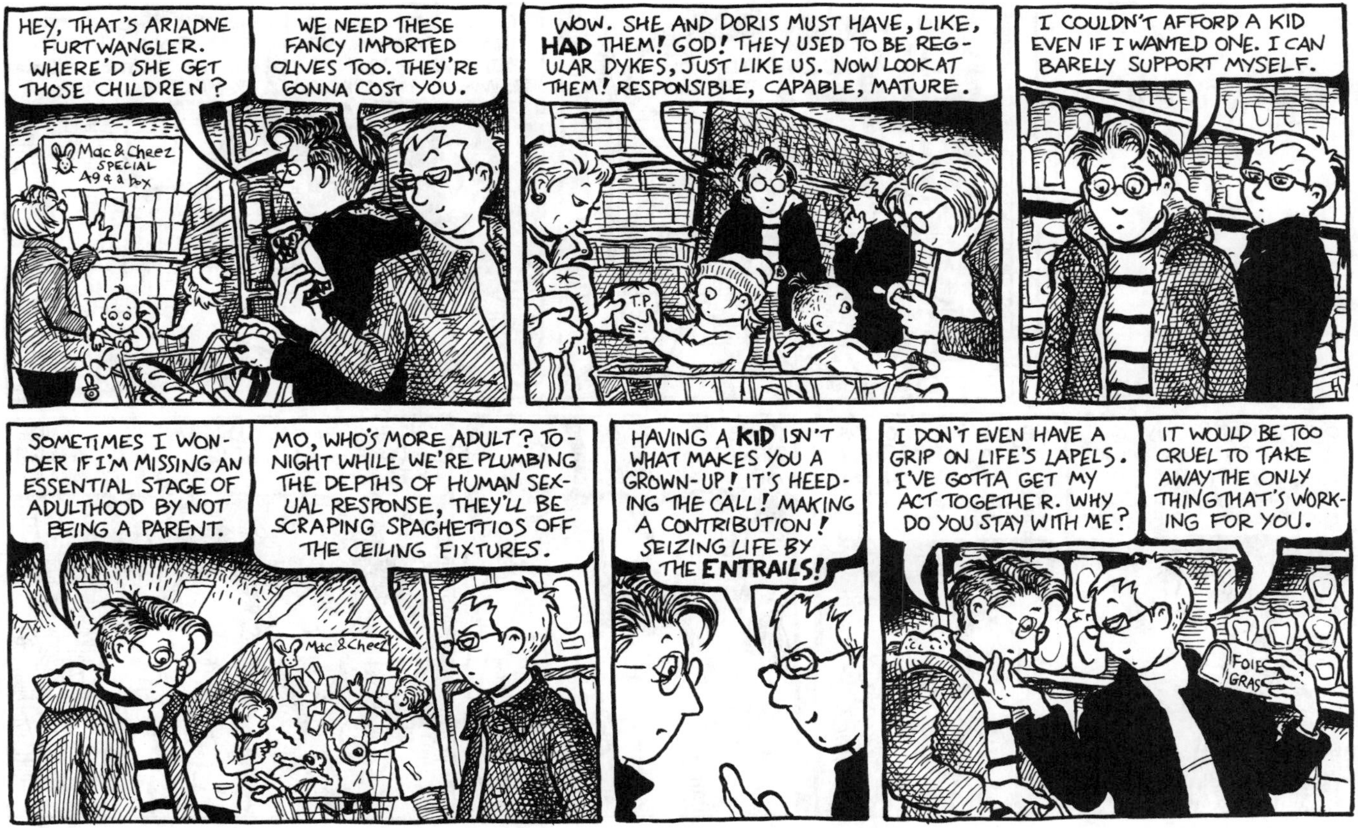
HEY, THAT'S ARIADNE FURTWANGLER. WHERE'D SHE GET THOSE CHILDREN?
WE NEED THESE FANCY IMPORTED OLIVES TOO. THEY'RE GONNA COST YOU.
Mac & Cheez SPECIAL 49¢ a box
WOW. SHE AND DORIS MUST HAVE, LIKE, **HAD** THEM! GOD! THEY USED TO BE REGULAR DYKES, JUST LIKE US. NOW LOOK AT THEM! RESPONSIBLE, CAPABLE, MATURE.
T.P.
I COULDN'T AFFORD A KID EVEN IF I WANTED ONE. I CAN BARELY SUPPORT MYSELF.
SOMETIMES I WONDER IF I'M MISSING AN ESSENTIAL STAGE OF ADULTHOOD BY NOT BEING A PARENT.
MO, WHO'S MORE ADULT? TONIGHT WHILE WE'RE PLUMBING THE DEPTHS OF HUMAN SEXUAL RESPONSE, THEY'LL BE SCRAPING SPAGHETTIOS OFF THE CEILING FIXTURES.
Mac & Cheez
HAVING A **KID** ISN'T WHAT MAKES YOU A GROWN-UP! IT'S HEEDING THE CALL! MAKING A CONTRIBUTION! SEIZING LIFE BY THE **ENTRAILS**!
I DON'T EVEN HAVE A GRIP ON LIFE'S LAPELS. I'VE GOTTA GET MY ACT TOGETHER. WHY DO YOU STAY WITH ME?
IT WOULD BE TOO CRUEL TO TAKE AWAY THE ONLY THING THAT'S WORKING FOR YOU.
FOIE GRAS

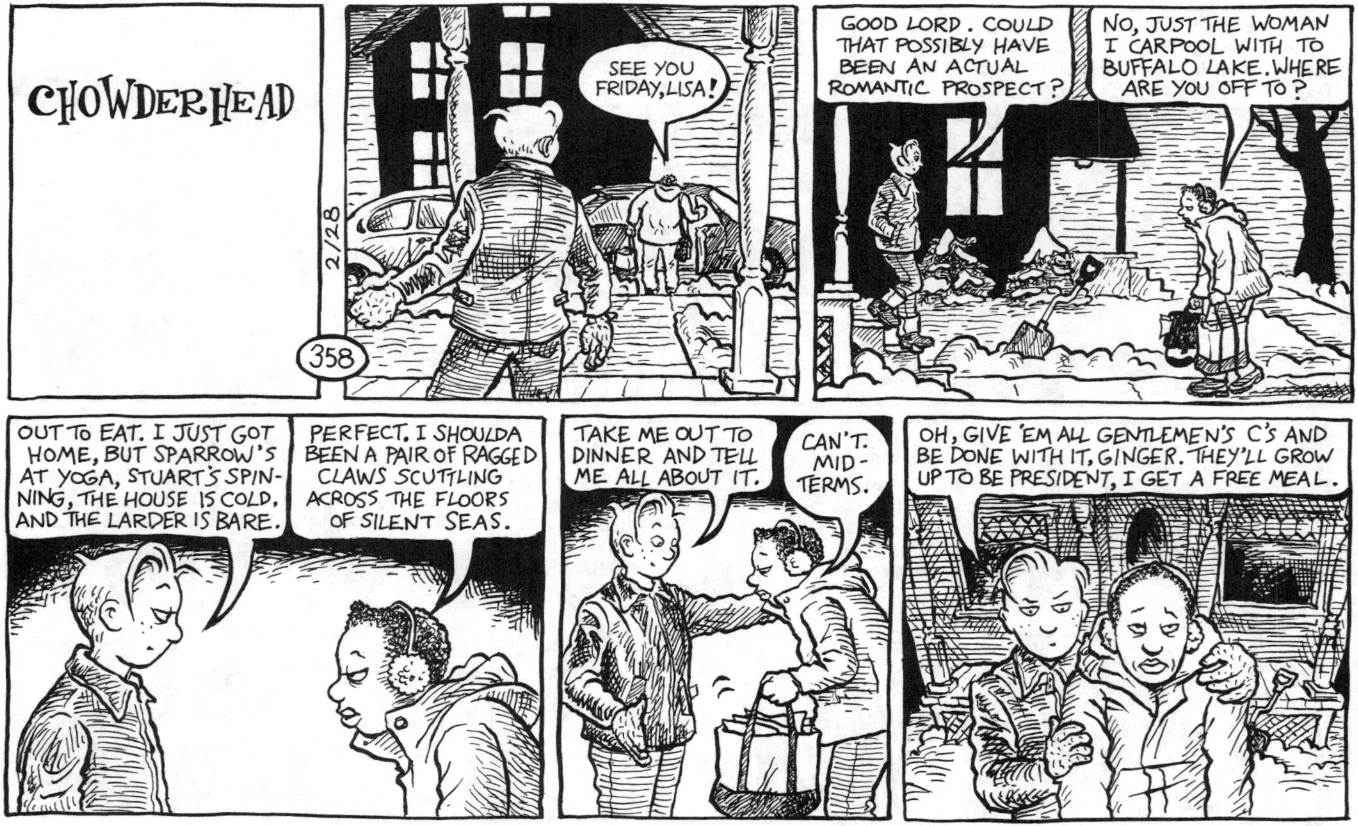
CHOWDERHEAD
2/28
358
SEE YOU FRIDAY, LISA!
GOOD LORD. COULD THAT POSSIBLY HAVE BEEN AN ACTUAL ROMANTIC PROSPECT?
NO, JUST THE WOMAN I CARPOOL WITH TO BUFFALO LAKE. WHERE ARE YOU OFF TO?
OUT TO EAT. I JUST GOT HOME, BUT SPARROW'S AT YOGA, STUART'S SPINNING, THE HOUSE IS COLD, AND THE LARDER IS BARE.
PERFECT. I SHOULDA BEEN A PAIR OF RAGGED CLAWS SCUTTLING ACROSS THE FLOORS OF SILENT SEAS.
TAKE ME OUT TO DINNER AND TELL ME ALL ABOUT IT.
CAN'T. MID-TERMS.
OH, GIVE 'EM ALL GENTLEMEN'S C'S AND BE DONE WITH IT, GINGER. THEY'LL GROW UP TO BE PRESIDENT, I GET A FREE MEAL.

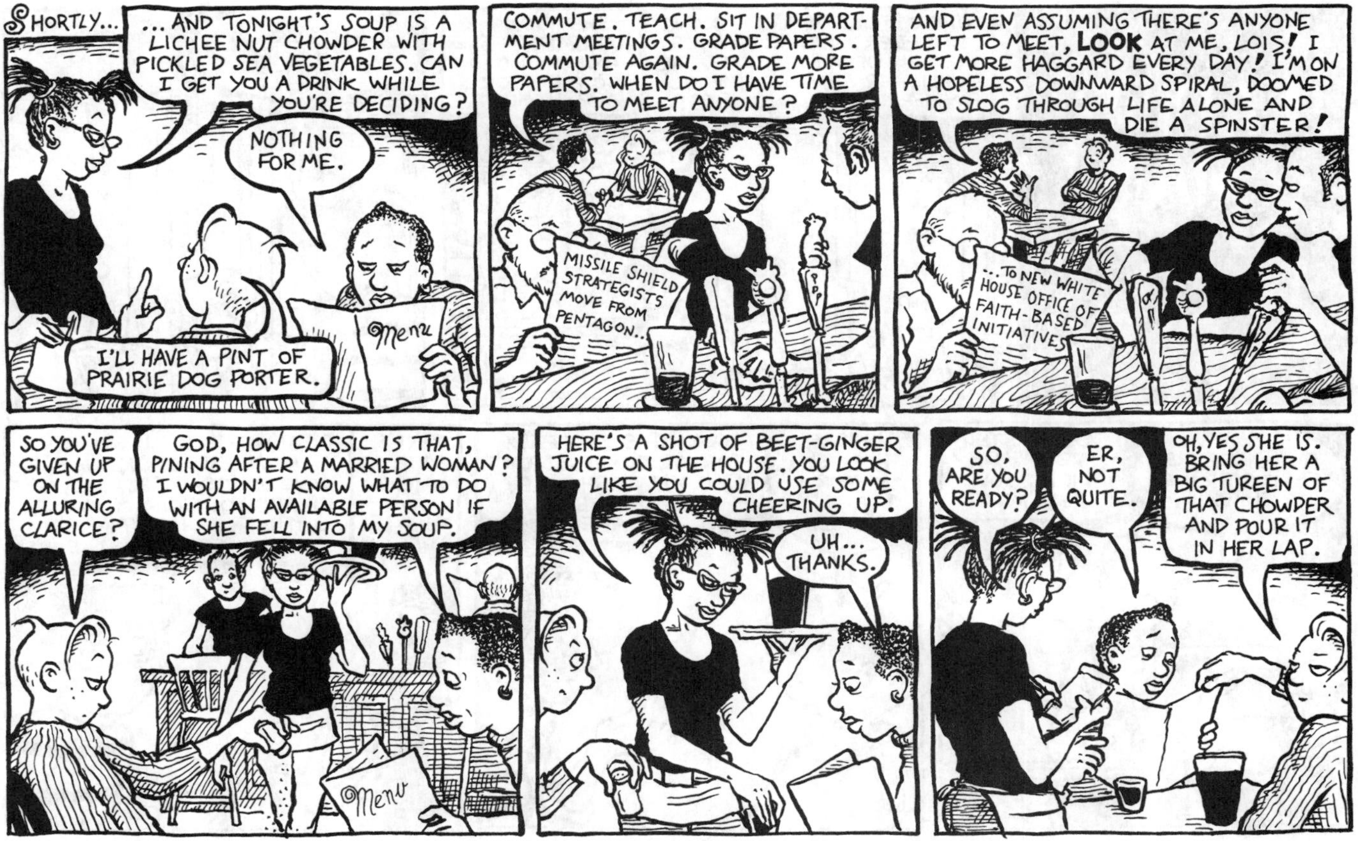
SHORTLY...
...AND TONIGHT'S SOUP IS A LICHEE NUT CHOWDER WITH PICKLED SEA VEGETABLES. CAN I GET YOU A DRINK WHILE YOU'RE DECIDING?
NOTHING FOR ME.
I'LL HAVE A PINT OF PRAIRIE DOG PORTER.
Menu
COMMUTE. TEACH. SIT IN DEPARTMENT MEETINGS. GRADE PAPERS. COMMUTE AGAIN. GRADE MORE PAPERS. WHEN DO I HAVE TIME TO MEET ANYONE?
MISSILE SHIELD STRATEGISTS MOVE FROM PENTAGON...
AND EVEN ASSUMING THERE'S ANYONE LEFT TO MEET, **LOOK** AT ME, LOIS! I GET MORE HAGGARD EVERY DAY! I'M ON A HOPELESS DOWNWARD SPIRAL, DOOMED TO SLOG THROUGH LIFE ALONE AND DIE A SPINSTER!
...TO NEW WHITE HOUSE OFFICE OF FAITH-BASED INITIATIVES
SO YOU'VE GIVEN UP ON THE ALLURING CLARICE?
GOD, HOW CLASSIC IS THAT, PINING AFTER A MARRIED WOMAN? I WOULDN'T KNOW WHAT TO DO WITH AN AVAILABLE PERSON IF SHE FELL INTO MY SOUP.
Menu
HERE'S A SHOT OF BEET-GINGER JUICE ON THE HOUSE. YOU LOOK LIKE YOU COULD USE SOME CHEERING UP.
UH... THANKS.
SO, ARE YOU READY?
ER, NOT QUITE.
OH, YES SHE IS. BRING HER A BIG TUREEN OF THAT CHOWDER AND POUR IT IN HER LAP.

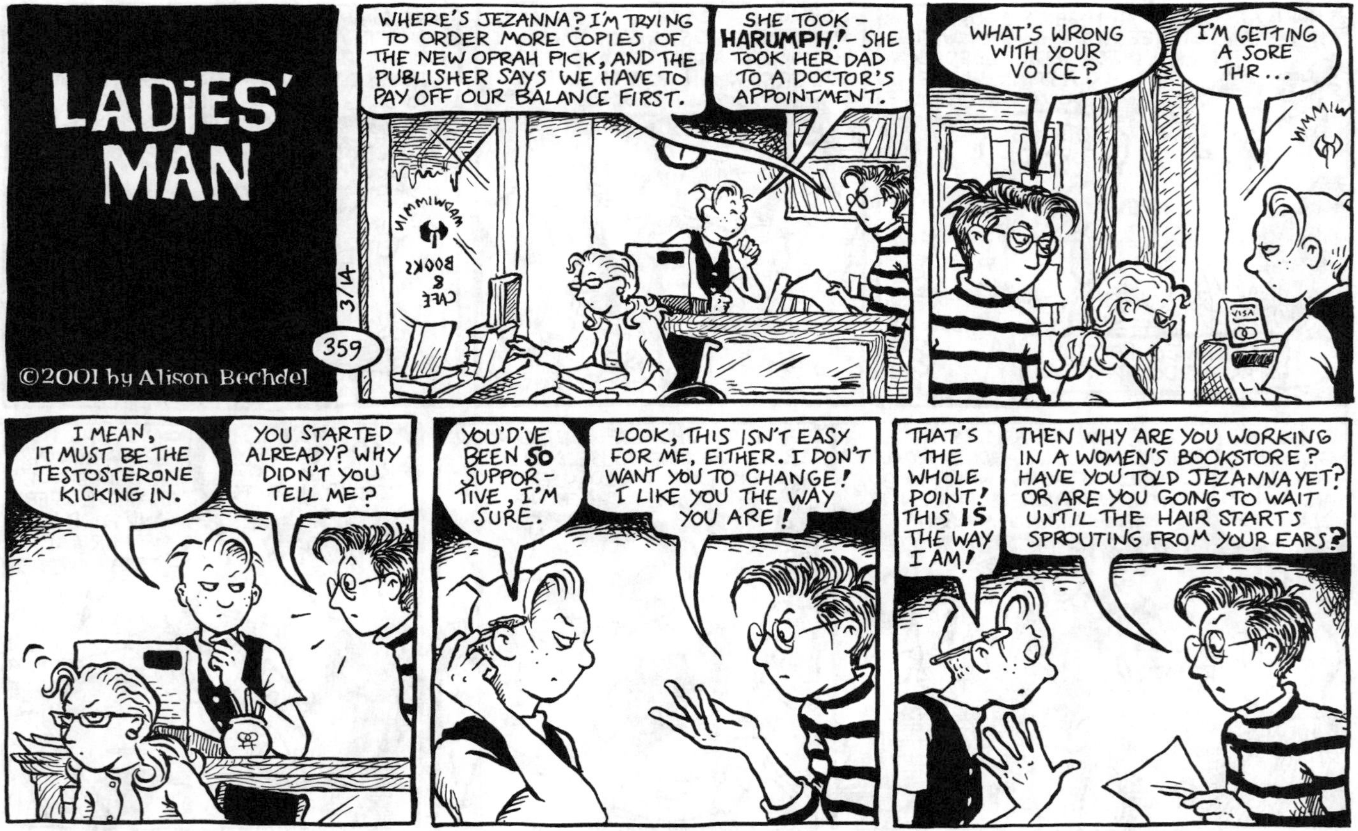
LADIES' MAN
©2001 by Alison Bechdel
359
3/14
WHERE'S JEZANNA? I'M TRYING TO ORDER MORE COPIES OF THE NEW OPRAH PICK, AND THE PUBLISHER SAYS WE HAVE TO PAY OFF OUR BALANCE FIRST.
SHE TOOK – HARUMPH! – SHE TOOK HER DAD TO A DOCTOR'S APPOINTMENT.
WHAT'S WRONG WITH YOUR VOICE?
I'M GETTING A SORE THR...
I MEAN, IT MUST BE THE TESTOSTERONE KICKING IN.
YOU STARTED ALREADY? WHY DIDN'T YOU TELL ME?
YOU'D'VE BEEN SO SUPPORTIVE, I'M SURE.
LOOK, THIS ISN'T EASY FOR ME, EITHER. I DON'T WANT YOU TO CHANGE! I LIKE YOU THE WAY YOU ARE!
THAT'S THE WHOLE POINT! THIS IS THE WAY I AM!
THEN WHY ARE YOU WORKING IN A WOMEN'S BOOKSTORE? HAVE YOU TOLD JEZANNA YET? OR ARE YOU GOING TO WAIT UNTIL THE HAIR STARTS SPROUTING FROM YOUR EARS?

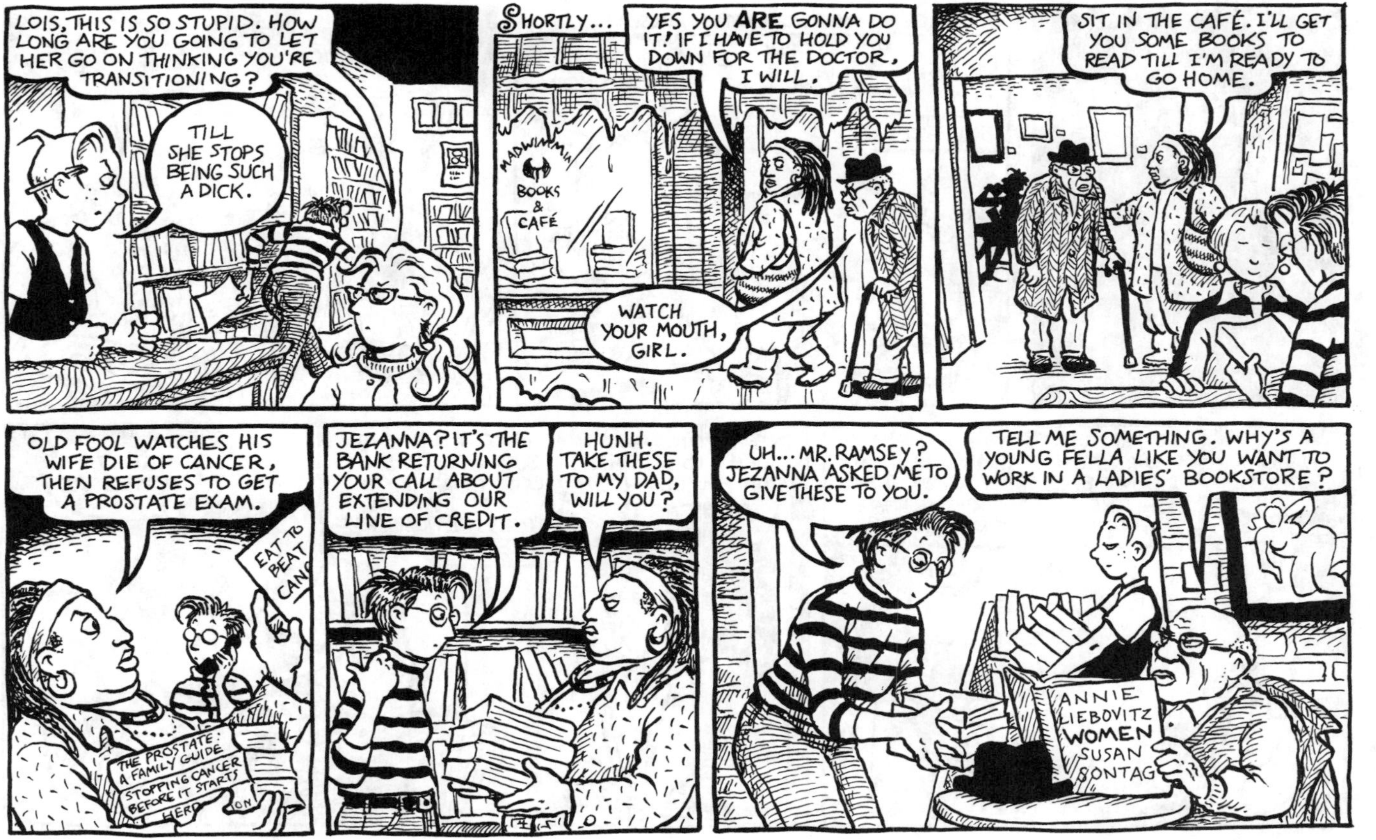
LOIS, THIS IS SO STUPID. HOW LONG ARE YOU GOING TO LET HER GO ON THINKING YOU'RE TRANSITIONING?
TILL SHE STOPS BEING SUCH A DICK.
SHORTLY...
YES YOU ARE GONNA DO IT! IF I HAVE TO HOLD YOU DOWN FOR THE DOCTOR, I WILL.
WATCH YOUR MOUTH, GIRL.
BOOKS & CAFÉ
SIT IN THE CAFÉ. I'LL GET YOU SOME BOOKS TO READ TILL I'M READY TO GO HOME.
OLD FOOL WATCHES HIS WIFE DIE OF CANCER, THEN REFUSES TO GET A PROSTATE EXAM.
EAT TO BEAT CAN
THE PROSTATE: A FAMILY GUIDE
STOPPING CANCER BEFORE IT STARTS
JEZANNA? IT'S THE BANK RETURNING YOUR CALL ABOUT EXTENDING OUR LINE OF CREDIT.
HUNH. TAKE THESE TO MY DAD, WILL YOU?
UH... MR. RAMSEY? JEZANNA ASKED ME TO GIVE THESE TO YOU.
TELL ME SOMETHING. WHY'S A YOUNG FELLA LIKE YOU WANT TO WORK IN A LADIES' BOOKSTORE?
ANNIE LIEBOVITZ WOMEN SUSAN SONTAG

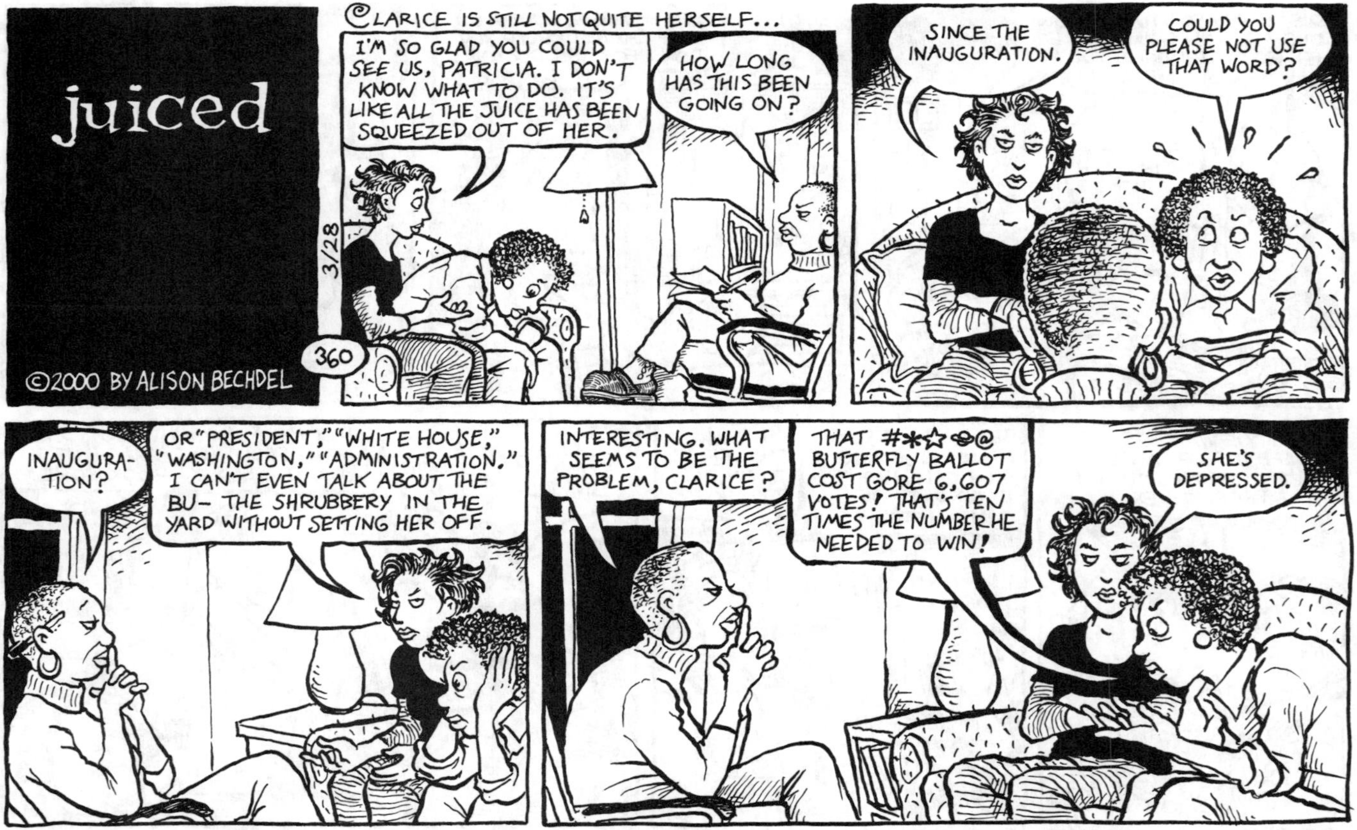
juiced
©2000 BY ALISON BECHDEL
360
3/28
CLARICE IS STILL NOT QUITE HERSELF...
I'M SO GLAD YOU COULD SEE US, PATRICIA. I DON'T KNOW WHAT TO DO. IT'S LIKE ALL THE JUICE HAS BEEN SQUEEZED OUT OF HER.
HOW LONG HAS THIS BEEN GOING ON?
SINCE THE INAUGURATION.
COULD YOU PLEASE NOT USE THAT WORD?
INAUGURATION?
OR "PRESIDENT," "WHITE HOUSE," "WASHINGTON," "ADMINISTRATION." I CAN'T EVEN TALK ABOUT THE BU– THE SHRUBBERY IN THE YARD WITHOUT SETTING HER OFF.
INTERESTING. WHAT SEEMS TO BE THE PROBLEM, CLARICE?
THAT #*☆@ BUTTERFLY BALLOT COST GORE 6,607 VOTES! THAT'S TEN TIMES THE NUMBER HE NEEDED TO WIN!
SHE'S DEPRESSED.

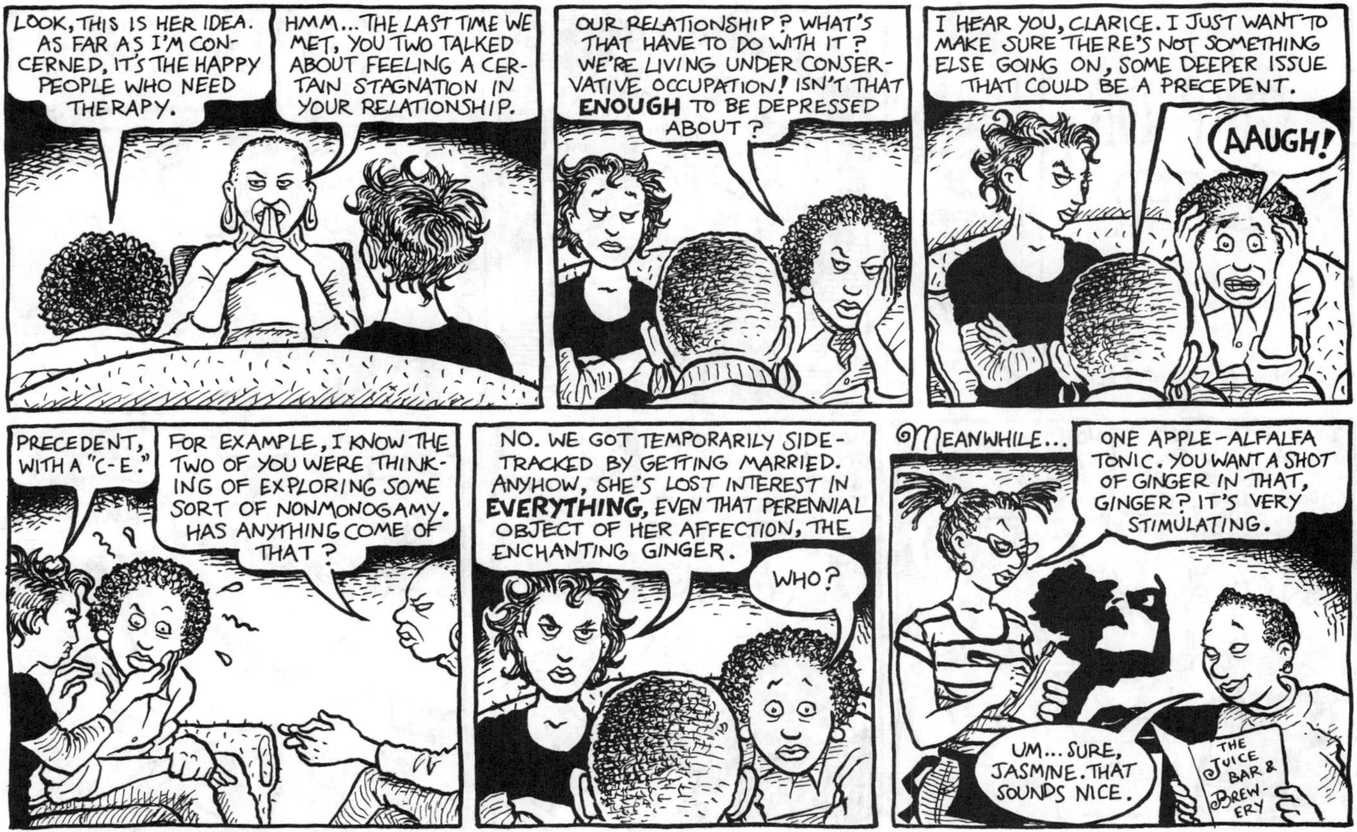
LOOK, THIS IS HER IDEA. AS FAR AS I'M CONCERNED, IT'S THE HAPPY PEOPLE WHO NEED THERAPY.
HMM... THE LAST TIME WE MET, YOU TWO TALKED ABOUT FEELING A CERTAIN STAGNATION IN YOUR RELATIONSHIP.
OUR RELATIONSHIP? WHAT'S THAT HAVE TO DO WITH IT? WE'RE LIVING UNDER CONSERVATIVE OCCUPATION! ISN'T THAT **ENOUGH** TO BE DEPRESSED ABOUT?
I HEAR YOU, CLARICE. I JUST WANT TO MAKE SURE THERE'S NOT SOMETHING ELSE GOING ON, SOME DEEPER ISSUE THAT COULD BE A PRECEDENT.
AAUGH!
PRECEDENT, WITH A "C-E."
FOR EXAMPLE, I KNOW THE TWO OF YOU WERE THINKING OF EXPLORING SOME SORT OF NONMONOGAMY. HAS ANYTHING COME OF THAT?
NO. WE GOT TEMPORARILY SIDETRACKED BY GETTING MARRIED. ANYHOW, SHE'S LOST INTEREST IN **EVERYTHING**, EVEN THAT PERENNIAL OBJECT OF HER AFFECTION, THE ENCHANTING GINGER.
WHO?
MEANWHILE...
ONE APPLE-ALFALFA TONIC. YOU WANT A SHOT OF GINGER IN THAT, GINGER? IT'S VERY STIMULATING.
UM... SURE, JASMINE. THAT SOUNDS NICE.
THE JUICE BAR & BREWERY

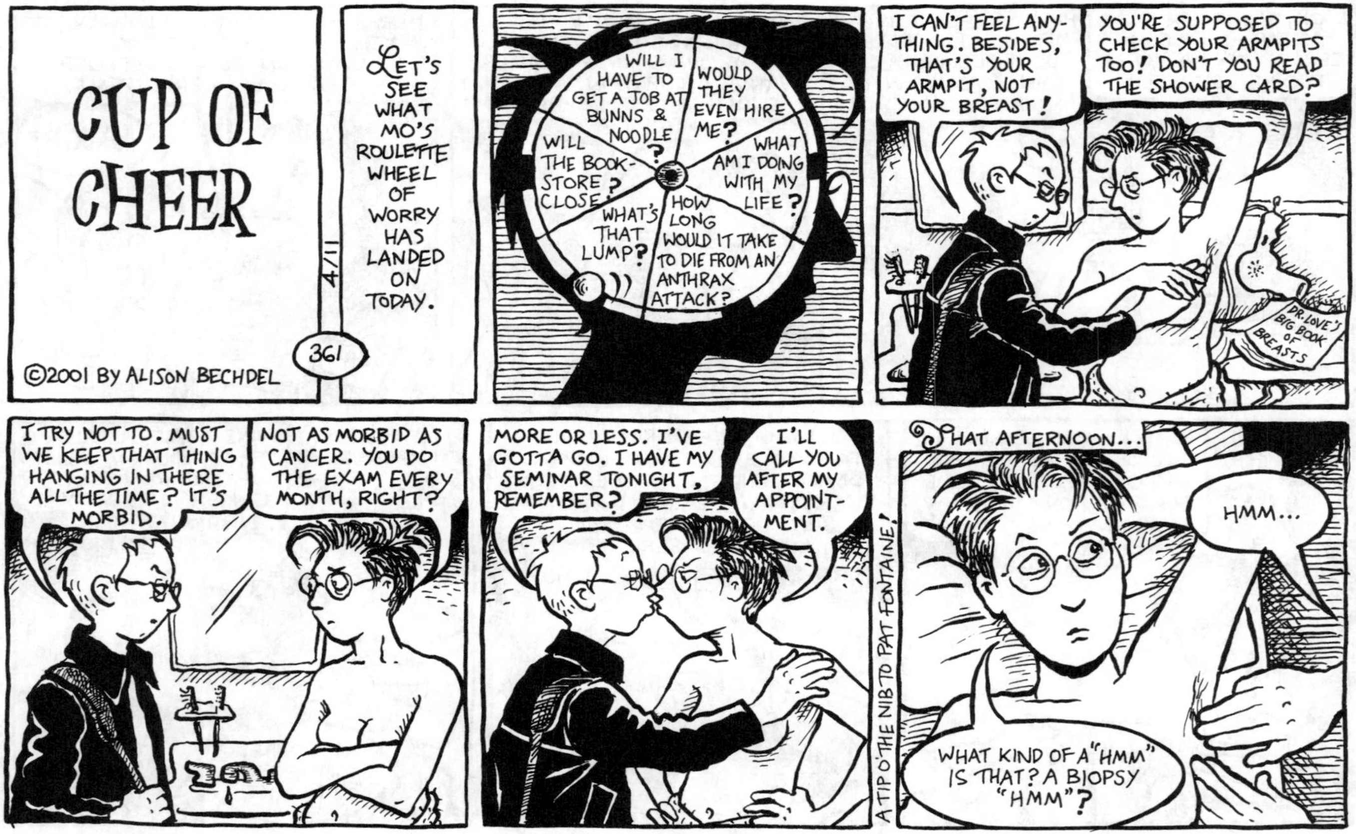
CUP OF CHEER
©2001 BY ALISON BECHDEL
361
4/11
LET'S SEE WHAT MO'S ROULETTE WHEEL OF WORRY HAS LANDED ON TODAY.
WILL I HAVE TO GET A JOB AT BUNNS & NOODLE?
WOULD THEY EVEN HIRE ME?
WHAT AM I DOING WITH MY LIFE?
HOW LONG WOULD IT TAKE TO DIE FROM AN ANTHRAX ATTACK?
WHAT'S THAT LUMP?
WILL THE BOOK-STORE CLOSE?
I CAN'T FEEL ANY-THING. BESIDES, THAT'S YOUR ARMPIT, NOT YOUR BREAST!
YOU'RE SUPPOSED TO CHECK YOUR ARMPITS TOO! DON'T YOU READ THE SHOWER CARD?
DR. LOVE'S BIG BOOK OF BREASTS
I TRY NOT TO. MUST WE KEEP THAT THING HANGING IN THERE ALL THE TIME? IT'S MORBID.
NOT AS MORBID AS CANCER. YOU DO THE EXAM EVERY MONTH, RIGHT?
MORE OR LESS. I'VE GOTTA GO. I HAVE MY SEMINAR TONIGHT, REMEMBER?
I'LL CALL YOU AFTER MY APPOINT-MENT.
A TIP O' THE NIB TO PAT FONTAINE!
THAT AFTERNOON...
HMM...
WHAT KIND OF A "HMM" IS THAT? A BIOPSY "HMM"?

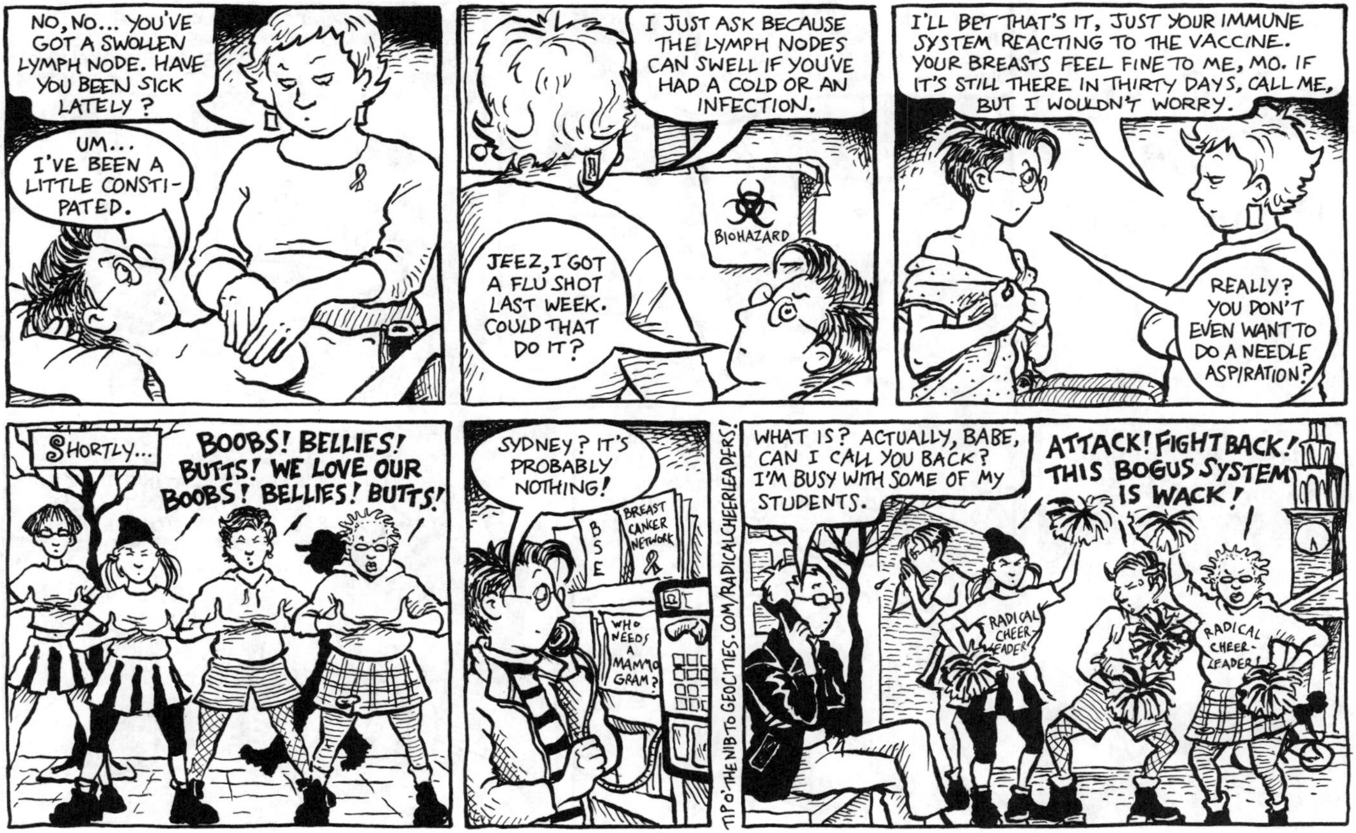
NO, NO... YOU'VE GOT A SWOLLEN LYMPH NODE. HAVE YOU BEEN SICK LATELY?
UM... I'VE BEEN A LITTLE CONSTI-PATED.
I JUST ASK BECAUSE THE LYMPH NODES CAN SWELL IF YOU'VE HAD A COLD OR AN INFECTION.
BIOHAZARD
JEEZ, I GOT A FLU SHOT LAST WEEK. COULD THAT DO IT?
I'LL BET THAT'S IT, JUST YOUR IMMUNE SYSTEM REACTING TO THE VACCINE. YOUR BREASTS FEEL FINE TO ME, MO. IF IT'S STILL THERE IN THIRTY DAYS, CALL ME, BUT I WOULDN'T WORRY.
REALLY? YOU DON'T EVEN WANT TO DO A NEEDLE ASPIRATION?
SHORTLY...
BOOBS! BELLIES! BUTTS! WE LOVE OUR BOOBS! BELLIES! BUTTS!
SYDNEY? IT'S PROBABLY NOTHING!
BSE
BREAST CANCER NETWORK
WHO NEEDS A MAMMOGRAM?
TIP O' THE NIB TO GEOCITIES.COM/RADICALCHEERLEADERS!
WHAT IS? ACTUALLY, BABE, CAN I CALL YOU BACK? I'M BUSY WITH SOME OF MY STUDENTS.
ATTACK! FIGHT BACK! THIS BOGUS SYSTEM IS WACK!
RADICAL CHEER-LEADER
RADICAL CHEER-LEADER!

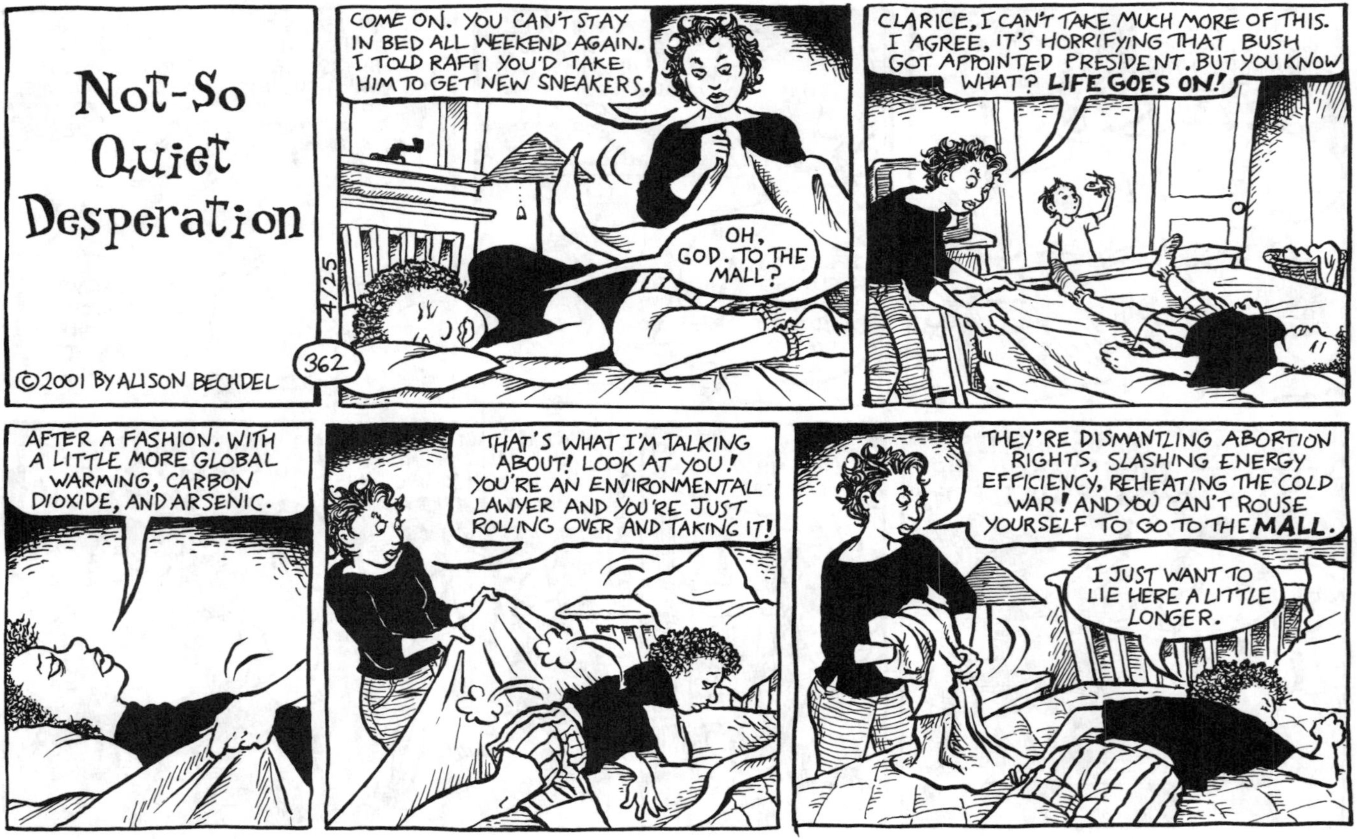

Not-So Quiet Desperation
©2001 BY ALISON BECHDEL
362
4/25
COME ON. YOU CAN'T STAY IN BED ALL WEEKEND AGAIN. I TOLD RAFFI YOU'D TAKE HIM TO GET NEW SNEAKERS.
OH, GOD. TO THE MALL?
CLARICE, I CAN'T TAKE MUCH MORE OF THIS. I AGREE, IT'S HORRIFYING THAT BUSH GOT APPOINTED PRESIDENT. BUT YOU KNOW WHAT? **LIFE GOES ON!**
AFTER A FASHION. WITH A LITTLE MORE GLOBAL WARMING, CARBON DIOXIDE, AND ARSENIC.
THAT'S WHAT I'M TALKING ABOUT! LOOK AT YOU! YOU'RE AN ENVIRONMENTAL LAWYER AND YOU'RE JUST ROLLING OVER AND TAKING IT!
THEY'RE DISMANTLING ABORTION RIGHTS, SLASHING ENERGY EFFICIENCY, REHEATING THE COLD WAR! AND YOU CAN'T ROUSE YOURSELF TO GO TO THE **MALL**.
I JUST WANT TO LIE HERE A LITTLE LONGER.

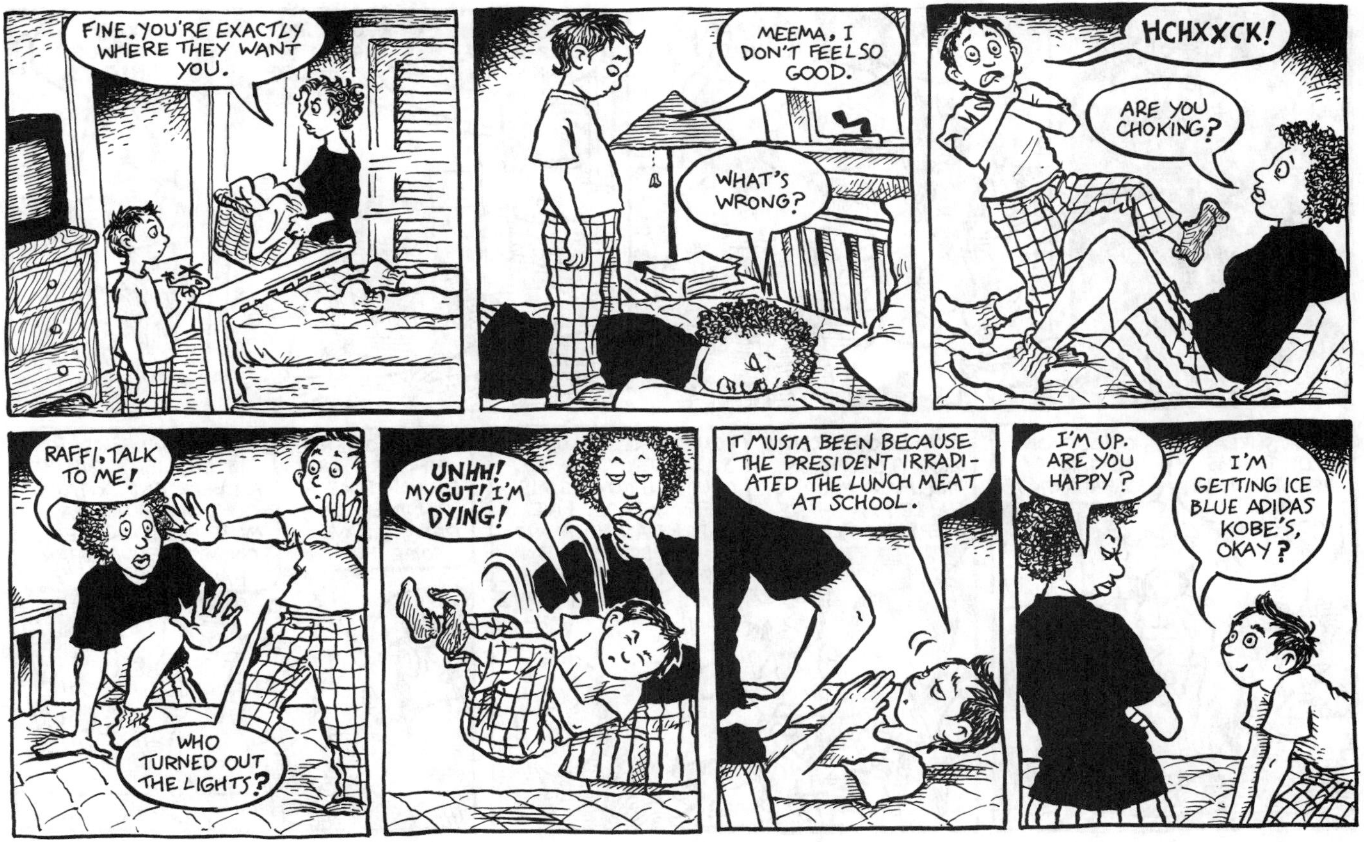
FINE. YOU'RE EXACTLY WHERE THEY WANT YOU.
MEEMA, I DON'T FEEL SO GOOD.
WHAT'S WRONG?
HCHXXCK!
ARE YOU CHOKING?
RAFFI, TALK TO ME!
WHO TURNED OUT THE LIGHTS?
UNHH! MY GUT! I'M DYING!
IT MUSTA BEEN BECAUSE THE PRESIDENT IRRADI-ATED THE LUNCH MEAT AT SCHOOL.
I'M UP. ARE YOU HAPPY?
I'M GETTING ICE BLUE ADIDAS KOBE'S, OKAY?

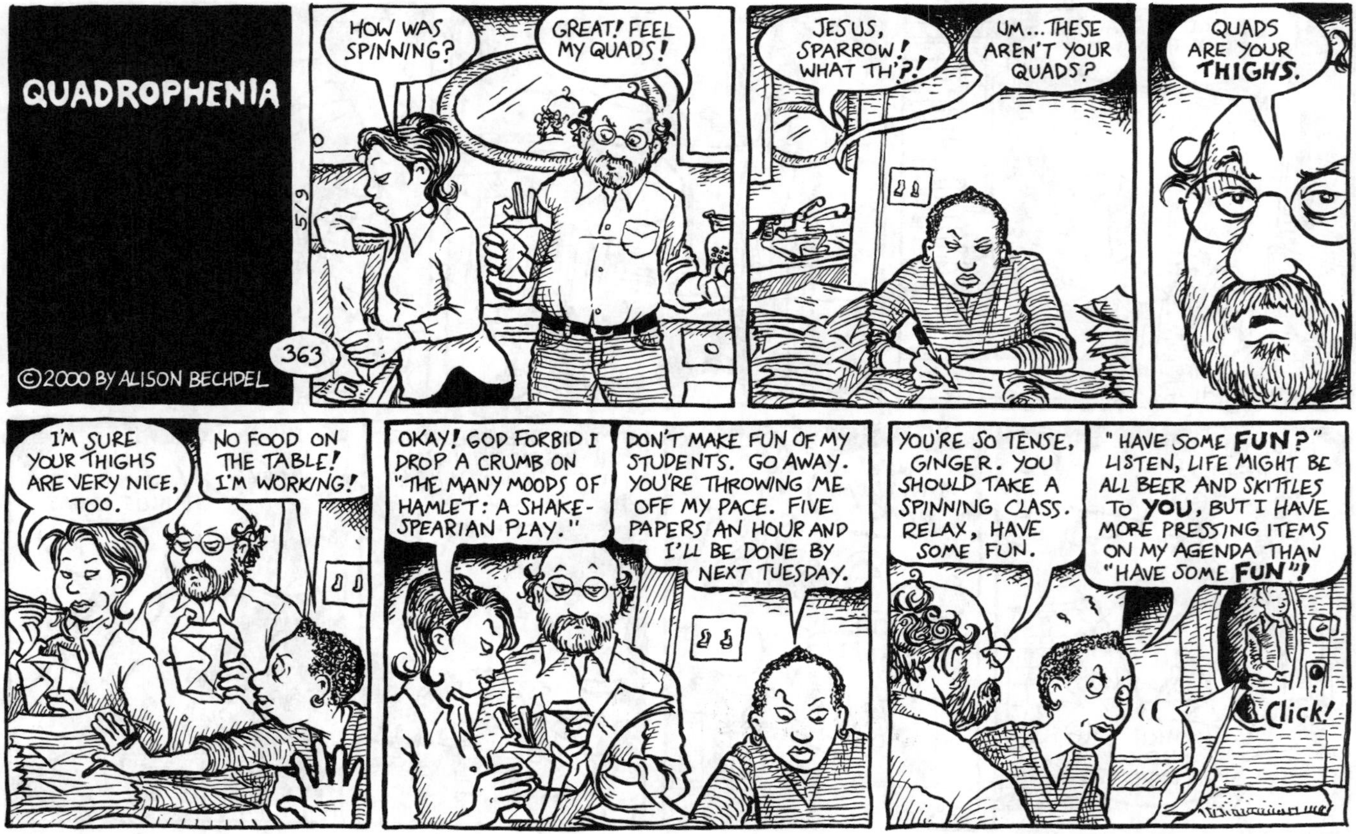
QUADROPHENIA
363
©2000 BY ALISON BECHDEL
5/9
HOW WAS SPINNING?
GREAT! FEEL MY QUADS!
JESUS, SPARROW! WHAT TH'?!
UM... THESE AREN'T YOUR QUADS?
QUADS ARE YOUR THIGHS.
I'M SURE YOUR THIGHS ARE VERY NICE, TOO.
NO FOOD ON THE TABLE! I'M WORKING!
OKAY! GOD FORBID I DROP A CRUMB ON "THE MANY MOODS OF HAMLET: A SHAKESPEARIAN PLAY."
DON'T MAKE FUN OF MY STUDENTS. GO AWAY. YOU'RE THROWING ME OFF MY PACE. FIVE PAPERS AN HOUR AND I'LL BE DONE BY NEXT TUESDAY.
YOU'RE SO TENSE, GINGER. YOU SHOULD TAKE A SPINNING CLASS. RELAX, HAVE SOME FUN.
"HAVE SOME FUN?" LISTEN, LIFE MIGHT BE ALL BEER AND SKITTLES TO YOU, BUT I HAVE MORE PRESSING ITEMS ON MY AGENDA THAN "HAVE SOME FUN"!
Click!

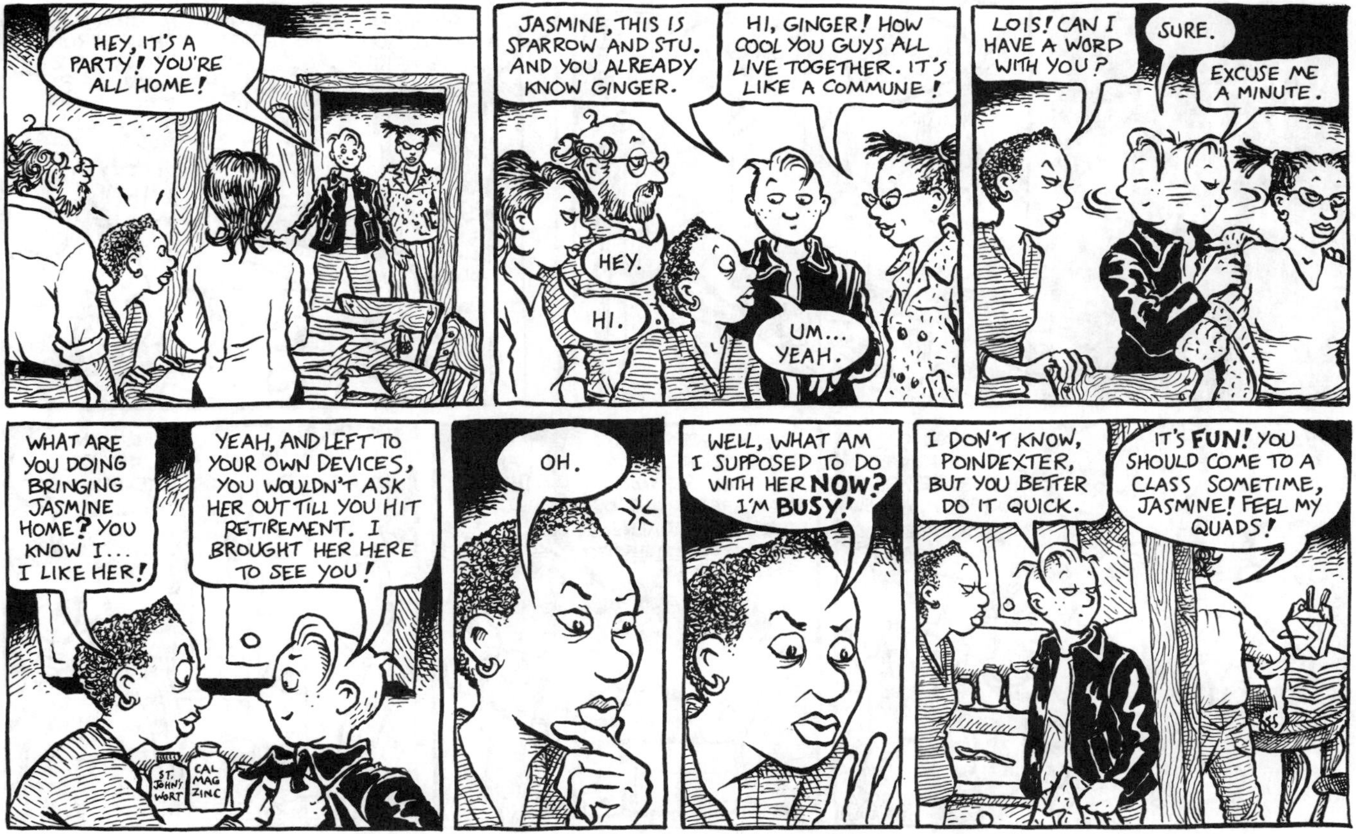
HEY, IT'S A PARTY! YOU'RE ALL HOME!
JASMINE, THIS IS SPARROW AND STU. AND YOU ALREADY KNOW GINGER.
HI, GINGER! HOW COOL YOU GUYS ALL LIVE TOGETHER. IT'S LIKE A COMMUNE!
HEY.
HI.
UM... YEAH.
LOIS! CAN I HAVE A WORD WITH YOU?
SURE.
EXCUSE ME A MINUTE.
WHAT ARE YOU DOING BRINGING JASMINE HOME? YOU KNOW I... I LIKE HER!
YEAH, AND LEFT TO YOUR OWN DEVICES, YOU WOULDN'T ASK HER OUT TILL YOU HIT RETIREMENT. I BROUGHT HER HERE TO SEE YOU!
ST. JOHN'S WORT
CAL MAG ZINC
OH.
WELL, WHAT AM I SUPPOSED TO DO WITH HER NOW? I'M BUSY!
I DON'T KNOW, POINDEXTER, BUT YOU BETTER DO IT QUICK.
IT'S FUN! YOU SHOULD COME TO A CLASS SOMETIME, JASMINE! FEEL MY QUADS!

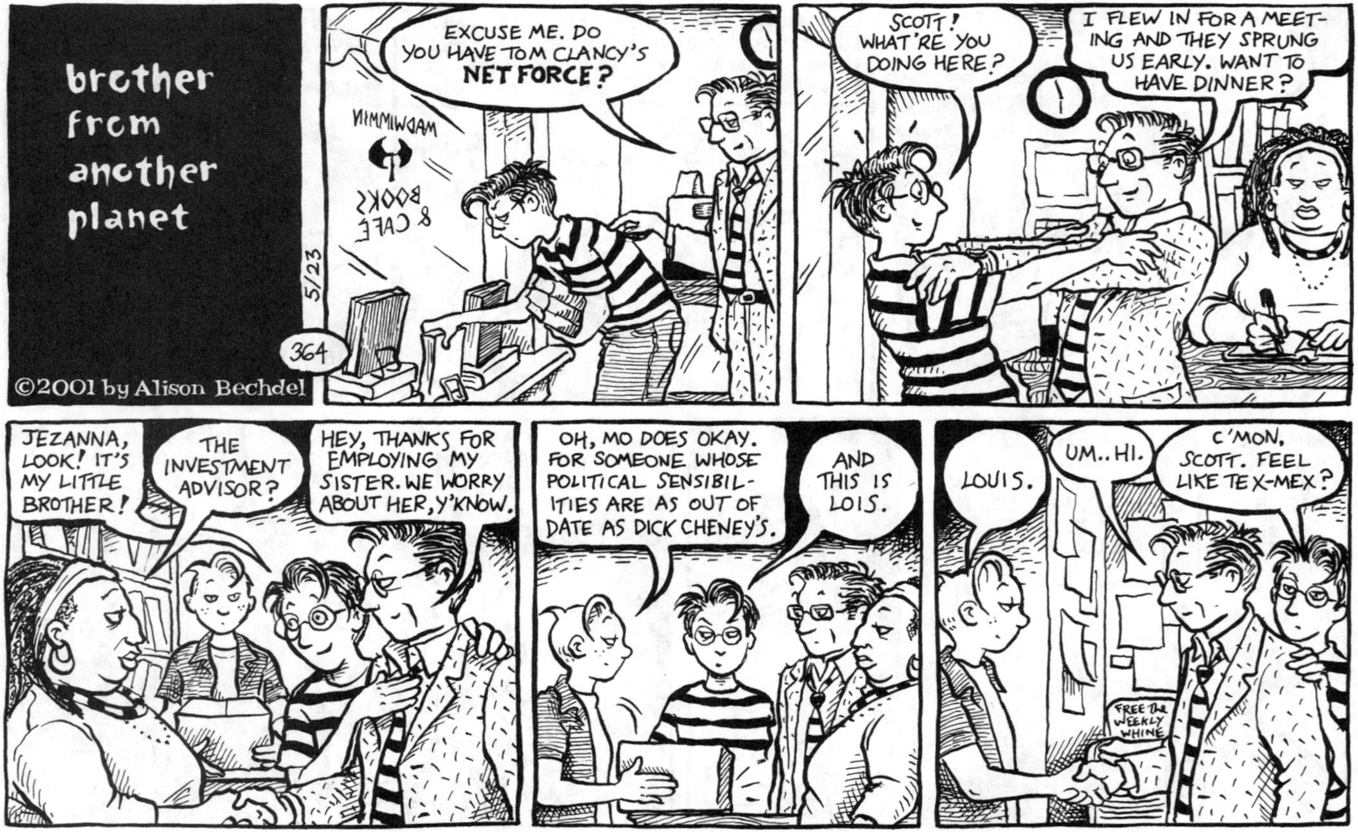

brother from another planet
©2001 by Alison Bechdel
364
5/23
MADWIMMIN BOOKS & CAFE
EXCUSE ME. DO YOU HAVE TOM CLANCY'S **NET FORCE?**
SCOTT! WHAT'RE YOU DOING HERE?
I FLEW IN FOR A MEETING AND THEY SPRUNG US EARLY. WANT TO HAVE DINNER?
JEZANNA, LOOK! IT'S MY LITTLE BROTHER!
THE INVESTMENT ADVISOR?
HEY, THANKS FOR EMPLOYING MY SISTER. WE WORRY ABOUT HER, Y'KNOW.
OH, MO DOES OKAY. FOR SOMEONE WHOSE POLITICAL SENSIBILITIES ARE AS OUT OF DATE AS DICK CHENEY'S.
AND THIS IS LOIS.
LOUIS.
UM.. HI.
C'MON, SCOTT. FEEL LIKE TEX-MEX?
FREE THE WEEKLY WHINE

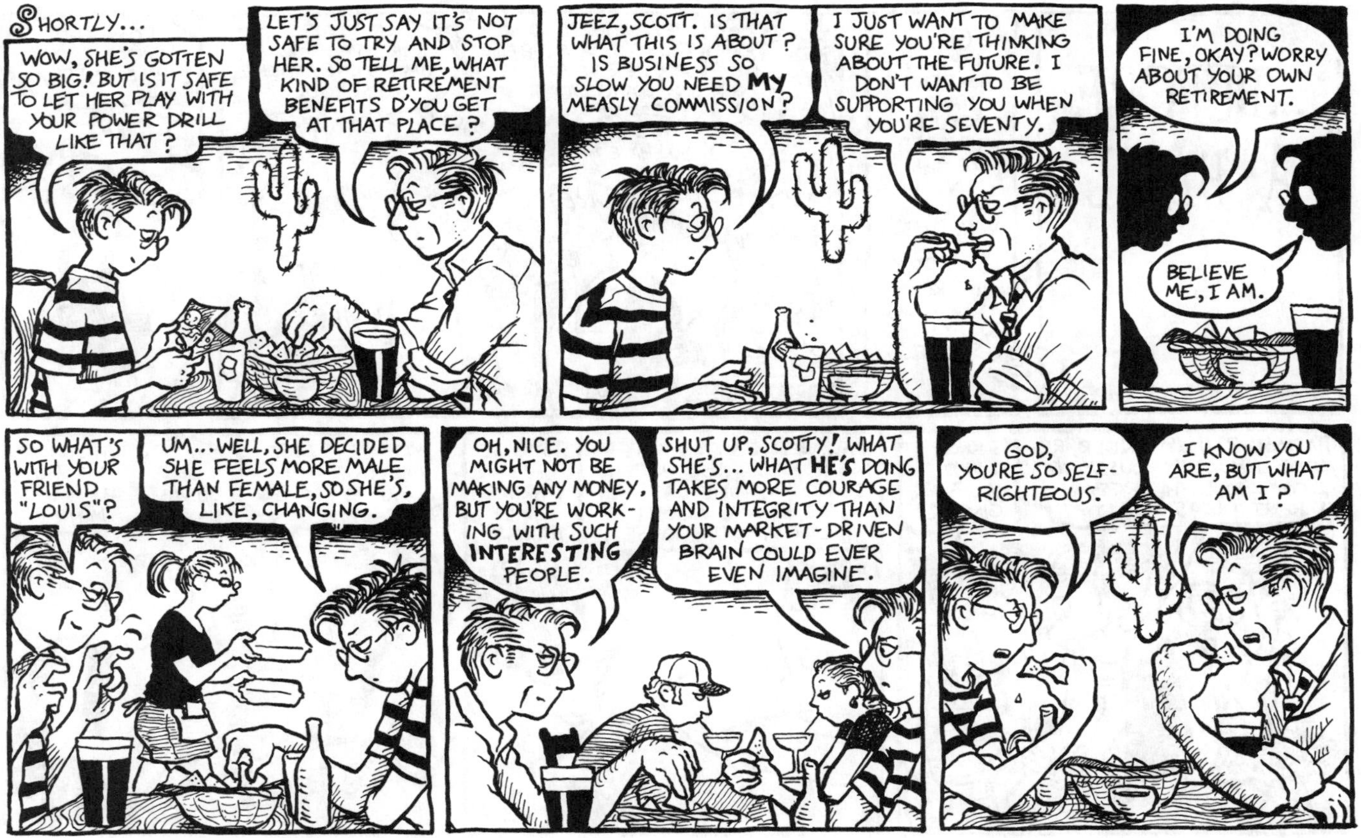
SHORTLY...
WOW, SHE'S GOTTEN SO BIG! BUT IS IT SAFE TO LET HER PLAY WITH YOUR POWER DRILL LIKE THAT?
LET'S JUST SAY IT'S NOT SAFE TO TRY AND STOP HER. SO TELL ME, WHAT KIND OF RETIREMENT BENEFITS D'YOU GET AT THAT PLACE?
JEEZ, SCOTT. IS THAT WHAT THIS IS ABOUT? IS BUSINESS SO SLOW YOU NEED MY MEASLY COMMISSION?
I JUST WANT TO MAKE SURE YOU'RE THINKING ABOUT THE FUTURE. I DON'T WANT TO BE SUPPORTING YOU WHEN YOU'RE SEVENTY.
I'M DOING FINE, OKAY? WORRY ABOUT YOUR OWN RETIREMENT.
BELIEVE ME, I AM.
SO WHAT'S WITH YOUR FRIEND "LOUIS"?
UM...WELL, SHE DECIDED SHE FEELS MORE MALE THAN FEMALE, SO SHE'S, LIKE, CHANGING.
OH, NICE. YOU MIGHT NOT BE MAKING ANY MONEY, BUT YOU'RE WORKING WITH SUCH INTERESTING PEOPLE.
SHUT UP, SCOTTY! WHAT SHE'S... WHAT HE'S DOING TAKES MORE COURAGE AND INTEGRITY THAN YOUR MARKET-DRIVEN BRAIN COULD EVER EVEN IMAGINE.
GOD, YOU'RE SO SELF-RIGHTEOUS.
I KNOW YOU ARE, BUT WHAT AM I?

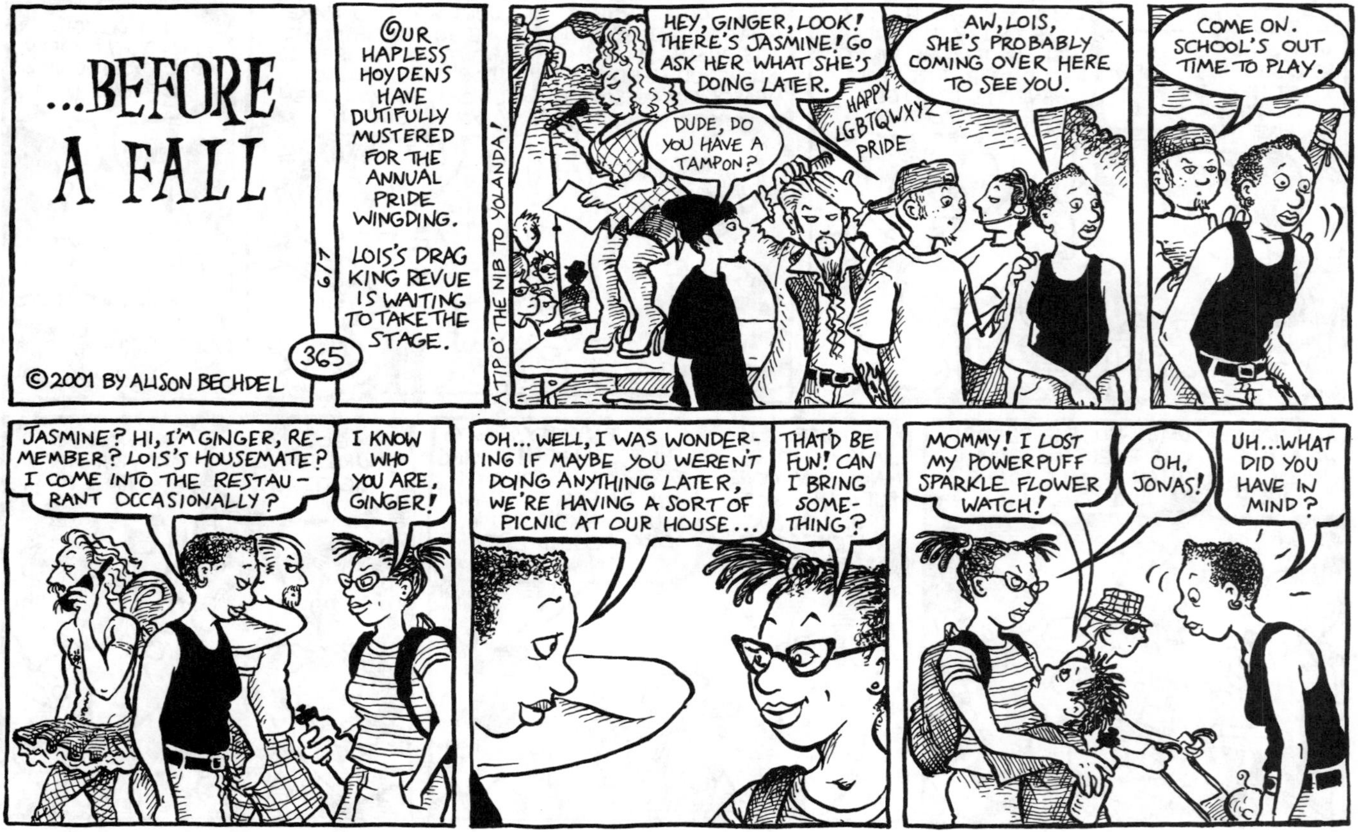

...BEFORE A FALL
©2001 BY ALISON BECHDEL
365
6/7
OUR HAPLESS HOYDENS HAVE DUTIFULLY MUSTERED FOR THE ANNUAL PRIDE WINGDING.
LOIS'S DRAG KING REVUE IS WAITING TO TAKE THE STAGE.
A TIP O' THE NIB TO YOLANDA!
HEY, GINGER, LOOK! THERE'S JASMINE! GO ASK HER WHAT SHE'S DOING LATER.
HAPPY LGBTQWXYZ PRIDE
DUDE, DO YOU HAVE A TAMPON?
AW, LOIS, SHE'S PROBABLY COMING OVER HERE TO SEE YOU.
COME ON. SCHOOL'S OUT TIME TO PLAY.
JASMINE? HI, I'M GINGER, REMEMBER? LOIS'S HOUSEMATE? I COME INTO THE RESTAURANT OCCASIONALLY?
I KNOW WHO YOU ARE, GINGER!
OH... WELL, I WAS WONDERING IF MAYBE YOU WEREN'T DOING ANYTHING LATER, WE'RE HAVING A SORT OF PICNIC AT OUR HOUSE...
THAT'D BE FUN! CAN I BRING SOMETHING?
MOMMY! I LOST MY POWERPUFF SPARKLE FLOWER WATCH!
OH, JONAS!
UH...WHAT DID YOU HAVE IN MIND?

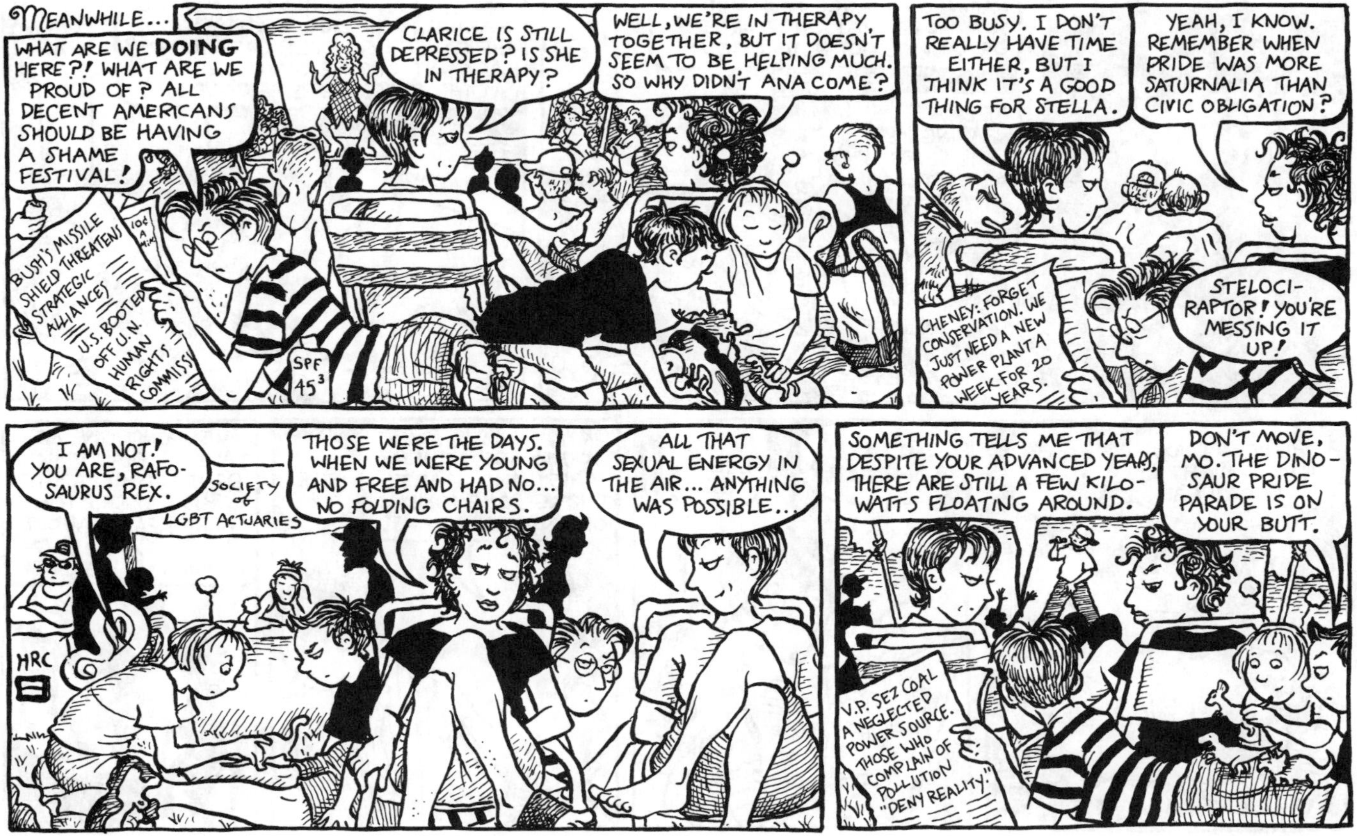
MEANWHILE...
WHAT ARE WE DOING HERE?! WHAT ARE WE PROUD OF? ALL DECENT AMERICANS SHOULD BE HAVING A SHAME FESTIVAL!
BUSH'S MISSILE SHIELD THREATENS STRATEGIC ALLIANCES
U.S. BOOTED OFF U.N. HUMAN RIGHTS COMMISS
SPF 45
CLARICE IS STILL DEPRESSED? IS SHE IN THERAPY?
WELL, WE'RE IN THERAPY TOGETHER, BUT IT DOESN'T SEEM TO BE HELPING MUCH. SO WHY DIDN'T ANA COME?
TOO BUSY. I DON'T REALLY HAVE TIME EITHER, BUT I THINK IT'S A GOOD THING FOR STELLA.
YEAH, I KNOW. REMEMBER WHEN PRIDE WAS MORE SATURNALIA THAN CIVIC OBLIGATION?
CHENEY: FORGET CONSERVATION. WE JUST NEED A NEW POWER PLANT A WEEK FOR 20 YEARS.
STELOCI-RAPTOR! YOU'RE MESSING IT UP!
I AM NOT! YOU ARE, RAFO-SAURUS REX.
SOCIETY of LGBT ACTUARIES
HRC
THOSE WERE THE DAYS. WHEN WE WERE YOUNG AND FREE AND HAD NO... NO FOLDING CHAIRS.
ALL THAT SEXUAL ENERGY IN THE AIR... ANYTHING WAS POSSIBLE...
SOMETHING TELLS ME THAT DESPITE YOUR ADVANCED YEARS, THERE ARE STILL A FEW KILO-WATTS FLOATING AROUND.
DON'T MOVE, MO. THE DINO-SAUR PRIDE PARADE IS ON YOUR BUTT.
V.P. SEZ COAL A NEGLECTED POWER SOURCE. THOSE WHO COMPLAIN OF POLLUTION "DENY REALITY."

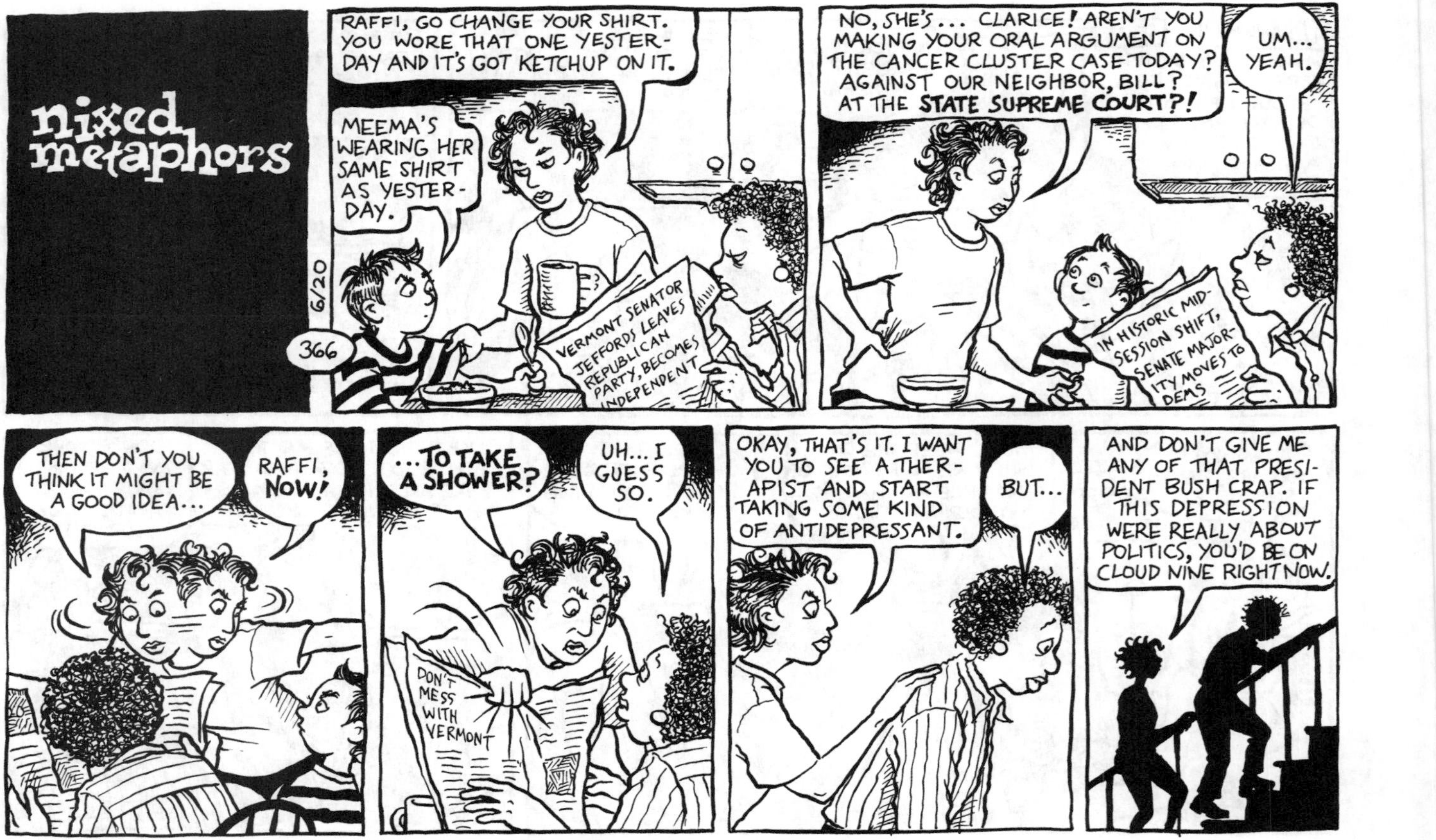
nixed metaphors
366
6/20
RAFFI, GO CHANGE YOUR SHIRT. YOU WORE THAT ONE YESTERDAY AND IT'S GOT KETCHUP ON IT.
MEEMA'S WEARING HER SAME SHIRT AS YESTERDAY.
VERMONT SENATOR JEFFORDS LEAVES REPUBLICAN PARTY, BECOMES INDEPENDENT
NO, SHE'S... CLARICE! AREN'T YOU MAKING YOUR ORAL ARGUMENT ON THE CANCER CLUSTER CASE TODAY? AGAINST OUR NEIGHBOR, BILL? AT THE **STATE SUPREME COURT**?!
UM... YEAH.
IN HISTORIC MID-SESSION SHIFT, SENATE MAJORITY MOVES TO DEMS
THEN DON'T YOU THINK IT MIGHT BE A GOOD IDEA...
RAFFI, **NOW!**
...**TO TAKE A SHOWER?**
UH... I GUESS SO.
DON'T MESS WITH VERMONT
OKAY, THAT'S IT. I WANT YOU TO SEE A THERAPIST AND START TAKING SOME KIND OF ANTIDEPRESSANT.
BUT...
AND DON'T GIVE ME ANY OF THAT PRESIDENT BUSH CRAP. IF THIS DEPRESSION WERE REALLY ABOUT POLITICS, YOU'D BE ON CLOUD NINE RIGHT NOW.

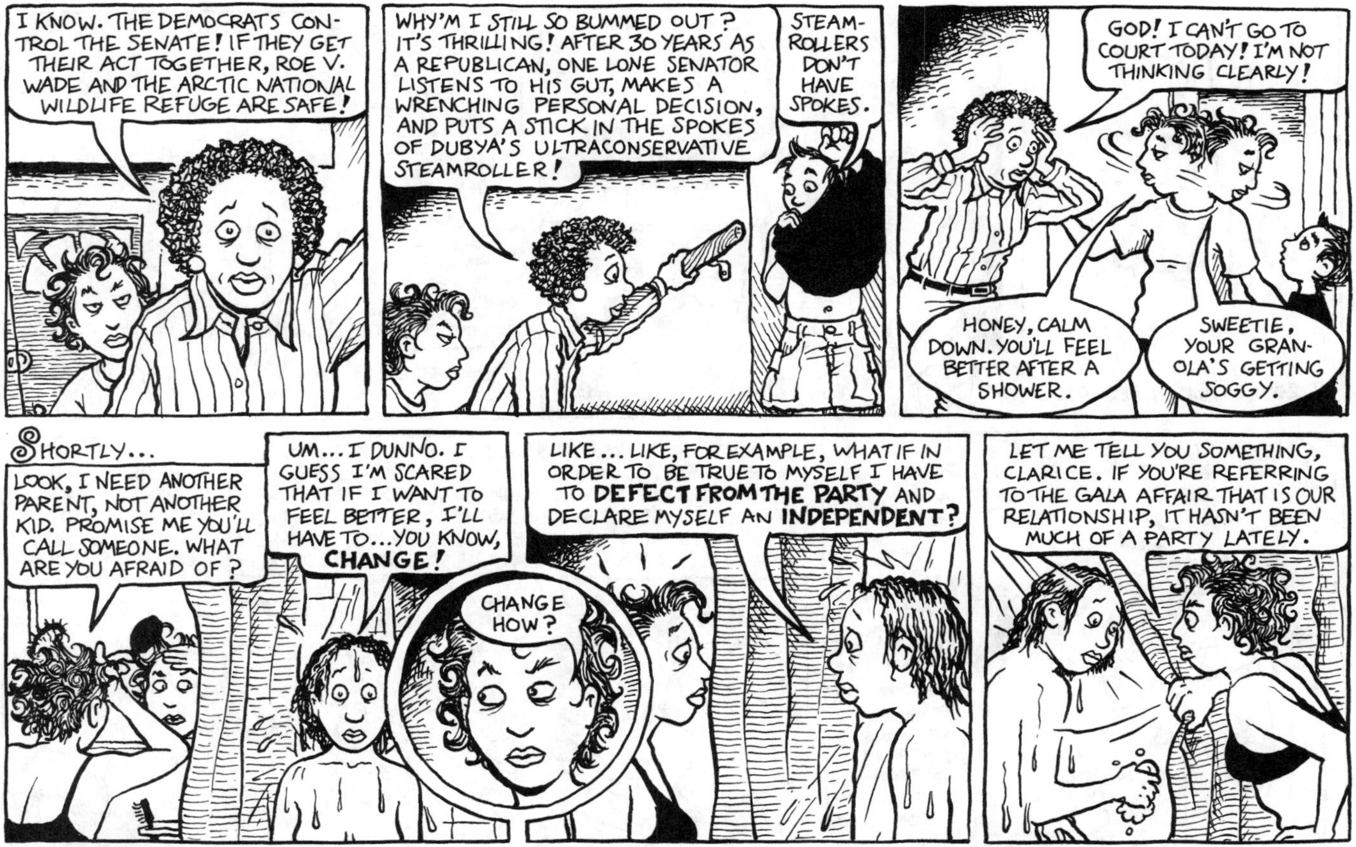

I KNOW. THE DEMOCRATS CONTROL THE SENATE! IF THEY GET THEIR ACT TOGETHER, ROE V. WADE AND THE ARCTIC NATIONAL WILDLIFE REFUGE ARE SAFE!
WHY'M I STILL SO BUMMED OUT? IT'S THRILLING! AFTER 30 YEARS AS A REPUBLICAN, ONE LONE SENATOR LISTENS TO HIS GUT, MAKES A WRENCHING PERSONAL DECISION, AND PUTS A STICK IN THE SPOKES OF DUBYA'S ULTRACONSERVATIVE STEAMROLLER!
STEAMROLLERS DON'T HAVE SPOKES.
GOD! I CAN'T GO TO COURT TODAY! I'M NOT THINKING CLEARLY!
HONEY, CALM DOWN. YOU'LL FEEL BETTER AFTER A SHOWER.
SWEETIE, YOUR GRANOLA'S GETTING SOGGY.
SHORTLY...
LOOK, I NEED ANOTHER PARENT, NOT ANOTHER KID. PROMISE ME YOU'LL CALL SOMEONE. WHAT ARE YOU AFRAID OF?
UM... I DUNNO. I GUESS I'M SCARED THAT IF I WANT TO FEEL BETTER, I'LL HAVE TO... YOU KNOW, CHANGE!
CHANGE HOW?
LIKE... LIKE, FOR EXAMPLE, WHAT IF IN ORDER TO BE TRUE TO MYSELF I HAVE TO DEFECT FROM THE PARTY AND DECLARE MYSELF AN INDEPENDENT?
LET ME TELL YOU SOMETHING, CLARICE. IF YOU'RE REFERRING TO THE GALA AFFAIR THAT IS OUR RELATIONSHIP, IT HASN'T BEEN MUCH OF A PARTY LATELY.

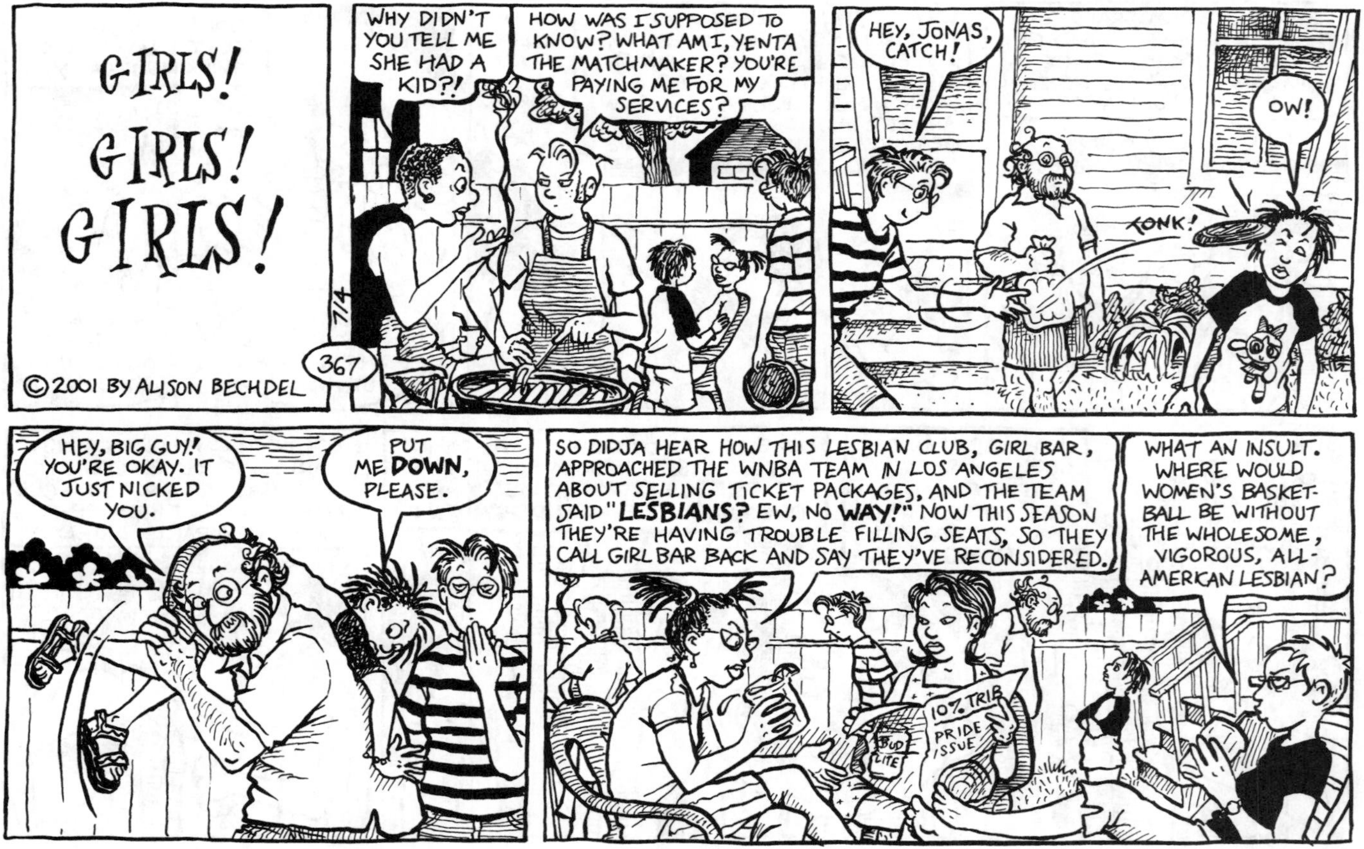

GIRLS! GIRLS! GIRLS!
©2001 BY ALISON BECHDEL
367
7/4
WHY DIDN'T YOU TELL ME SHE HAD A KID?!
HOW WAS I SUPPOSED TO KNOW? WHAT AM I, YENTA THE MATCHMAKER? YOU'RE PAYING ME FOR MY SERVICES?
HEY, JONAS, CATCH!
OW!
TONK!
HEY, BIG GUY! YOU'RE OKAY. IT JUST NICKED YOU.
PUT ME DOWN, PLEASE.
SO DIDJA HEAR HOW THIS LESBIAN CLUB, GIRL BAR, APPROACHED THE WNBA TEAM IN LOS ANGELES ABOUT SELLING TICKET PACKAGES, AND THE TEAM SAID "LESBIANS? EW, NO WAY!" NOW THIS SEASON THEY'RE HAVING TROUBLE FILLING SEATS, SO THEY CALL GIRL BAR BACK AND SAY THEY'VE RECONSIDERED.
10% TRIB PRIDE ISSUE
BUD LITE
WHAT AN INSULT. WHERE WOULD WOMEN'S BASKETBALL BE WITHOUT THE WHOLESOME, VIGOROUS, ALL-AMERICAN LESBIAN?

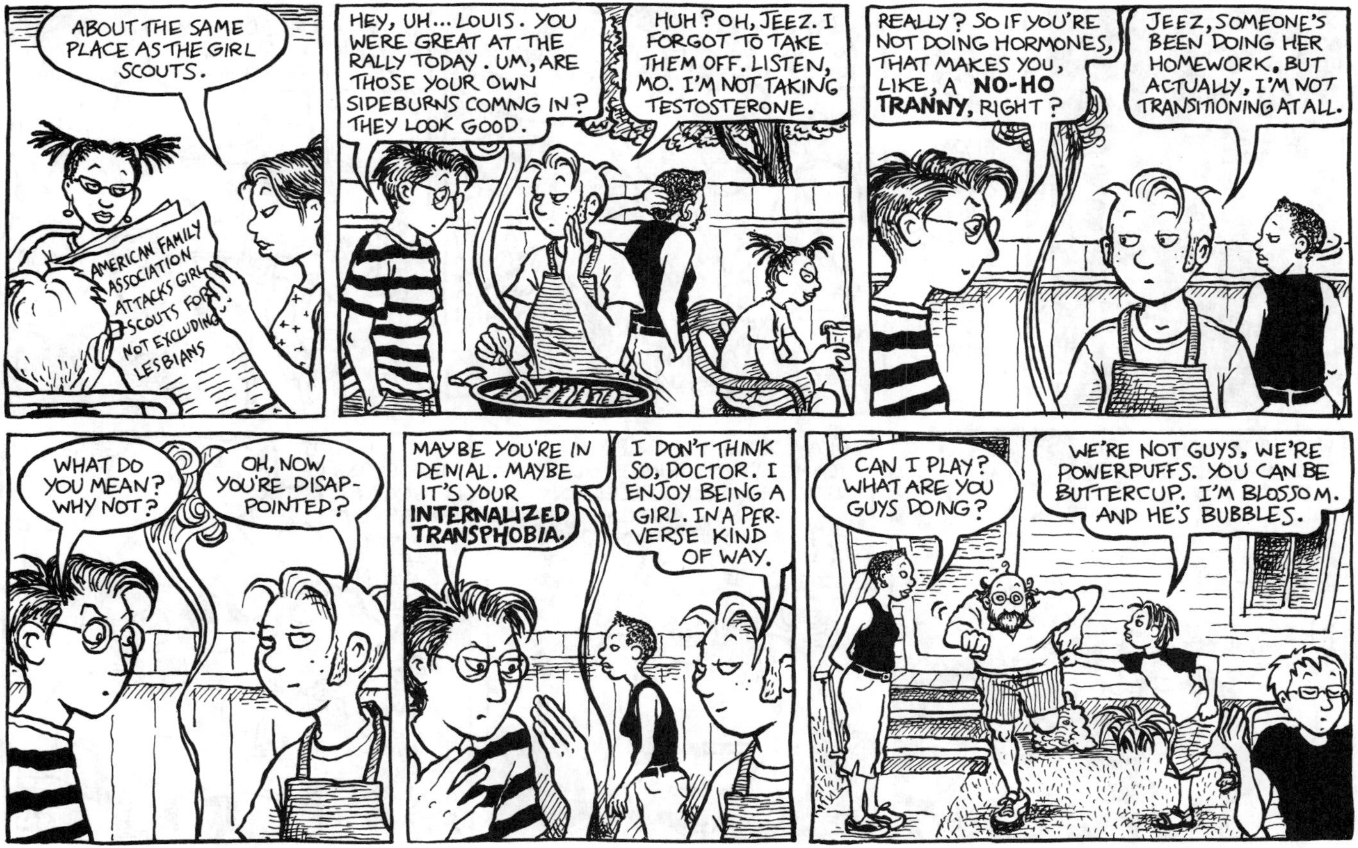
ABOUT THE SAME PLACE AS THE GIRL SCOUTS.
AMERICAN FAMILY ASSOCIATION ATTACKS GIRL SCOUTS FOR NOT EXCLUDING LESBIANS
HEY, UH... LOUIS. YOU WERE GREAT AT THE RALLY TODAY. UM, ARE THOSE YOUR OWN SIDEBURNS COMING IN? THEY LOOK GOOD.
HUH? OH, JEEZ. I FORGOT TO TAKE THEM OFF. LISTEN, MO. I'M NOT TAKING TESTOSTERONE.
REALLY? SO IF YOU'RE NOT DOING HORMONES, THAT MAKES YOU, LIKE, A **NO-HO TRANNY**, RIGHT?
JEEZ, SOMEONE'S BEEN DOING HER HOMEWORK. BUT ACTUALLY, I'M NOT TRANSITIONING AT ALL.
WHAT DO YOU MEAN? WHY NOT?
OH, NOW YOU'RE DISAPPOINTED?
MAYBE YOU'RE IN DENIAL. MAYBE IT'S YOUR **INTERNALIZED TRANSPHOBIA.**
I DON'T THINK SO, DOCTOR. I ENJOY BEING A GIRL. IN A PERVERSE KIND OF WAY.
CAN I PLAY? WHAT ARE YOU GUYS DOING?
WE'RE NOT GUYS, WE'RE POWERPUFFS. YOU CAN BE BUTTERCUP. I'M BLOSSOM. AND HE'S BUBBLES.

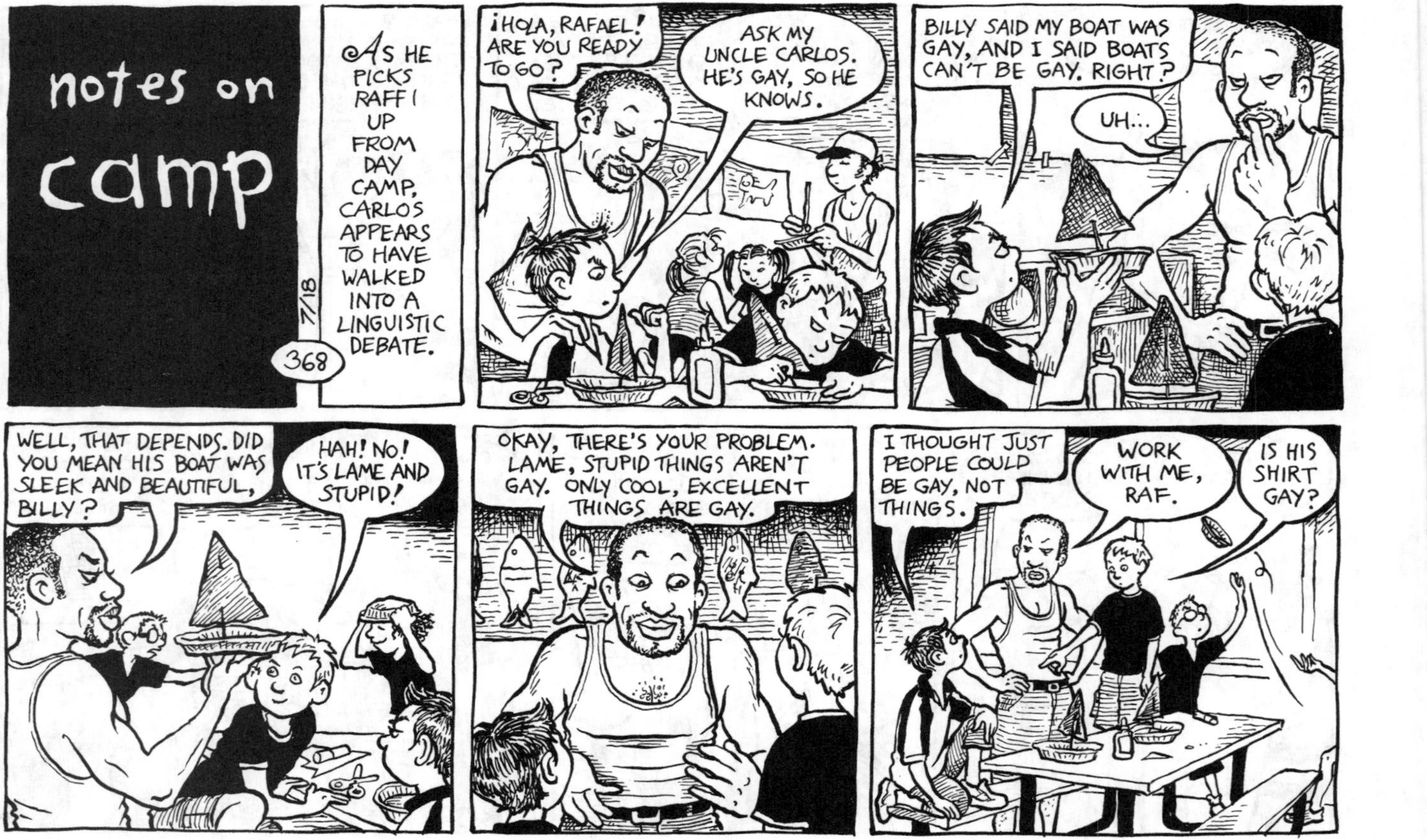
notes on camp
7/18
368
AS HE PICKS RAFFI UP FROM DAY CAMP, CARLOS APPEARS TO HAVE WALKED INTO A LINGUISTIC DEBATE.
¡HOLA, RAFAEL! ARE YOU READY TO GO?
ASK MY UNCLE CARLOS. HE'S GAY, SO HE KNOWS.
BILLY SAID MY BOAT WAS GAY, AND I SAID BOATS CAN'T BE GAY. RIGHT?
UH...
WELL, THAT DEPENDS. DID YOU MEAN HIS BOAT WAS SLEEK AND BEAUTIFUL, BILLY?
HAH! NO! IT'S LAME AND STUPID!
OKAY, THERE'S YOUR PROBLEM. LAME, STUPID THINGS AREN'T GAY. ONLY COOL, EXCELLENT THINGS ARE GAY.
I THOUGHT JUST PEOPLE COULD BE GAY, NOT THINGS.
WORK WITH ME, RAF.
IS HIS SHIRT GAY?

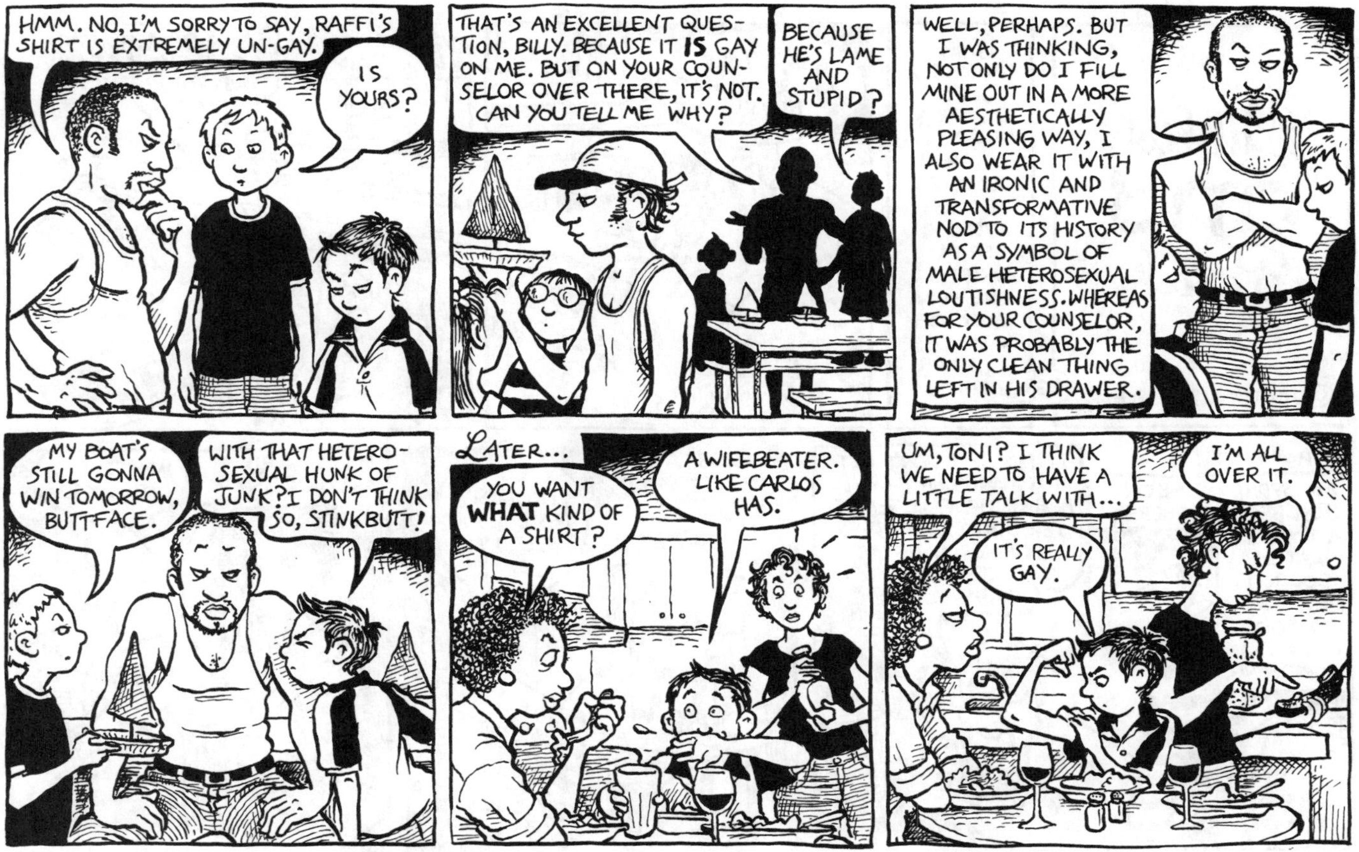
HMM. NO, I'M SORRY TO SAY, RAFFI'S SHIRT IS EXTREMELY UN-GAY.
IS YOURS?
THAT'S AN EXCELLENT QUESTION, BILLY. BECAUSE IT **IS** GAY ON ME. BUT ON YOUR COUNSELOR OVER THERE, IT'S NOT. CAN YOU TELL ME WHY?
BECAUSE HE'S LAME AND STUPID?
WELL, PERHAPS. BUT I WAS THINKING, NOT ONLY DO I FILL MINE OUT IN A MORE AESTHETICALLY PLEASING WAY, I ALSO WEAR IT WITH AN IRONIC AND TRANSFORMATIVE NOD TO ITS HISTORY AS A SYMBOL OF MALE HETEROSEXUAL LOUTISHNESS. WHEREAS FOR YOUR COUNSELOR, IT WAS PROBABLY THE ONLY CLEAN THING LEFT IN HIS DRAWER.
MY BOAT'S STILL GONNA WIN TOMORROW, BUTTFACE.
WITH THAT HETEROSEXUAL HUNK OF JUNK? I DON'T THINK SO, STINKBUTT!
LATER...
YOU WANT **WHAT** KIND OF A SHIRT?
A WIFEBEATER. LIKE CARLOS HAS.
UM, TONI? I THINK WE NEED TO HAVE A LITTLE TALK WITH...
I'M ALL OVER IT.
IT'S REALLY GAY.

Publish and Perish

© 2001 BY ALISON BECHDEL

8/1 369

OUR CROTCHETY COUPLE HAS TAKEN THE DAY OFF— MO, FROM SELLING BOOKS; SYDNEY, FROM WRITING ONE — IN QUEST OF A LITTLE SUMMER FUN.

GOD, I LOVE YOU SO MUCH IT HURTS.

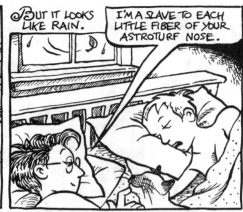

BUT IT LOOKS LIKE RAIN.

I'M A SLAVE TO EACH LITTLE FIBER OF YOUR ASTROTURF NOSE.

SHORTLY...

AW, SYDNEY, COME ON. JUST BECAUSE THERE'S A TORNADO WATCH DOESN'T MEAN WE CAN'T GO OUT AND DO SOMETHING!

LISTEN, IF I DON'T GET THIS MANUSCRIPT DONE BEFORE THE FALL SEMESTER STARTS, MY ASS IS UNTENURED GRASS. LEMME JUST GET A FEW NOTES DOWN.

3 HOURS LATER...

BZZZT!

BZZZT!

NO, NO. DON'T DISTURB YOURSELF, I'LL GET IT.

HYPOCRITE! CONSERVATIVE GAY JOURNALIST ANDREW SULLIVAN TROLLS INTERNET...

SYDNEY KRU... KREWKUTSKI?

WHATEVER. THANKS.

...FOR DATES WITH NADER-VOTING PETA MEMBERS...

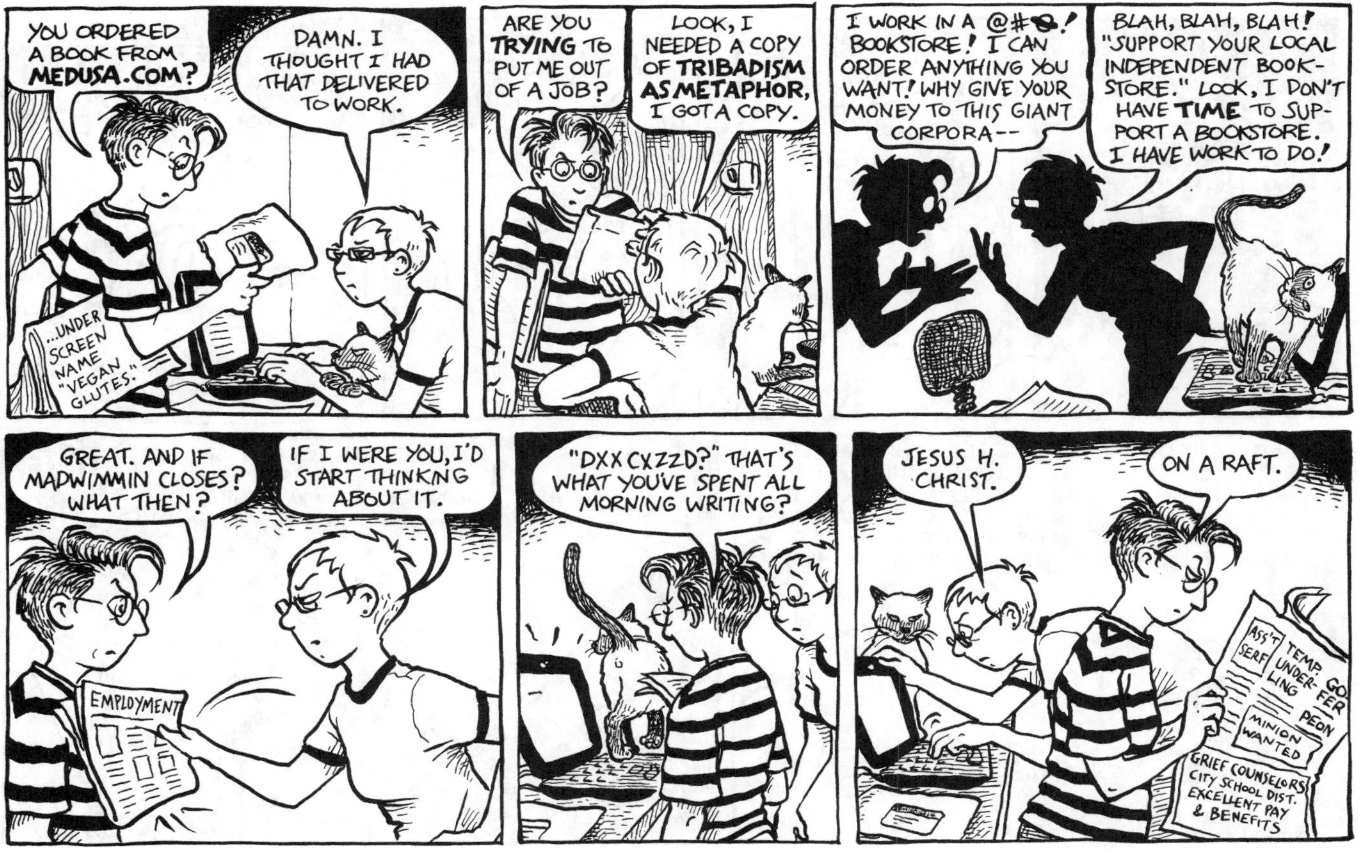
YOU ORDERED A BOOK FROM MEDUSA.COM?
DAMN. I THOUGHT I HAD THAT DELIVERED TO WORK.
...UNDER SCREEN NAME "VEGAN GLUTES."
ARE YOU TRYING TO PUT ME OUT OF A JOB?
LOOK, I NEEDED A COPY OF TRIBADISM AS METAPHOR, I GOT A COPY.
I WORK IN A @#✪! BOOKSTORE! I CAN ORDER ANYTHING YOU WANT! WHY GIVE YOUR MONEY TO THIS GIANT CORPORA--
BLAH, BLAH, BLAH! "SUPPORT YOUR LOCAL INDEPENDENT BOOKSTORE." LOOK, I DON'T HAVE TIME TO SUPPORT A BOOKSTORE. I HAVE WORK TO DO!
GREAT. AND IF MADWIMMIN CLOSES? WHAT THEN?
IF I WERE YOU, I'D START THINKING ABOUT IT.
EMPLOYMENT
"DXX CXZZD?" THAT'S WHAT YOU'VE SPENT ALL MORNING WRITING?
JESUS H. CHRIST.
ON A RAFT.
ASS'T SERF
TEMP GOFER UNDERLING
PEON
MINION WANTED
GRIEF COUNSELORS CITY SCHOOL DIST. EXCELLENT PAY & BENEFITS

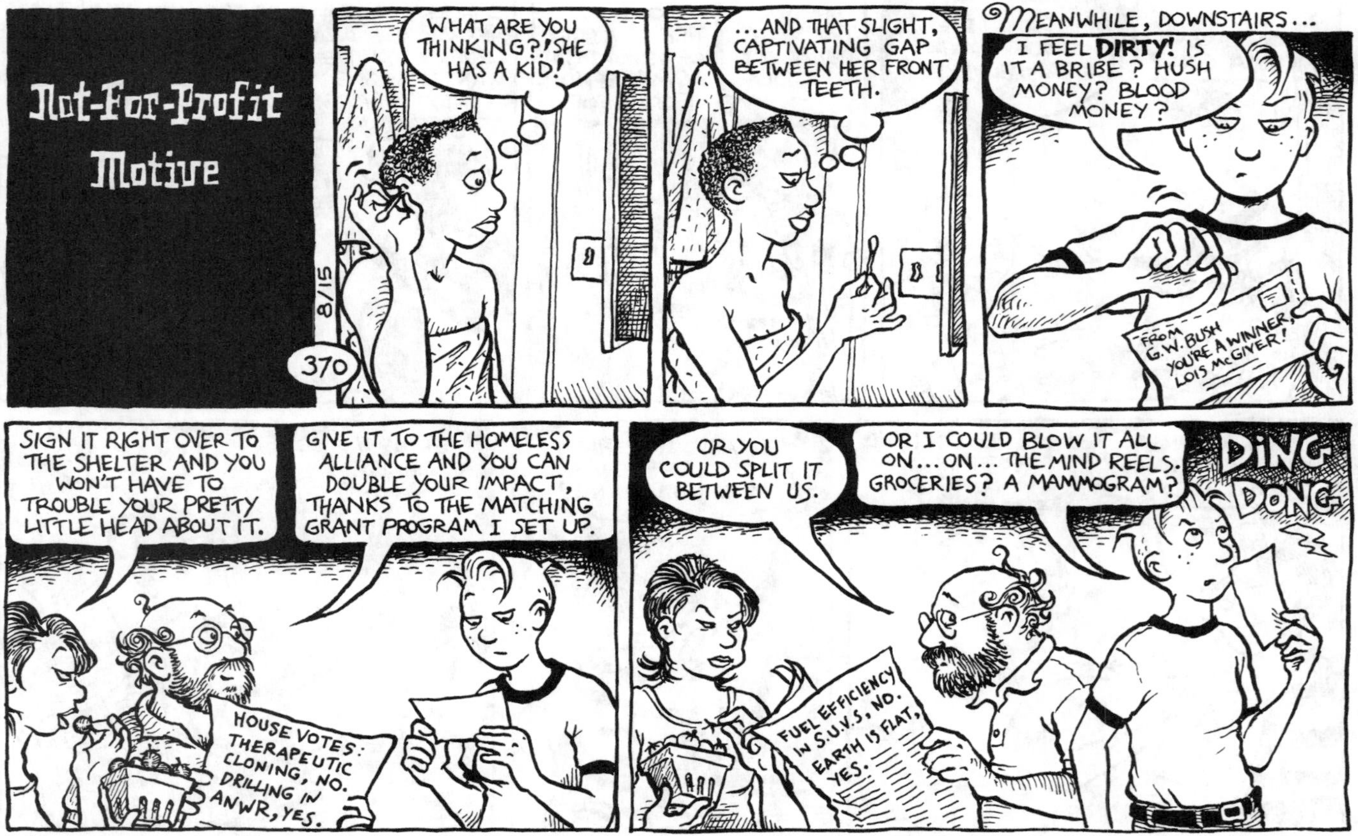
Not-For-Profit Motive
370
8/15
WHAT ARE YOU THINKING?! SHE HAS A KID!
...AND THAT SLIGHT, CAPTIVATING GAP BETWEEN HER FRONT TEETH.
MEANWHILE, DOWNSTAIRS...
I FEEL DIRTY! IS IT A BRIBE? HUSH MONEY? BLOOD MONEY?
FROM G.W. BUSH
YOU'RE A WINNER, LOIS McGIVER!
SIGN IT RIGHT OVER TO THE SHELTER AND YOU WON'T HAVE TO TROUBLE YOUR PRETTY LITTLE HEAD ABOUT IT.
GIVE IT TO THE HOMELESS ALLIANCE AND YOU CAN DOUBLE YOUR IMPACT, THANKS TO THE MATCHING GRANT PROGRAM I SET UP.
HOUSE VOTES: THERAPEUTIC CLONING, NO. DRILLING IN ANWR, YES.
OR YOU COULD SPLIT IT BETWEEN US.
OR I COULD BLOW IT ALL ON... ON... THE MIND REELS. GROCERIES? A MAMMOGRAM?
DING DONG
FUEL EFFICIENCY IN S.U.V.S, NO. EARTH IS FLAT, YES.

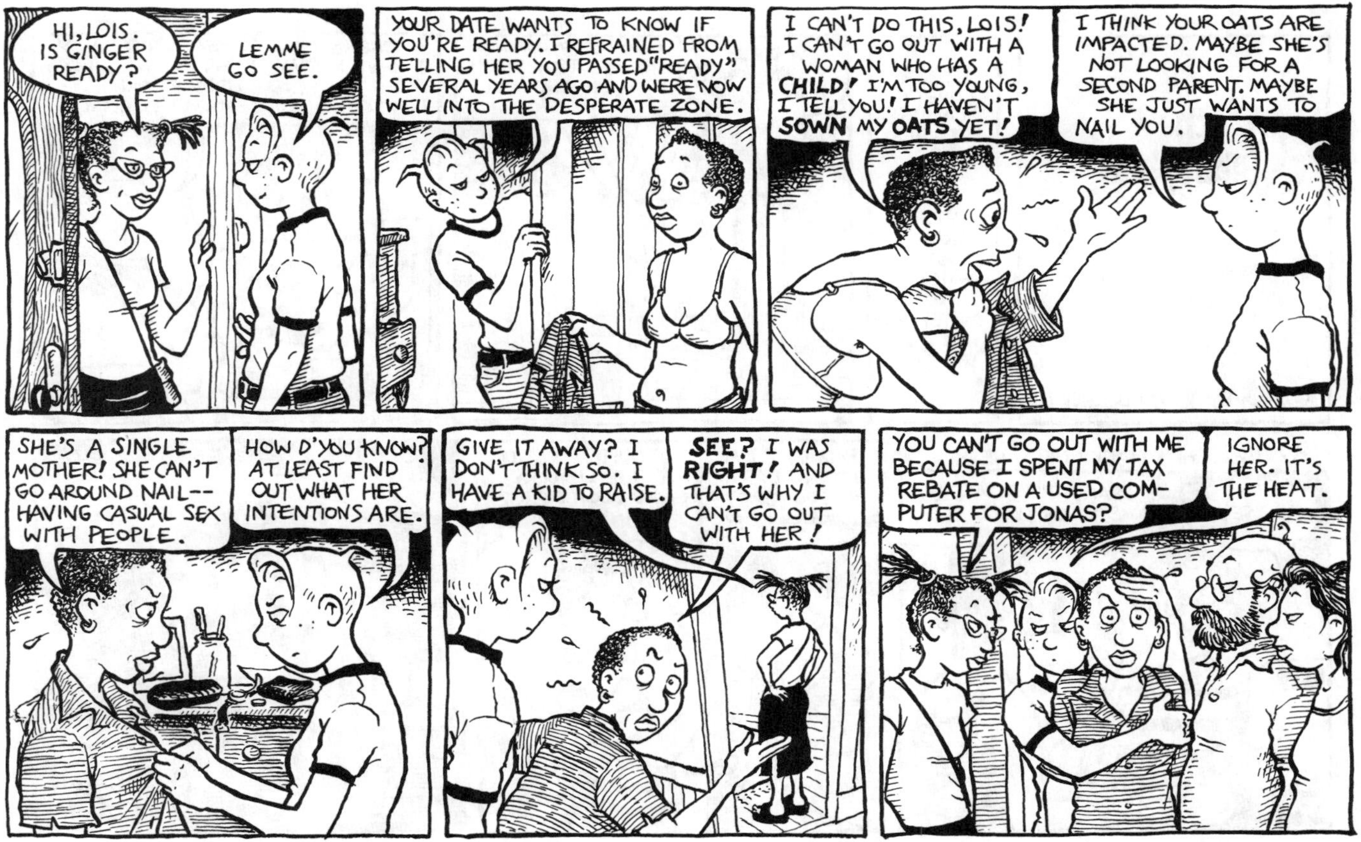
HI, LOIS. IS GINGER READY?
LEMME GO SEE.
YOUR DATE WANTS TO KNOW IF YOU'RE READY. I REFRAINED FROM TELLING HER YOU PASSED "READY" SEVERAL YEARS AGO AND WERE NOW WELL INTO THE DESPERATE ZONE.
I CAN'T DO THIS, LOIS! I CAN'T GO OUT WITH A WOMAN WHO HAS A CHILD! I'M TOO YOUNG, I TELL YOU! I HAVEN'T SOWN MY OATS YET!
I THINK YOUR OATS ARE IMPACTED. MAYBE SHE'S NOT LOOKING FOR A SECOND PARENT. MAYBE SHE JUST WANTS TO NAIL YOU.
SHE'S A SINGLE MOTHER! SHE CAN'T GO AROUND NAIL-- HAVING CASUAL SEX WITH PEOPLE.
HOW D'YOU KNOW? AT LEAST FIND OUT WHAT HER INTENTIONS ARE.
GIVE IT AWAY? I DON'T THINK SO. I HAVE A KID TO RAISE.
SEE? I WAS RIGHT! AND THAT'S WHY I CAN'T GO OUT WITH HER!
YOU CAN'T GO OUT WITH ME BECAUSE I SPENT MY TAX REBATE ON A USED COM-PUTER FOR JONAS?
IGNORE HER. IT'S THE HEAT.

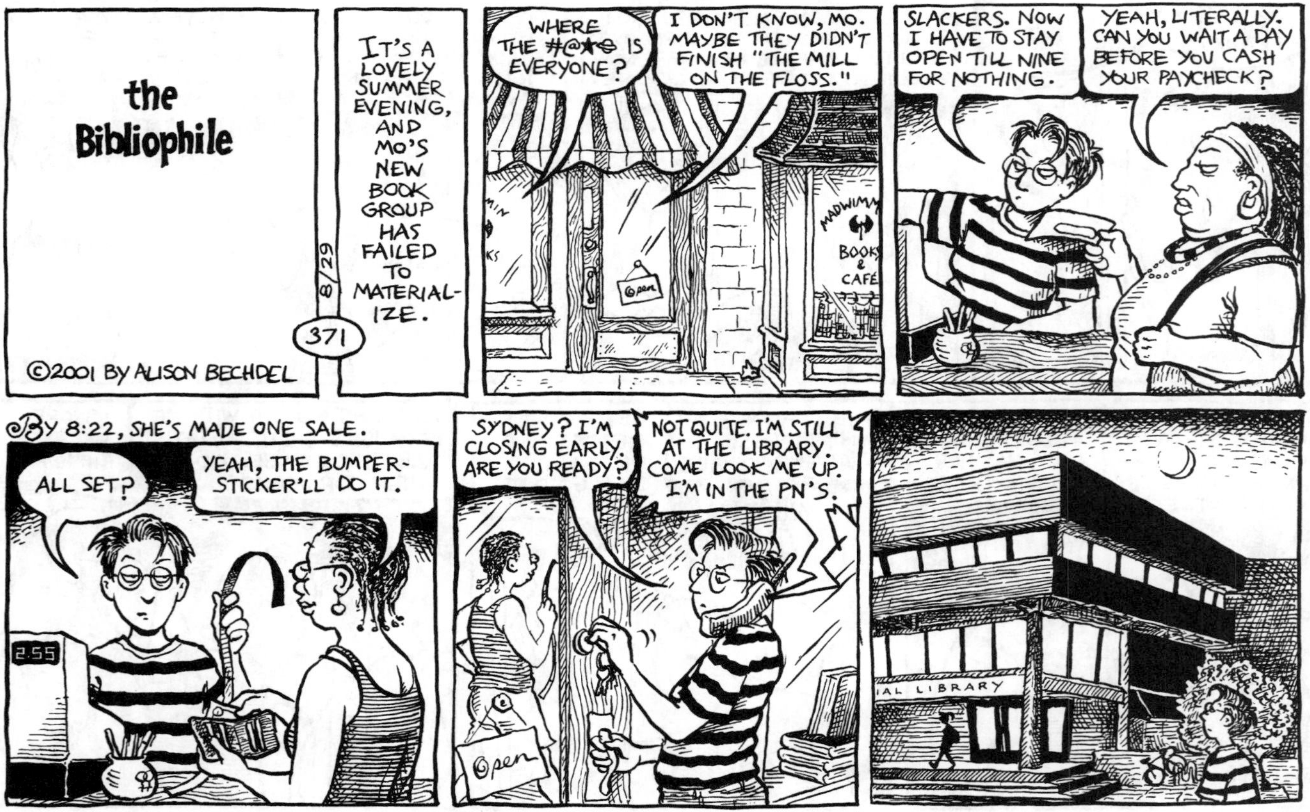
the Bibliophile
©2001 BY ALISON BECHDEL
371
8/29
IT'S A LOVELY SUMMER EVENING, AND MO'S NEW BOOK GROUP HAS FAILED TO MATERIALIZE.
WHERE THE #@*@ IS EVERYONE?
I DON'T KNOW, MO. MAYBE THEY DIDN'T FINISH "THE MILL ON THE FLOSS."
Open
MADWIMMIN BOOKS & CAFE
SLACKERS. NOW I HAVE TO STAY OPEN TILL NINE FOR NOTHING.
YEAH, LITERALLY. CAN YOU WAIT A DAY BEFORE YOU CASH YOUR PAYCHECK?
BY 8:22, SHE'S MADE ONE SALE.
ALL SET?
YEAH, THE BUMPER-STICKER'LL DO IT.
2.55
SYDNEY? I'M CLOSING EARLY. ARE YOU READY?
NOT QUITE. I'M STILL AT THE LIBRARY. COME LOOK ME UP. I'M IN THE PN'S.
Open
IAL LIBRARY

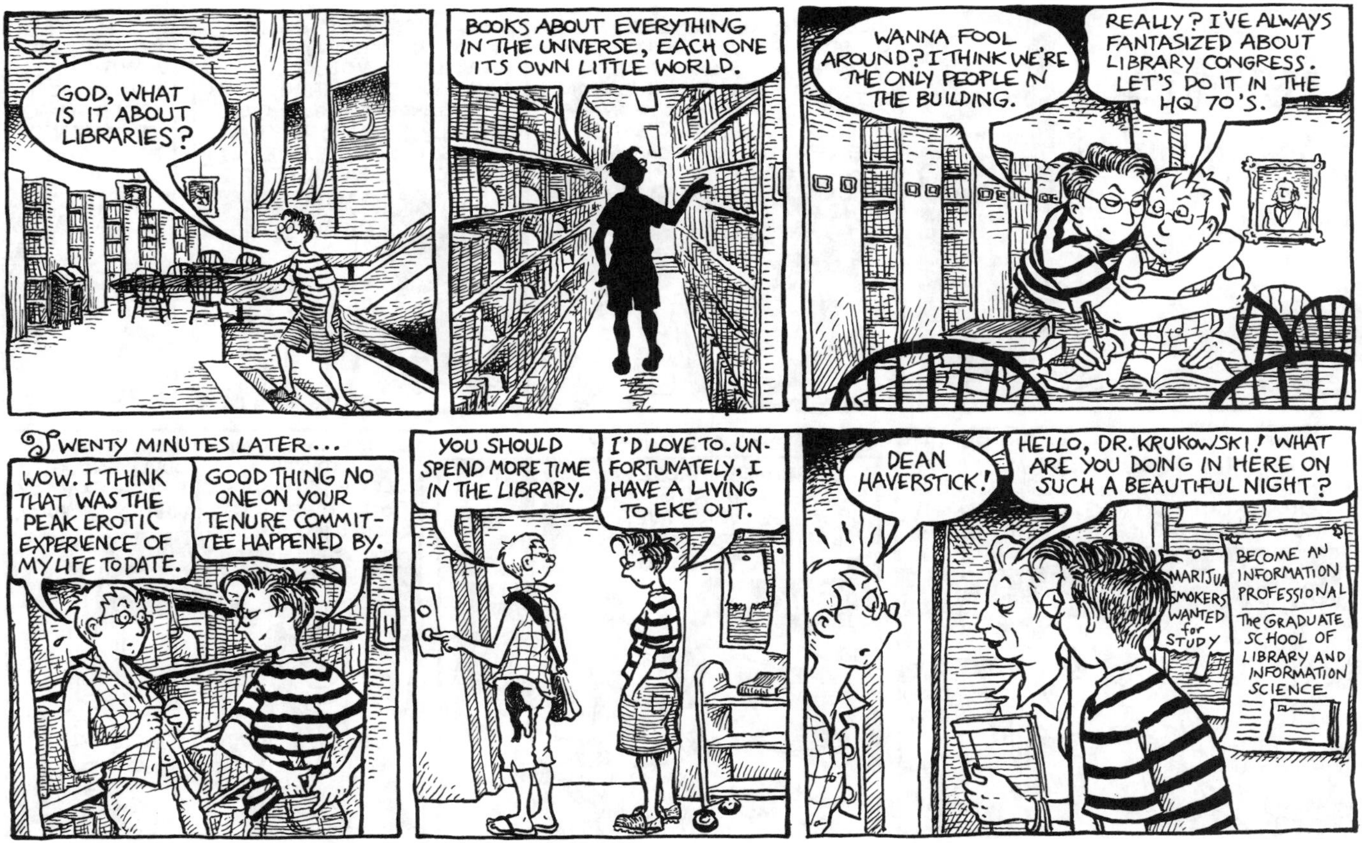
GOD, WHAT IS IT ABOUT LIBRARIES?
BOOKS ABOUT EVERYTHING IN THE UNIVERSE, EACH ONE ITS OWN LITTLE WORLD.
WANNA FOOL AROUND? I THINK WE'RE THE ONLY PEOPLE IN THE BUILDING.
REALLY? I'VE ALWAYS FANTASIZED ABOUT LIBRARY CONGRESS. LET'S DO IT IN THE HQ 70'S.
TWENTY MINUTES LATER...
WOW. I THINK THAT WAS THE PEAK EROTIC EXPERIENCE OF MY LIFE TO DATE.
GOOD THING NO ONE ON YOUR TENURE COMMITTEE HAPPENED BY.
YOU SHOULD SPEND MORE TIME IN THE LIBRARY.
I'D LOVE TO. UNFORTUNATELY, I HAVE A LIVING TO EKE OUT.
DEAN HAVERSTICK!
HELLO, DR. KRUKOWSKI! WHAT ARE YOU DOING IN HERE ON SUCH A BEAUTIFUL NIGHT?
MARIJUA SMOKERS WANTED for STUDY
BECOME AN INFORMATION PROFESSIONAL
The GRADUATE SCHOOL OF LIBRARY AND INFORMATION SCIENCE

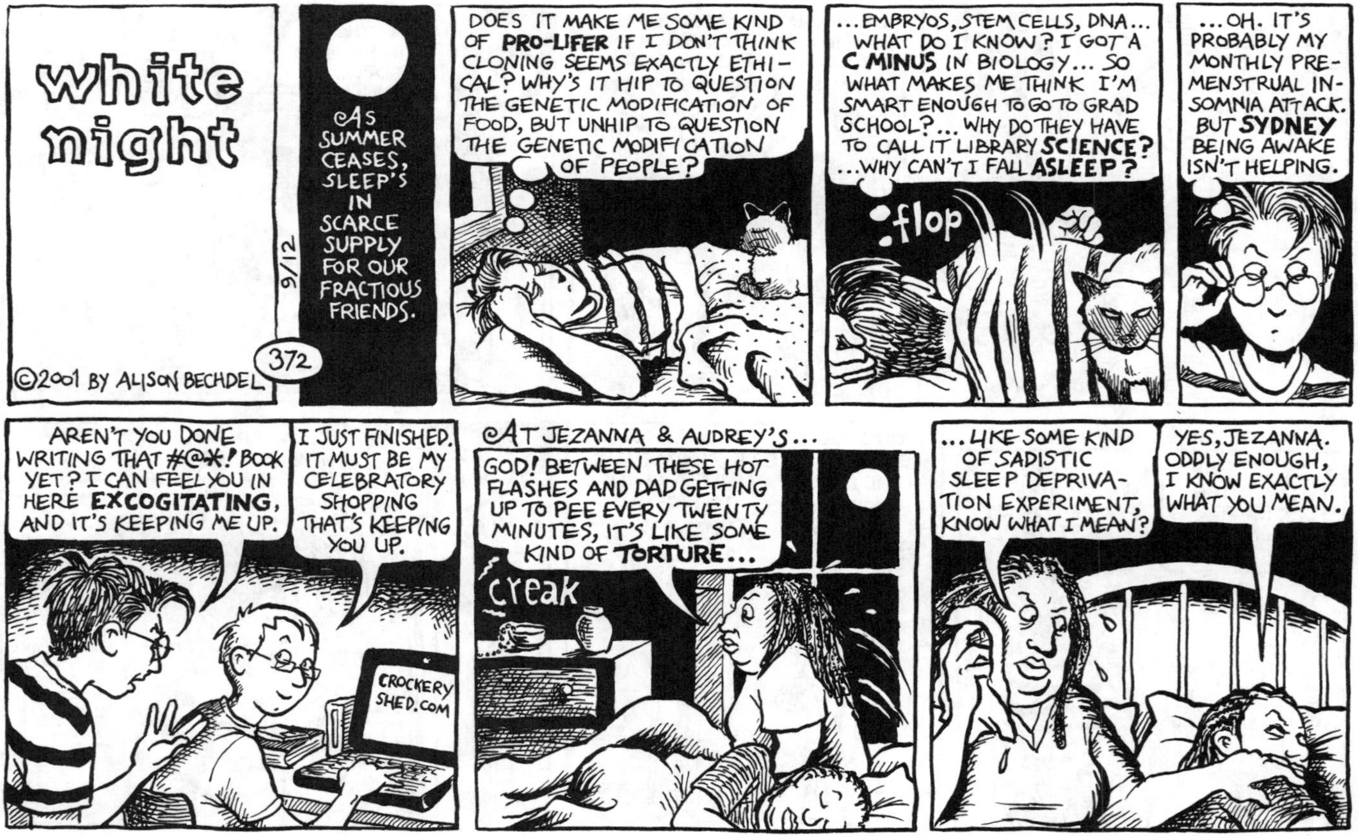
white night
©2001 BY ALISON BECHDEL
372
9/12
AS SUMMER CEASES, SLEEP'S IN SCARCE SUPPLY FOR OUR FRACTIOUS FRIENDS.
DOES IT MAKE ME SOME KIND OF PRO-LIFER IF I DON'T THINK CLONING SEEMS EXACTLY ETHICAL? WHY'S IT HIP TO QUESTION THE GENETIC MODIFICATION OF FOOD, BUT UNHIP TO QUESTION THE GENETIC MODIFICATION OF PEOPLE?
...EMBRYOS, STEM CELLS, DNA... WHAT DO I KNOW? I GOT A C MINUS IN BIOLOGY... SO WHAT MAKES ME THINK I'M SMART ENOUGH TO GO TO GRAD SCHOOL?... WHY DO THEY HAVE TO CALL IT LIBRARY SCIENCE? ...WHY CAN'T I FALL ASLEEP?
flop
...OH. IT'S PROBABLY MY MONTHLY PRE-MENSTRUAL INSOMNIA ATTACK. BUT SYDNEY BEING AWAKE ISN'T HELPING.
AREN'T YOU DONE WRITING THAT #@*! BOOK YET? I CAN FEEL YOU IN HERE EXCOGITATING, AND IT'S KEEPING ME UP.
I JUST FINISHED. IT MUST BE MY CELEBRATORY SHOPPING THAT'S KEEPING YOU UP.
CROCKERY SHED.COM
AT JEZANNA & AUDREY'S...
GOD! BETWEEN THESE HOT FLASHES AND DAD GETTING UP TO PEE EVERY TWENTY MINUTES, IT'S LIKE SOME KIND OF TORTURE...
creak
...LIKE SOME KIND OF SADISTIC SLEEP DEPRIVATION EXPERIMENT, KNOW WHAT I MEAN?
YES, JEZANNA. ODDLY ENOUGH, I KNOW EXACTLY WHAT YOU MEAN.

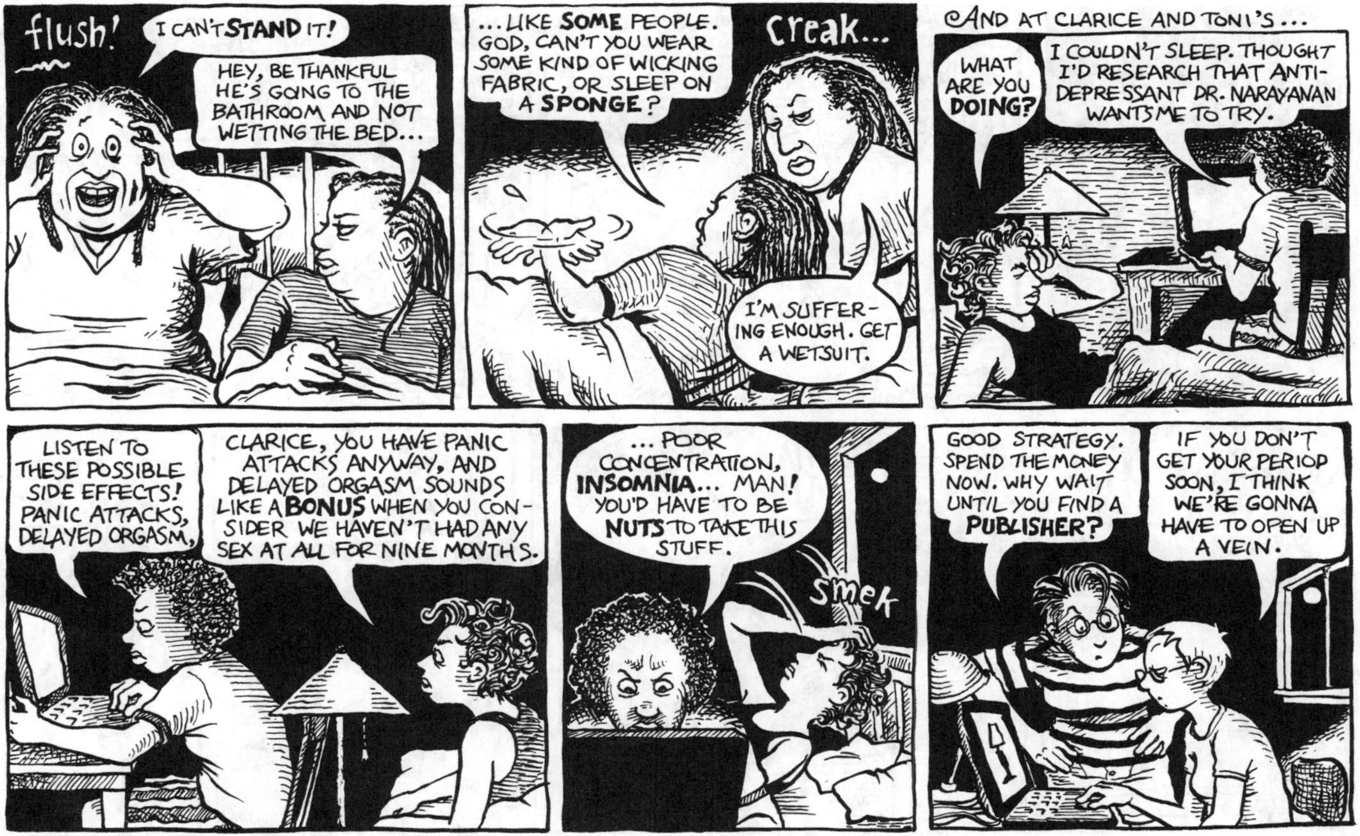
flush!
I CAN'T **STAND** IT!
HEY, BE THANKFUL HE'S GOING TO THE BATHROOM AND NOT WETTING THE BED...
...LIKE **SOME** PEOPLE. GOD, CAN'T YOU WEAR SOME KIND OF WICKING FABRIC, OR SLEEP ON A **SPONGE**?
Creak...
I'M SUFFERING ENOUGH. GET A WETSUIT.
AND AT CLARICE AND TONI'S...
WHAT ARE YOU **DOING?**
I COULDN'T SLEEP. THOUGHT I'D RESEARCH THAT ANTI-DEPRESSANT DR. NARAYANAN WANTS ME TO TRY.
LISTEN TO THESE POSSIBLE SIDE EFFECTS! PANIC ATTACKS, DELAYED ORGASM,
CLARICE, YOU HAVE PANIC ATTACKS ANYWAY, AND DELAYED ORGASM SOUNDS LIKE A **BONUS** WHEN YOU CONSIDER WE HAVEN'T HAD ANY SEX AT ALL FOR NINE MONTHS.
...POOR CONCENTRATION, **INSOMNIA**... MAN! YOU'D HAVE TO BE **NUTS** TO TAKE THIS STUFF.
SMEK
GOOD STRATEGY. SPEND THE MONEY NOW. WHY WAIT UNTIL YOU FIND A **PUBLISHER?**
IF YOU DON'T GET YOUR PERIOD SOON, I THINK WE'RE GONNA HAVE TO OPEN UP A VEIN.

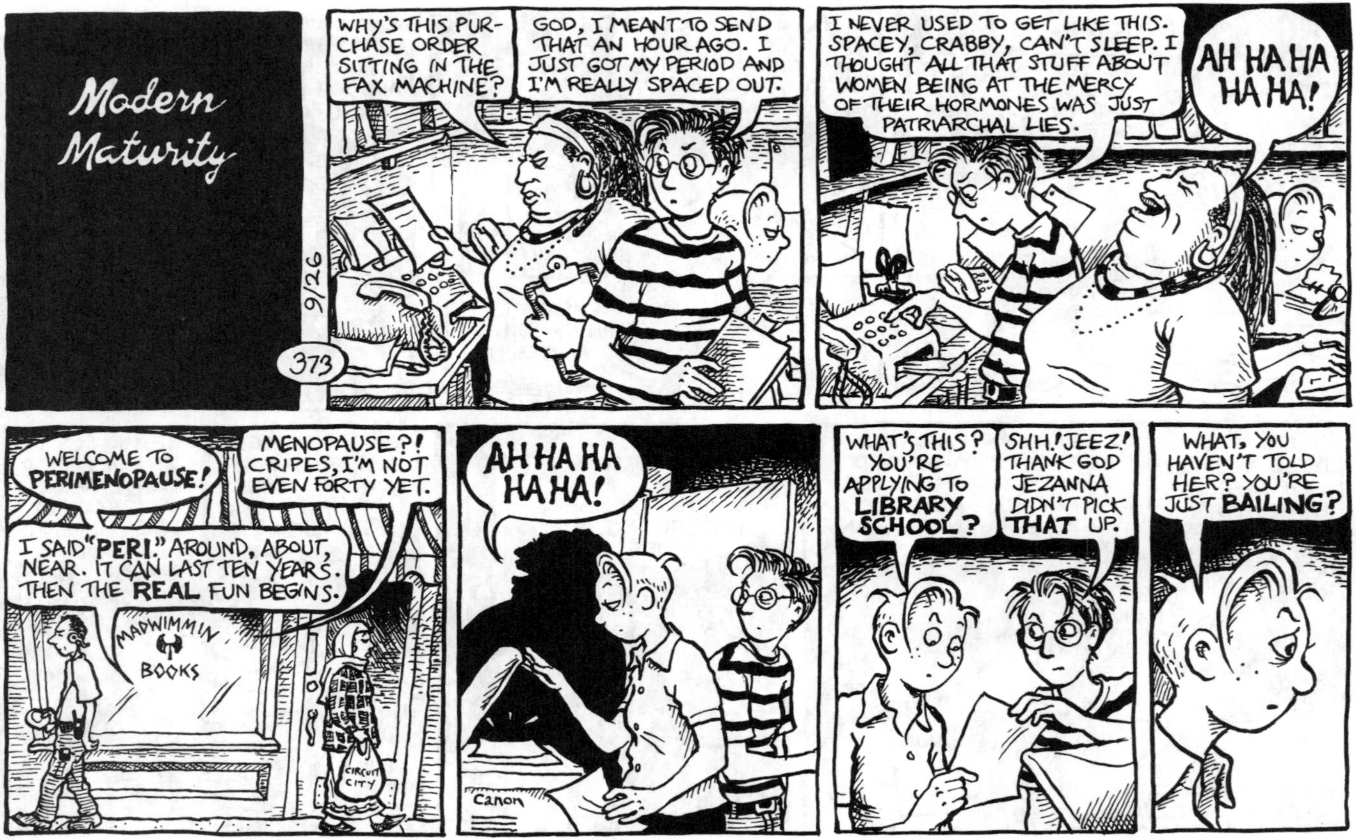
Modern Maturity
373
9/26
WHY'S THIS PURCHASE ORDER SITTING IN THE FAX MACHINE?
GOD, I MEANT TO SEND THAT AN HOUR AGO. I JUST GOT MY PERIOD AND I'M REALLY SPACED OUT.
I NEVER USED TO GET LIKE THIS. SPACEY, CRABBY, CAN'T SLEEP. I THOUGHT ALL THAT STUFF ABOUT WOMEN BEING AT THE MERCY OF THEIR HORMONES WAS JUST PATRIARCHAL LIES.
AH HA HA HA HA!
WELCOME TO PERIMENOPAUSE!
MENOPAUSE?! CRIPES, I'M NOT EVEN FORTY YET.
I SAID "PERI." AROUND, ABOUT, NEAR. IT CAN LAST TEN YEARS. THEN THE REAL FUN BEGINS.
MADWIMMIN BOOKS
CIRCUIT CITY
AH HA HA HA HA!
Canon
WHAT'S THIS? YOU'RE APPLYING TO LIBRARY SCHOOL?
SHH! JEEZ! THANK GOD JEZANNA DIDN'T PICK THAT UP.
WHAT, YOU HAVEN'T TOLD HER? YOU'RE JUST BAILING?

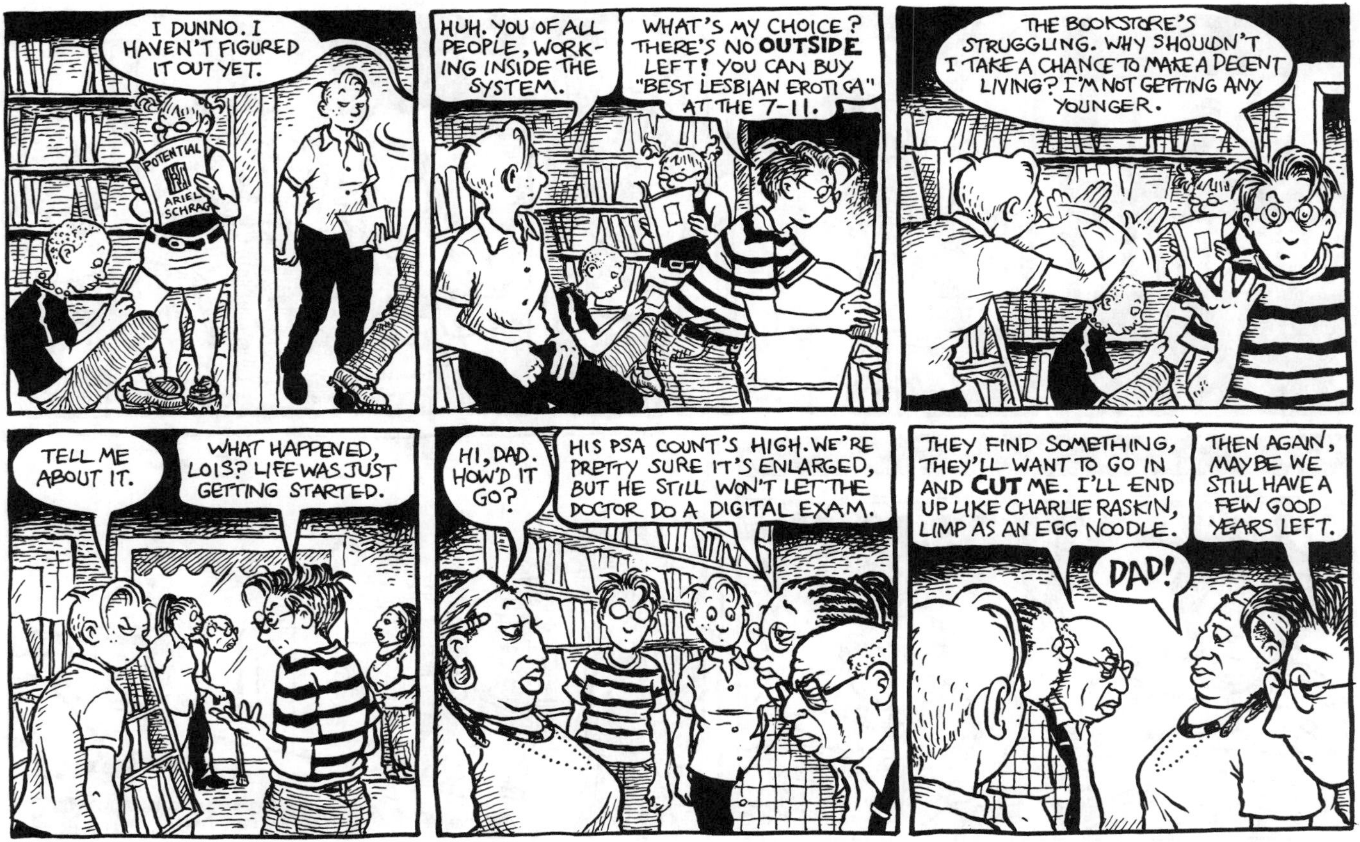
I DUNNO. I HAVEN'T FIGURED IT OUT YET.
POTENTIAL
ARIEL SCHRAG
HUH. YOU OF ALL PEOPLE, WORKING INSIDE THE SYSTEM.
WHAT'S MY CHOICE? THERE'S NO **OUTSIDE** LEFT! YOU CAN BUY "BEST LESBIAN EROTICA" AT THE 7-11.
THE BOOKSTORE'S STRUGGLING. WHY SHOULDN'T I TAKE A CHANCE TO MAKE A DECENT LIVING? I'M NOT GETTING ANY YOUNGER.
TELL ME ABOUT IT.
WHAT HAPPENED, LOIS? LIFE WAS JUST GETTING STARTED.
HI, DAD. HOW'D IT GO?
HIS PSA COUNT'S HIGH. WE'RE PRETTY SURE IT'S ENLARGED, BUT HE STILL WON'T LET THE DOCTOR DO A DIGITAL EXAM.
THEY FIND SOMETHING, THEY'LL WANT TO GO IN AND **CUT** ME. I'LL END UP LIKE CHARLIE RASKIN, LIMP AS AN EGG NOODLE.
DAD!
THEN AGAIN, MAYBE WE STILL HAVE A FEW GOOD YEARS LEFT.

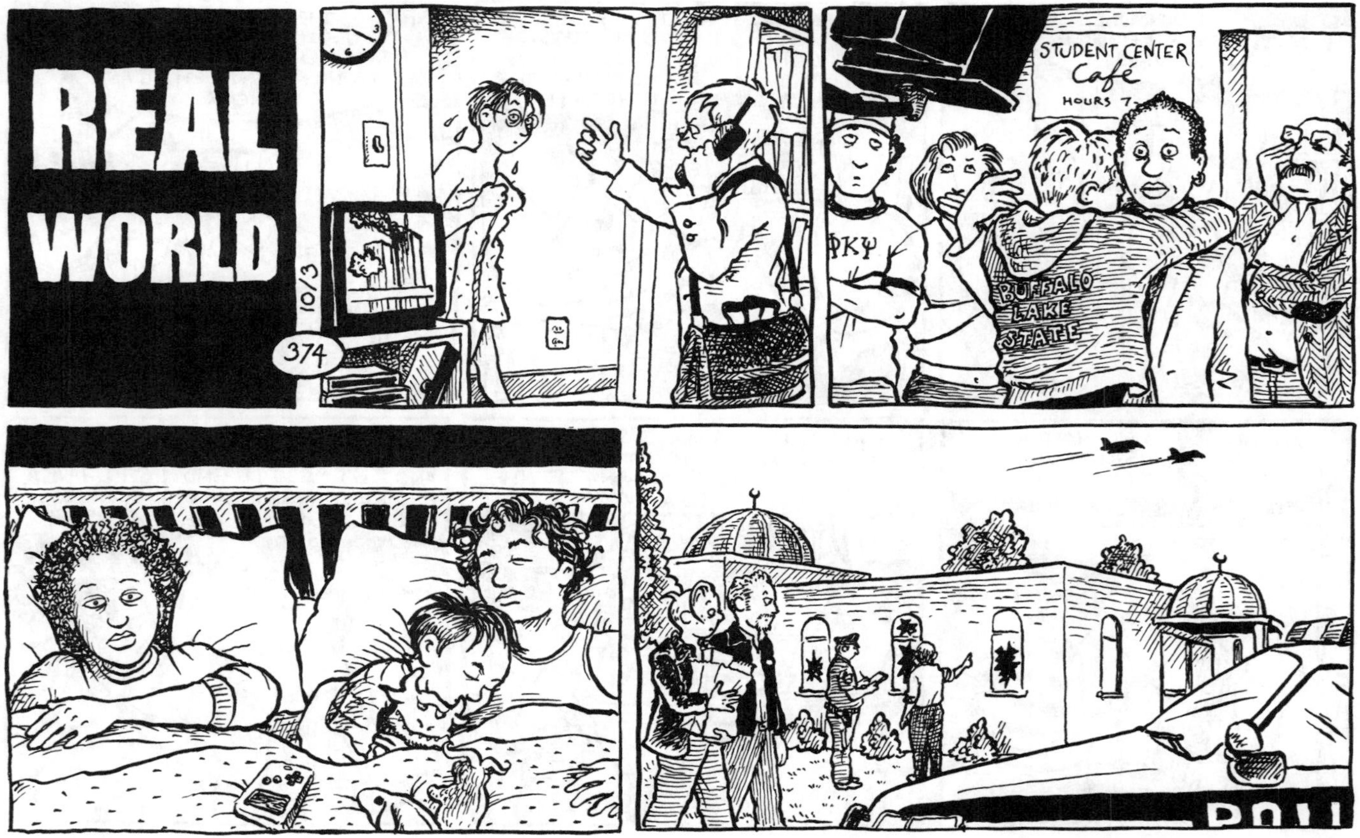
REAL WORLD
10/3
374
STUDENT CENTER
Café
HOURS 7-
ΦKΨ
BUFFALO LAKE STATE

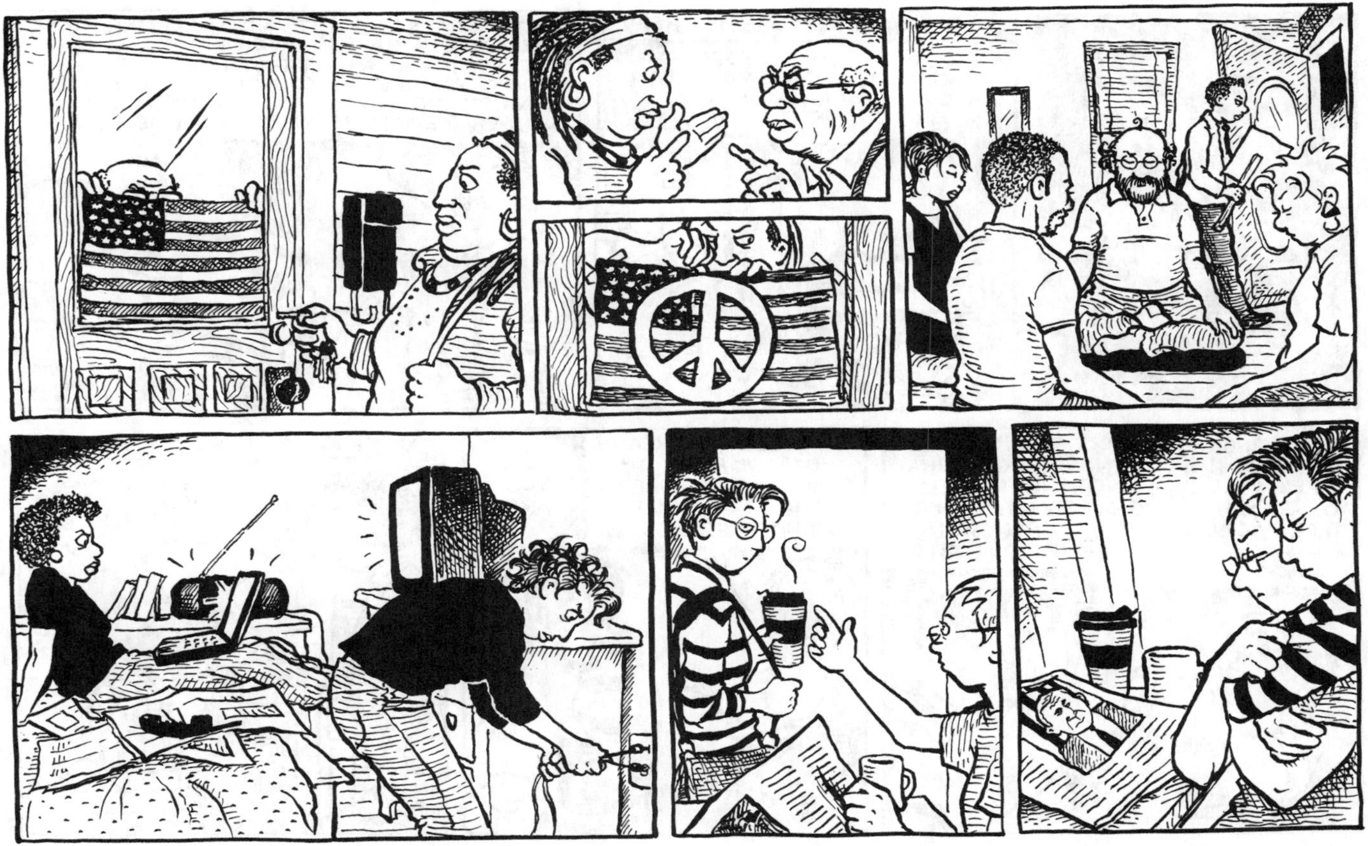

idealpolitik

©2001 by Alison Bechdel

10/24
375

DON'T KNOW MUCH ABOUT HISTORY...

DON'T GIVE ME THAT SELF-FLAGELLATING CRAP, MO. WHAT ARE YOU SAYING, WE BROUGHT THIS ON OURSELVES?!

THAT'S...THAT'S LIKE JERRY FALWELL, BLAMING IT ON THE "ABORTIONISTS AND THE FEMINISTS AND THE GAYS AND THE **ACLU**"!

IT'S NOTHING LIKE THAT! I'M SAYING THAT GIVEN THE VIOLENCE OUR OWN COUNTRY PERPETRATES, WE SHOULDN'T BE SO SURPRISED WHEN SOME OF IT COMES BACK AT US.

CHIPS

BY PLACING THE BLAME ON U.S. FOREIGN POLICY, YOU'RE EXCUSING THESE VICIOUS, FUNDAMENTALIST WACKOS!

NO, I'M NOT. **YOU'RE** USING THE EXCUSE THAT SINCE THEY'RE RELIGIOUS FANATICS, OUR FOREIGN POLICY HAS NOTHING TO DO WITH IT!

?

IT'S EGOCENTRIC, REALLY. YOU THINK EVERY TIME SOMETHING BAD HAPPENS IN THE WORLD, YOU'RE SOMEHOW RESPONSIBLE.

NO, YOU ARE.

PISS 'N' VINEGAR

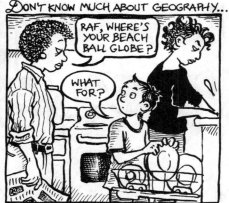

DON'T KNOW MUCH ABOUT GEOGRAPHY...

RAF, WHERE'S YOUR BEACH BALL GLOBE?

WHAT FOR?

84

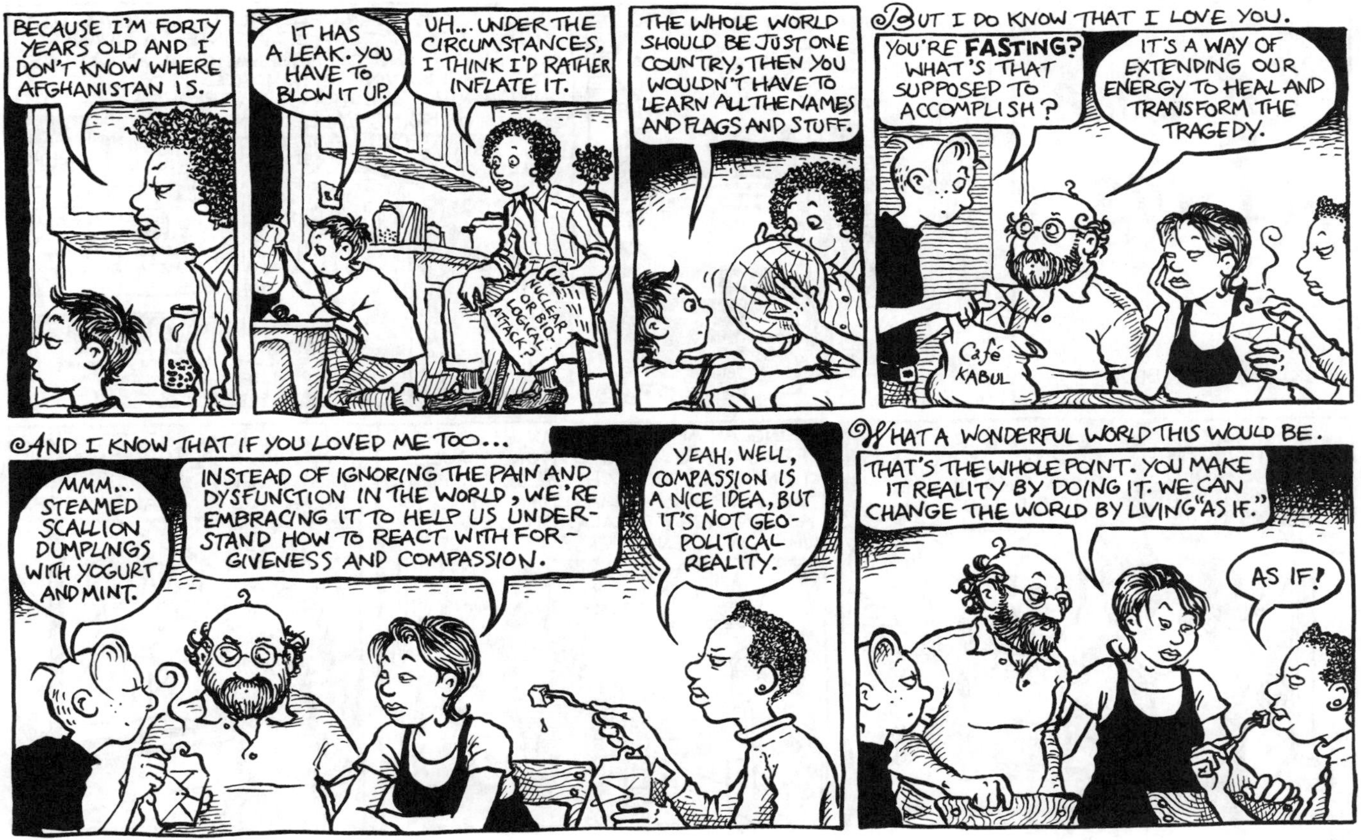
BECAUSE I'M FORTY YEARS OLD AND I DON'T KNOW WHERE AFGHANISTAN IS.
IT HAS A LEAK. YOU HAVE TO BLOW IT UP.
UH... UNDER THE CIRCUMSTANCES, I THINK I'D RATHER INFLATE IT.
NUCLEAR OR BIOLOGICAL ATTACK?
THE WHOLE WORLD SHOULD BE JUST ONE COUNTRY, THEN YOU WOULDN'T HAVE TO LEARN ALL THE NAMES AND FLAGS AND STUFF.
BUT I DO KNOW THAT I LOVE YOU.
YOU'RE **FASTING?** WHAT'S THAT SUPPOSED TO ACCOMPLISH?
IT'S A WAY OF EXTENDING OUR ENERGY TO HEAL AND TRANSFORM THE TRAGEDY.
Café KABUL
AND I KNOW THAT IF YOU LOVED ME TOO...
MMM... STEAMED SCALLION DUMPLINGS WITH YOGURT AND MINT.
INSTEAD OF IGNORING THE PAIN AND DYSFUNCTION IN THE WORLD, WE'RE EMBRACING IT TO HELP US UNDERSTAND HOW TO REACT WITH FORGIVENESS AND COMPASSION.
YEAH, WELL, COMPASSION IS A NICE IDEA, BUT IT'S NOT GEOPOLITICAL REALITY.
WHAT A WONDERFUL WORLD THIS WOULD BE.
THAT'S THE WHOLE POINT. YOU MAKE IT REALITY BY DOING IT. WE CAN CHANGE THE WORLD BY LIVING "AS IF."
AS IF!

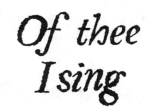

Of thee
I sing

©2001 BY ALISON BECHDEL

11/7

376

WILL YOU STOP WHINING ABOUT ALL THE FLAGS, MO? THEY GIVE PEOPLE A SENSE OF SOLIDARITY. IS THAT SO BAD?

GOD BLESS America

LOTTO

ATM INSIDE

GUZZLER

Marlboro

LUCKY STRIKE

THEY ALSO MAKE PEOPLE STUPID. CHANTING "USA! USA!" DOESN'T EXACTLY FOSTER A NUANCED UNDERSTANDING OF INTERNATIONAL RELATIONS. AND FLAG-WAVING INTIMIDATES PEOPLE INTO NOT ASKING QUESTIONS. EVERYONE'S SCARED OF BEING CALLED "UNPATRIOTIC."

NEWSST

WALL ST. JOURNAL RESULTS OF MEDIA VOTE RECOUNT IN FLORIDA? WHAT MEDIA RECOUNT?

New York Times BUSH HAS NEW GRAVITAS, SPEAKS 45 MINUTES WITH HARDLY A SLIP

WHAT IS PATRIOTISM, ANYWAY? DO PEOPLE THINK ABOUT WHAT IT MEANS TO BE AN AMERICAN?

GOD, FIVE TRILLION DRINK SELECTIONS, AND THERE'S NO UNSWEET-ENED ICED TEA!

UM...

NEW

STICKERS $1.99

TIME

THEY HATE US! THEY REALLY HATE US!

USA

BEING AN AMERICAN MEANS HAVING THE FREEDOM TO ASK QUESTIONS! QUES- TIONS LIKE, WHAT THE HELL IS BOMBING THE RUBBLE IN AFGHANISTAN GOING TO ACCOMPLISH? ESCALATION IS EXACTLY WHAT BIN LADEN WANTS!

The Daily DISTRESS

ALL WE'RE DOING IS MAKING MORE PEOPLE WANT TO KILL US!

JEEZ, YEAH. WOULDN'T WANT TO PISS THE TALIBAN OFF.

PAPAYA REPUBLIC

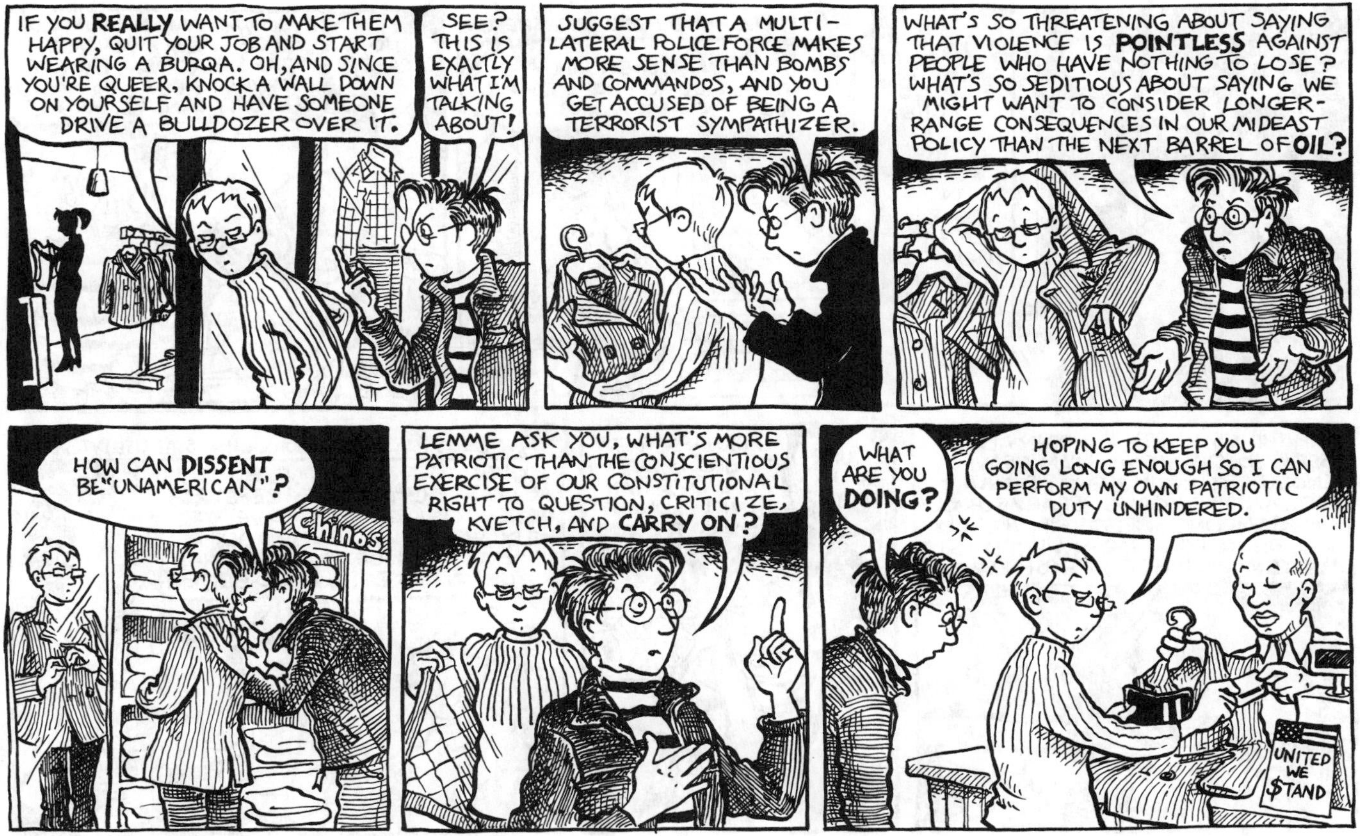
IF YOU **REALLY** WANT TO MAKE THEM HAPPY, QUIT YOUR JOB AND START WEARING A BURQA. OH, AND SINCE YOU'RE QUEER, KNOCK A WALL DOWN ON YOURSELF AND HAVE SOMEONE DRIVE A BULLDOZER OVER IT.
SEE? THIS IS EXACTLY WHAT I'M TALKING ABOUT!
SUGGEST THAT A MULTI-LATERAL POLICE FORCE MAKES MORE SENSE THAN BOMBS AND COMMANDOS, AND YOU GET ACCUSED OF BEING A TERRORIST SYMPATHIZER.
WHAT'S SO THREATENING ABOUT SAYING THAT VIOLENCE IS **POINTLESS** AGAINST PEOPLE WHO HAVE NOTHING TO LOSE? WHAT'S SO SEDITIOUS ABOUT SAYING WE MIGHT WANT TO CONSIDER LONGER-RANGE CONSEQUENCES IN OUR MIDEAST POLICY THAN THE NEXT BARREL OF **OIL?**
HOW CAN **DISSENT** BE "UNAMERICAN"?
Chinos
LEMME ASK YOU, WHAT'S MORE PATRIOTIC THAN THE CONSCIENTIOUS EXERCISE OF OUR CONSTITUTIONAL RIGHT TO QUESTION, CRITICIZE, KVETCH, AND **CARRY ON?**
WHAT ARE YOU **DOING?**
HOPING TO KEEP YOU GOING LONG ENOUGH SO I CAN PERFORM MY OWN PATRIOTIC DUTY UNHINDERED.
UNITED WE $TAND

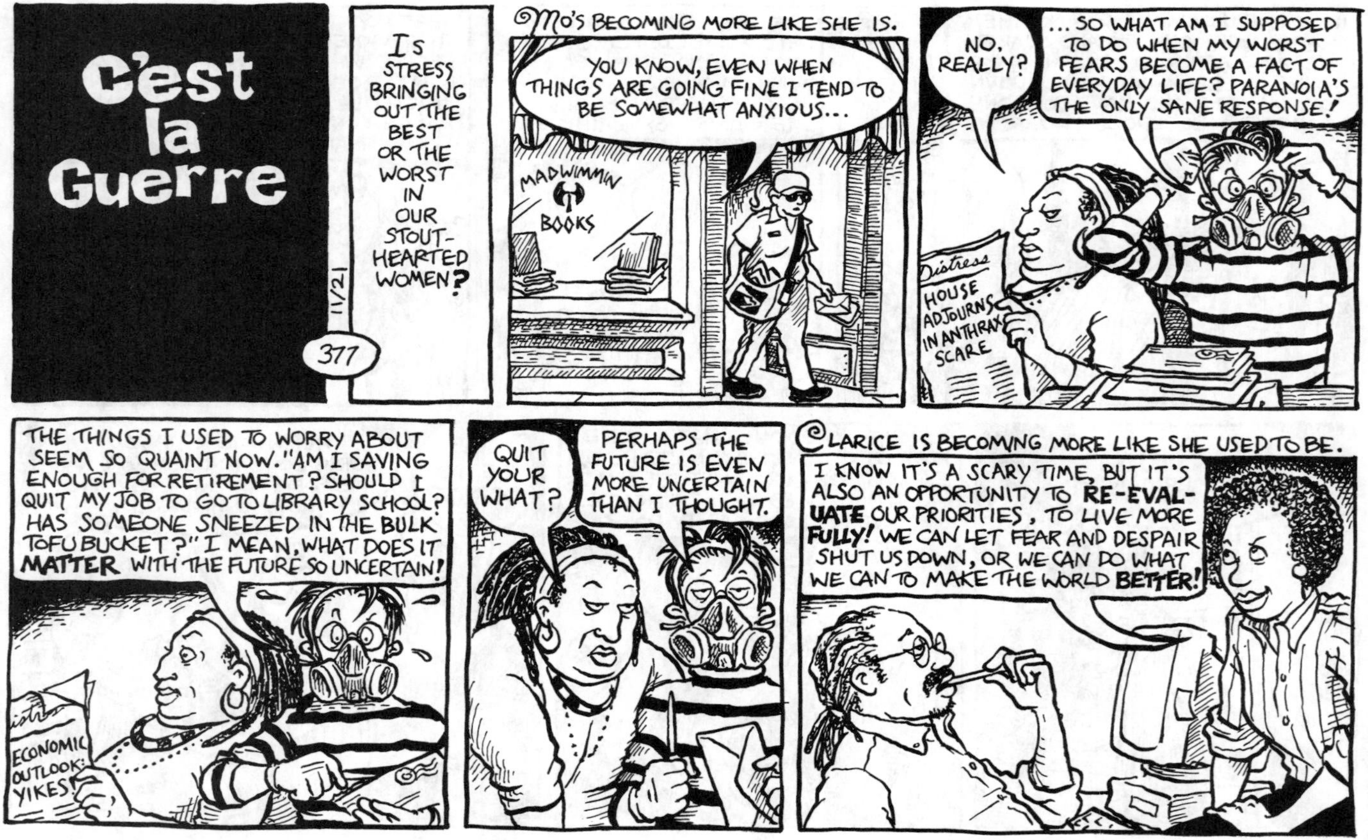
C'est la Guerre
377
11/21
IS STRESS BRINGING OUT THE BEST OR THE WORST IN OUR STOUT-HEARTED WOMEN?
MO'S BECOMING MORE LIKE SHE IS.
YOU KNOW, EVEN WHEN THINGS ARE GOING FINE I TEND TO BE SOMEWHAT ANXIOUS...
MADWIMMIN BOOKS
NO, REALLY?
... SO WHAT AM I SUPPOSED TO DO WHEN MY WORST FEARS BECOME A FACT OF EVERYDAY LIFE? PARANOIA'S THE ONLY SANE RESPONSE!
Distress
HOUSE ADJOURNS IN ANTHRAX SCARE
THE THINGS I USED TO WORRY ABOUT SEEM SO QUAINT NOW. "AM I SAVING ENOUGH FOR RETIREMENT? SHOULD I QUIT MY JOB TO GO TO LIBRARY SCHOOL? HAS SOMEONE SNEEZED IN THE BULK TOFU BUCKET?" I MEAN, WHAT DOES IT MATTER WITH THE FUTURE SO UNCERTAIN!
ECONOMIC OUTLOOK: YIKES!
QUIT YOUR WHAT?
PERHAPS THE FUTURE IS EVEN MORE UNCERTAIN THAN I THOUGHT.
CLARICE IS BECOMING MORE LIKE SHE USED TO BE.
I KNOW IT'S A SCARY TIME, BUT IT'S ALSO AN OPPORTUNITY TO RE-EVALUATE OUR PRIORITIES, TO LIVE MORE FULLY! WE CAN LET FEAR AND DESPAIR SHUT US DOWN, OR WE CAN DO WHAT WE CAN TO MAKE THE WORLD BETTER!

I'M GLAD TO HEAR YOU SAY SO. YOU'VE BEEN SO DOWN FOR MONTHS NOW, I WAS GETTING WORRIED. I GUESS ADVERSITY CAN REALLY GALVANIZE SOME PEOPLE.

ADVERSITY AND 150 MILLIGRAMS OF **EFFEXOR.**

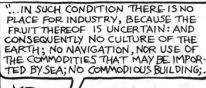
SYDNEY'S VEERING OFF-CURRICULUM.

I KNOW THIS IS INTRO TO WOMEN'S STUDIES, BUT I WANT TO SHARE WHAT ONE OF MY FAVORITE DEAD WHITE MEN HAS TO SAY ABOUT OUR HUMAN PROPENSITY TOWARD "...THAT CONDITION WHICH IS CALLED WAR."

HOBBES LEVIATHAN

"...IN SUCH CONDITION THERE IS NO PLACE FOR INDUSTRY, BECAUSE THE FRUIT THEREOF IS UNCERTAIN: AND CONSEQUENTLY NO CULTURE OF THE EARTH; NO NAVIGATION, NOR USE OF THE COMMODITIES THAT MAY BE IMPORTED BY SEA; NO COMMODIOUS BUILDING;...

...NO ARTS; NO LETTERS; NO SOCIETY; AND WHICH IS WORST OF ALL, CONTINUAL FEAR, AND DANGER OF VIOLENT DEATH; AND THE LIFE OF MAN, SOLITARY, POOR, NASTY, BRUTISH, AND SHORT."

GINGER HAS REGRESSED SADLY.

LET'S DO THIS EVERY DAY.

WE CAN'T PRETEND WE'RE SICK EVERY DAY. EVENTUALLY WE'D GET FIRED.

WONDER HOW LONG IT'D TAKE?

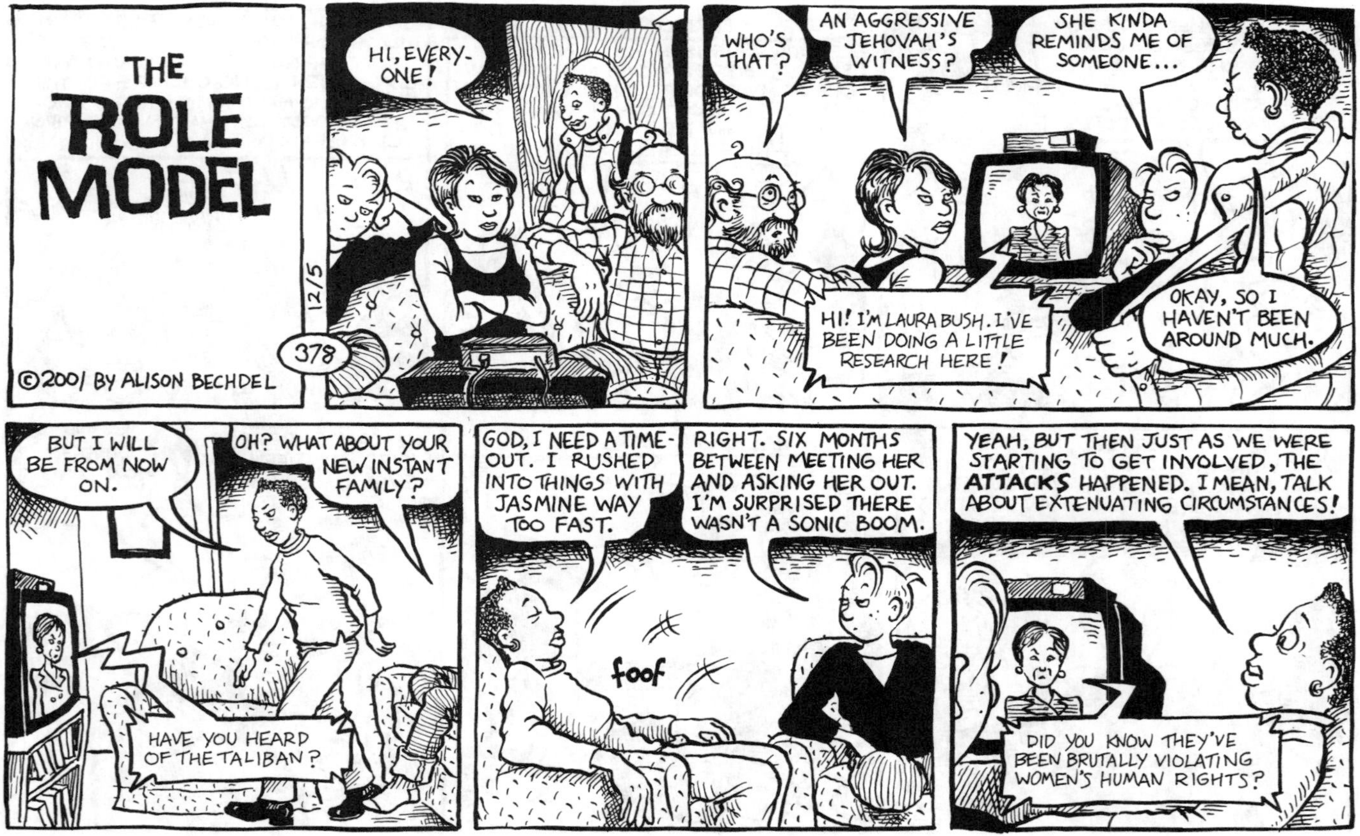
THE ROLE MODEL
©2001 BY ALISON BECHDEL
378
12/5
HI, EVERY-ONE!
WHO'S THAT?
AN AGGRESSIVE JEHOVAH'S WITNESS?
SHE KINDA REMINDS ME OF SOMEONE...
HI! I'M LAURA BUSH. I'VE BEEN DOING A LITTLE RESEARCH HERE!
OKAY, SO I HAVEN'T BEEN AROUND MUCH.
BUT I WILL BE FROM NOW ON.
OH? WHAT ABOUT YOUR NEW INSTANT FAMILY?
HAVE YOU HEARD OF THE TALIBAN?
GOD, I NEED A TIME-OUT. I RUSHED INTO THINGS WITH JASMINE WAY TOO FAST.
foof
RIGHT. SIX MONTHS BETWEEN MEETING HER AND ASKING HER OUT. I'M SURPRISED THERE WASN'T A SONIC BOOM.
YEAH, BUT THEN JUST AS WE WERE STARTING TO GET INVOLVED, THE ATTACKS HAPPENED. I MEAN, TALK ABOUT EXTENUATING CIRCUMSTANCES!
DID YOU KNOW THEY'VE BEEN BRUTALLY VIOLATING WOMEN'S HUMAN RIGHTS?

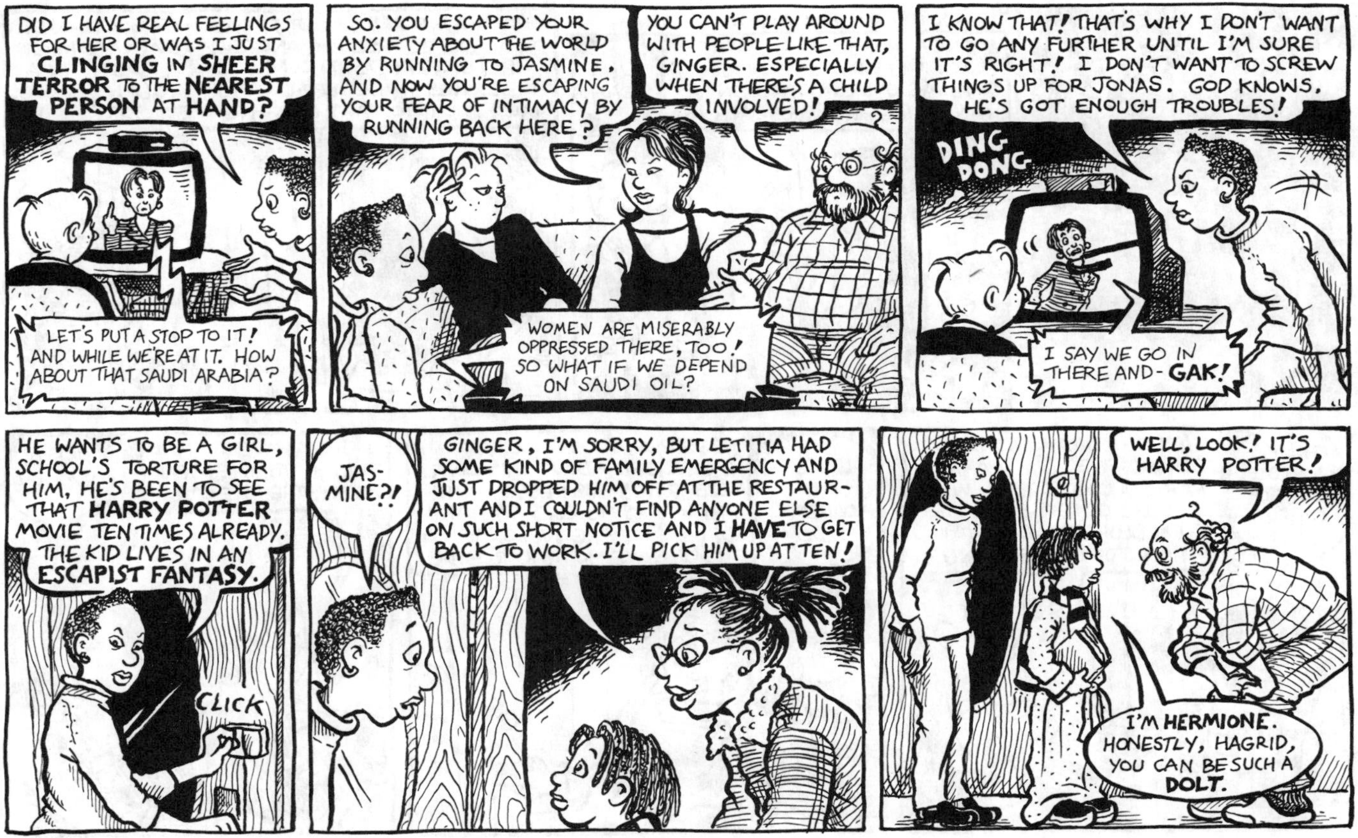

DID I HAVE REAL FEELINGS FOR HER OR WAS I JUST **CLINGING** IN **SHEER TERROR** TO THE **NEAREST PERSON** AT **HAND?**
LET'S PUT A STOP TO IT! AND WHILE WE'RE AT IT. HOW ABOUT THAT SAUDI ARABIA?
SO. YOU ESCAPED YOUR ANXIETY ABOUT THE WORLD BY RUNNING TO JASMINE. AND NOW YOU'RE ESCAPING YOUR FEAR OF INTIMACY BY RUNNING BACK HERE?
YOU CAN'T PLAY AROUND WITH PEOPLE LIKE THAT, GINGER. ESPECIALLY WHEN THERE'S A CHILD INVOLVED!
WOMEN ARE MISERABLY OPPRESSED THERE, TOO! SO WHAT IF WE DEPEND ON SAUDI OIL?
I KNOW THAT! THAT'S WHY I DON'T WANT TO GO ANY FURTHER UNTIL I'M SURE IT'S RIGHT! I DON'T WANT TO SCREW THINGS UP FOR JONAS. GOD KNOWS. HE'S GOT ENOUGH TROUBLES!
DING DONG
I SAY WE GO IN THERE AND- **GAK!**
HE WANTS TO BE A GIRL, SCHOOL'S TORTURE FOR HIM, HE'S BEEN TO SEE THAT **HARRY POTTER** MOVIE TEN TIMES ALREADY. THE KID LIVES IN AN **ESCAPIST FANTASY.**
CLICK
JAS-MINE?!
GINGER, I'M SORRY, BUT LETITIA HAD SOME KIND OF FAMILY EMERGENCY AND JUST DROPPED HIM OFF AT THE RESTAURANT AND I COULDN'T FIND ANYONE ELSE ON SUCH SHORT NOTICE AND I **HAVE** TO GET BACK TO WORK. I'LL PICK HIM UP AT TEN!
WELL, LOOK! IT'S HARRY POTTER!
I'M **HERMIONE**. HONESTLY, HAGRID, YOU CAN BE SUCH A **DOLT**.

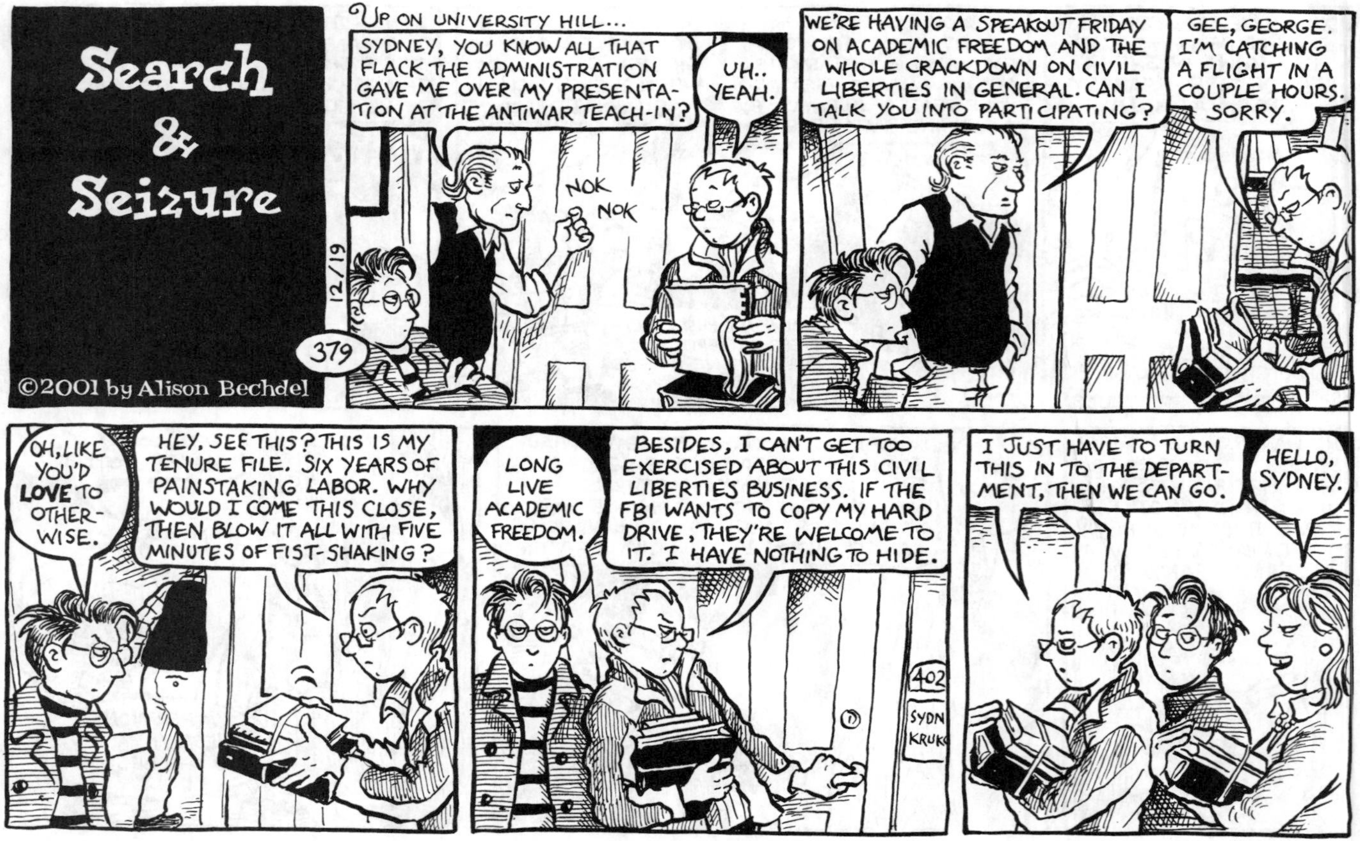
Search & Seizure
©2001 by Alison Bechdel
379
12/19
UP ON UNIVERSITY HILL...
SYDNEY, YOU KNOW ALL THAT FLACK THE ADMINISTRATION GAVE ME OVER MY PRESENTATION AT THE ANTIWAR TEACH-IN?
UH.. YEAH.
NOK NOK
WE'RE HAVING A SPEAKOUT FRIDAY ON ACADEMIC FREEDOM AND THE WHOLE CRACKDOWN ON CIVIL LIBERTIES IN GENERAL. CAN I TALK YOU INTO PARTICIPATING?
GEE, GEORGE. I'M CATCHING A FLIGHT IN A COUPLE HOURS. SORRY.
OH, LIKE YOU'D **LOVE** TO OTHERWISE.
HEY. SEE THIS? THIS IS MY TENURE FILE. SIX YEARS OF PAINSTAKING LABOR. WHY WOULD I COME THIS CLOSE, THEN BLOW IT ALL WITH FIVE MINUTES OF FIST-SHAKING?
LONG LIVE ACADEMIC FREEDOM.
BESIDES, I CAN'T GET TOO EXERCISED ABOUT THIS CIVIL LIBERTIES BUSINESS. IF THE FBI WANTS TO COPY MY HARD DRIVE, THEY'RE WELCOME TO IT. I HAVE NOTHING TO HIDE.
402
SYDN
KRUK
I JUST HAVE TO TURN THIS IN TO THE DEPARTMENT, THEN WE CAN GO.
HELLO, SYDNEY.

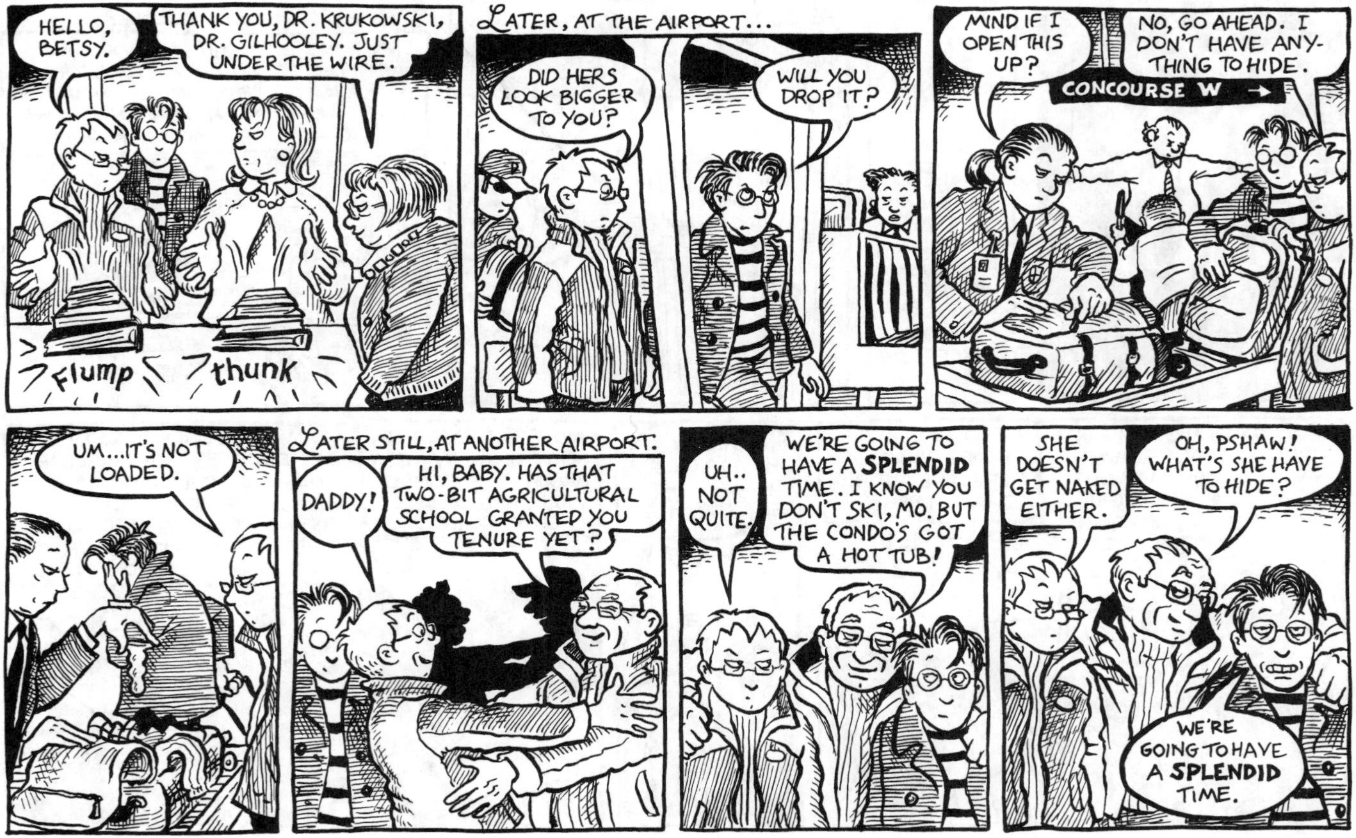
HELLO, BETSY.
THANK YOU, DR. KRUKOWSKI, DR. GILHOOLEY. JUST UNDER THE WIRE.
Flump
thunk
LATER, AT THE AIRPORT...
DID HERS LOOK BIGGER TO YOU?
WILL YOU DROP IT?
MIND IF I OPEN THIS UP?
NO, GO AHEAD. I DON'T HAVE ANYTHING TO HIDE.
CONCOURSE W →
UM...IT'S NOT LOADED.
LATER STILL, AT ANOTHER AIRPORT.
DADDY!
HI, BABY. HAS THAT TWO-BIT AGRICULTURAL SCHOOL GRANTED YOU TENURE YET?
UH.. NOT QUITE.
WE'RE GOING TO HAVE A **SPLENDID** TIME. I KNOW YOU DON'T SKI, MO. BUT THE CONDO'S GOT A HOT TUB!
SHE DOESN'T GET NAKED EITHER.
OH, PSHAW! WHAT'S SHE HAVE TO HIDE?
WE'RE GOING TO HAVE A **SPLENDID** TIME.

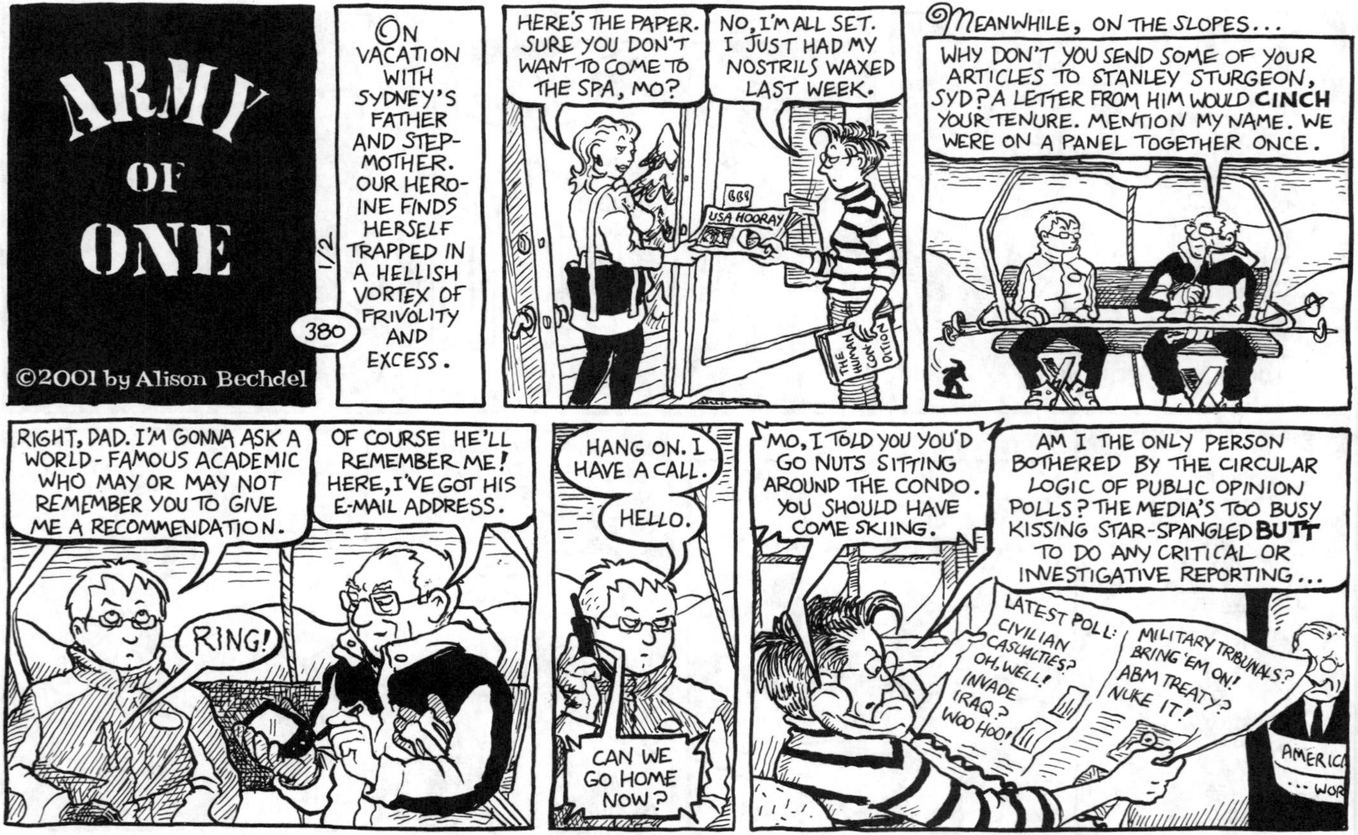
ARMY OF ONE
©2001 by Alison Bechdel
1/2
380
ON VACATION WITH SYDNEY'S FATHER AND STEP-MOTHER. OUR HEROINE FINDS HERSELF TRAPPED IN A HELLISH VORTEX OF FRIVOLITY AND EXCESS.
HERE'S THE PAPER. SURE YOU DON'T WANT TO COME TO THE SPA, MO?
NO, I'M ALL SET. I JUST HAD MY NOSTRILS WAXED LAST WEEK.
USA HOORAY
THE HUMAN CONDITION
MEANWHILE, ON THE SLOPES...
WHY DON'T YOU SEND SOME OF YOUR ARTICLES TO STANLEY STURGEON, SYD? A LETTER FROM HIM WOULD **CINCH** YOUR TENURE. MENTION MY NAME. WE WERE ON A PANEL TOGETHER ONCE.
RIGHT, DAD. I'M GONNA ASK A WORLD-FAMOUS ACADEMIC WHO MAY OR MAY NOT REMEMBER YOU TO GIVE ME A RECOMMENDATION.
OF COURSE HE'LL REMEMBER ME! HERE, I'VE GOT HIS E-MAIL ADDRESS.
RING!
HANG ON. I HAVE A CALL.
HELLO.
CAN WE GO HOME NOW?
MO, I TOLD YOU YOU'D GO NUTS SITTING AROUND THE CONDO. YOU SHOULD HAVE COME SKIING.
AM I THE ONLY PERSON BOTHERED BY THE CIRCULAR LOGIC OF PUBLIC OPINION POLLS? THE MEDIA'S TOO BUSY KISSING STAR-SPANGLED **BUTT** TO DO ANY CRITICAL OR INVESTIGATIVE REPORTING...
LATEST POLL:
CIVILIAN CASUALTIES? OH, WELL!
INVADE IRAQ? WOO HOO!
MILITARY TRIBUNALS? BRING 'EM ON!
ABM TREATY? NUKE IT!

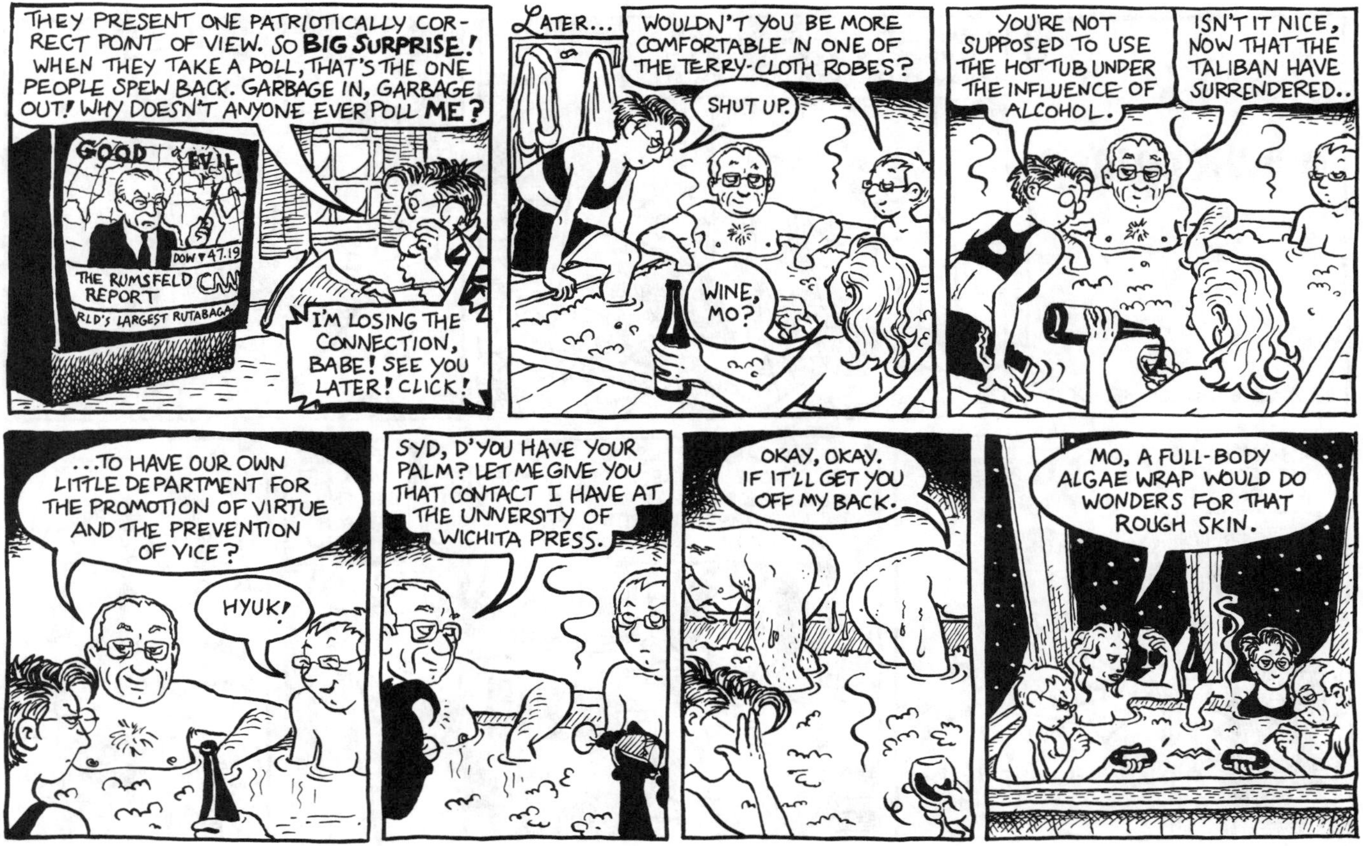
THEY PRESENT ONE PATRIOTICALLY CORRECT POINT OF VIEW. SO **BIG SURPRISE**! WHEN THEY TAKE A POLL, THAT'S THE ONE PEOPLE SPEW BACK. GARBAGE IN, GARBAGE OUT! WHY DOESN'T ANYONE EVER POLL **ME**?
GOOD
EVIL
DOW ▼47.19
THE RUMSFELD REPORT
CNN
RLD'S LARGEST RUTABAGA
I'M LOSING THE CONNECTION, BABE! SEE YOU LATER! CLICK!
LATER...
WOULDN'T YOU BE MORE COMFORTABLE IN ONE OF THE TERRY-CLOTH ROBES?
SHUT UP.
WINE, MO?
YOU'RE NOT SUPPOSED TO USE THE HOT TUB UNDER THE INFLUENCE OF ALCOHOL.
ISN'T IT NICE, NOW THAT THE TALIBAN HAVE SURRENDERED..
...TO HAVE OUR OWN LITTLE DEPARTMENT FOR THE PROMOTION OF VIRTUE AND THE PREVENTION OF VICE?
HYUK!
SYD, D'YOU HAVE YOUR PALM? LET ME GIVE YOU THAT CONTACT I HAVE AT THE UNIVERSITY OF WICHITA PRESS.
OKAY, OKAY. IF IT'LL GET YOU OFF MY BACK.
MO, A FULL-BODY ALGAE WRAP WOULD DO WONDERS FOR THAT ROUGH SKIN.

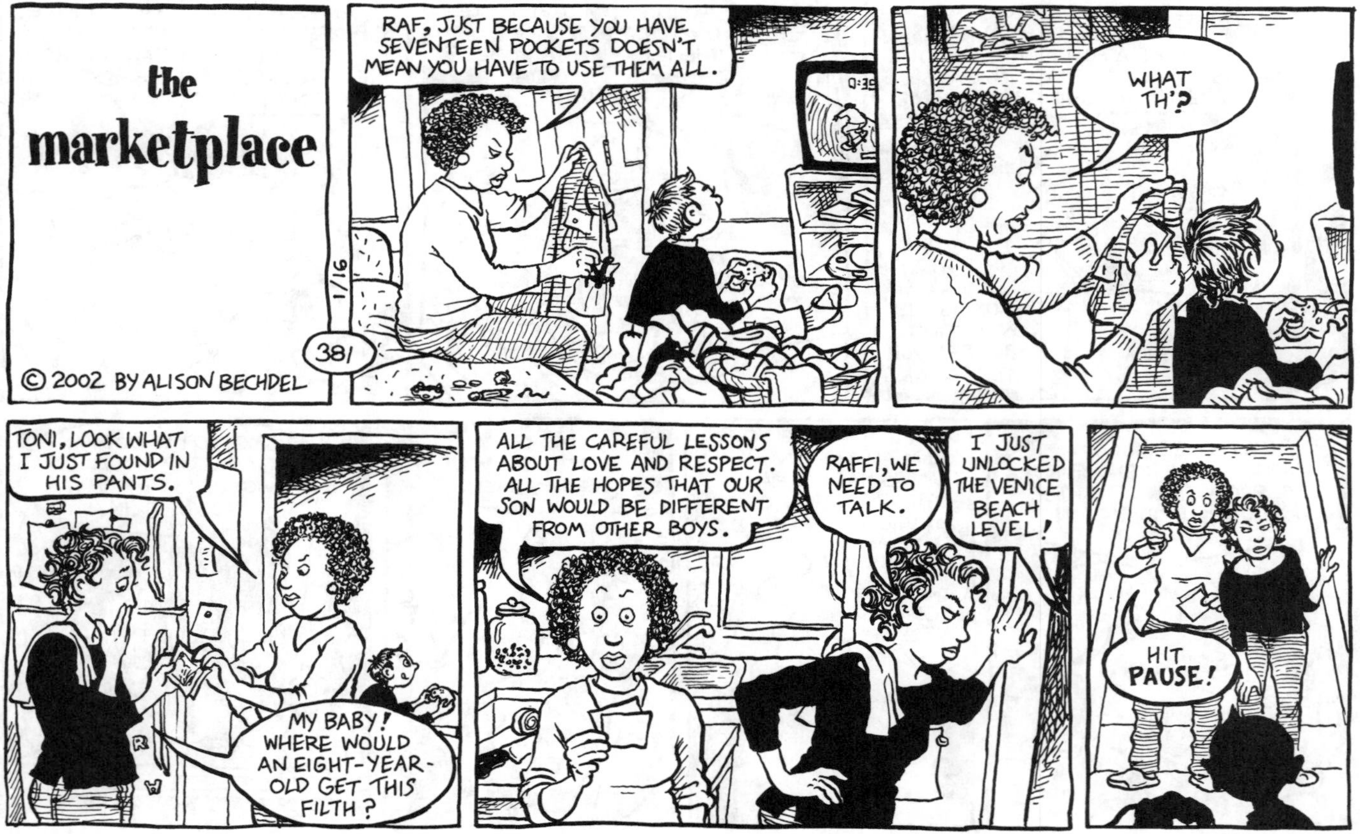
the marketplace
© 2002 BY ALISON BECHDEL
381
1/16
RAF, JUST BECAUSE YOU HAVE SEVENTEEN POCKETS DOESN'T MEAN YOU HAVE TO USE THEM ALL.
WHAT TH'?
TONI, LOOK WHAT I JUST FOUND IN HIS PANTS.
MY BABY! WHERE WOULD AN EIGHT-YEAR-OLD GET THIS FILTH?
ALL THE CAREFUL LESSONS ABOUT LOVE AND RESPECT. ALL THE HOPES THAT OUR SON WOULD BE DIFFERENT FROM OTHER BOYS.
RAFFI, WE NEED TO TALK.
I JUST UNLOCKED THE VENICE BEACH LEVEL!
HIT PAUSE!

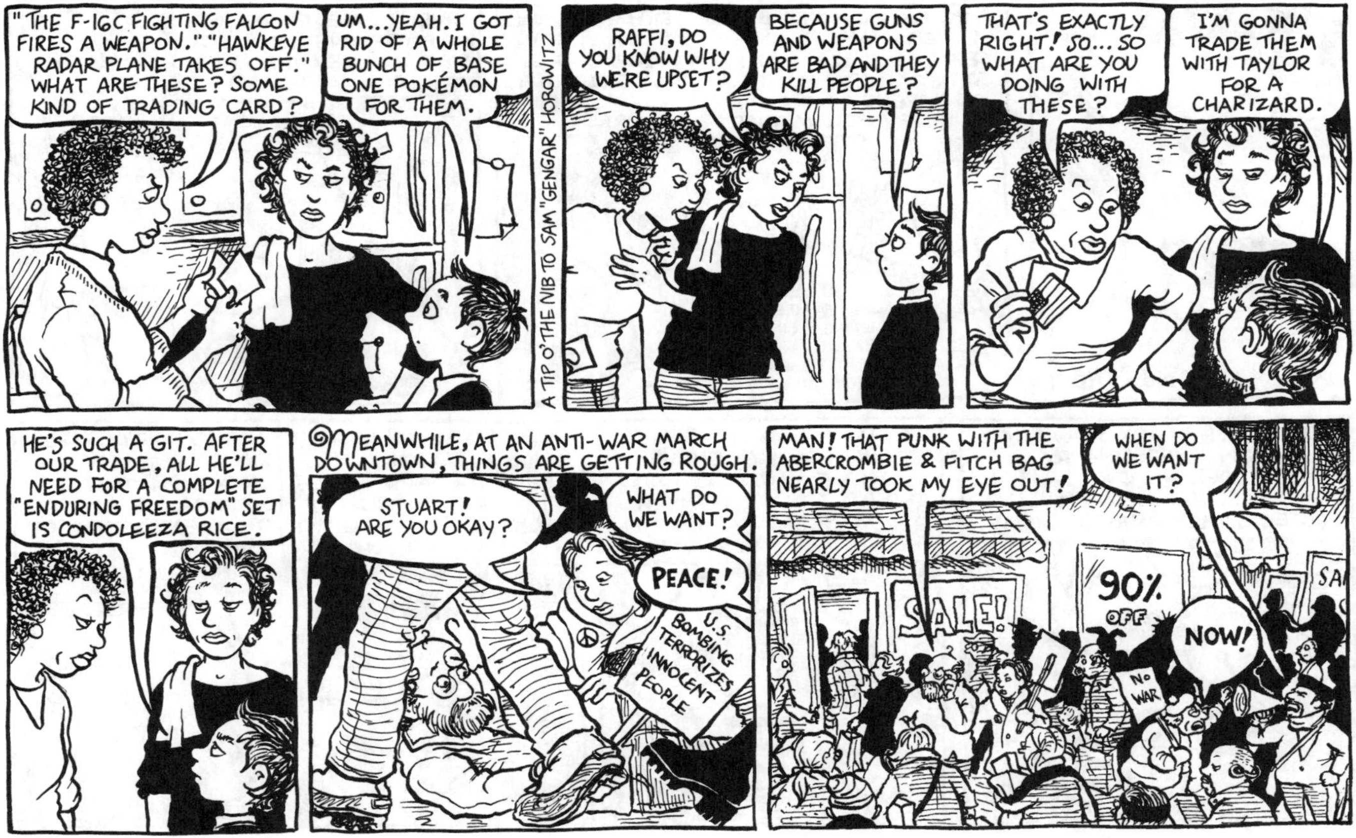
"THE F-16C FIGHTING FALCON FIRES A WEAPON." "HAWKEYE RADAR PLANE TAKES OFF." WHAT ARE THESE? SOME KIND OF TRADING CARD?
UM... YEAH. I GOT RID OF A WHOLE BUNCH OF BASE ONE POKÉMON FOR THEM.
A TIP O' THE NIB TO SAM "GENGAR" HOROWITZ
RAFFI, DO YOU KNOW WHY WE'RE UPSET?
BECAUSE GUNS AND WEAPONS ARE BAD AND THEY KILL PEOPLE?
THAT'S EXACTLY RIGHT! SO... SO WHAT ARE YOU DOING WITH THESE?
I'M GONNA TRADE THEM WITH TAYLOR FOR A CHARIZARD.
HE'S SUCH A GIT. AFTER OUR TRADE, ALL HE'LL NEED FOR A COMPLETE "ENDURING FREEDOM" SET IS CONDOLEEZA RICE.
MEANWHILE, AT AN ANTI-WAR MARCH DOWNTOWN, THINGS ARE GETTING ROUGH.
STUART! ARE YOU OKAY?
WHAT DO WE WANT?
PEACE!
U.S. BOMBING TERRORIZES INNOCENT PEOPLE
MAN! THAT PUNK WITH THE ABERCROMBIE & FITCH BAG NEARLY TOOK MY EYE OUT!
WHEN DO WE WANT IT?
SALE!
90% OFF
NOW!
NO WAR

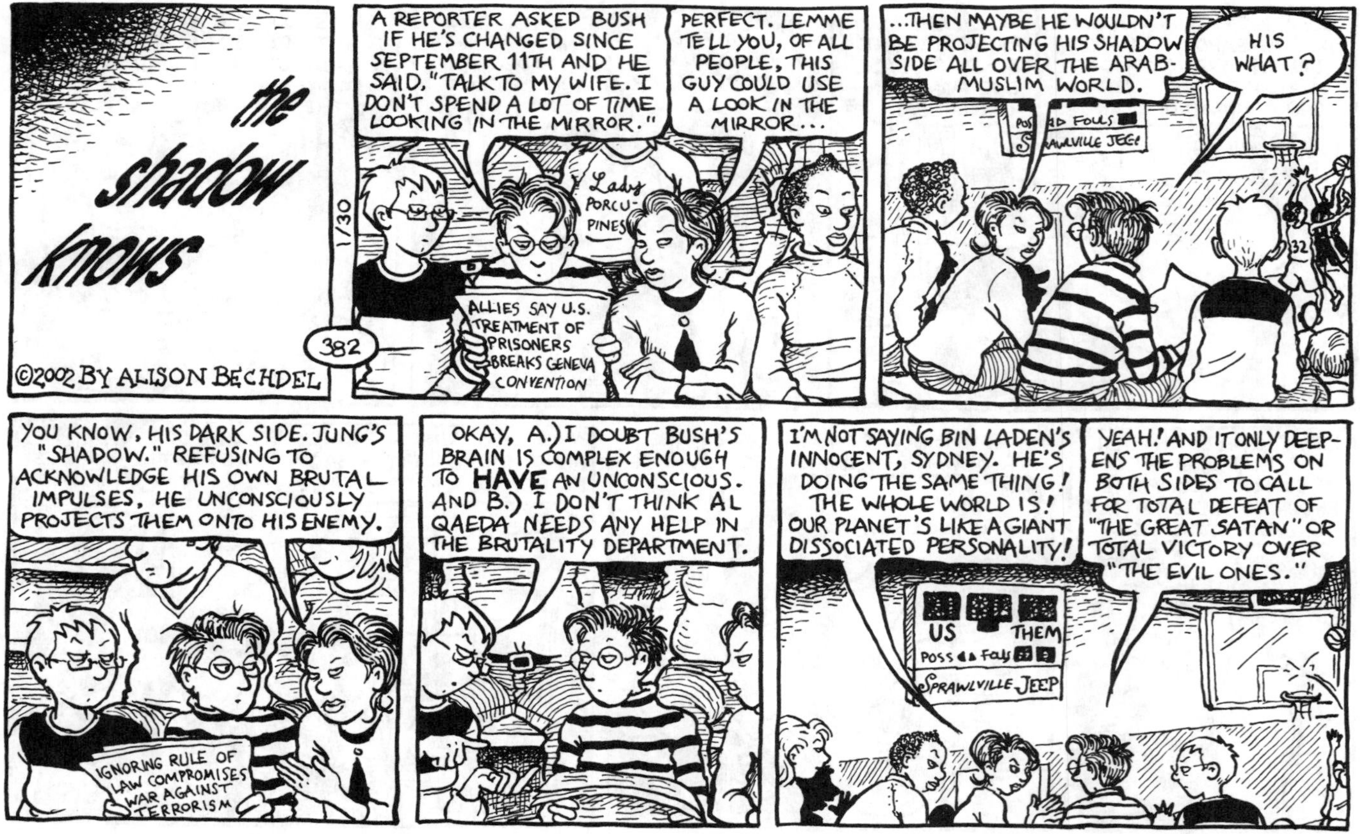
the shadow knows
©2002 BY ALISON BECHDEL
382
1/30
A REPORTER ASKED BUSH IF HE'S CHANGED SINCE SEPTEMBER 11TH AND HE SAID, "TALK TO MY WIFE. I DON'T SPEND A LOT OF TIME LOOKING IN THE MIRROR."
PERFECT. LEMME TELL YOU, OF ALL PEOPLE, THIS GUY COULD USE A LOOK IN THE MIRROR...
Lady PORCUPINES
ALLIES SAY U.S. TREATMENT OF PRISONERS BREAKS GENEVA CONVENTION
...THEN MAYBE HE WOULDN'T BE PROJECTING HIS SHADOW SIDE ALL OVER THE ARAB-MUSLIM WORLD.
HIS WHAT?
32
YOU KNOW, HIS DARK SIDE. JUNG'S "SHADOW." REFUSING TO ACKNOWLEDGE HIS OWN BRUTAL IMPULSES, HE UNCONSCIOUSLY PROJECTS THEM ONTO HIS ENEMY.
IGNORING RULE OF LAW COMPROMISES WAR AGAINST TERRORISM
OKAY, A.) I DOUBT BUSH'S BRAIN IS COMPLEX ENOUGH TO HAVE AN UNCONSCIOUS. AND B.) I DON'T THINK AL QAEDA NEEDS ANY HELP IN THE BRUTALITY DEPARTMENT.
I'M NOT SAYING BIN LADEN'S INNOCENT, SYDNEY. HE'S DOING THE SAME THING! THE WHOLE WORLD IS! OUR PLANET'S LIKE A GIANT DISSOCIATED PERSONALITY!
YEAH! AND IT ONLY DEEPENS THE PROBLEMS ON BOTH SIDES TO CALL FOR TOTAL DEFEAT OF "THE GREAT SATAN" OR TOTAL VICTORY OVER "THE EVIL ONES."
US
THEM
POSS
FOULS
SPRAWLVILLE JEEP

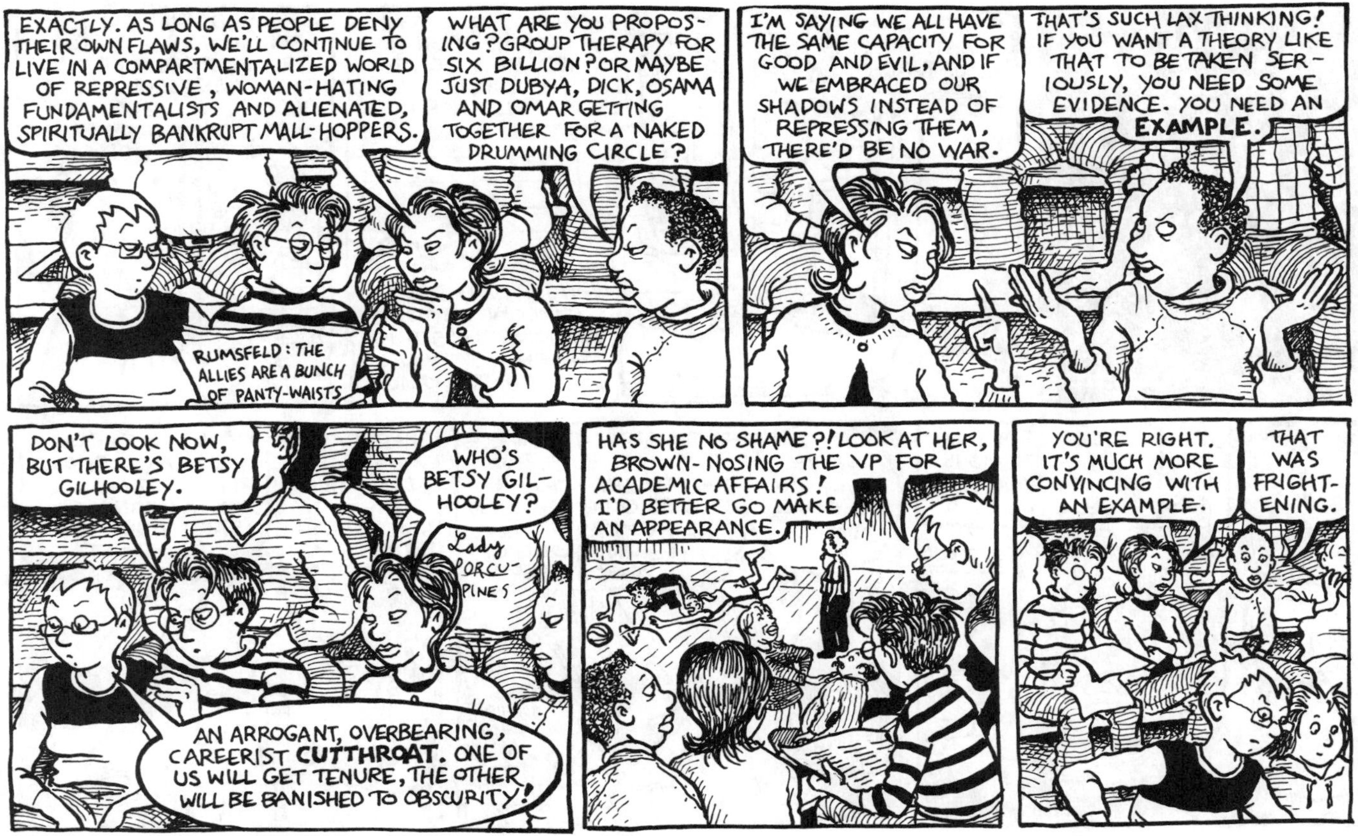
EXACTLY. AS LONG AS PEOPLE DENY THEIR OWN FLAWS, WE'LL CONTINUE TO LIVE IN A COMPARTMENTALIZED WORLD OF REPRESSIVE, WOMAN-HATING FUNDAMENTALISTS AND ALIENATED, SPIRITUALLY BANKRUPT MALL-HOPPERS.
WHAT ARE YOU PROPOSING? GROUP THERAPY FOR SIX BILLION? OR MAYBE JUST DUBYA, DICK, OSAMA AND OMAR GETTING TOGETHER FOR A NAKED DRUMMING CIRCLE?
RUMSFELD: THE ALLIES ARE A BUNCH OF PANTY-WAISTS
I'M SAYING WE ALL HAVE THE SAME CAPACITY FOR GOOD AND EVIL, AND IF WE EMBRACED OUR SHADOWS INSTEAD OF REPRESSING THEM, THERE'D BE NO WAR.
THAT'S SUCH LAX THINKING! IF YOU WANT A THEORY LIKE THAT TO BE TAKEN SERIOUSLY, YOU NEED SOME EVIDENCE. YOU NEED AN **EXAMPLE**.
DON'T LOOK NOW, BUT THERE'S BETSY GILHOOLEY.
WHO'S BETSY GILHOOLEY?
Lady PORCUPINES
AN ARROGANT, OVERBEARING, CAREERIST **CUTTHROAT**. ONE OF US WILL GET TENURE, THE OTHER WILL BE BANISHED TO OBSCURITY!
HAS SHE NO SHAME?! LOOK AT HER, BROWN-NOSING THE VP FOR ACADEMIC AFFAIRS! I'D BETTER GO MAKE AN APPEARANCE.
YOU'RE RIGHT. IT'S MUCH MORE CONVINCING WITH AN EXAMPLE.
THAT WAS FRIGHTENING.

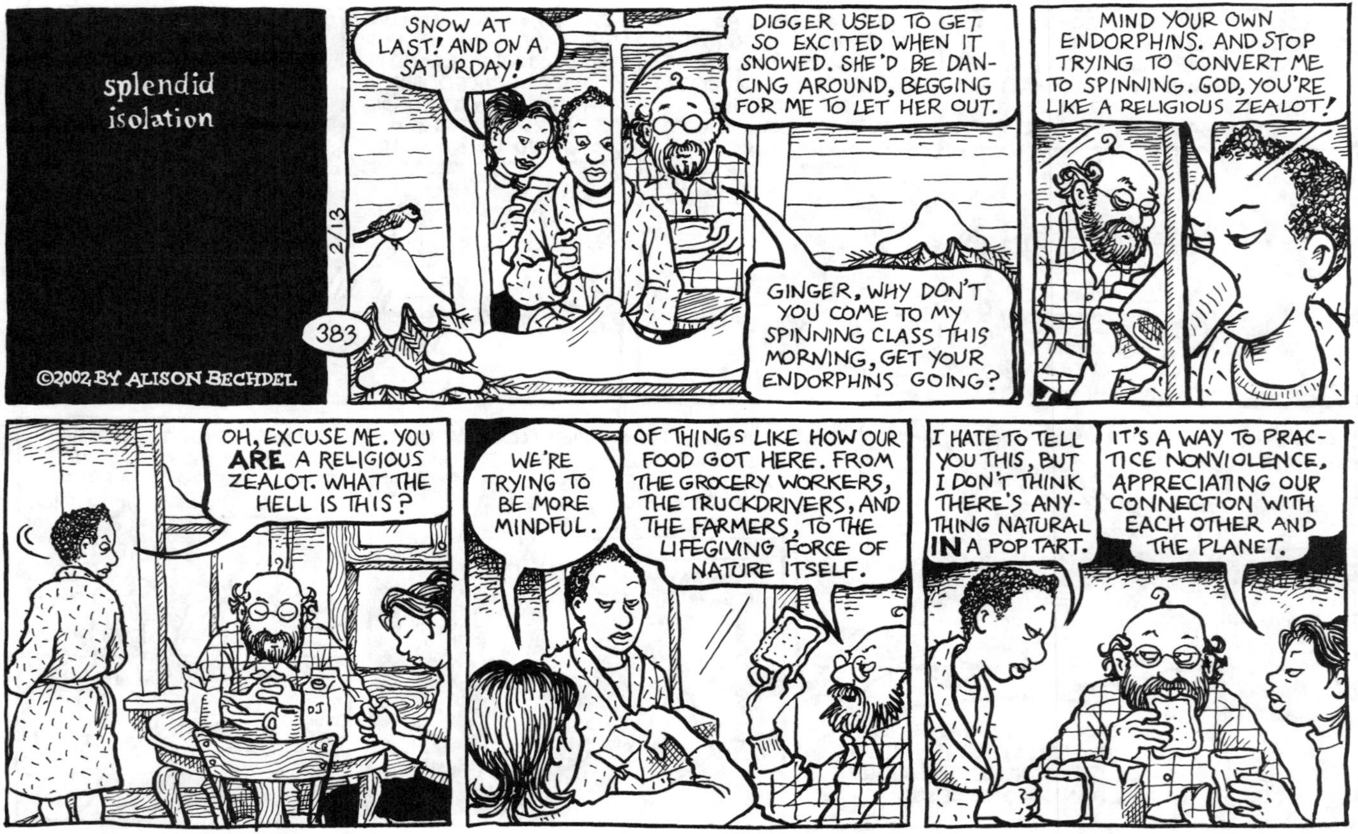
splendid
isolation
©2002 BY ALISON BECHDEL
383
2/13
SNOW AT LAST! AND ON A SATURDAY!
DIGGER USED TO GET SO EXCITED WHEN IT SNOWED. SHE'D BE DANCING AROUND, BEGGING FOR ME TO LET HER OUT.
GINGER, WHY DON'T YOU COME TO MY SPINNING CLASS THIS MORNING, GET YOUR ENDORPHINS GOING?
MIND YOUR OWN ENDORPHINS. AND STOP TRYING TO CONVERT ME TO SPINNING. GOD, YOU'RE LIKE A RELIGIOUS ZEALOT!
OH, EXCUSE ME. YOU **ARE** A RELIGIOUS ZEALOT. WHAT THE HELL IS THIS?
OJ
WE'RE TRYING TO BE MORE MINDFUL.
OF THINGS LIKE HOW OUR FOOD GOT HERE. FROM THE GROCERY WORKERS, THE TRUCKDRIVERS, AND THE FARMERS, TO THE LIFEGIVING FORCE OF NATURE ITSELF.
I HATE TO TELL YOU THIS, BUT I DON'T THINK THERE'S ANYTHING NATURAL **IN** A POP TART.
IT'S A WAY TO PRACTICE NONVIOLENCE, APPRECIATING OUR CONNECTION WITH EACH OTHER AND THE PLANET.

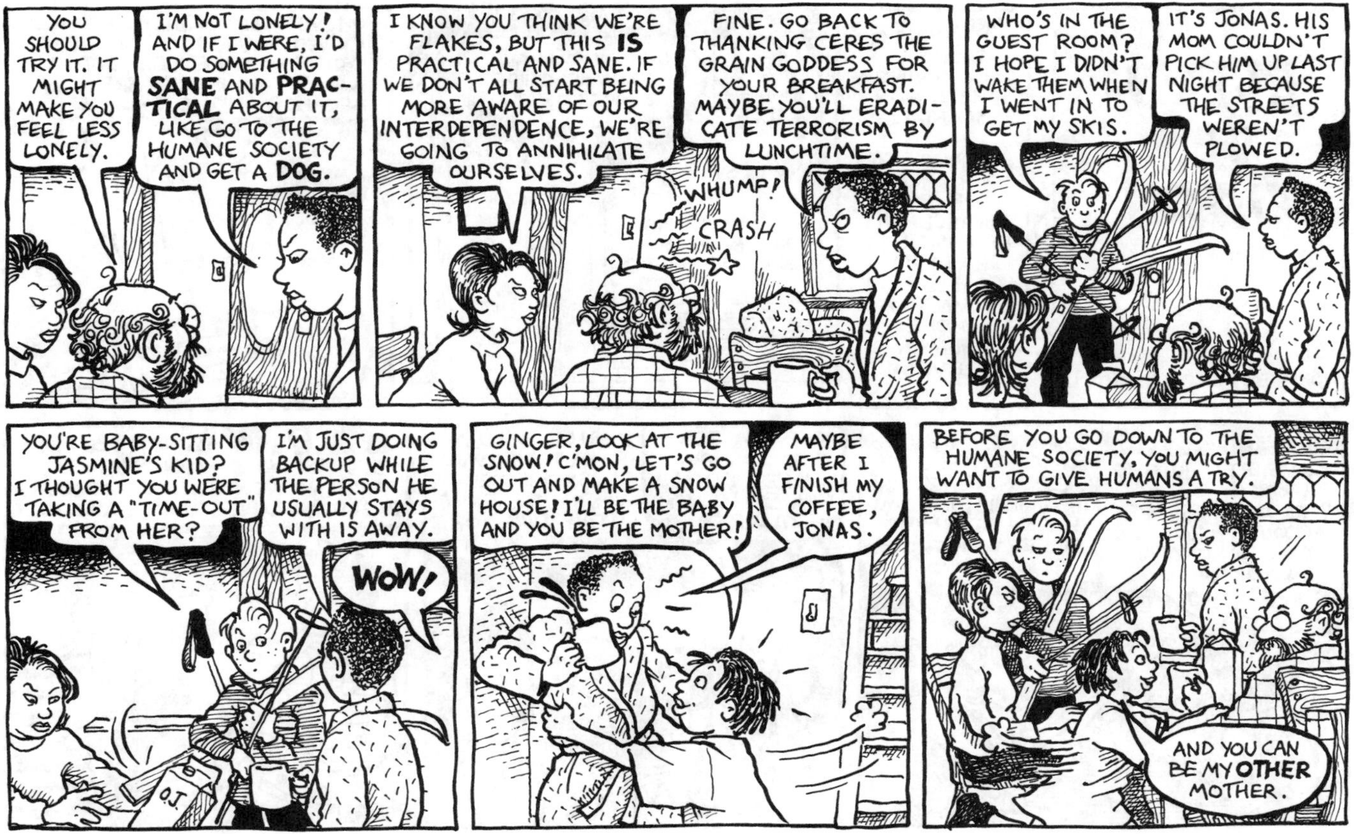
YOU SHOULD TRY IT. IT MIGHT MAKE YOU FEEL LESS LONELY.
I'M NOT LONELY! AND IF I WERE, I'D DO SOMETHING **SANE** AND **PRACTICAL** ABOUT IT, LIKE GO TO THE HUMANE SOCIETY AND GET A **DOG**.
I KNOW YOU THINK WE'RE FLAKES, BUT THIS **IS** PRACTICAL AND SANE. IF WE DON'T ALL START BEING MORE AWARE OF OUR INTERDEPENDENCE, WE'RE GOING TO ANNIHILATE OURSELVES.
WHUMP!
CRASH
FINE. GO BACK TO THANKING CERES THE GRAIN GODDESS FOR YOUR BREAKFAST. MAYBE YOU'LL ERADICATE TERRORISM BY LUNCHTIME.
WHO'S IN THE GUEST ROOM? I HOPE I DIDN'T WAKE THEM WHEN I WENT IN TO GET MY SKIS.
IT'S JONAS. HIS MOM COULDN'T PICK HIM UP LAST NIGHT BECAUSE THE STREETS WEREN'T PLOWED.
YOU'RE BABY-SITTING JASMINE'S KID? I THOUGHT YOU WERE TAKING A "TIME-OUT" FROM HER?
I'M JUST DOING BACKUP WHILE THE PERSON HE USUALLY STAYS WITH IS AWAY.
WOW!
O.J.
GINGER, LOOK AT THE SNOW! C'MON, LET'S GO OUT AND MAKE A SNOW HOUSE! I'LL BE THE BABY AND YOU BE THE MOTHER!
MAYBE AFTER I FINISH MY COFFEE, JONAS.
BEFORE YOU GO DOWN TO THE HUMANE SOCIETY, YOU MIGHT WANT TO GIVE HUMANS A TRY.
AND YOU CAN BE MY **OTHER** MOTHER.

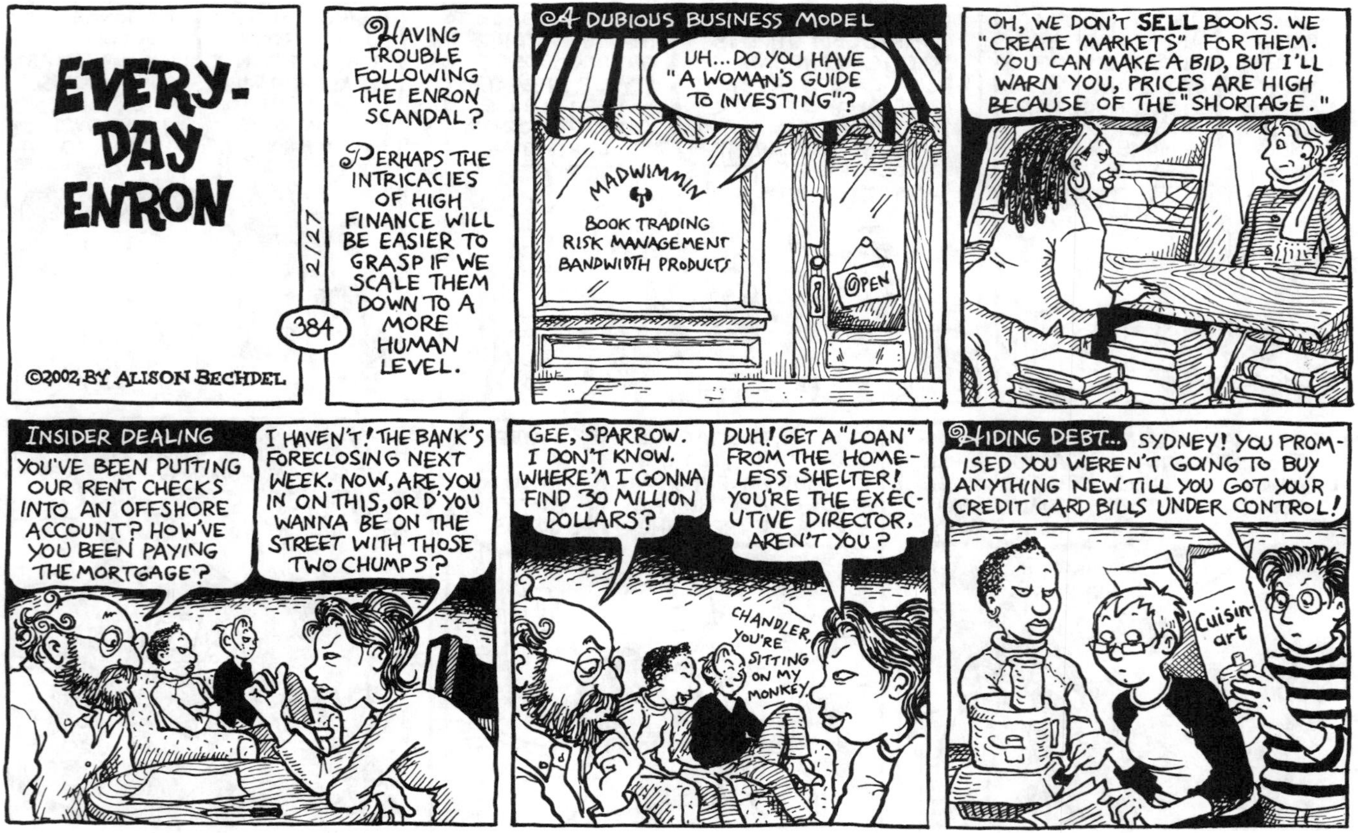
EVERY-DAY ENRON
©2002 BY ALISON BECHDEL
384
2/27
HAVING TROUBLE FOLLOWING THE ENRON SCANDAL?
PERHAPS THE INTRICACIES OF HIGH FINANCE WILL BE EASIER TO GRASP IF WE SCALE THEM DOWN TO A MORE HUMAN LEVEL.
A DUBIOUS BUSINESS MODEL
UH...DO YOU HAVE "A WOMAN'S GUIDE TO INVESTING"?
MADWIMMIN
BOOK TRADING
RISK MANAGEMENT
BANDWIDTH PRODUCTS
OPEN
OH, WE DON'T SELL BOOKS. WE "CREATE MARKETS" FOR THEM. YOU CAN MAKE A BID, BUT I'LL WARN YOU, PRICES ARE HIGH BECAUSE OF THE "SHORTAGE."
INSIDER DEALING
YOU'VE BEEN PUTTING OUR RENT CHECKS INTO AN OFFSHORE ACCOUNT? HOW'VE YOU BEEN PAYING THE MORTGAGE?
I HAVEN'T! THE BANK'S FORECLOSING NEXT WEEK. NOW, ARE YOU IN ON THIS, OR D'YOU WANNA BE ON THE STREET WITH THOSE TWO CHUMPS?
GEE, SPARROW. I DON'T KNOW. WHERE'M I GONNA FIND 30 MILLION DOLLARS?
DUH! GET A "LOAN" FROM THE HOMELESS SHELTER! YOU'RE THE EXECUTIVE DIRECTOR, AREN'T YOU?
CHANDLER, YOU'RE SITTING ON MY MONKEY.
HIDING DEBT...
SYDNEY! YOU PROMISED YOU WEREN'T GOING TO BUY ANYTHING NEW TILL YOU GOT YOUR CREDIT CARD BILLS UNDER CONTROL!
Cuisinart

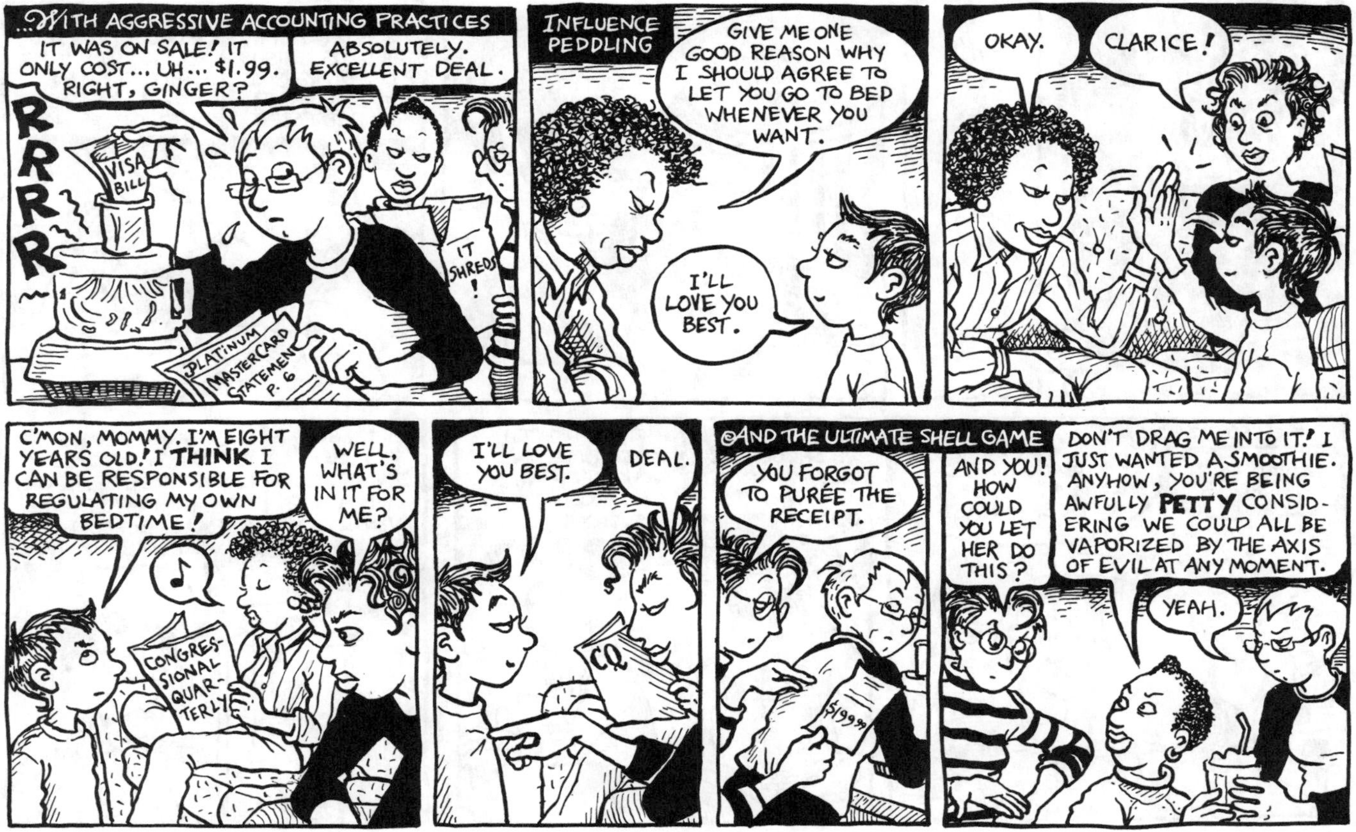
...WITH AGGRESSIVE ACCOUNTING PRACTICES
IT WAS ON SALE! IT ONLY COST... UH... $1.99. RIGHT, GINGER?
ABSOLUTELY. EXCELLENT DEAL.
RRRR
VISA BILL
IT SHREDS!
PLATINUM MASTERCARD STATEMENT P. 6
INFLUENCE PEDDLING
GIVE ME ONE GOOD REASON WHY I SHOULD AGREE TO LET YOU GO TO BED WHENEVER YOU WANT.
I'LL LOVE YOU BEST.
OKAY.
CLARICE!
C'MON, MOMMY. I'M EIGHT YEARS OLD! I THINK I CAN BE RESPONSIBLE FOR REGULATING MY OWN BEDTIME!
WELL, WHAT'S IN IT FOR ME?
♪
CONGRESSIONAL QUARTERLY
I'LL LOVE YOU BEST.
DEAL.
CQ
...AND THE ULTIMATE SHELL GAME
YOU FORGOT TO PURÉE THE RECEIPT.
$199.99
AND YOU! HOW COULD YOU LET HER DO THIS?
DON'T DRAG ME INTO IT! I JUST WANTED A SMOOTHIE. ANYHOW, YOU'RE BEING AWFULLY PETTY CONSIDERING WE COULD ALL BE VAPORIZED BY THE AXIS OF EVIL AT ANY MOMENT.
YEAH.

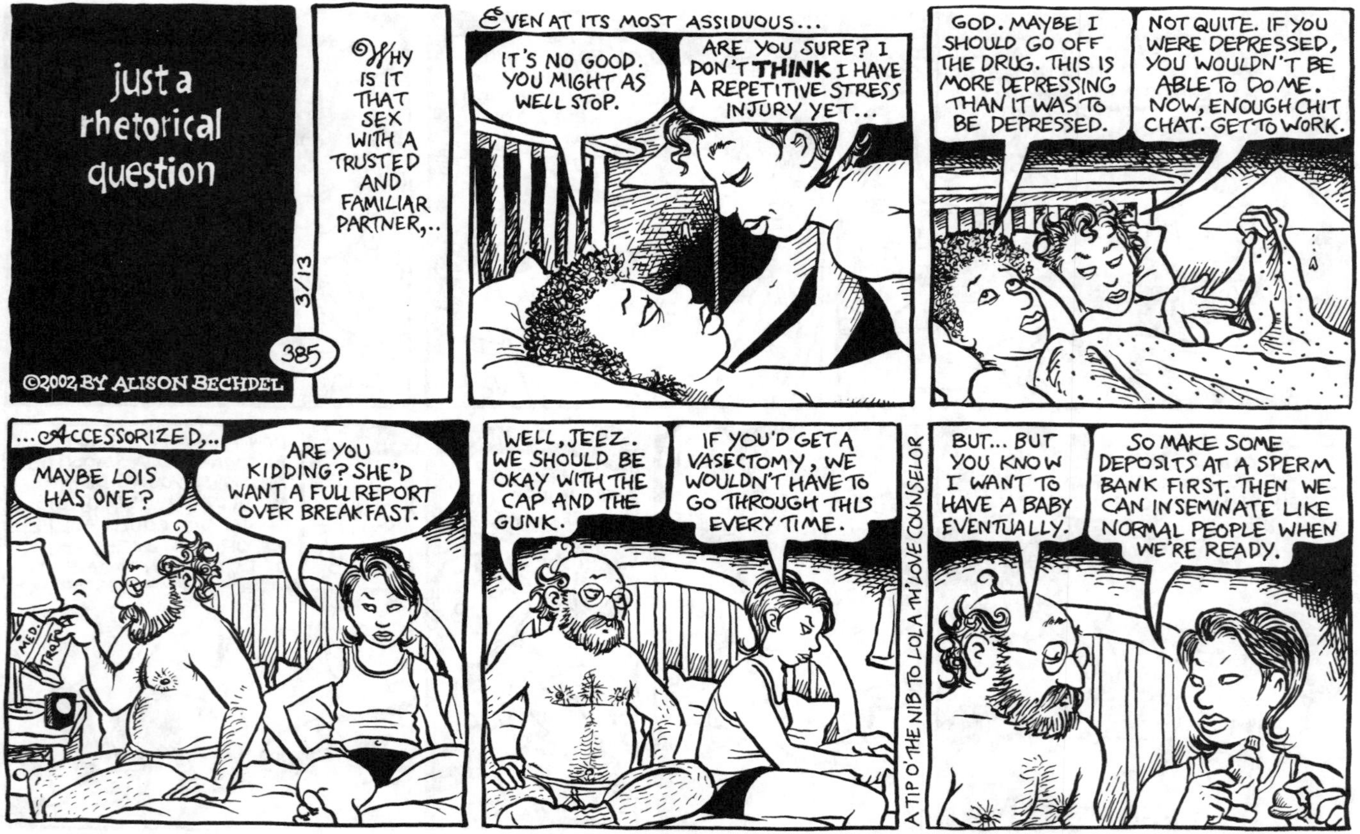
just a rhetorical question
©2002 BY ALISON BECHDEL
385
3/13
WHY IS IT THAT SEX WITH A TRUSTED AND FAMILIAR PARTNER,..
EVEN AT ITS MOST ASSIDUOUS...
IT'S NO GOOD. YOU MIGHT AS WELL STOP.
ARE YOU SURE? I DON'T **THINK** I HAVE A REPETITIVE STRESS INJURY YET...
GOD. MAYBE I SHOULD GO OFF THE DRUG. THIS IS MORE DEPRESSING THAN IT WAS TO BE DEPRESSED.
NOT QUITE. IF YOU WERE DEPRESSED, YOU WOULDN'T BE ABLE TO DO ME. NOW, ENOUGH CHIT CHAT. GET TO WORK.
...ACCESSORIZED,..
MAYBE LOIS HAS ONE?
ARE YOU KIDDING? SHE'D WANT A FULL REPORT OVER BREAKFAST.
MED.
TROJ
WELL, JEEZ. WE SHOULD BE OKAY WITH THE CAP AND THE GUNK.
IF YOU'D GET A VASECTOMY, WE WOULDN'T HAVE TO GO THROUGH THIS EVERY TIME.
A TIP O' THE NIB TO LOLA TH' LOVE COUNSELOR
BUT... BUT YOU KNOW I WANT TO HAVE A BABY EVENTUALLY.
SO MAKE SOME DEPOSITS AT A SPERM BANK FIRST. THEN WE CAN INSEMINATE LIKE NORMAL PEOPLE WHEN WE'RE READY.

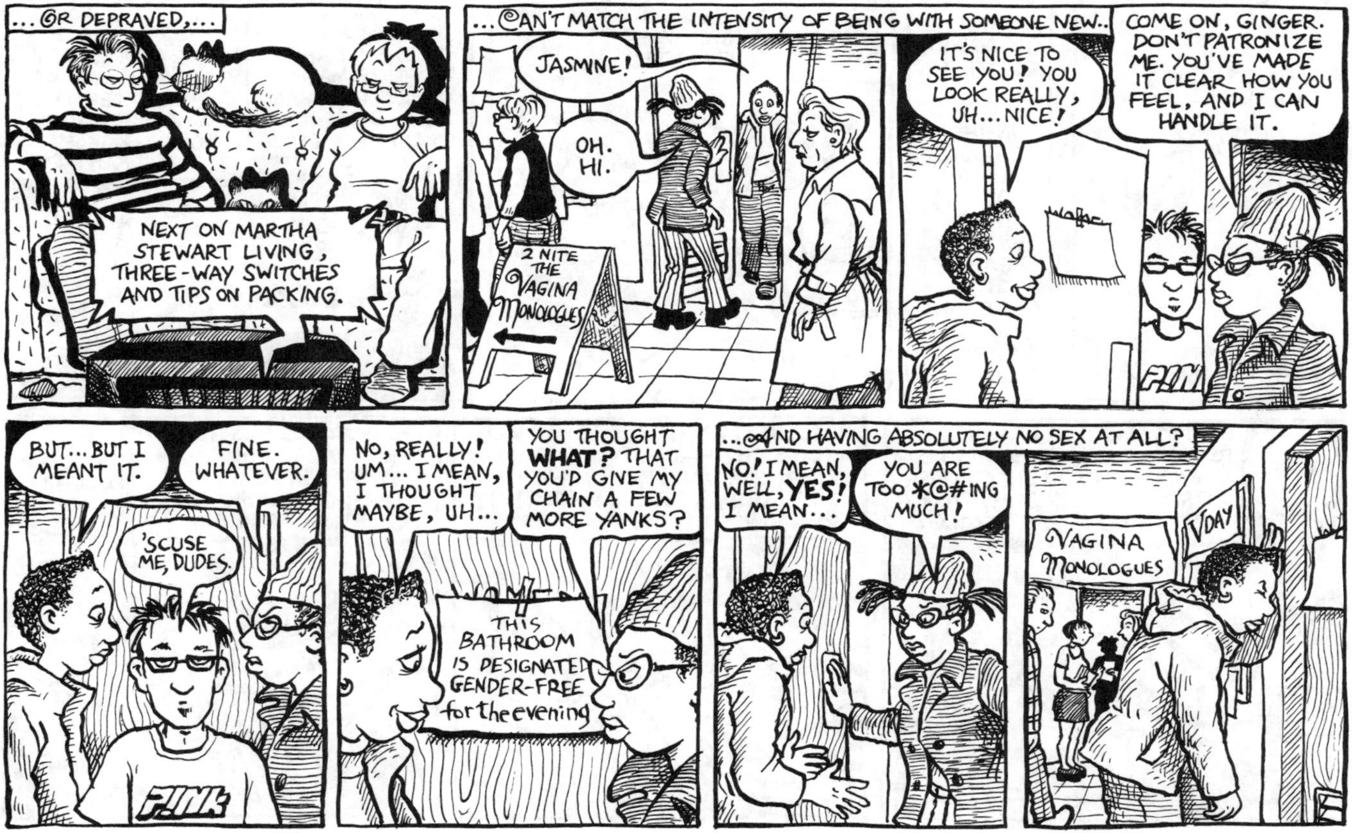

...OR DEPRAVED,...
NEXT ON MARTHA STEWART LIVING, THREE-WAY SWITCHES AND TIPS ON PACKING.
...CAN'T MATCH THE INTENSITY OF BEING WITH SOMEONE NEW...
JASMINE!
OH. HI.
2 NITE THE VAGINA MONOLOGUES
IT'S NICE TO SEE YOU! YOU LOOK REALLY, UH... NICE!
COME ON, GINGER. DON'T PATRONIZE ME. YOU'VE MADE IT CLEAR HOW YOU FEEL, AND I CAN HANDLE IT.
PINK
BUT... BUT I MEANT IT.
FINE. WHATEVER.
'SCUSE ME, DUDES.
PINK
NO, REALLY! UM... I MEAN, I THOUGHT MAYBE, UH...
YOU THOUGHT WHAT? THAT YOU'D GIVE MY CHAIN A FEW MORE YANKS?
THIS BATHROOM IS DESIGNATED GENDER-FREE for the evening
...AND HAVING ABSOLUTELY NO SEX AT ALL?
NO! I MEAN, WELL, YES! I MEAN...
YOU ARE TOO *@#ING MUCH!
VAGINA MONOLOGUES
VDAY

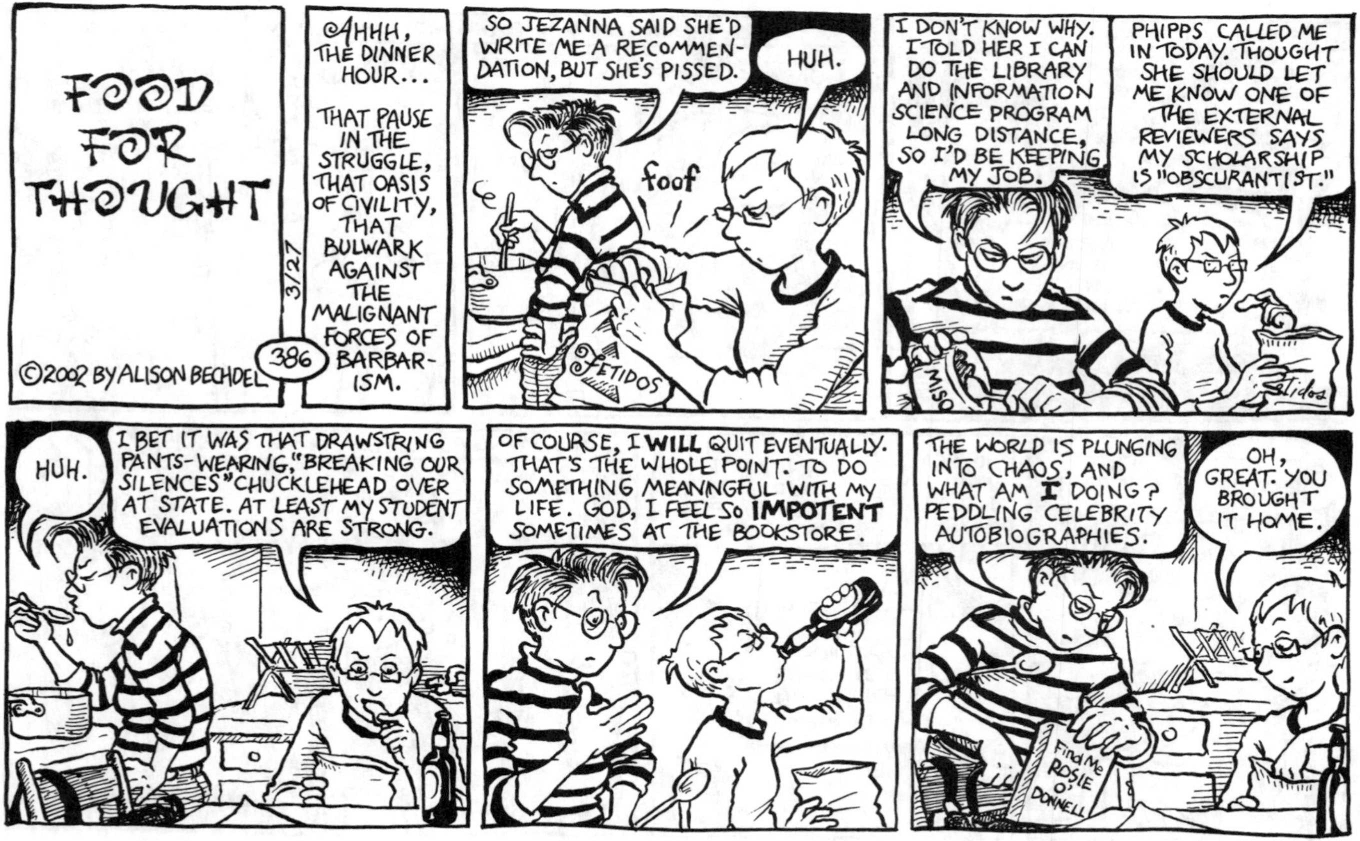
FOOD FOR THOUGHT
©2002 BY ALISON BECHDEL
386
3/27
AHHH, THE DINNER HOUR...
THAT PAUSE IN THE STRUGGLE, THAT OASIS OF CIVILITY, THAT BULWARK AGAINST THE MALIGNANT FORCES OF BARBARISM.
SO JEZANNA SAID SHE'D WRITE ME A RECOMMENDATION, BUT SHE'S PISSED.
HUH.
foof
FETIDOS
I DON'T KNOW WHY. I TOLD HER I CAN DO THE LIBRARY AND INFORMATION SCIENCE PROGRAM LONG DISTANCE, SO I'D BE KEEPING MY JOB.
PHIPPS CALLED ME IN TODAY. THOUGHT SHE SHOULD LET ME KNOW ONE OF THE EXTERNAL REVIEWERS SAYS MY SCHOLARSHIP IS "OBSCURANTIST."
MISO
HUH.
I BET IT WAS THAT DRAWSTRING PANTS-WEARING, "BREAKING OUR SILENCES" CHUCKLEHEAD OVER AT STATE. AT LEAST MY STUDENT EVALUATIONS ARE STRONG.
OF COURSE, I **WILL** QUIT EVENTUALLY. THAT'S THE WHOLE POINT. TO DO SOMETHING MEANINGFUL WITH MY LIFE. GOD, I FEEL SO **IMPOTENT** SOMETIMES AT THE BOOKSTORE.
THE WORLD IS PLUNGING INTO CHAOS, AND WHAT AM **I** DOING? PEDDLING CELEBRITY AUTOBIOGRAPHIES.
OH, GREAT. YOU BROUGHT IT HOME.
Find Me ROSIE O' DONNELL

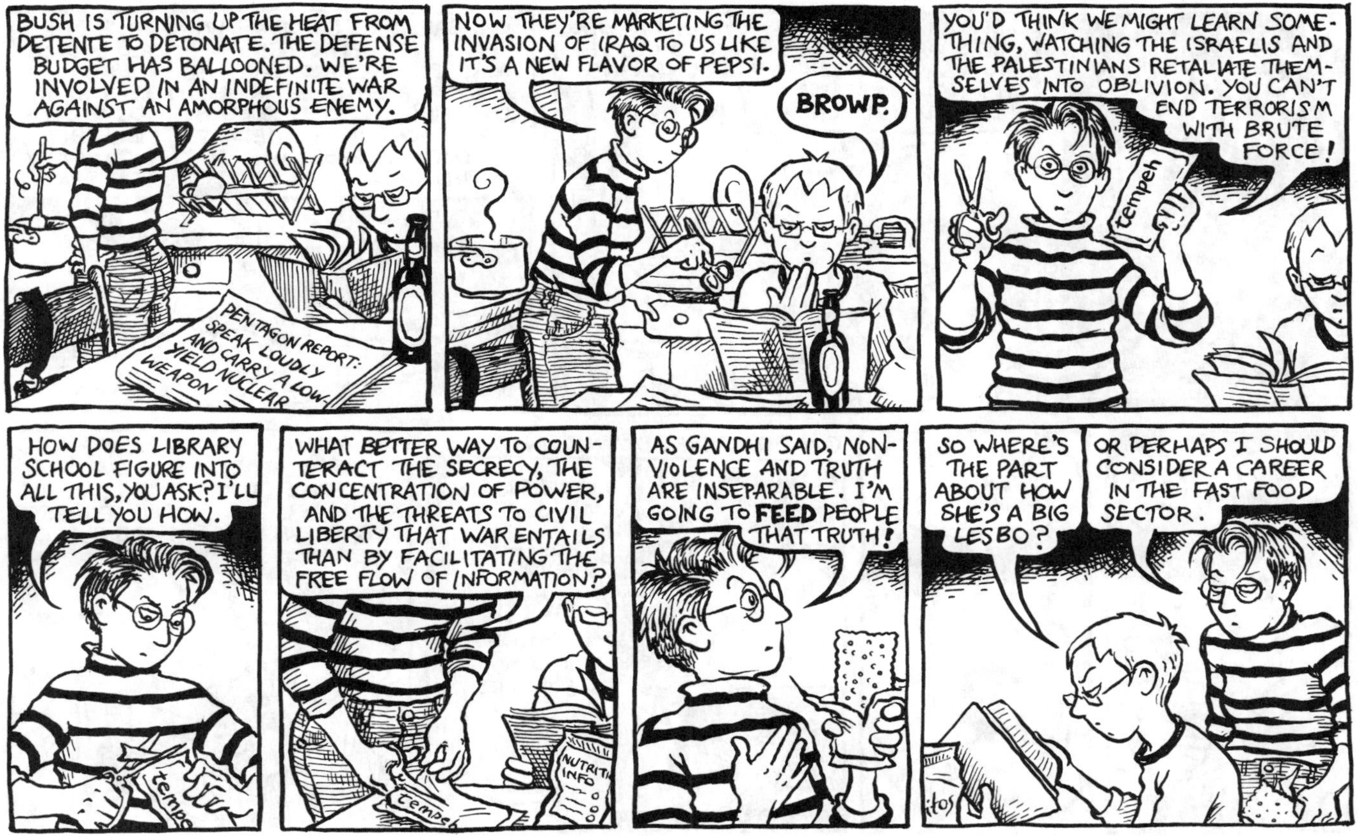

BUSH IS TURNING UP THE HEAT FROM DETENTE TO DETONATE. THE DEFENSE BUDGET HAS BALLOONED. WE'RE INVOLVED IN AN INDEFINITE WAR AGAINST AN AMORPHOUS ENEMY.
PENTAGON REPORT: SPEAK LOUDLY AND CARRY A LOW-YIELD NUCLEAR WEAPON
NOW THEY'RE MARKETING THE INVASION OF IRAQ TO US LIKE IT'S A NEW FLAVOR OF PEPSI.
BROWP.
YOU'D THINK WE MIGHT LEARN SOMETHING, WATCHING THE ISRAELIS AND THE PALESTINIANS RETALIATE THEMSELVES INTO OBLIVION. YOU CAN'T END TERRORISM WITH BRUTE FORCE!
tempeh
HOW DOES LIBRARY SCHOOL FIGURE INTO ALL THIS, YOU ASK? I'LL TELL YOU HOW.
WHAT BETTER WAY TO COUNTERACT THE SECRECY, THE CONCENTRATION OF POWER, AND THE THREATS TO CIVIL LIBERTY THAT WAR ENTAILS THAN BY FACILITATING THE FREE FLOW OF INFORMATION?
tempeh
AS GANDHI SAID, NONVIOLENCE AND TRUTH ARE INSEPARABLE. I'M GOING TO **FEED** PEOPLE THAT TRUTH!
SO WHERE'S THE PART ABOUT HOW SHE'S A BIG LESBO?
OR PERHAPS I SHOULD CONSIDER A CAREER IN THE FAST FOOD SECTOR.

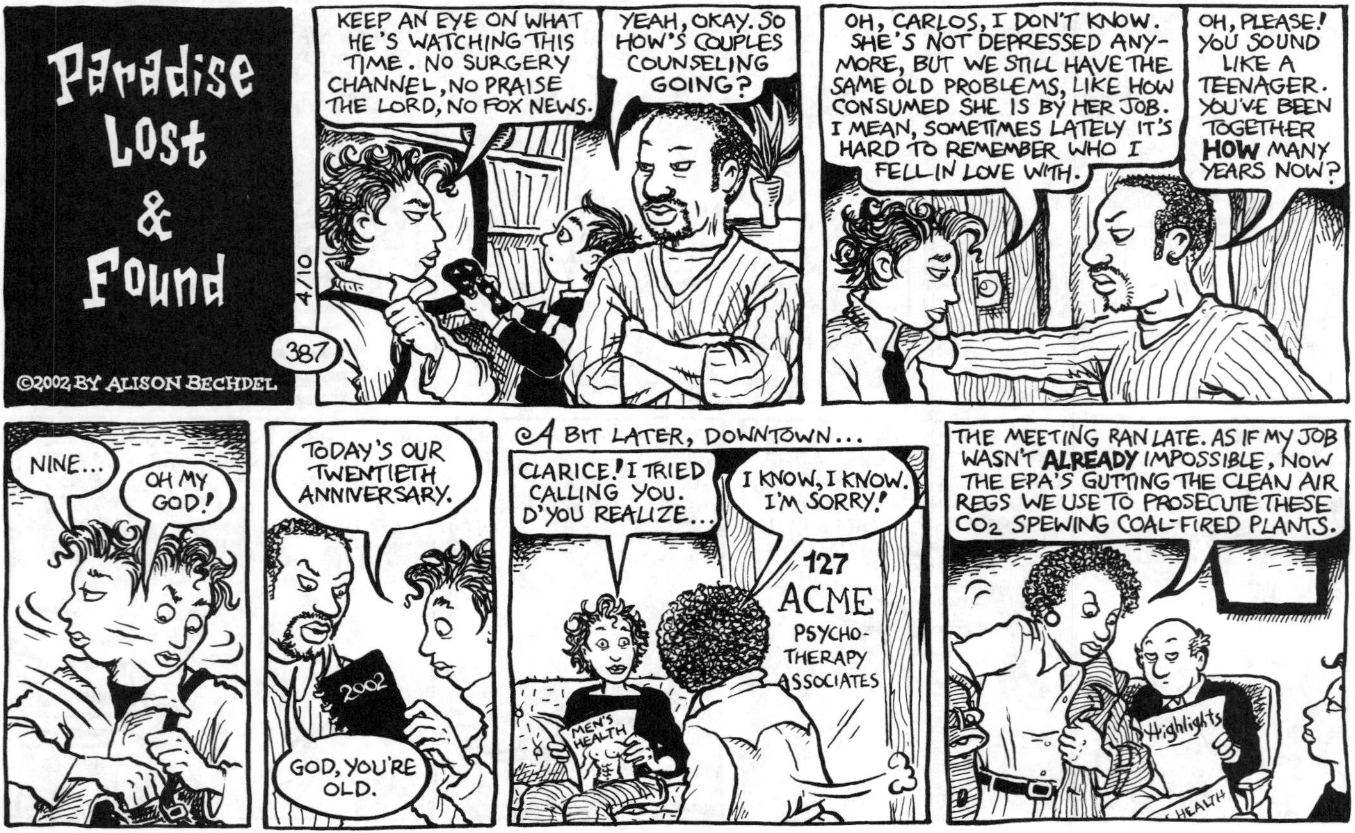
Paradise Lost & Found
©2002 BY ALISON BECHDEL
387
4/10
KEEP AN EYE ON WHAT HE'S WATCHING THIS TIME. NO SURGERY CHANNEL, NO PRAISE THE LORD, NO FOX NEWS.
YEAH, OKAY. SO HOW'S COUPLES COUNSELING GOING?
OH, CARLOS, I DON'T KNOW. SHE'S NOT DEPRESSED ANYMORE, BUT WE STILL HAVE THE SAME OLD PROBLEMS, LIKE HOW CONSUMED SHE IS BY HER JOB. I MEAN, SOMETIMES LATELY IT'S HARD TO REMEMBER WHO I FELL IN LOVE WITH.
OH, PLEASE! YOU SOUND LIKE A TEENAGER. YOU'VE BEEN TOGETHER HOW MANY YEARS NOW?
NINE...
OH MY GOD!
TODAY'S OUR TWENTIETH ANNIVERSARY.
2002
GOD, YOU'RE OLD.
A BIT LATER, DOWNTOWN...
CLARICE! I TRIED CALLING YOU. D'YOU REALIZE...
I KNOW, I KNOW. I'M SORRY!
127
ACME
PSYCHO-THERAPY ASSOCIATES
MEN'S HEALTH
THE MEETING RAN LATE. AS IF MY JOB WASN'T ALREADY IMPOSSIBLE, NOW THE EPA'S GUTTING THE CLEAN AIR REGS WE USE TO PROSECUTE THESE CO2 SPEWING COAL-FIRED PLANTS.
Highlights
HEALTH

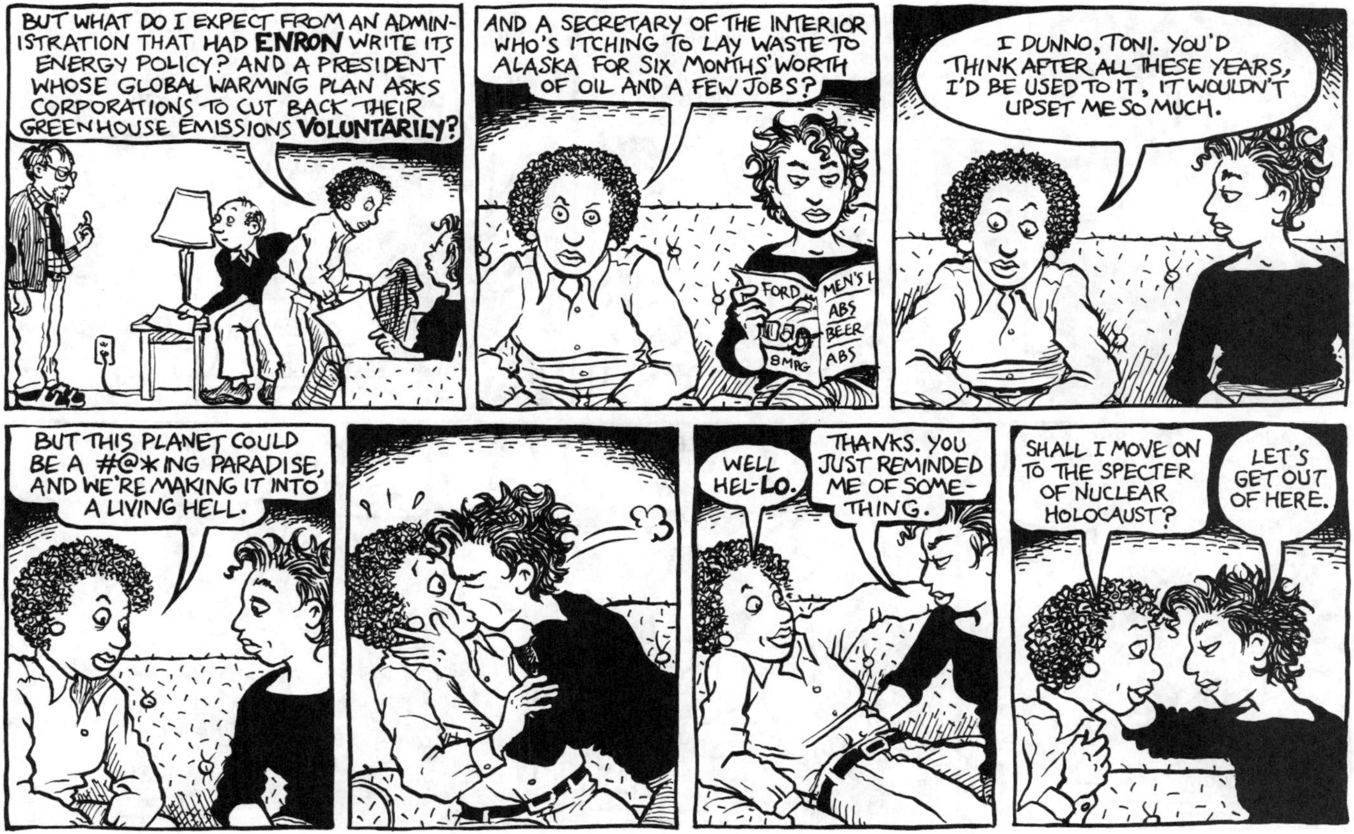
BUT WHAT DO I EXPECT FROM AN ADMINISTRATION THAT HAD ENRON WRITE ITS ENERGY POLICY? AND A PRESIDENT WHOSE GLOBAL WARMING PLAN ASKS CORPORATIONS TO CUT BACK THEIR GREENHOUSE EMISSIONS VOLUNTARILY?
AND A SECRETARY OF THE INTERIOR WHO'S ITCHING TO LAY WASTE TO ALASKA FOR SIX MONTHS' WORTH OF OIL AND A FEW JOBS?
FORD
8 MPG
MEN'S
ABS
BEER
ABS
I DUNNO, TONI. YOU'D THINK AFTER ALL THESE YEARS, I'D BE USED TO IT, IT WOULDN'T UPSET ME SO MUCH.
BUT THIS PLANET COULD BE A #@*ING PARADISE, AND WE'RE MAKING IT INTO A LIVING HELL.
WELL HEL-LO.
THANKS. YOU JUST REMINDED ME OF SOMETHING.
SHALL I MOVE ON TO THE SPECTER OF NUCLEAR HOLOCAUST?
LET'S GET OUT OF HERE.

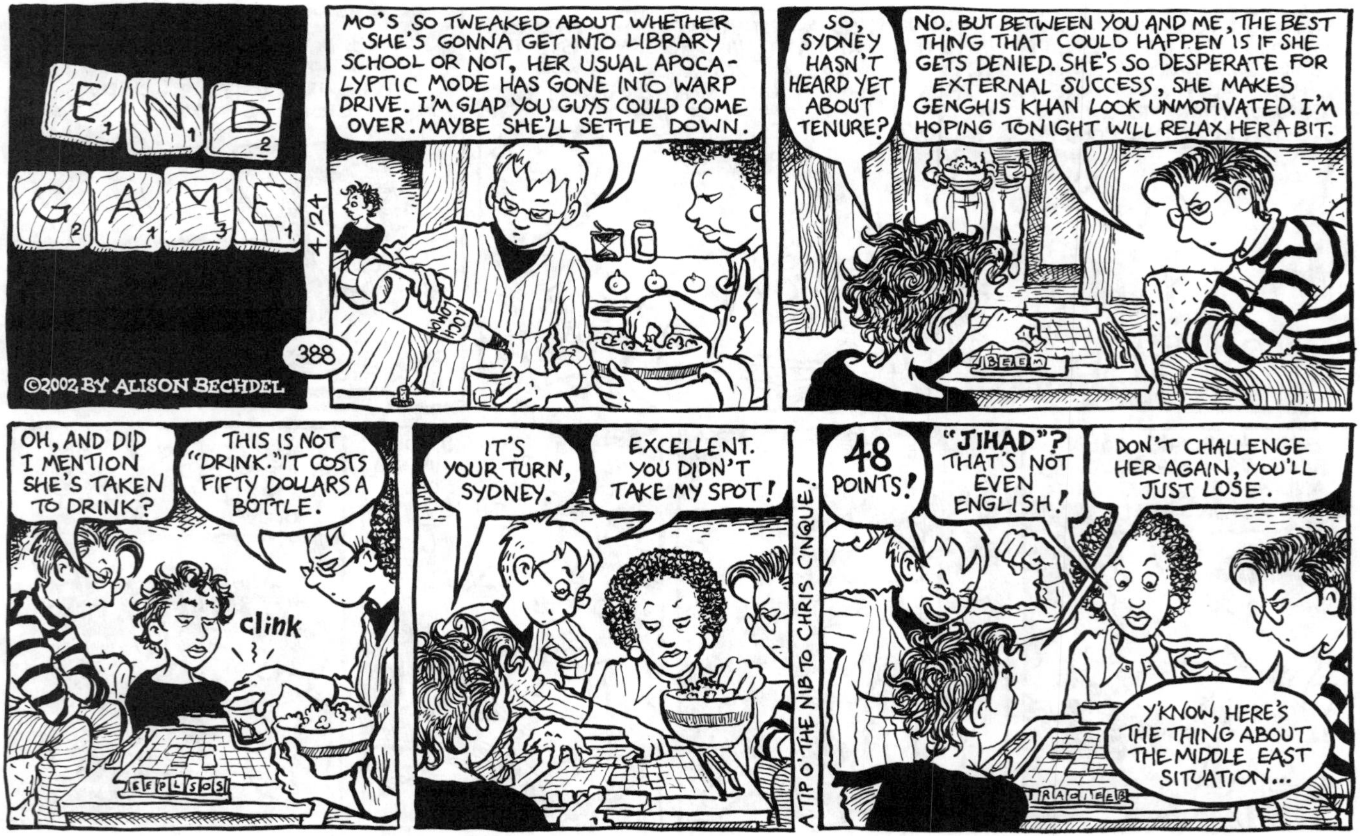
END GAME
©2002 BY ALISON BECHDEL
4/24
388
MO'S SO TWEAKED ABOUT WHETHER SHE'S GONNA GET INTO LIBRARY SCHOOL OR NOT, HER USUAL APOCALYPTIC MODE HAS GONE INTO WARP DRIVE. I'M GLAD YOU GUYS COULD COME OVER. MAYBE SHE'LL SETTLE DOWN.
LOCH LOMOND
SO, SYDNEY HASN'T HEARD YET ABOUT TENURE?
NO. BUT BETWEEN YOU AND ME, THE BEST THING THAT COULD HAPPEN IS IF SHE GETS DENIED. SHE'S SO DESPERATE FOR EXTERNAL SUCCESS, SHE MAKES GENGHIS KHAN LOOK UNMOTIVATED. I'M HOPING TONIGHT WILL RELAX HER A BIT.
OH, AND DID I MENTION SHE'S TAKEN TO DRINK?
THIS IS NOT "DRINK." IT COSTS FIFTY DOLLARS A BOTTLE.
clink
IT'S YOUR TURN, SYDNEY.
EXCELLENT. YOU DIDN'T TAKE MY SPOT!
A TIP O' THE NIB TO CHRIS CINQUE!
48 POINTS!
"JIHAD"? THAT'S NOT EVEN ENGLISH!
DON'T CHALLENGE HER AGAIN, YOU'LL JUST LOSE.
Y'KNOW, HERE'S THE THING ABOUT THE MIDDLE EAST SITUATION...

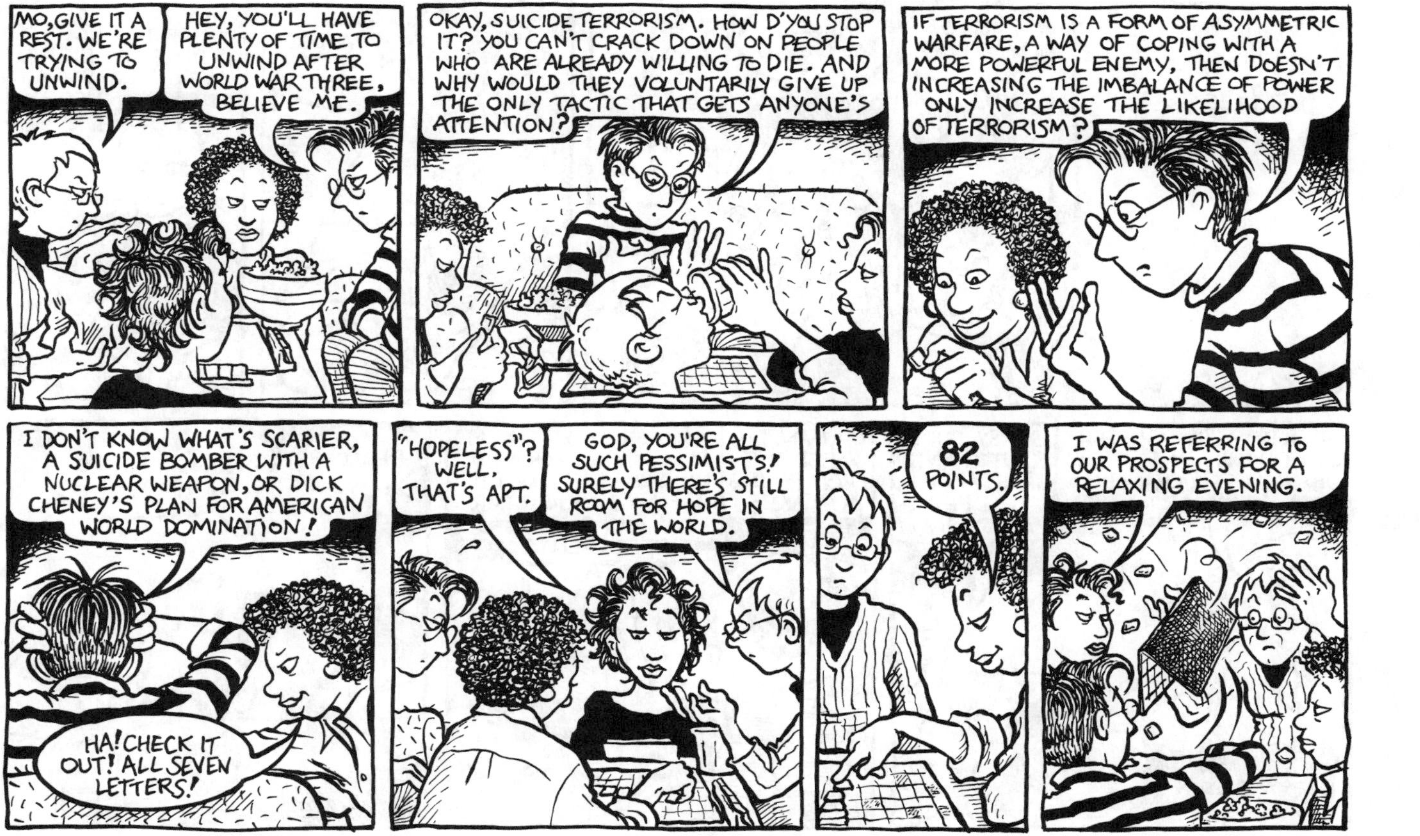
MO, GIVE IT A REST. WE'RE TRYING TO UNWIND.
HEY, YOU'LL HAVE PLENTY OF TIME TO UNWIND AFTER WORLD WAR THREE, BELIEVE ME.
OKAY, SUICIDE TERRORISM. HOW D'YOU STOP IT? YOU CAN'T CRACK DOWN ON PEOPLE WHO ARE ALREADY WILLING TO DIE. AND WHY WOULD THEY VOLUNTARILY GIVE UP THE ONLY TACTIC THAT GETS ANYONE'S ATTENTION?
IF TERRORISM IS A FORM OF ASYMMETRIC WARFARE, A WAY OF COPING WITH A MORE POWERFUL ENEMY, THEN DOESN'T INCREASING THE IMBALANCE OF POWER ONLY INCREASE THE LIKELIHOOD OF TERRORISM?
I DON'T KNOW WHAT'S SCARIER, A SUICIDE BOMBER WITH A NUCLEAR WEAPON, OR DICK CHENEY'S PLAN FOR AMERICAN WORLD DOMINATION!
HA! CHECK IT OUT! ALL SEVEN LETTERS!
GOD, YOU'RE ALL SUCH PESSIMISTS! SURELY THERE'S STILL ROOM FOR HOPE IN THE WORLD.
"HOPELESS"? WELL. THAT'S APT.
82 POINTS.
I WAS REFERRING TO OUR PROSPECTS FOR A RELAXING EVENING.

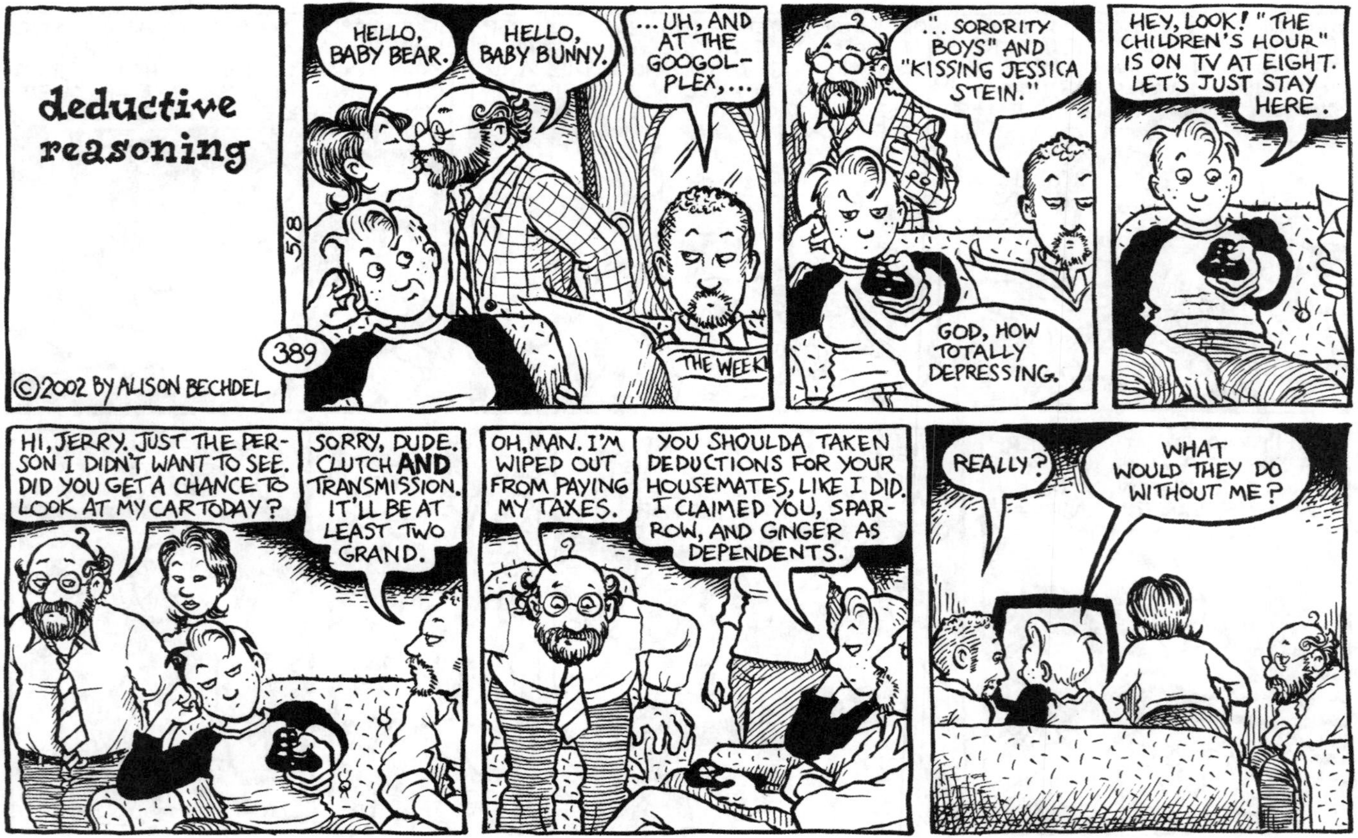

deductive reasoning
©2002 BY ALISON BECHDEL
5/8
389
HELLO, BABY BEAR.
HELLO, BABY BUNNY.
...UH, AND AT THE GOOGOL-PLEX,...
THE WEEK
"...SORORITY BOYS" AND "KISSING JESSICA STEIN."
GOD, HOW TOTALLY DEPRESSING.
HEY, LOOK! "THE CHILDREN'S HOUR" IS ON TV AT EIGHT. LET'S JUST STAY HERE.
HI, JERRY. JUST THE PERSON I DIDN'T WANT TO SEE. DID YOU GET A CHANCE TO LOOK AT MY CAR TODAY?
SORRY, DUDE. CLUTCH **AND** TRANSMISSION. IT'LL BE AT LEAST TWO GRAND.
OH, MAN. I'M WIPED OUT FROM PAYING MY TAXES.
YOU SHOULDA TAKEN DEDUCTIONS FOR YOUR HOUSEMATES, LIKE I DID. I CLAIMED YOU, SPARROW, AND GINGER AS DEPENDENTS.
REALLY?
WHAT WOULD THEY DO WITHOUT ME?

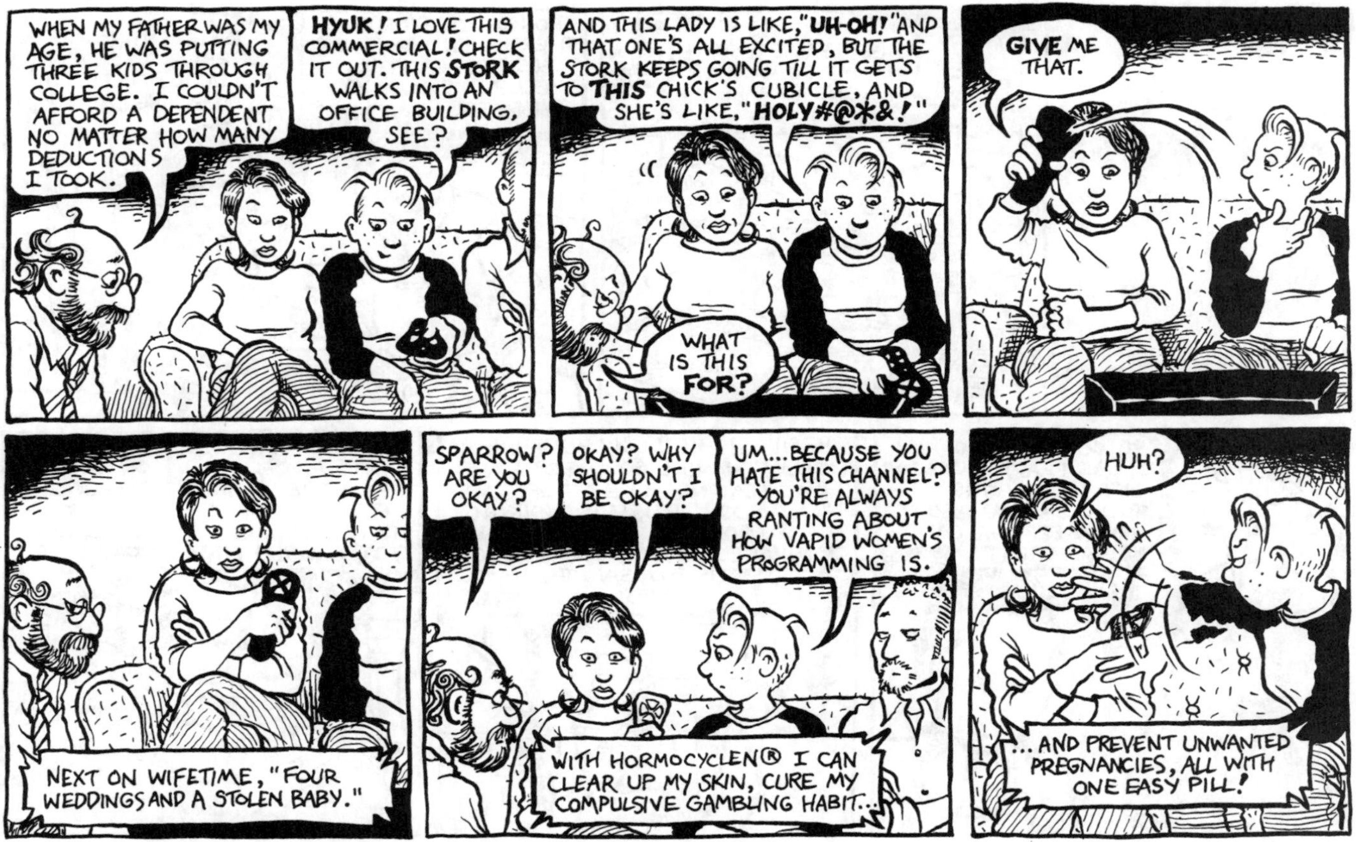
WHEN MY FATHER WAS MY AGE, HE WAS PUTTING THREE KIDS THROUGH COLLEGE. I COULDN'T AFFORD A DEPENDENT NO MATTER HOW MANY DEDUCTIONS I TOOK.
HYUK! I LOVE THIS COMMERCIAL! CHECK IT OUT. THIS STORK WALKS INTO AN OFFICE BUILDING, SEE?
AND THIS LADY IS LIKE, "UH-OH!" AND THAT ONE'S ALL EXCITED, BUT THE STORK KEEPS GOING TILL IT GETS TO THIS CHICK'S CUBICLE, AND SHE'S LIKE, "HOLY#@*&!"
WHAT IS THIS FOR?
GIVE ME THAT.
NEXT ON WIFETIME, "FOUR WEDDINGS AND A STOLEN BABY."
SPARROW? ARE YOU OKAY?
OKAY? WHY SHOULDN'T I BE OKAY?
UM...BECAUSE YOU HATE THIS CHANNEL? YOU'RE ALWAYS RANTING ABOUT HOW VAPID WOMEN'S PROGRAMMING IS.
WITH HORMOCYCLEN® I CAN CLEAR UP MY SKIN, CURE MY COMPULSIVE GAMBLING HABIT...
HUH?
...AND PREVENT UNWANTED PREGNANCIES, ALL WITH ONE EASY PILL!

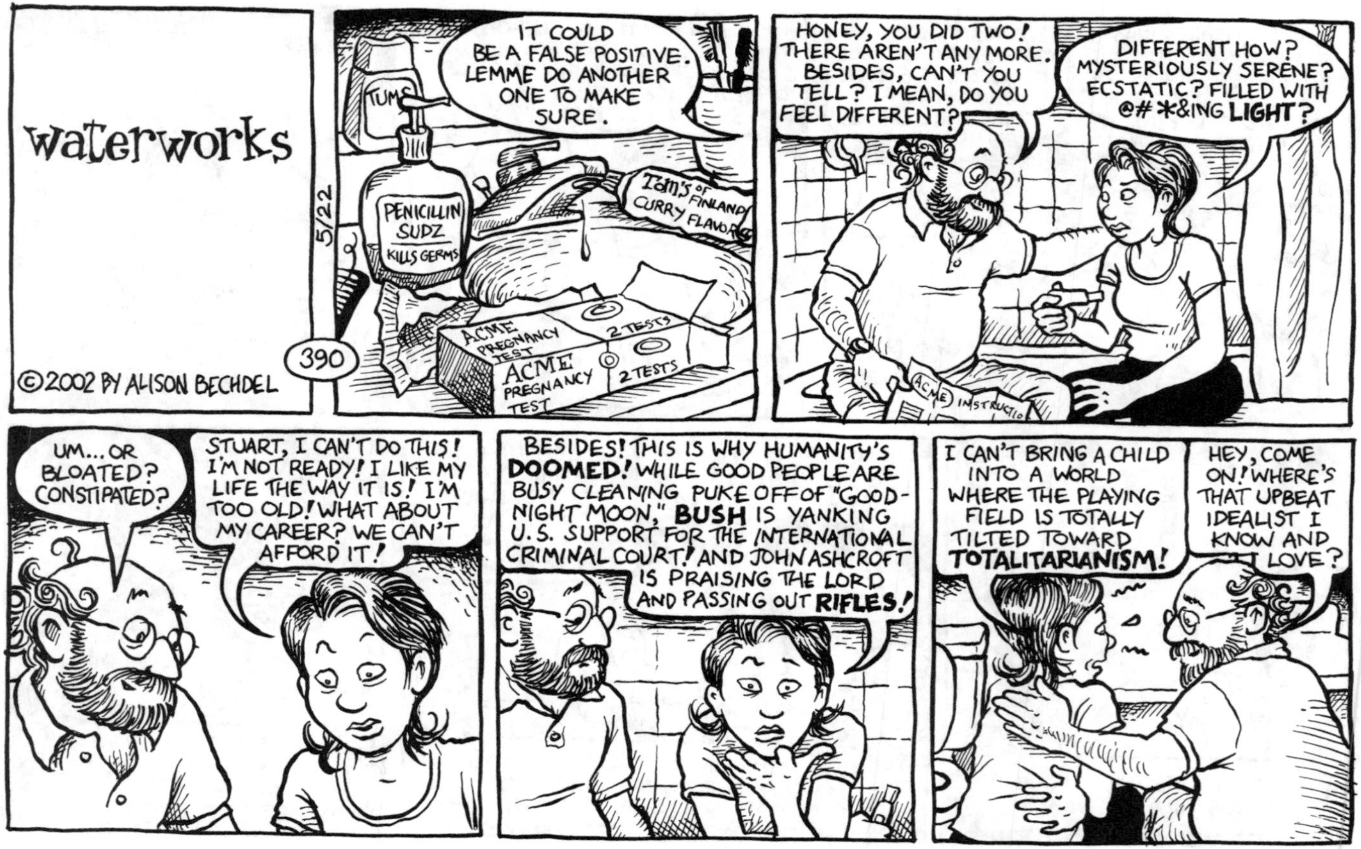
waterworks
©2002 BY ALISON BECHDEL
390
5/22
IT COULD BE A FALSE POSITIVE. LEMME DO ANOTHER ONE TO MAKE SURE.
TUMS
PENICILLIN SUDZ KILLS GERMS
Tom's OF FINLAND CURRY FLAVOR
ACME PREGNANCY TEST 2 TESTS
ACME PREGNANCY TEST 2 TESTS
HONEY, YOU DID TWO! THERE AREN'T ANY MORE. BESIDES, CAN'T YOU TELL? I MEAN, DO YOU FEEL DIFFERENT?
DIFFERENT HOW? MYSTERIOUSLY SERENE? ECSTATIC? FILLED WITH @#*&ING LIGHT?
ACME INSTRUCTIO
UM... OR BLOATED? CONSTIPATED?
STUART, I CAN'T DO THIS! I'M NOT READY! I LIKE MY LIFE THE WAY IT IS! I'M TOO OLD! WHAT ABOUT MY CAREER? WE CAN'T AFFORD IT!
BESIDES! THIS IS WHY HUMANITY'S DOOMED! WHILE GOOD PEOPLE ARE BUSY CLEANING PUKE OFF OF "GOOD-NIGHT MOON," BUSH IS YANKING U.S. SUPPORT FOR THE INTERNATIONAL CRIMINAL COURT! AND JOHN ASHCROFT IS PRAISING THE LORD AND PASSING OUT RIFLES!
I CAN'T BRING A CHILD INTO A WORLD WHERE THE PLAYING FIELD IS TOTALLY TILTED TOWARD TOTALITARIANISM!
HEY, COME ON! WHERE'S THAT UPBEAT IDEALIST I KNOW AND LOVE?

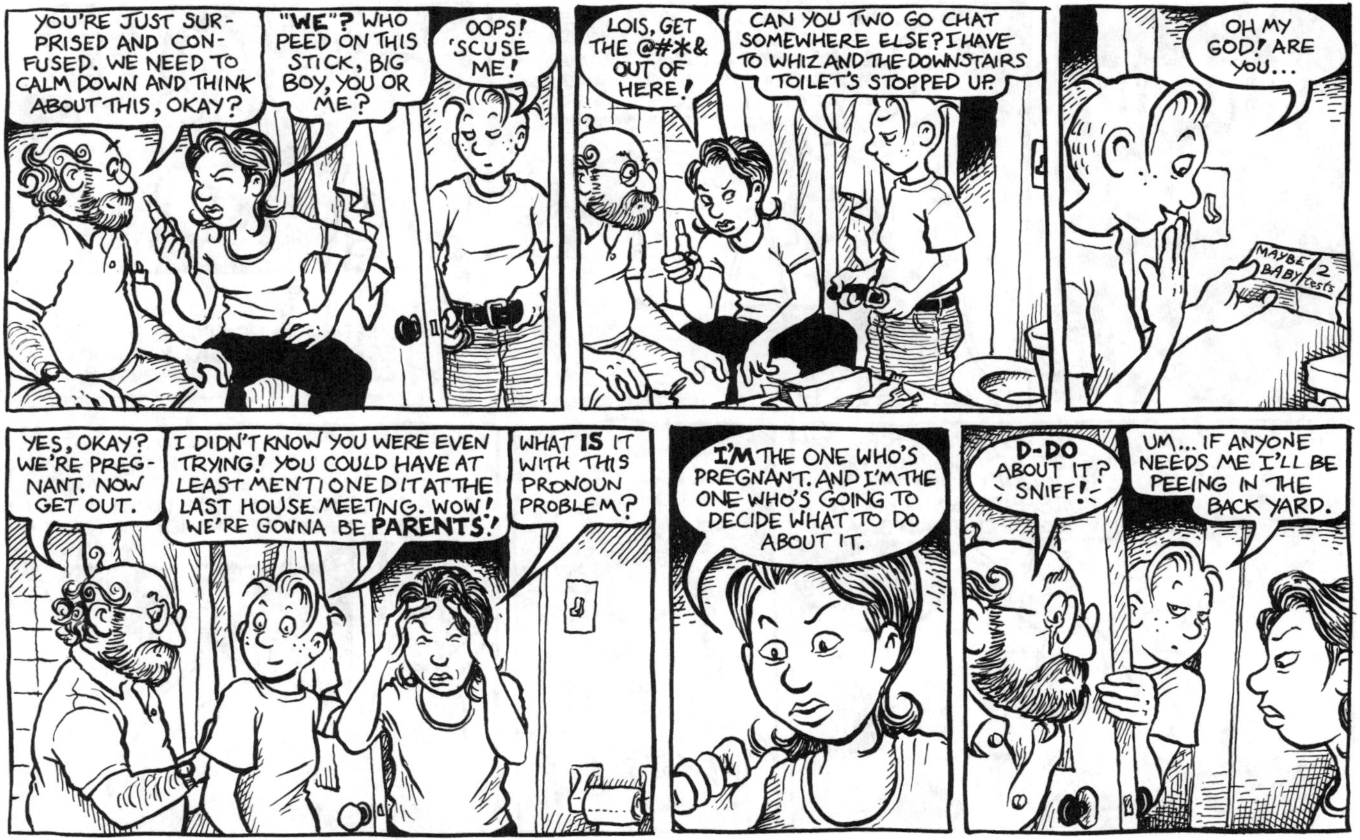
YOU'RE JUST SURPRISED AND CONFUSED. WE NEED TO CALM DOWN AND THINK ABOUT THIS, OKAY?
"WE"? WHO PEED ON THIS STICK, BIG BOY, YOU OR ME?
OOPS! 'SCUSE ME!
LOIS, GET THE @#*& OUT OF HERE!
CAN YOU TWO GO CHAT SOMEWHERE ELSE? I HAVE TO WHIZ AND THE DOWNSTAIRS TOILET'S STOPPED UP.
OH MY GOD! ARE YOU...
MAYBE BABY 2 tests
YES, OKAY? WE'RE PREGNANT. NOW GET OUT.
I DIDN'T KNOW YOU WERE EVEN TRYING! YOU COULD HAVE AT LEAST MENTIONED IT AT THE LAST HOUSE MEETING. WOW! WE'RE GONNA BE PARENTS!
WHAT IS IT WITH THIS PRONOUN PROBLEM?
I'M THE ONE WHO'S PREGNANT. AND I'M THE ONE WHO'S GOING TO DECIDE WHAT TO DO ABOUT IT.
D-DO ABOUT IT? SNIFF!
UM... IF ANYONE NEEDS ME I'LL BE PEEING IN THE BACK YARD.

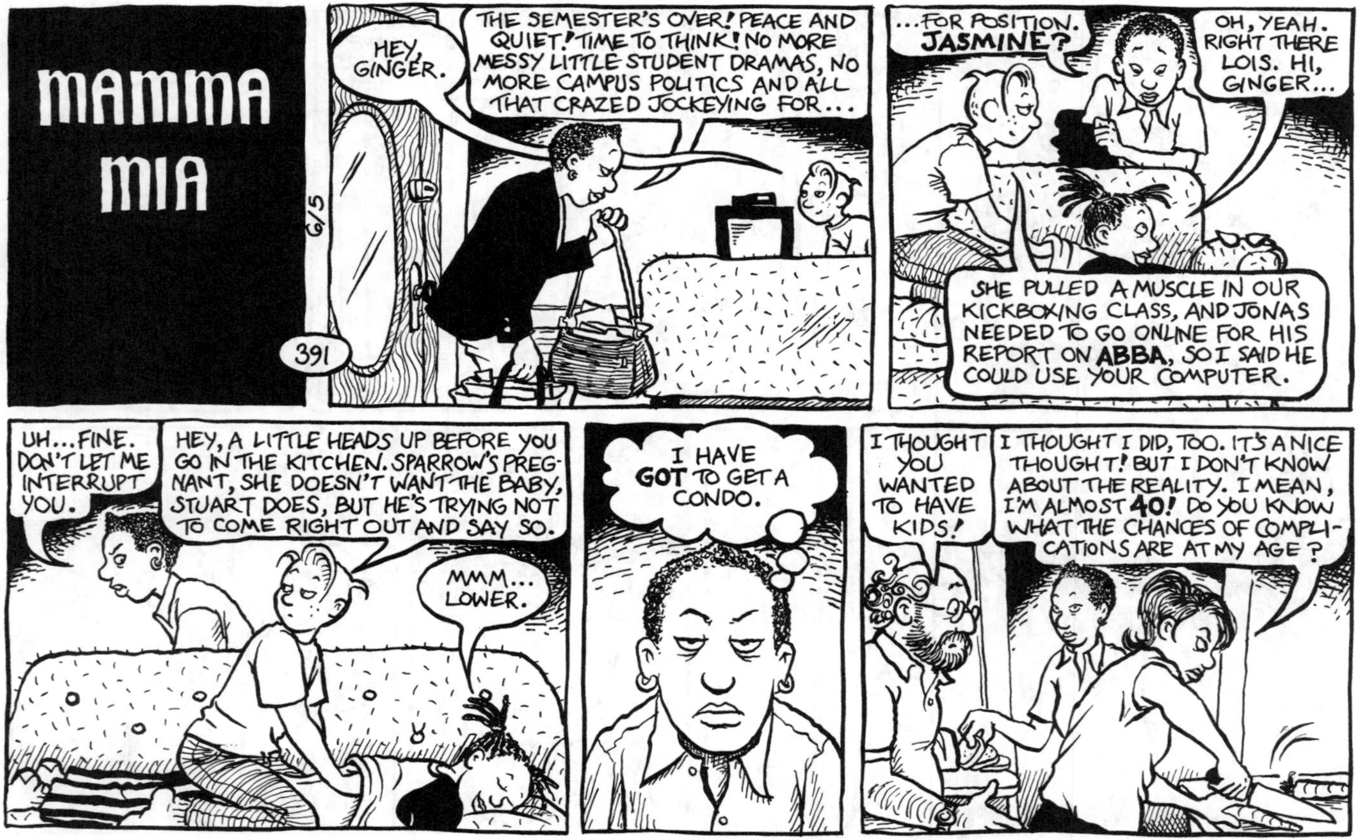
MAMMA MIA
6/5
391
HEY, GINGER.
THE SEMESTER'S OVER! PEACE AND QUIET! TIME TO THINK! NO MORE MESSY LITTLE STUDENT DRAMAS, NO MORE CAMPUS POLITICS AND ALL THAT CRAZED JOCKEYING FOR...
...FOR POSITION. JASMINE?
OH, YEAH. RIGHT THERE LOIS. HI, GINGER...
SHE PULLED A MUSCLE IN OUR KICKBOXING CLASS, AND JONAS NEEDED TO GO ONLINE FOR HIS REPORT ON ABBA, SO I SAID HE COULD USE YOUR COMPUTER.
UH...FINE. DON'T LET ME INTERRUPT YOU.
HEY, A LITTLE HEADS UP BEFORE YOU GO IN THE KITCHEN. SPARROW'S PREGNANT, SHE DOESN'T WANT THE BABY, STUART DOES, BUT HE'S TRYING NOT TO COME RIGHT OUT AND SAY SO.
MMM... LOWER.
I HAVE GOT TO GET A CONDO.
I THOUGHT YOU WANTED TO HAVE KIDS!
I THOUGHT I DID, TOO. IT'S A NICE THOUGHT! BUT I DON'T KNOW ABOUT THE REALITY. I MEAN, I'M ALMOST 40! DO YOU KNOW WHAT THE CHANCES OF COMPLICATIONS ARE AT MY AGE?

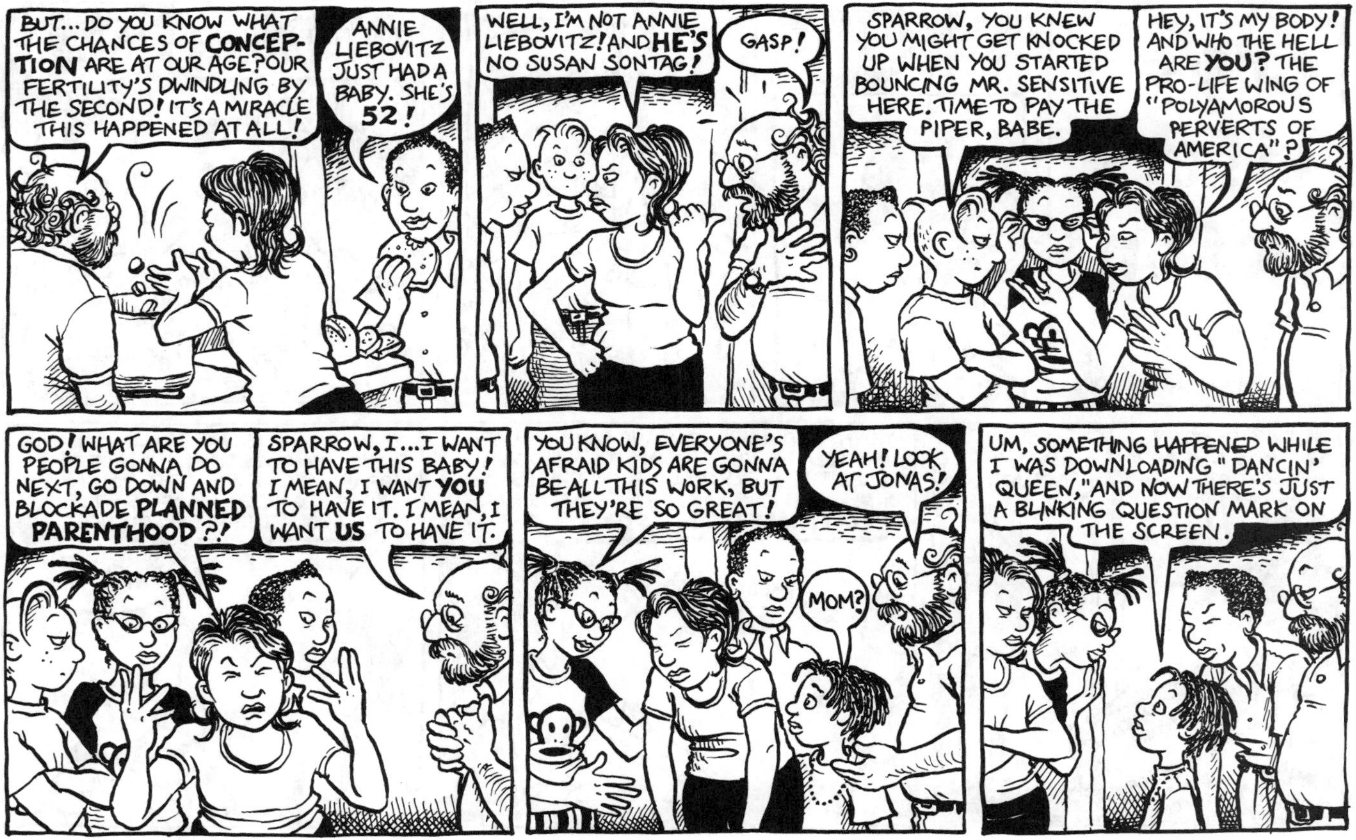

BUT... DO YOU KNOW WHAT THE CHANCES OF **CONCEPTION** ARE AT OUR AGE? OUR FERTILITY'S DWINDLING BY THE SECOND! IT'S A MIRACLE THIS HAPPENED AT ALL!
ANNIE LIEBOVITZ JUST HAD A BABY. SHE'S **52**!
WELL, I'M NOT ANNIE LIEBOVITZ! AND **HE'S** NO SUSAN SONTAG!
GASP!
SPARROW, YOU KNEW YOU MIGHT GET KNOCKED UP WHEN YOU STARTED BOUNCING MR. SENSITIVE HERE. TIME TO PAY THE PIPER, BABE.
HEY, IT'S MY BODY! AND WHO THE HELL ARE **YOU**? THE PRO-LIFE WING OF "POLYAMOROUS PERVERTS OF AMERICA"?
GOD! WHAT ARE YOU PEOPLE GONNA DO NEXT, GO DOWN AND BLOCKADE **PLANNED PARENTHOOD**?!
SPARROW, I... I WANT TO HAVE THIS BABY! I MEAN, I WANT **YOU** TO HAVE IT. I MEAN, I WANT **US** TO HAVE IT.
YOU KNOW, EVERYONE'S AFRAID KIDS ARE GONNA BE ALL THIS WORK, BUT THEY'RE SO GREAT!
YEAH! LOOK AT JONAS!
MOM?
UM, SOMETHING HAPPENED WHILE I WAS DOWNLOADING "DANCIN' QUEEN," AND NOW THERE'S JUST A BLINKING QUESTION MARK ON THE SCREEN.

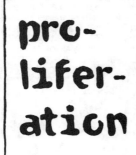

**pro-
lifer-
ation**

©2002 BY ALISON BECHDEL

392

WHILE BROWSING AT THE BOOKSTORE, OUR HEROINE HAS SUFFERED A BRIEF BOUT OF NAUSEA.

OH NO! I FORGOT TO HAVE CHILDREN!

PSORIASIS 10K

APOCALYPTICS ANONYMOUS TUESDAYS 7 PM

HEY, SPARROW. I DIDN'T SEE YOU COME IN. HOW'S IT GOING?

UH...HI, MO. I'M FINE. YOU?

RESTROOM

U.S. AND RUSSIA SIGN "HISTORIC" ARMS CONTROL AGREEMENT

OH, UP AND DOWN. I GOT INTO LIBRARY SCHOOL.

YOU DID? THAT'S GREAT!

RESTROOM

FIRST NUCLEAR TREATY IN HISTORY TO INCREASE RISK OF PROLIFERATION

YEAH, AND NOW INDIA AND PAKISTAN ARE POISED TO NUKE US ALL TO KINGDOM COME. BUT I TRY TO LOOK ON THE BRIGHT SIDE. YOU KNOW ME, THE GLASS IS HALF FULL. **HALF-FULL OF STRONTIUM-90!**

MMMIWØAM

BOOKS

CAFE &

JAPAN: PACIFISM BLOWS. LET'S GO NUCLEAR!

YEAH, WELL, LISTEN. I'M LOOKING FOR BOOKS ON ABORTION. UM, FOR THE LIBRARY AT THE SHELTER. YOU KNOW, RESOURCE GUIDES, WOMEN'S STORIES ABOUT THEIR EXPERIENCES...

SURE, RIGHT OVER HERE.

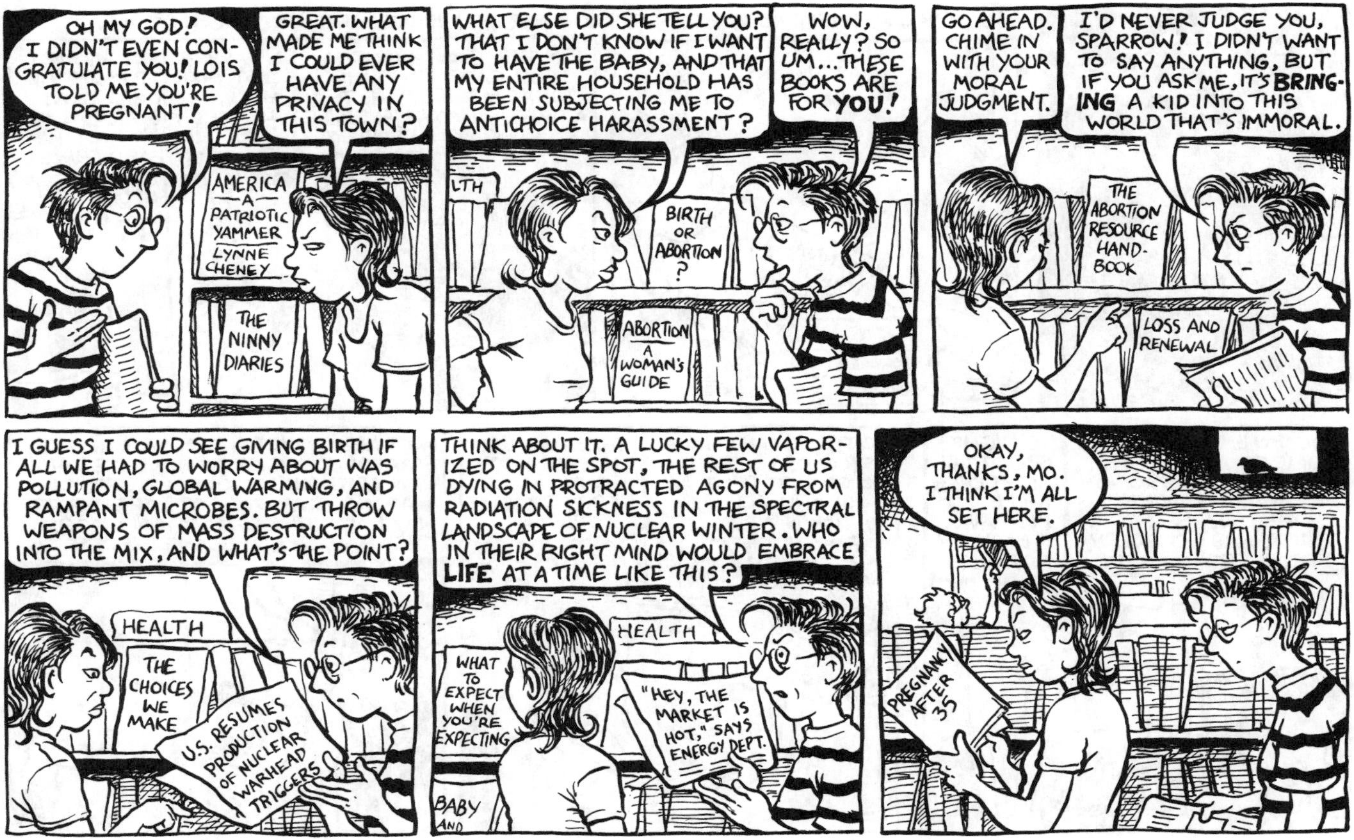
OH MY GOD! I DIDN'T EVEN CONGRATULATE YOU! LOIS TOLD ME YOU'RE PREGNANT!
AMERICA A PATRIOTIC YAMMER LYNNE CHENEY
THE NINNY DIARIES
GREAT. WHAT MADE ME THINK I COULD EVER HAVE ANY PRIVACY IN THIS TOWN?
WHAT ELSE DID SHE TELL YOU? THAT I DON'T KNOW IF I WANT TO HAVE THE BABY, AND THAT MY ENTIRE HOUSEHOLD HAS BEEN SUBJECTING ME TO ANTICHOICE HARASSMENT?
WOW, REALLY? SO UM... THESE BOOKS ARE FOR **YOU**!
BIRTH OR ABORTION ?
ABORTION A WOMAN'S GUIDE
GO AHEAD. CHIME IN WITH YOUR MORAL JUDGMENT.
I'D NEVER JUDGE YOU, SPARROW! I DIDN'T WANT TO SAY ANYTHING, BUT IF YOU ASK ME, IT'S **BRINGING** A KID INTO THIS WORLD THAT'S IMMORAL.
THE ABORTION RESOURCE HANDBOOK
LOSS AND RENEWAL
I GUESS I COULD SEE GIVING BIRTH IF ALL WE HAD TO WORRY ABOUT WAS POLLUTION, GLOBAL WARMING, AND RAMPANT MICROBES. BUT THROW WEAPONS OF MASS DESTRUCTION INTO THE MIX, AND WHAT'S THE POINT?
HEALTH
THE CHOICES WE MAKE
U.S. RESUMES PRODUCTION OF NUCLEAR WARHEAD TRIGGERS
THINK ABOUT IT. A LUCKY FEW VAPORIZED ON THE SPOT, THE REST OF US DYING IN PROTRACTED AGONY FROM RADIATION SICKNESS IN THE SPECTRAL LANDSCAPE OF NUCLEAR WINTER. WHO IN THEIR RIGHT MIND WOULD EMBRACE **LIFE** AT A TIME LIKE THIS?
HEALTH
WHAT TO EXPECT WHEN YOU'RE EXPECTING
"HEY, THE MARKET IS HOT," SAYS ENERGY DEPT.
BABY AND
OKAY, THANKS, MO. I THINK I'M ALL SET HERE.
PREGNANCY AFTER 35

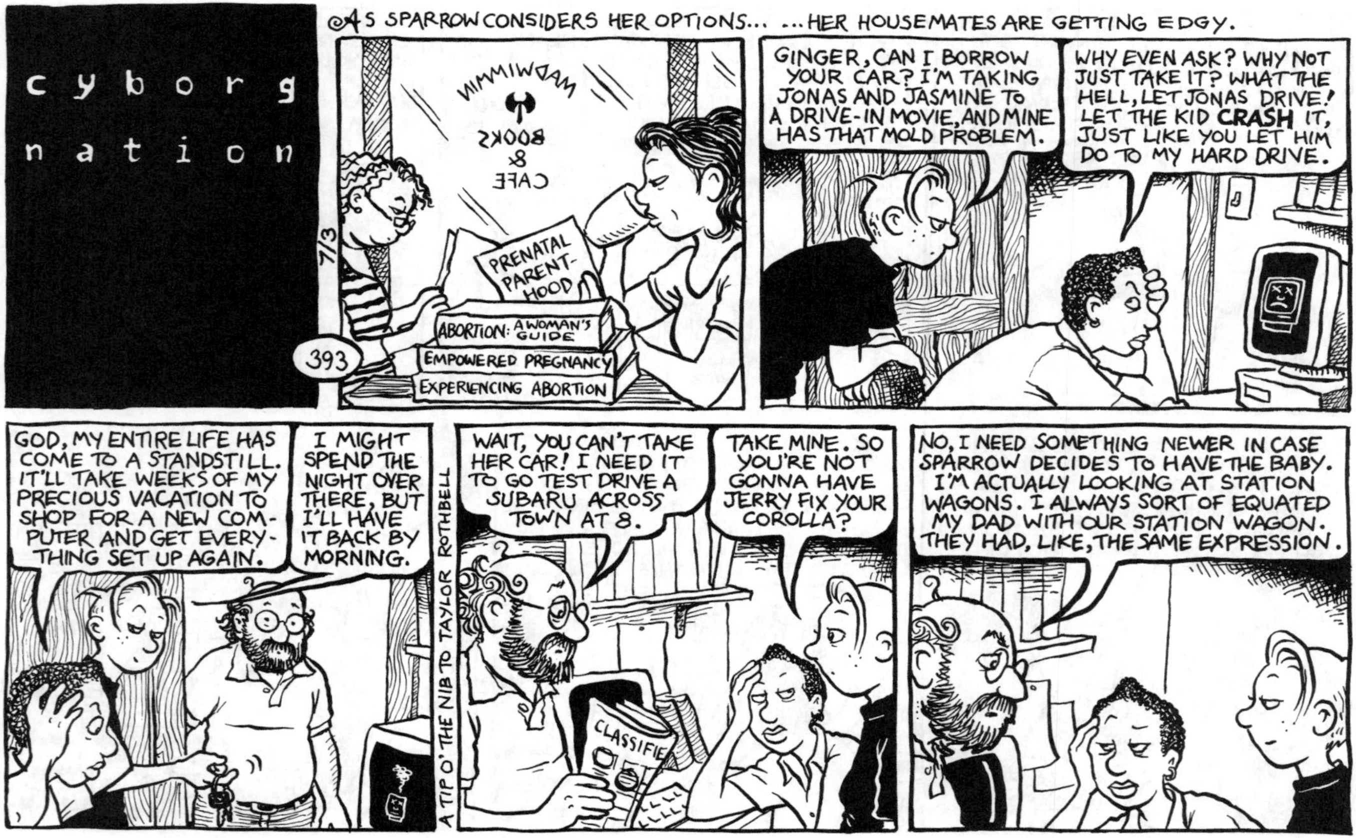
cyborg nation
AS SPARROW CONSIDERS HER OPTIONS... ...HER HOUSEMATES ARE GETTING EDGY.
MADWIMMIN BOOKS & CAFE
7/3
393
PRENATAL PARENTHOOD
ABORTION: A WOMAN'S GUIDE
EMPOWERED PREGNANCY
EXPERIENCING ABORTION
GINGER, CAN I BORROW YOUR CAR? I'M TAKING JONAS AND JASMINE TO A DRIVE-IN MOVIE, AND MINE HAS THAT MOLD PROBLEM.
WHY EVEN ASK? WHY NOT JUST TAKE IT? WHAT THE HELL, LET JONAS DRIVE! LET THE KID **CRASH** IT, JUST LIKE YOU LET HIM DO TO MY HARD DRIVE.
GOD, MY ENTIRE LIFE HAS COME TO A STANDSTILL. IT'LL TAKE WEEKS OF MY PRECIOUS VACATION TO SHOP FOR A NEW COMPUTER AND GET EVERYTHING SET UP AGAIN.
I MIGHT SPEND THE NIGHT OVER THERE, BUT I'LL HAVE IT BACK BY MORNING.
A TIP O' THE NIB TO TAYLOR ROTHBELL
WAIT, YOU CAN'T TAKE HER CAR! I NEED IT TO GO TEST DRIVE A SUBARU ACROSS TOWN AT 8.
CLASSIFIE
TAKE MINE. SO YOU'RE NOT GONNA HAVE JERRY FIX YOUR COROLLA?
NO, I NEED SOMETHING NEWER IN CASE SPARROW DECIDES TO HAVE THE BABY. I'M ACTUALLY LOOKING AT STATION WAGONS. I ALWAYS SORT OF EQUATED MY DAD WITH OUR STATION WAGON. THEY HAD, LIKE, THE SAME EXPRESSION.

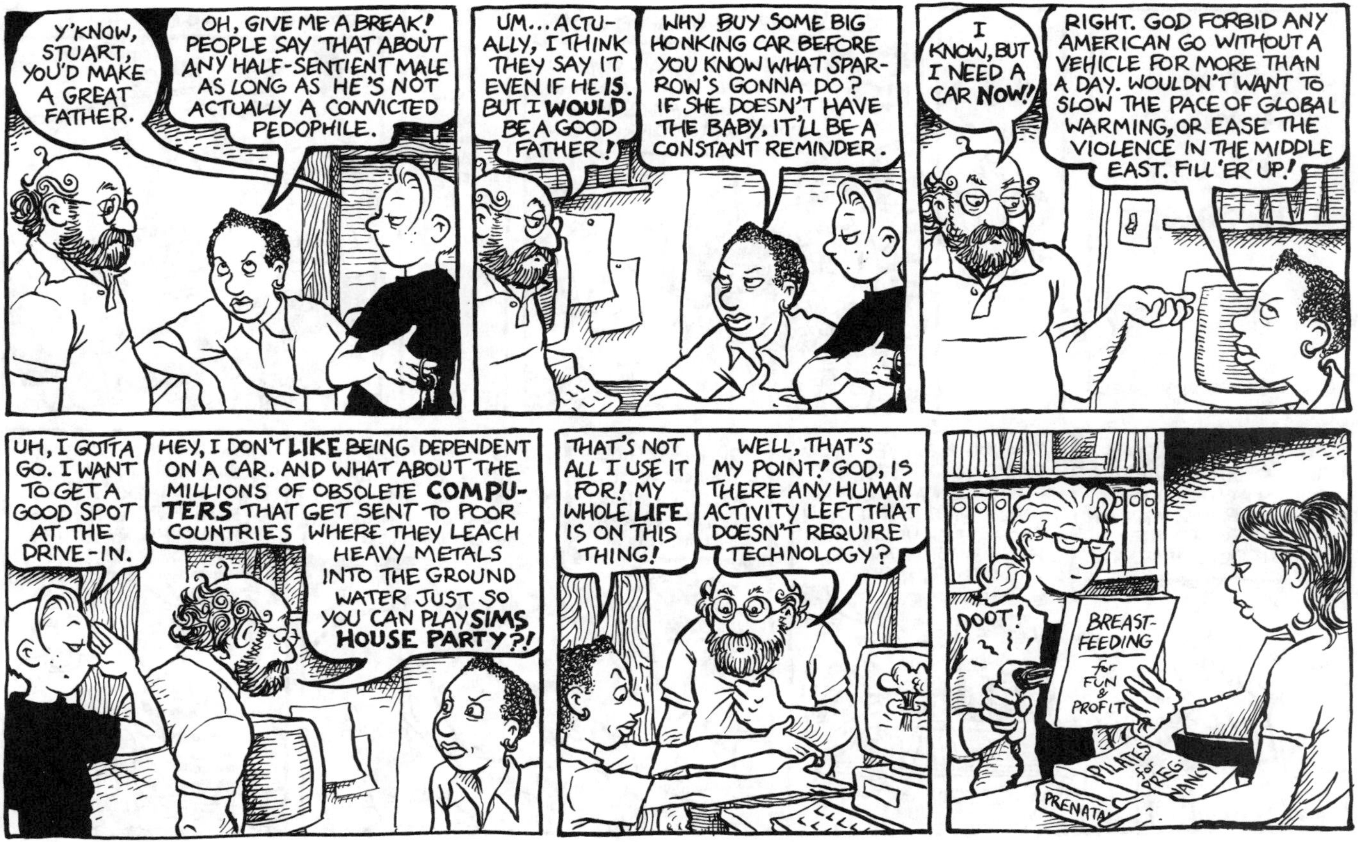
Y'KNOW, STUART, YOU'D MAKE A GREAT FATHER.
OH, GIVE ME A BREAK! PEOPLE SAY THAT ABOUT ANY HALF-SENTIENT MALE AS LONG AS HE'S NOT ACTUALLY A CONVICTED PEDOPHILE.
UM... ACTUALLY, I THINK THEY SAY IT EVEN IF HE **IS**. BUT I **WOULD** BE A GOOD FATHER!
WHY BUY SOME BIG HONKING CAR BEFORE YOU KNOW WHAT SPARROW'S GONNA DO? IF SHE DOESN'T HAVE THE BABY, IT'LL BE A CONSTANT REMINDER.
I KNOW, BUT I NEED A CAR **NOW**!
RIGHT. GOD FORBID ANY AMERICAN GO WITHOUT A VEHICLE FOR MORE THAN A DAY. WOULDN'T WANT TO SLOW THE PACE OF GLOBAL WARMING, OR EASE THE VIOLENCE IN THE MIDDLE EAST. FILL 'ER UP!
UH, I GOTTA GO. I WANT TO GET A GOOD SPOT AT THE DRIVE-IN.
HEY, I DON'T **LIKE** BEING DEPENDENT ON A CAR. AND WHAT ABOUT THE MILLIONS OF OBSOLETE **COMPUTERS** THAT GET SENT TO POOR COUNTRIES WHERE THEY LEACH HEAVY METALS INTO THE GROUND WATER JUST SO YOU CAN PLAY **SIMS HOUSE PARTY**?!
THAT'S NOT ALL I USE IT FOR! MY WHOLE **LIFE** IS ON THIS THING!
WELL, THAT'S MY POINT! GOD, IS THERE ANY HUMAN ACTIVITY LEFT THAT DOESN'T REQUIRE TECHNOLOGY?
DOOT!
BREAST-FEEDING for FUN & PROFIT
PILATES for PREGNANCY
PRENATA

the Summer of Our Discontent

©2002 BY ALISON BECHDEL

394

AH, SUMMER-TIME!

TIME TO KICK BACK AND HAVE A NICE, COOL GLASS OF LEMON-ADE...

...OR PERHAPS A FIT OF APOPLEXY.

NGH!

...TODAY, THE PALESTINIAN PEOPLE LIVE IN ECONOMIC STAGNATION, MADE WORSE BY OFFICIAL CORRUPTION...

FISH ARE JUMPIN'! AND THE COTTON IS HIGH!

...OR PERHAPS NOT.

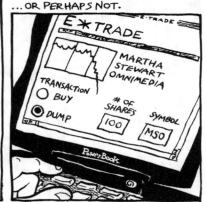

E*TRADE

MARTHA STEWART OMNIMEDIA

TRANSACTION
○ BUY
● DUMP

OF SHARES
100

SYMBOL
MSO

PowerBook

...A PALESTINIAN STATE WILL REQUIRE A VIBRANT ECONOMY, WHERE HONEST ENTERPRISE IS ENCOURAGED BY HONEST GOVERNMENT...

CAN YOU BELIEVE THIS DYNASTIC **DIPSTICK**?! IF IT WEREN'T FOR DIS-HONEST ENTERPRISE AND DISHONEST GOVERNMENT, HE'D BE SELLING PRE-OWNED **BUICKS**.

BIRDS

GOD. EVERY TIME I DOWNLOAD THE LATEST QUOTES, MY NET WORTH PLUNGES.

THIS IS HIS MIDEAST "PLAN"? HOPE THAT ARAFAT GOES AWAY, AND LET ISRAEL CONTINUE THE OCCUPATION?

SOUNDS A LOT LIKE HIS GLOBAL WARMING "PLAN." PRETEND THERE'S NOT A RAGING **FIRE** GOING ON, BUT AT THE SAME TIME, THROW MORE **FUEL** ON IT.

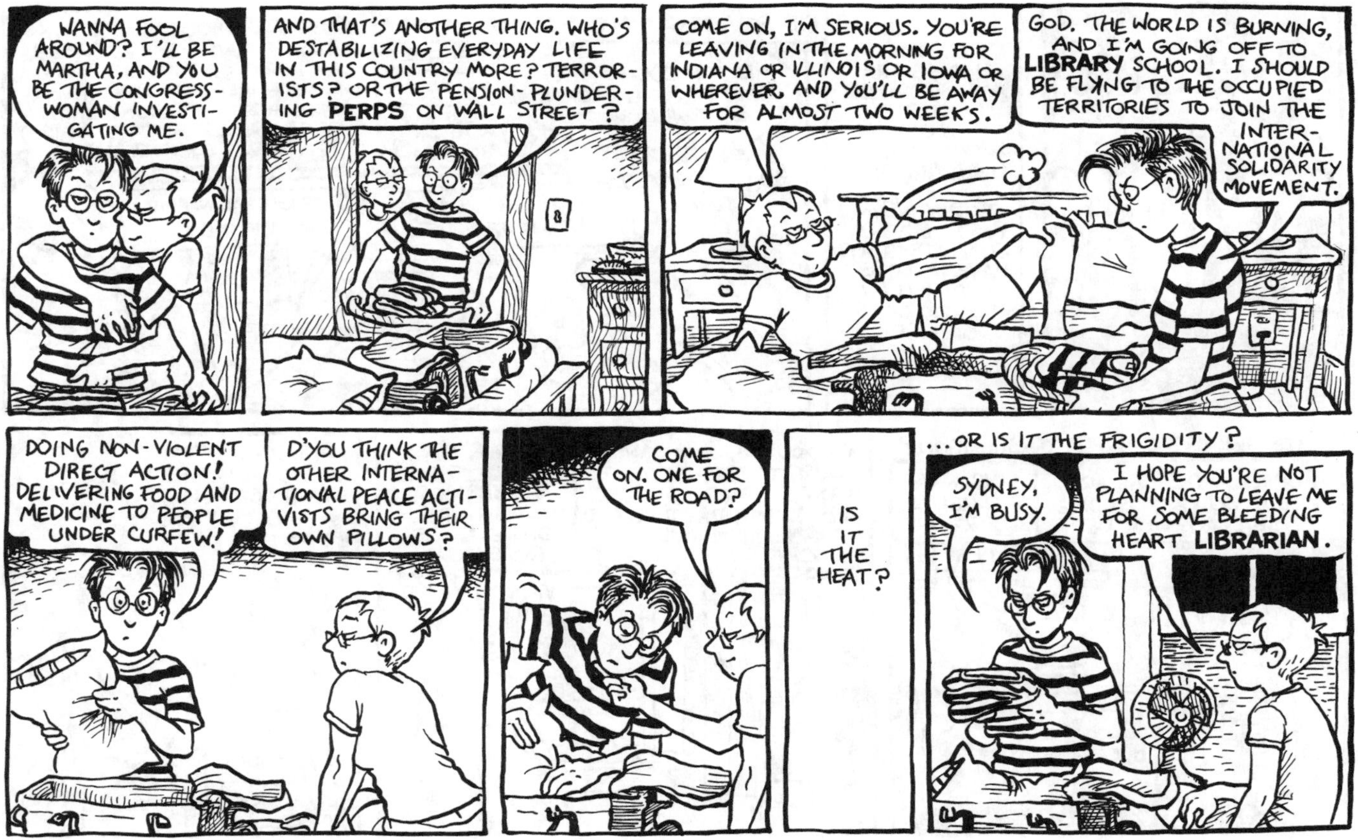
WANNA FOOL AROUND? I'LL BE MARTHA, AND YOU BE THE CONGRESS-WOMAN INVESTI-GATING ME.
AND THAT'S ANOTHER THING. WHO'S DESTABILIZING EVERYDAY LIFE IN THIS COUNTRY MORE? TERROR-ISTS? OR THE PENSION-PLUNDER-ING PERPS ON WALL STREET?
COME ON, I'M SERIOUS. YOU'RE LEAVING IN THE MORNING FOR INDIANA OR ILLINOIS OR IOWA OR WHEREVER, AND YOU'LL BE AWAY FOR ALMOST TWO WEEKS.
GOD. THE WORLD IS BURNING, AND I'M GOING OFF TO LIBRARY SCHOOL. I SHOULD BE FLYING TO THE OCCUPIED TERRITORIES TO JOIN THE INTER-NATIONAL SOLIDARITY MOVEMENT.
DOING NON-VIOLENT DIRECT ACTION! DELIVERING FOOD AND MEDICINE TO PEOPLE UNDER CURFEW!
D'YOU THINK THE OTHER INTERNA-TIONAL PEACE ACTI-VISTS BRING THEIR OWN PILLOWS?
COME ON. ONE FOR THE ROAD?
IS IT THE HEAT?
...OR IS IT THE FRIGIDITY?
SYDNEY, I'M BUSY.
I HOPE YOU'RE NOT PLANNING TO LEAVE ME FOR SOME BLEEDING HEART LIBRARIAN.

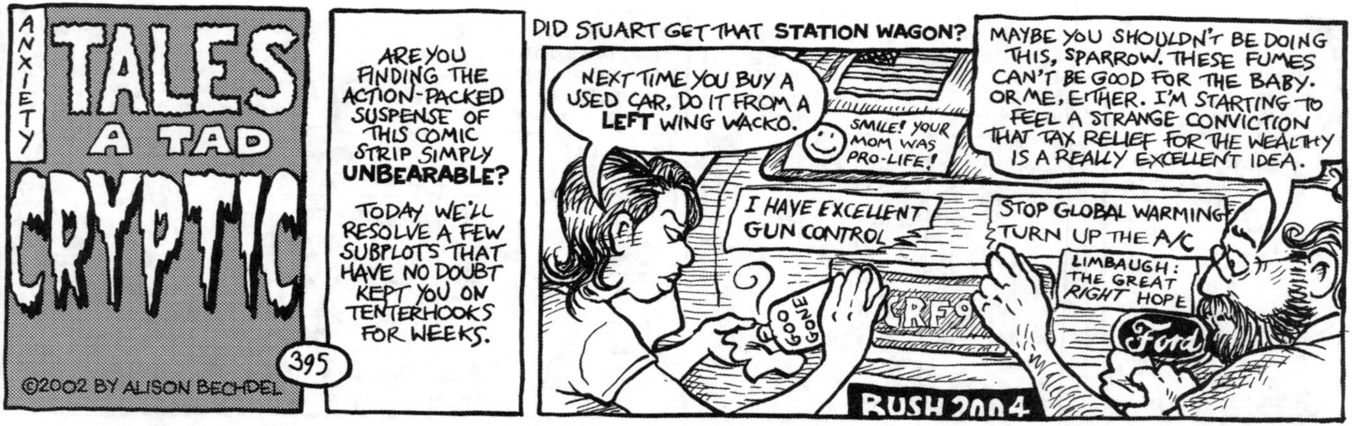
ANXIETY
TALES A TAD CRYPTIC
395
©2002 BY ALISON BECHDEL
ARE YOU FINDING THE ACTION-PACKED SUSPENSE OF THIS COMIC STRIP SIMPLY UNBEARABLE?
TODAY WE'LL RESOLVE A FEW SUBPLOTS THAT HAVE NO DOUBT KEPT YOU ON TENTERHOOKS FOR WEEKS.
DID STUART GET THAT STATION WAGON?
NEXT TIME YOU BUY A USED CAR, DO IT FROM A LEFT WING WACKO.
SMILE! YOUR MOM WAS PRO-LIFE!
I HAVE EXCELLENT GUN CONTROL
GOO GONE
CRF9
BUSH 2004
MAYBE YOU SHOULDN'T BE DOING THIS, SPARROW. THESE FUMES CAN'T BE GOOD FOR THE BABY. OR ME, EITHER. I'M STARTING TO FEEL A STRANGE CONVICTION THAT TAX RELIEF FOR THE WEALTHY IS A REALLY EXCELLENT IDEA.
STOP GLOBAL WARMING TURN UP THE A/C
LIMBAUGH: THE GREAT RIGHT HOPE
Ford

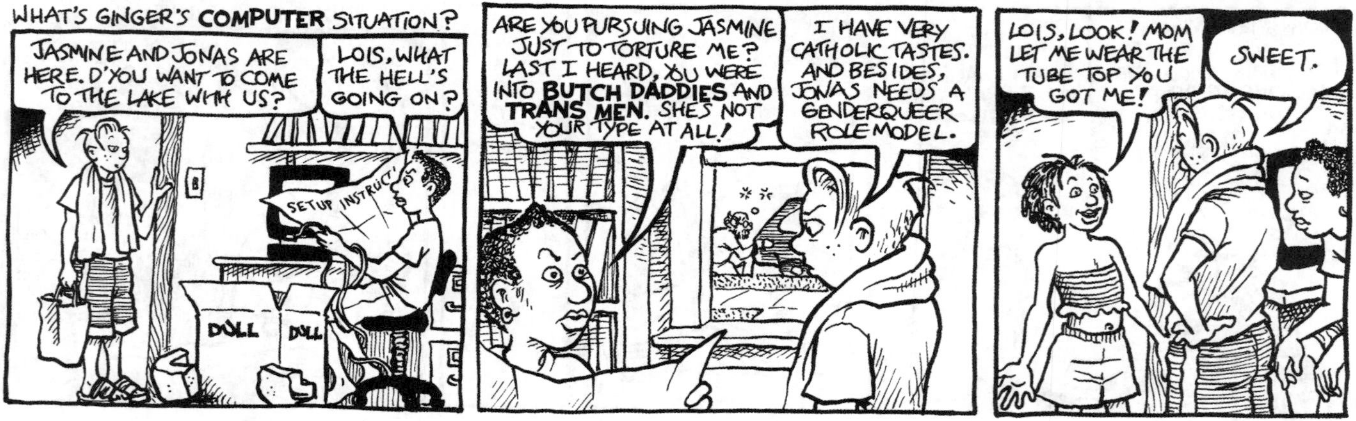
WHAT'S GINGER'S COMPUTER SITUATION?
JASMINE AND JONAS ARE HERE. D'YOU WANT TO COME TO THE LAKE WITH US?
LOIS, WHAT THE HELL'S GOING ON?
SETUP INSTRUCT
DOLL
DOLL
ARE YOU PURSUING JASMINE JUST TO TORTURE ME? LAST I HEARD, YOU WERE INTO BUTCH DADDIES AND TRANS MEN. SHE'S NOT YOUR TYPE AT ALL!
I HAVE VERY CATHOLIC TASTES. AND BESIDES, JONAS NEEDS A GENDERQUEER ROLE MODEL.
LOIS, LOOK! MOM LET ME WEAR THE TUBE TOP YOU GOT ME!
SWEET.

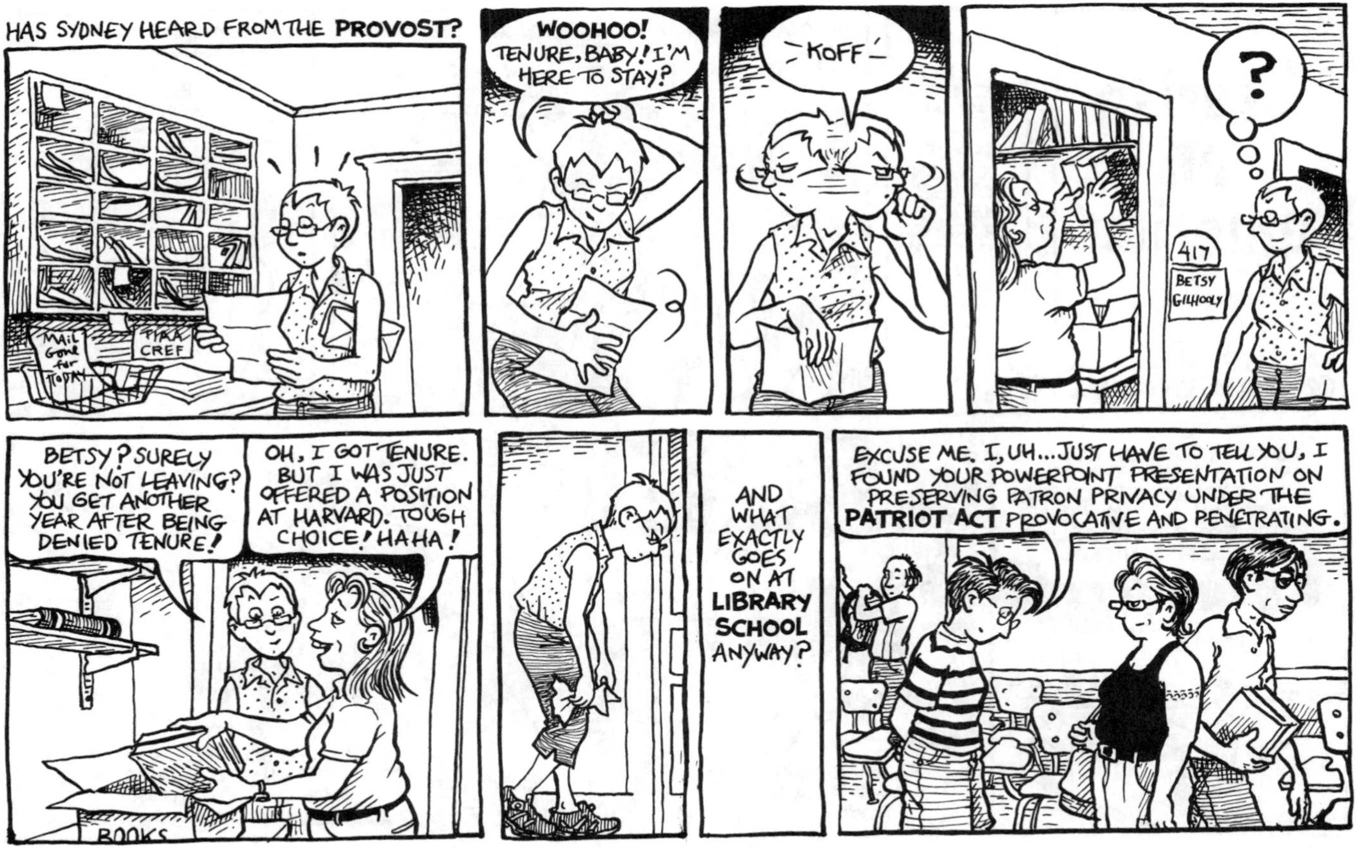
HAS SYDNEY HEARD FROM THE PROVOST?
MAIL GONE FOR TODAY
TIAA CREF
WOOHOO! TENURE, BABY! I'M HERE TO STAY!
KOFF
?
417
BETSY GILHOOLY
BETSY? SURELY YOU'RE NOT LEAVING? YOU GET ANOTHER YEAR AFTER BEING DENIED TENURE!
OH, I GOT TENURE. BUT I WAS JUST OFFERED A POSITION AT HARVARD. TOUGH CHOICE! HAHA!
BOOKS
AND WHAT EXACTLY GOES ON AT LIBRARY SCHOOL ANYWAY?
EXCUSE ME. I, UH...JUST HAVE TO TELL YOU, I FOUND YOUR POWERPOINT PRESENTATION ON PRESERVING PATRON PRIVACY UNDER THE PATRIOT ACT PROVOCATIVE AND PENETRATING.

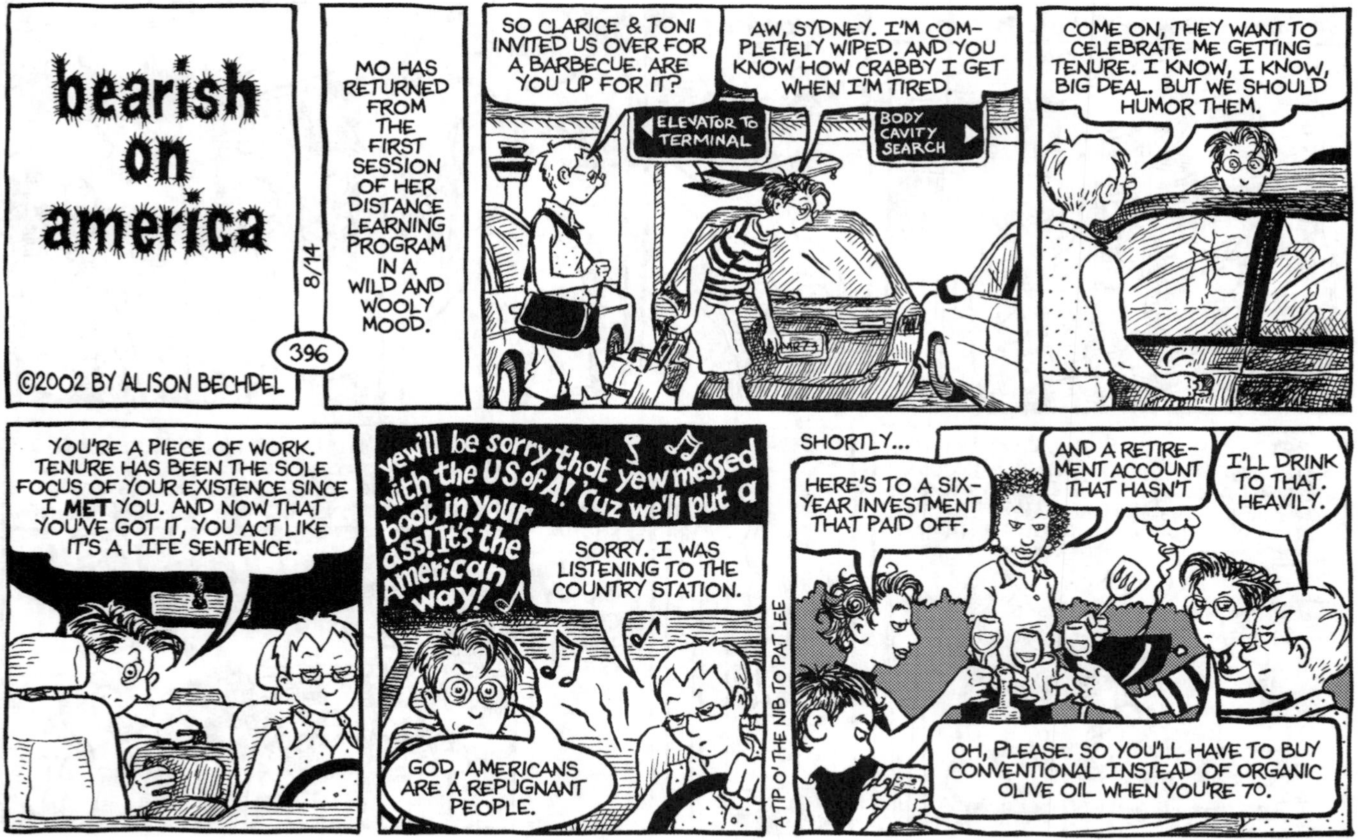
bearish on america
©2002 BY ALISON BECHDEL
396
8/14
MO HAS RETURNED FROM THE FIRST SESSION OF HER DISTANCE LEARNING PROGRAM IN A WILD AND WOOLY MOOD.
SO CLARICE & TONI INVITED US OVER FOR A BARBECUE. ARE YOU UP FOR IT?
AW, SYDNEY. I'M COMPLETELY WIPED. AND YOU KNOW HOW CRABBY I GET WHEN I'M TIRED.
ELEVATOR TO TERMINAL
BODY CAVITY SEARCH
COME ON, THEY WANT TO CELEBRATE ME GETTING TENURE. I KNOW, I KNOW, BIG DEAL. BUT WE SHOULD HUMOR THEM.
YOU'RE A PIECE OF WORK. TENURE HAS BEEN THE SOLE FOCUS OF YOUR EXISTENCE SINCE I MET YOU. AND NOW THAT YOU'VE GOT IT, YOU ACT LIKE IT'S A LIFE SENTENCE.
yew'll be sorry that yew messed with the US of A! 'Cuz we'll put a boot in your ass! It's the American way!
SORRY. I WAS LISTENING TO THE COUNTRY STATION.
GOD, AMERICANS ARE A REPUGNANT PEOPLE.
A TIP O' THE NIB TO PAT LEE
SHORTLY...
HERE'S TO A SIX-YEAR INVESTMENT THAT PAID OFF.
AND A RETIREMENT ACCOUNT THAT HASN'T
I'LL DRINK TO THAT. HEAVILY.
OH, PLEASE. SO YOU'LL HAVE TO BUY CONVENTIONAL INSTEAD OF ORGANIC OLIVE OIL WHEN YOU'RE 70.

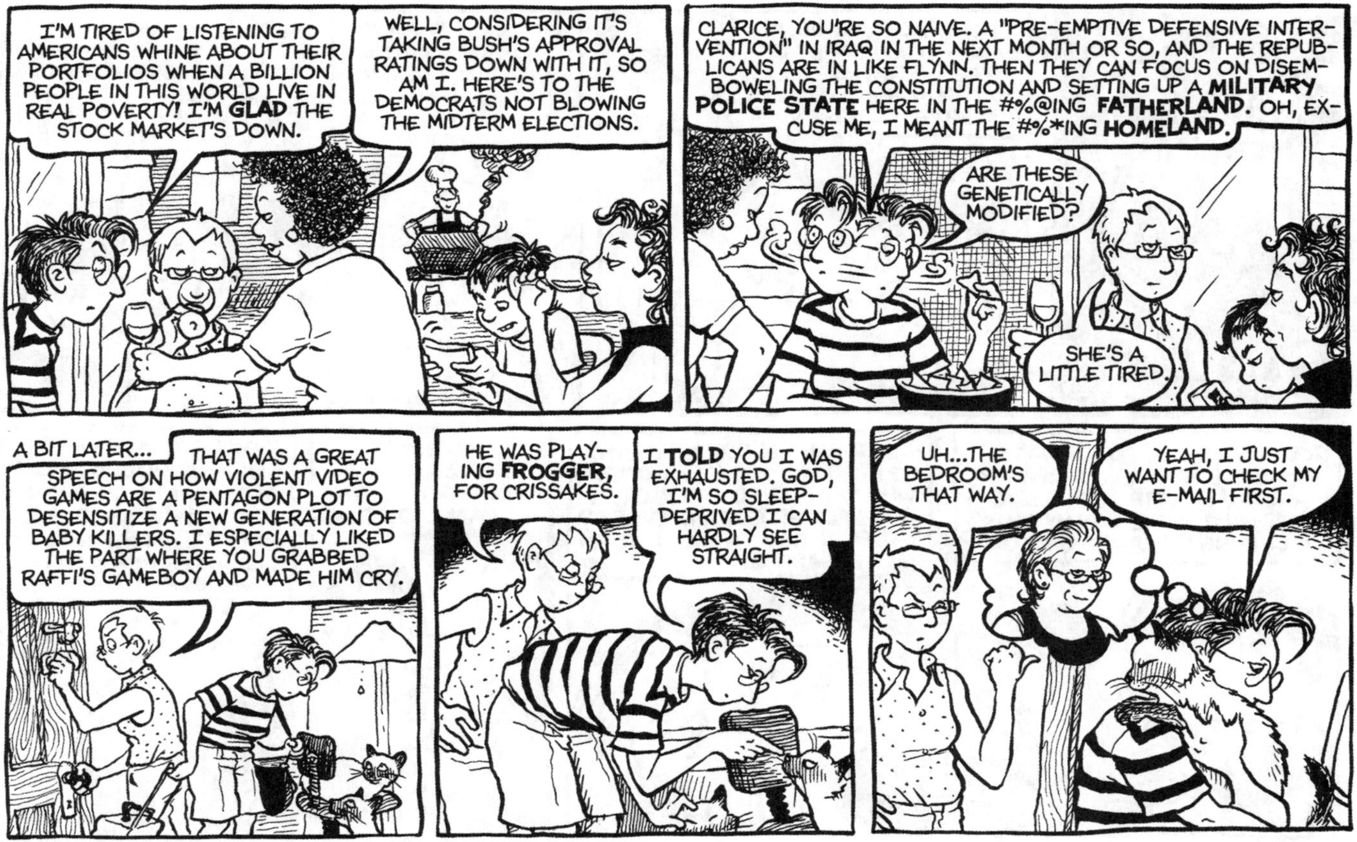
I'M TIRED OF LISTENING TO AMERICANS WHINE ABOUT THEIR PORTFOLIOS WHEN A BILLION PEOPLE IN THIS WORLD LIVE IN REAL POVERTY! I'M **GLAD** THE STOCK MARKET'S DOWN.
WELL, CONSIDERING IT'S TAKING BUSH'S APPROVAL RATINGS DOWN WITH IT, SO AM I. HERE'S TO THE DEMOCRATS NOT BLOWING THE MIDTERM ELECTIONS.
CLARICE, YOU'RE SO NAIVE. A "PRE-EMPTIVE DEFENSIVE INTERVENTION" IN IRAQ IN THE NEXT MONTH OR SO, AND THE REPUBLICANS ARE IN LIKE FLYNN. THEN THEY CAN FOCUS ON DISEMBOWELING THE CONSTITUTION AND SETTING UP A **MILITARY POLICE STATE** HERE IN THE #%@ING **FATHERLAND**. OH, EXCUSE ME, I MEANT THE #%*ING **HOMELAND**.
ARE THESE GENETICALLY MODIFIED?
SHE'S A LITTLE TIRED.
A BIT LATER...
THAT WAS A GREAT SPEECH ON HOW VIOLENT VIDEO GAMES ARE A PENTAGON PLOT TO DESENSITIZE A NEW GENERATION OF BABY KILLERS. I ESPECIALLY LIKED THE PART WHERE YOU GRABBED RAFFI'S GAMEBOY AND MADE HIM CRY.
HE WAS PLAYING **FROGGER**, FOR CRISSAKES.
I **TOLD** YOU I WAS EXHAUSTED. GOD, I'M SO SLEEP-DEPRIVED I CAN HARDLY SEE STRAIGHT.
UH...THE BEDROOM'S THAT WAY.
YEAH, I JUST WANT TO CHECK MY E-MAIL FIRST.

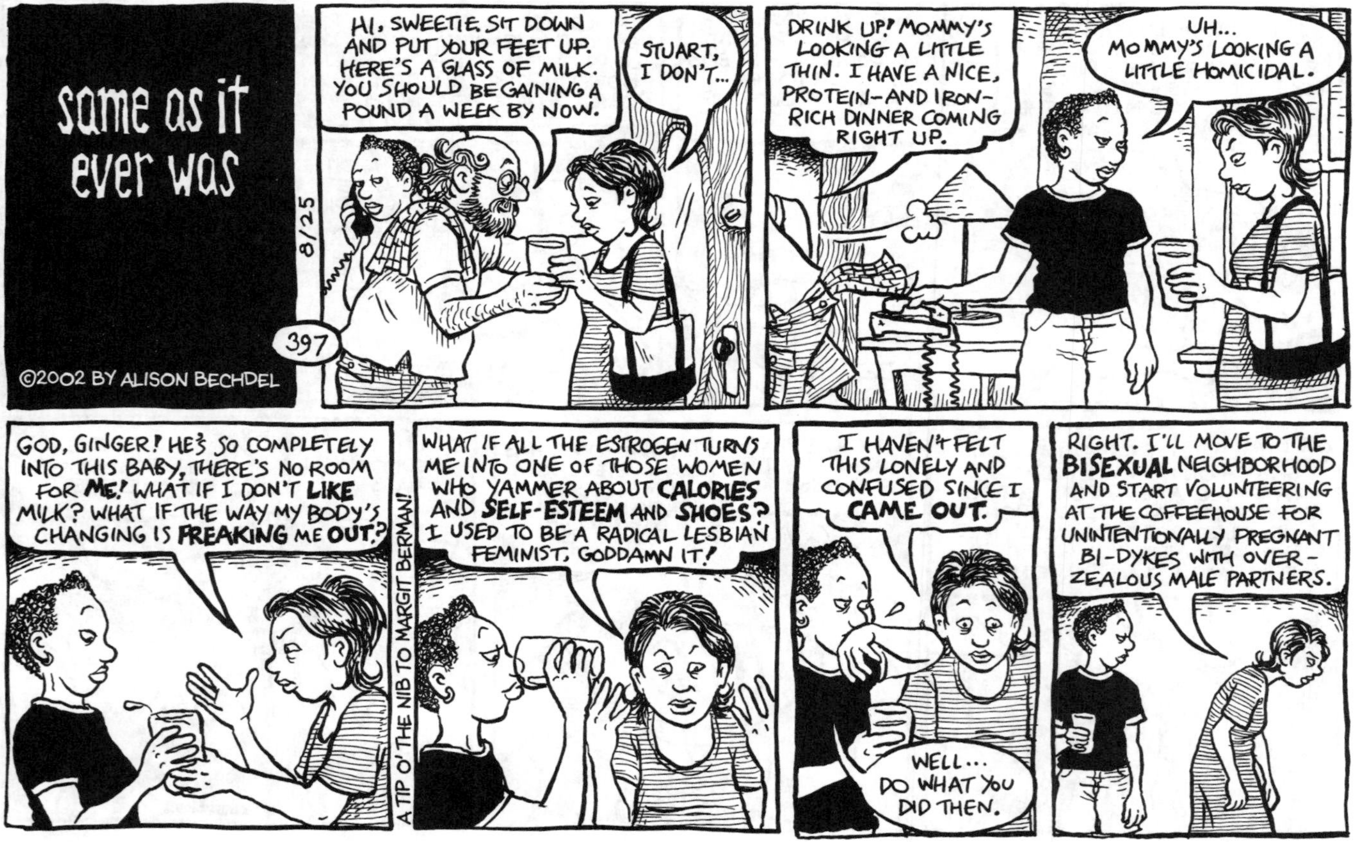
same as it ever was
©2002 BY ALISON BECHDEL
397
8/25
HI, SWEETIE. SIT DOWN AND PUT YOUR FEET UP. HERE'S A GLASS OF MILK. YOU SHOULD BE GAINING A POUND A WEEK BY NOW.
STUART, I DON'T...
DRINK UP! MOMMY'S LOOKING A LITTLE THIN. I HAVE A NICE, PROTEIN- AND IRON-RICH DINNER COMING RIGHT UP.
UH... MOMMY'S LOOKING A LITTLE HOMICIDAL.
GOD, GINGER! HE'S SO COMPLETELY INTO THIS BABY, THERE'S NO ROOM FOR ME! WHAT IF I DON'T LIKE MILK? WHAT IF THE WAY MY BODY'S CHANGING IS FREAKING ME OUT?
A TIP O' THE NIB TO MARGIT BERMAN!
WHAT IF ALL THE ESTROGEN TURNS ME INTO ONE OF THOSE WOMEN WHO YAMMER ABOUT CALORIES AND SELF-ESTEEM AND SHOES? I USED TO BE A RADICAL LESBIAN FEMINIST, GODDAMN IT!
I HAVEN'T FELT THIS LONELY AND CONFUSED SINCE I CAME OUT.
WELL... DO WHAT YOU DID THEN.
RIGHT. I'LL MOVE TO THE BISEXUAL NEIGHBORHOOD AND START VOLUNTEERING AT THE COFFEEHOUSE FOR UNINTENTIONALLY PREGNANT BI-DYKES WITH OVER-ZEALOUS MALE PARTNERS.

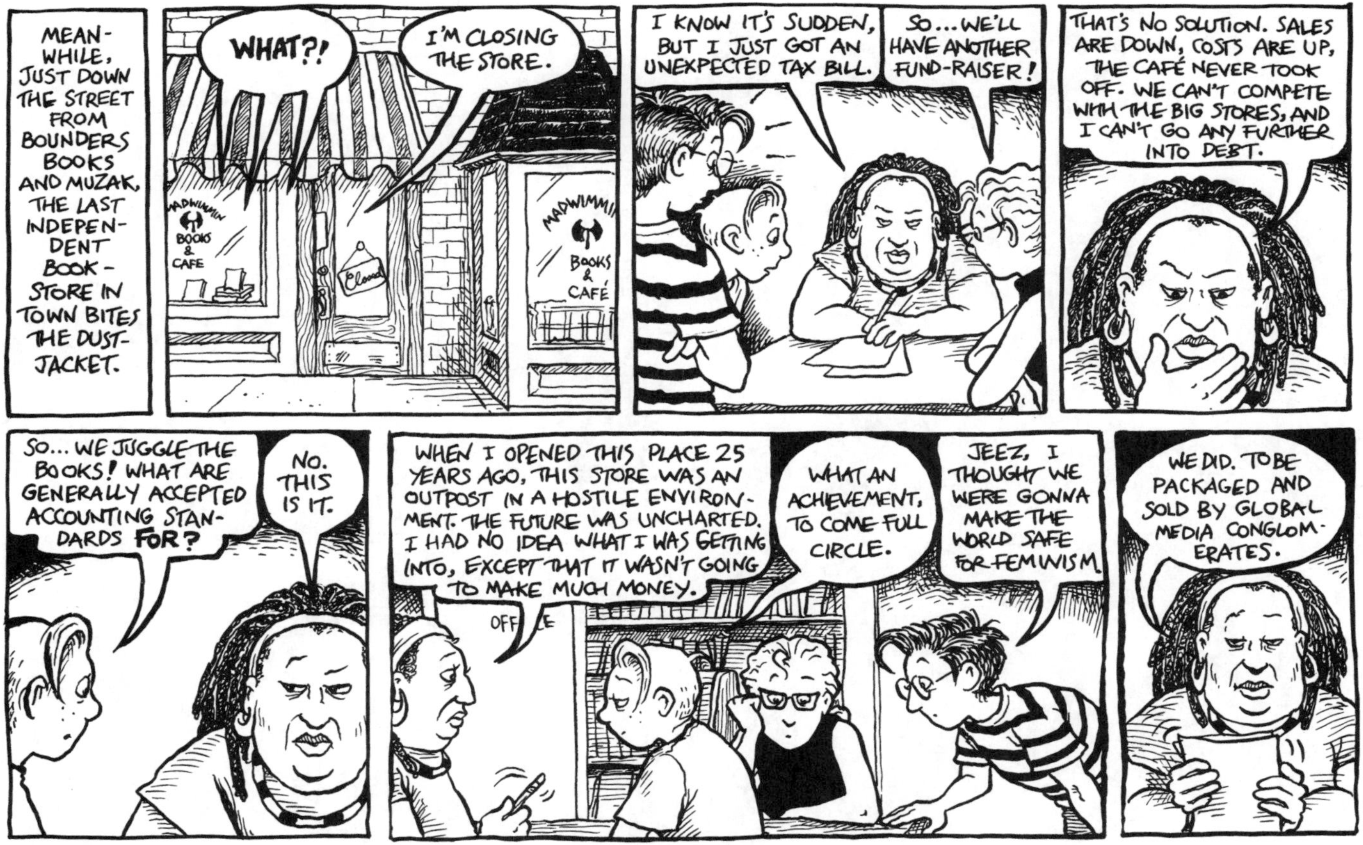
MEAN-WHILE, JUST DOWN THE STREET FROM BOUNDERS BOOKS AND MUZAK, THE LAST INDEPEN-DENT BOOK-STORE IN TOWN BITES THE DUST-JACKET.
WHAT?!
I'M CLOSING THE STORE.
MADWIMMIN BOOKS & CAFE
Closed
MADWIMMIN BOOKS & CAFÉ
I KNOW IT'S SUDDEN, BUT I JUST GOT AN UNEXPECTED TAX BILL.
SO... WE'LL HAVE ANOTHER FUND-RAISER!
THAT'S NO SOLUTION. SALES ARE DOWN, COSTS ARE UP, THE CAFÉ NEVER TOOK OFF. WE CAN'T COMPETE WITH THE BIG STORES, AND I CAN'T GO ANY FURTHER INTO DEBT.
SO... WE JUGGLE THE BOOKS! WHAT ARE GENERALLY ACCEPTED ACCOUNTING STAN-DARDS FOR?
NO. THIS IS IT.
WHEN I OPENED THIS PLACE 25 YEARS AGO, THIS STORE WAS AN OUTPOST IN A HOSTILE ENVIRON-MENT. THE FUTURE WAS UNCHARTED. I HAD NO IDEA WHAT I WAS GETTING INTO, EXCEPT THAT IT WASN'T GOING TO MAKE MUCH MONEY.
WHAT AN ACHIEVEMENT, TO COME FULL CIRCLE.
JEEZ, I THOUGHT WE WERE GONNA MAKE THE WORLD SAFE FOR FEMINISM.
WE DID. TO BE PACKAGED AND SOLD BY GLOBAL MEDIA CONGLOM-ERATES.

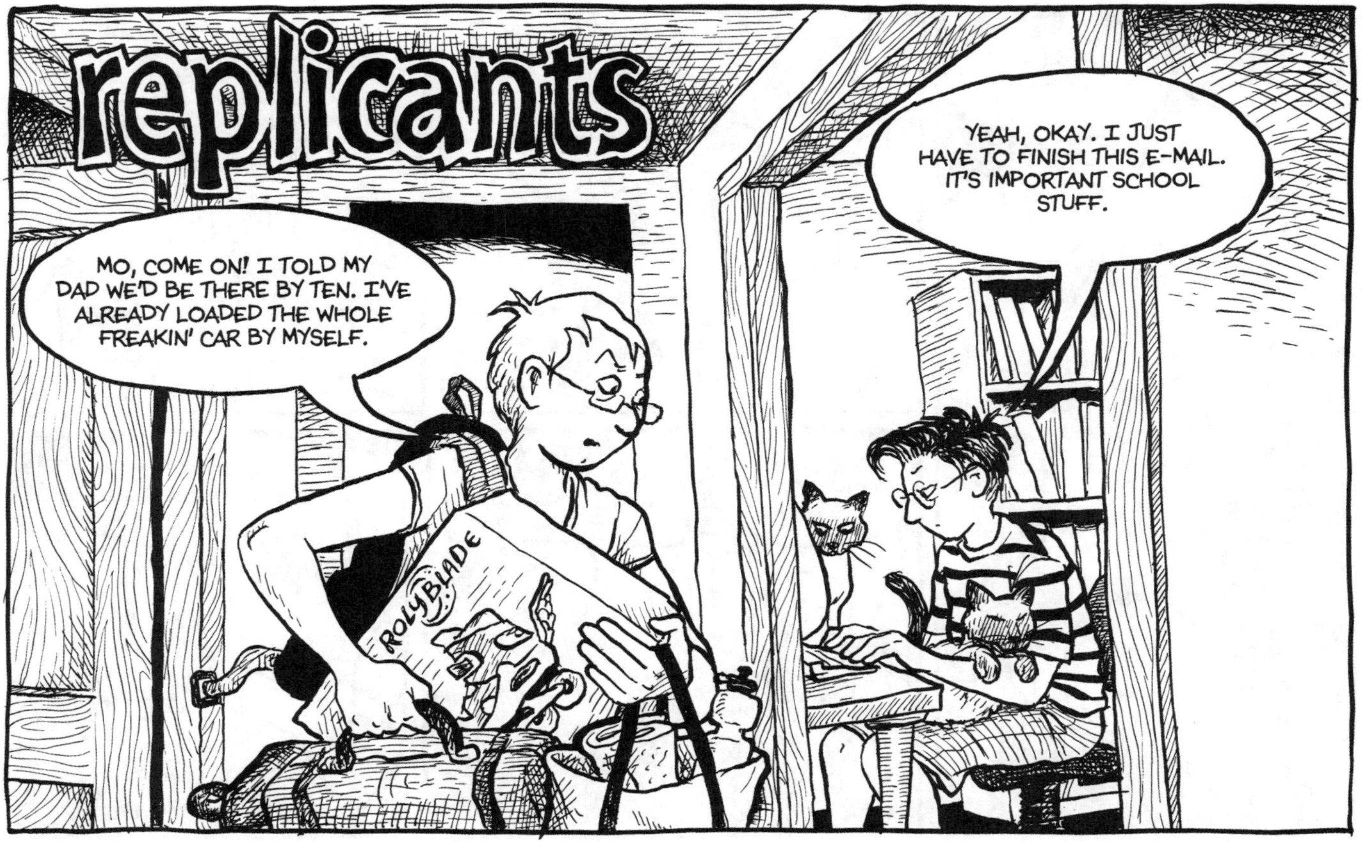
replicants
MO, COME ON! I TOLD MY DAD WE'D BE THERE BY TEN. I'VE ALREADY LOADED THE WHOLE FREAKIN' CAR BY MYSELF.
YEAH, OKAY. I JUST HAVE TO FINISH THIS E-MAIL. IT'S IMPORTANT SCHOOL STUFF.
ROLYBLADE

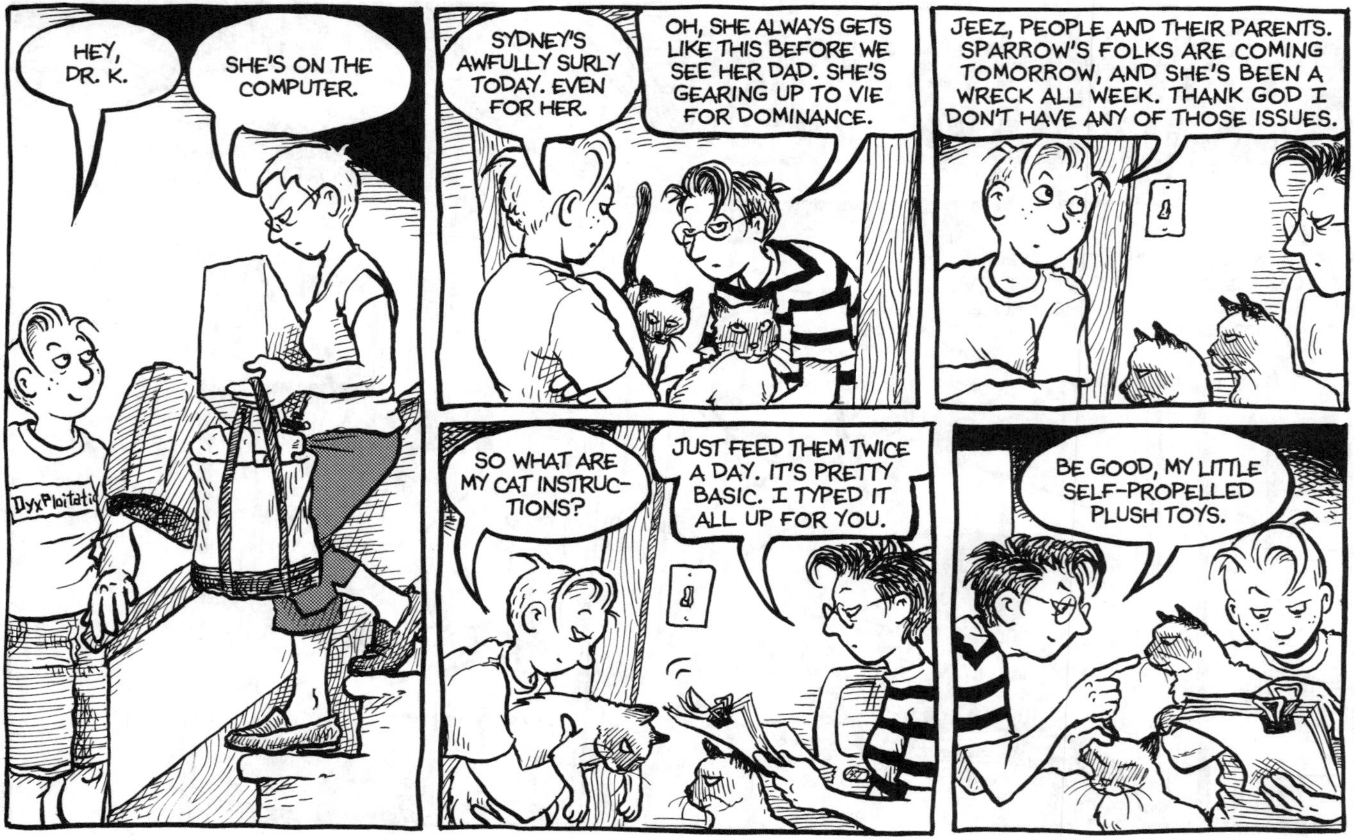
HEY, DR. K.
SHE'S ON THE COMPUTER.
DyxPloitatio
SYDNEY'S AWFULLY SURLY TODAY. EVEN FOR HER.
OH, SHE ALWAYS GETS LIKE THIS BEFORE WE SEE HER DAD. SHE'S GEARING UP TO VIE FOR DOMINANCE.
JEEZ, PEOPLE AND THEIR PARENTS. SPARROW'S FOLKS ARE COMING TOMORROW, AND SHE'S BEEN A WRECK ALL WEEK. THANK GOD I DON'T HAVE ANY OF THOSE ISSUES.
SO WHAT ARE MY CAT INSTRUCTIONS?
JUST FEED THEM TWICE A DAY. IT'S PRETTY BASIC. I TYPED IT ALL UP FOR YOU.
BE GOOD, MY LITTLE SELF-PROPELLED PLUSH TOYS.

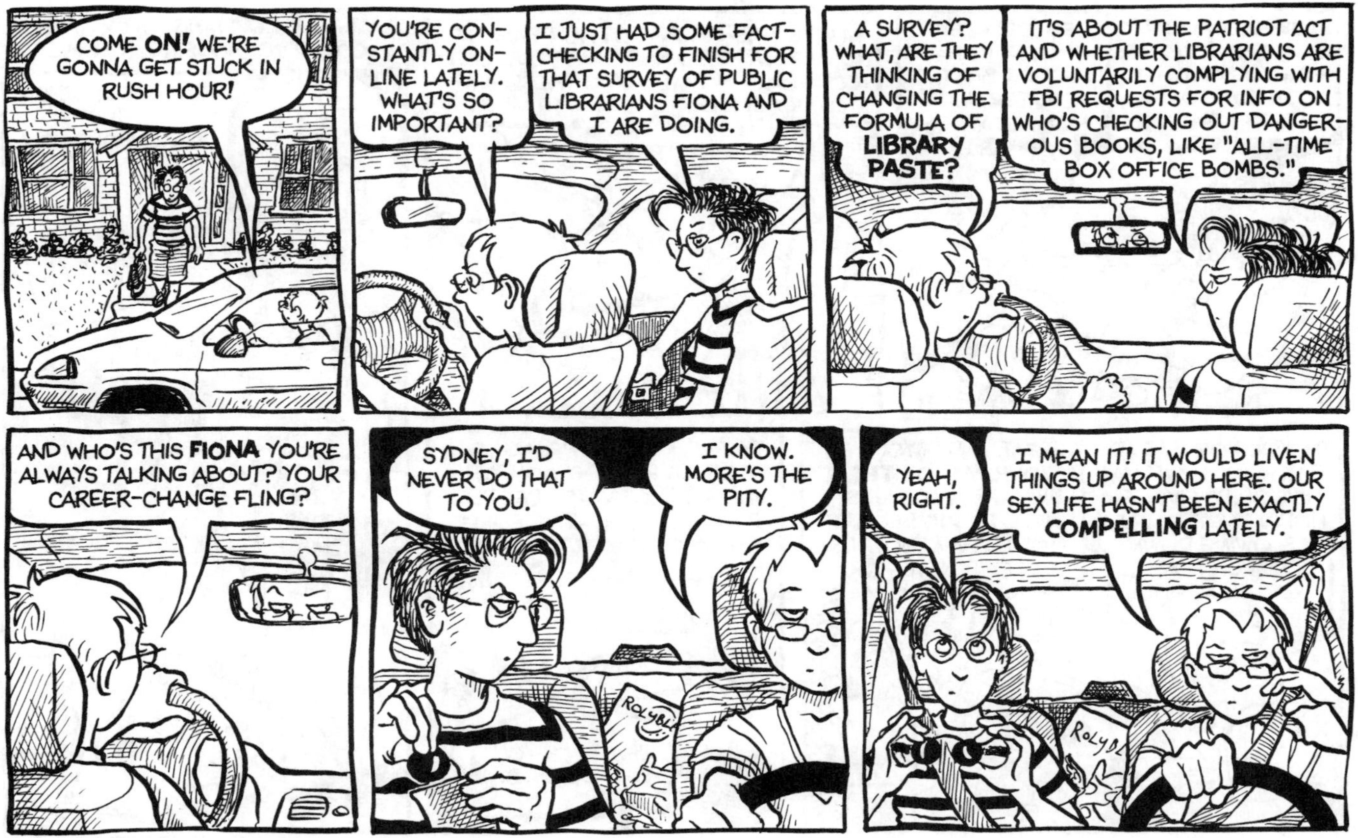
COME ON! WE'RE GONNA GET STUCK IN RUSH HOUR!
YOU'RE CONSTANTLY ONLINE LATELY. WHAT'S SO IMPORTANT?
I JUST HAD SOME FACT-CHECKING TO FINISH FOR THAT SURVEY OF PUBLIC LIBRARIANS FIONA AND I ARE DOING.
A SURVEY? WHAT, ARE THEY THINKING OF CHANGING THE FORMULA OF LIBRARY PASTE?
IT'S ABOUT THE PATRIOT ACT AND WHETHER LIBRARIANS ARE VOLUNTARILY COMPLYING WITH FBI REQUESTS FOR INFO ON WHO'S CHECKING OUT DANGEROUS BOOKS, LIKE "ALL-TIME BOX OFFICE BOMBS."
AND WHO'S THIS FIONA YOU'RE ALWAYS TALKING ABOUT? YOUR CAREER-CHANGE FLING?
SYDNEY, I'D NEVER DO THAT TO YOU.
I KNOW. MORE'S THE PITY.
YEAH, RIGHT.
I MEAN IT! IT WOULD LIVEN THINGS UP AROUND HERE. OUR SEX LIFE HASN'T BEEN EXACTLY COMPELLING LATELY.

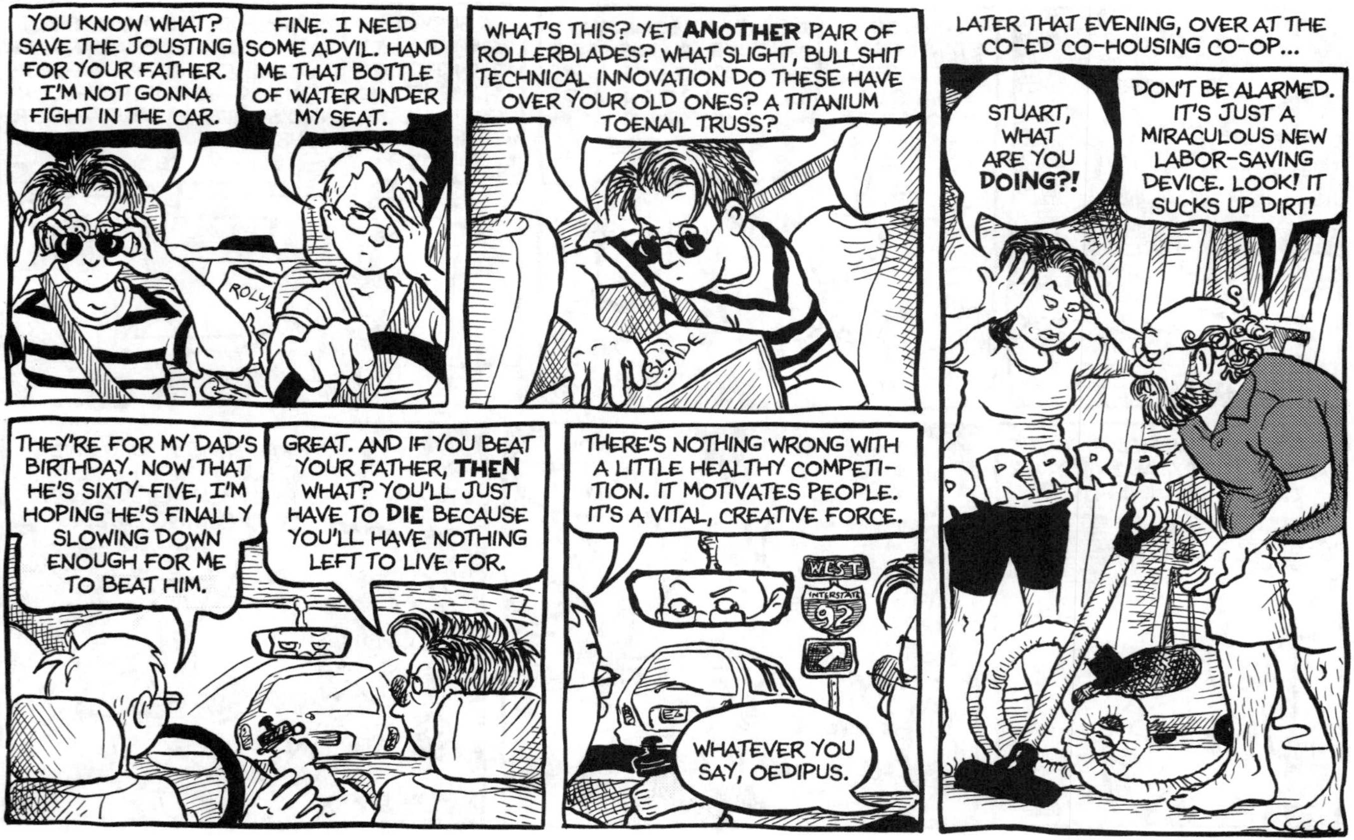
YOU KNOW WHAT? SAVE THE JOUSTING FOR YOUR FATHER. I'M NOT GONNA FIGHT IN THE CAR.
FINE. I NEED SOME ADVIL. HAND ME THAT BOTTLE OF WATER UNDER MY SEAT.
ROLY
WHAT'S THIS? YET **ANOTHER** PAIR OF ROLLERBLADES? WHAT SLIGHT, BULLSHIT TECHNICAL INNOVATION DO THESE HAVE OVER YOUR OLD ONES? A TITANIUM TOENAIL TRUSS?
BLADE
LATER THAT EVENING, OVER AT THE CO-ED CO-HOUSING CO-OP...
STUART, WHAT ARE YOU **DOING?!**
DON'T BE ALARMED. IT'S JUST A MIRACULOUS NEW LABOR-SAVING DEVICE. LOOK! IT SUCKS UP DIRT!
RRRRR
THEY'RE FOR MY DAD'S BIRTHDAY. NOW THAT HE'S SIXTY-FIVE, I'M HOPING HE'S FINALLY SLOWING DOWN ENOUGH FOR ME TO BEAT HIM.
GREAT. AND IF YOU BEAT YOUR FATHER, **THEN** WHAT? YOU'LL JUST HAVE TO **DIE** BECAUSE YOU'LL HAVE NOTHING LEFT TO LIVE FOR.
THERE'S NOTHING WRONG WITH A LITTLE HEALTHY COMPETITION. IT MOTIVATES PEOPLE. IT'S A VITAL, CREATIVE FORCE.
WEST
INTERSTATE 92
WHATEVER YOU SAY, OEDIPUS.

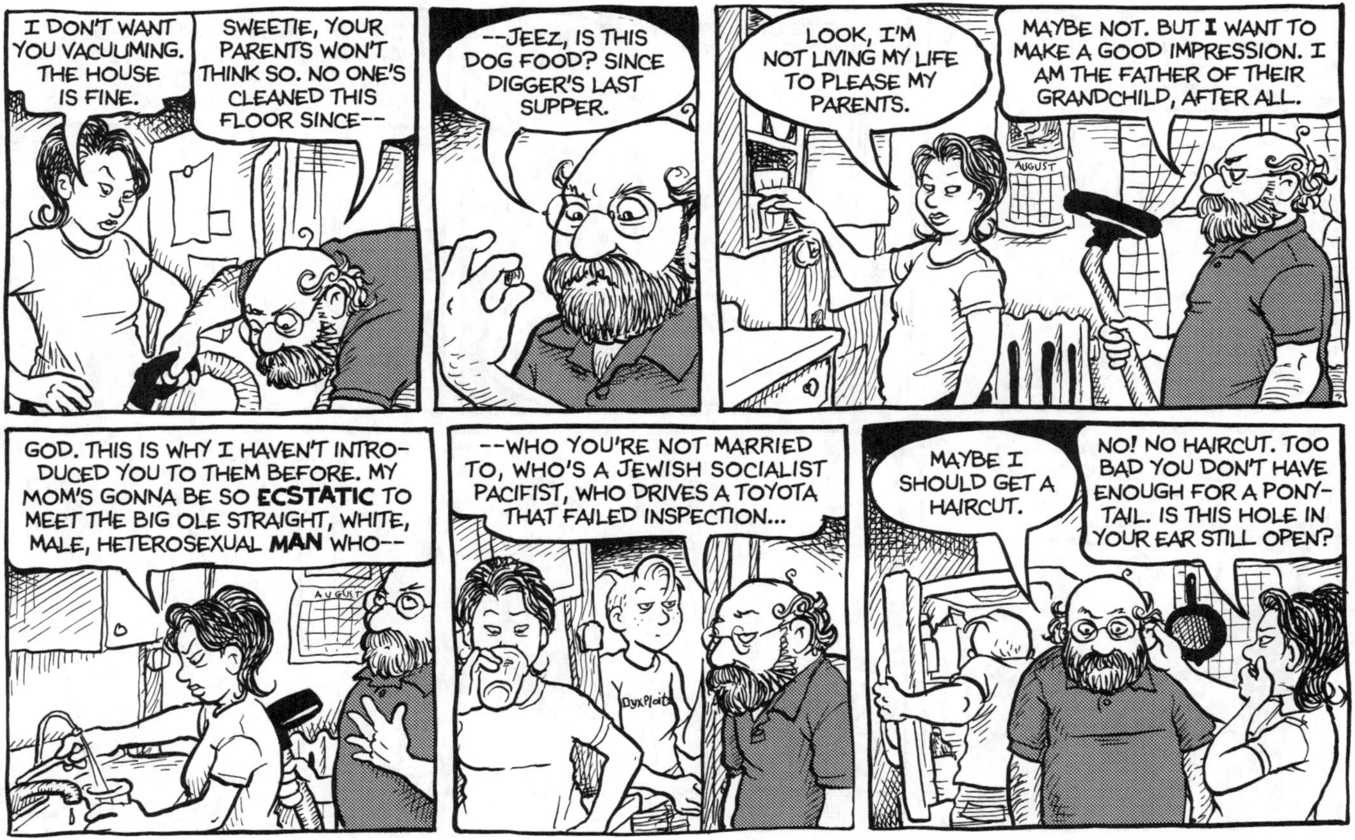
I DON'T WANT YOU VACUUMING. THE HOUSE IS FINE.
SWEETIE, YOUR PARENTS WON'T THINK SO. NO ONE'S CLEANED THIS FLOOR SINCE--
--JEEZ, IS THIS DOG FOOD? SINCE DIGGER'S LAST SUPPER.
LOOK, I'M NOT LIVING MY LIFE TO PLEASE MY PARENTS.
MAYBE NOT. BUT **I** WANT TO MAKE A GOOD IMPRESSION. I AM THE FATHER OF THEIR GRANDCHILD, AFTER ALL.
AUGUST
GOD. THIS IS WHY I HAVEN'T INTRODUCED YOU TO THEM BEFORE. MY MOM'S GONNA BE SO **ECSTATIC** TO MEET THE BIG OLE STRAIGHT, WHITE, MALE, HETEROSEXUAL **MAN** WHO--
AUGUST
--WHO YOU'RE NOT MARRIED TO, WHO'S A JEWISH SOCIALIST PACIFIST, WHO DRIVES A TOYOTA THAT FAILED INSPECTION...
MAYBE I SHOULD GET A HAIRCUT.
NO! NO HAIRCUT. TOO BAD YOU DON'T HAVE ENOUGH FOR A PONYTAIL. IS THIS HOLE IN YOUR EAR STILL OPEN?

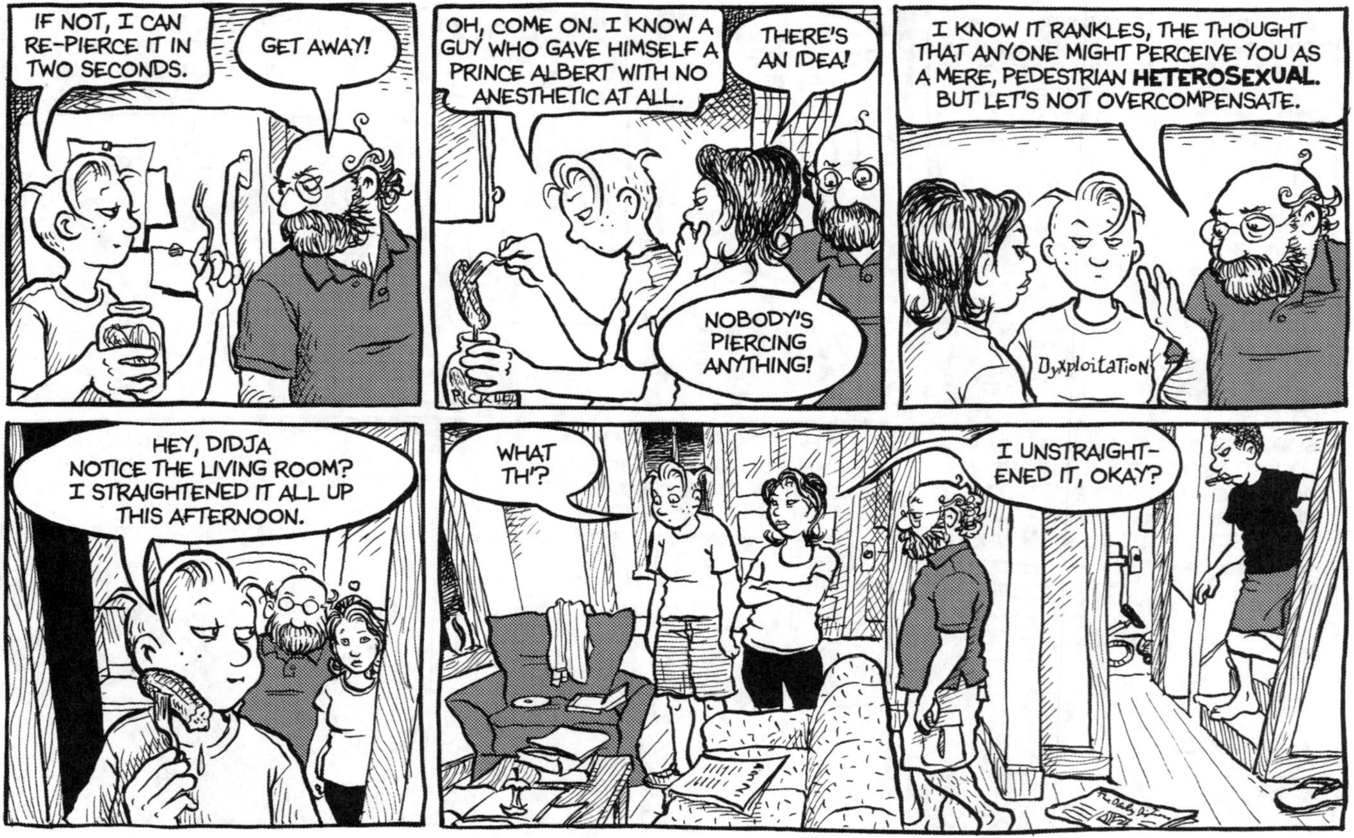

IF NOT, I CAN RE-PIERCE IT IN TWO SECONDS.
GET AWAY!
OH, COME ON. I KNOW A GUY WHO GAVE HIMSELF A PRINCE ALBERT WITH NO ANESTHETIC AT ALL.
THERE'S AN IDEA!
NOBODY'S PIERCING ANYTHING!
PICKLES
I KNOW IT RANKLES, THE THOUGHT THAT ANYONE MIGHT PERCEIVE YOU AS A MERE, PEDESTRIAN **HETEROSEXUAL.** BUT LET'S NOT OVERCOMPENSATE.
DyXploitaTioN
HEY, DIDJA NOTICE THE LIVING ROOM? I STRAIGHTENED IT ALL UP THIS AFTERNOON.
WHAT TH'?
I UNSTRAIGHT-ENED IT, OKAY?

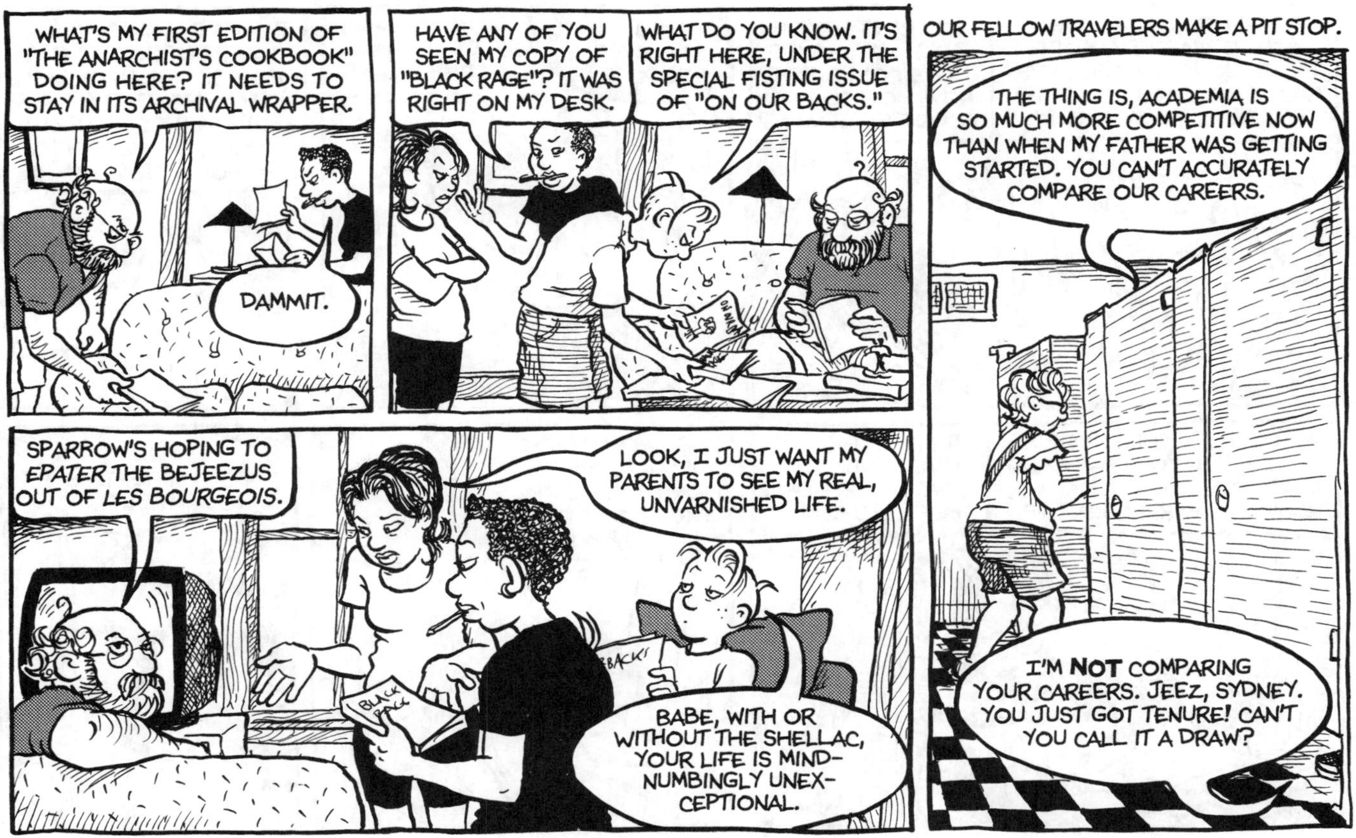
WHAT'S MY FIRST EDITION OF "THE ANARCHIST'S COOKBOOK" DOING HERE? IT NEEDS TO STAY IN ITS ARCHIVAL WRAPPER.
DAMMIT.
HAVE ANY OF YOU SEEN MY COPY OF "BLACK RAGE"? IT WAS RIGHT ON MY DESK.
WHAT DO YOU KNOW. IT'S RIGHT HERE, UNDER THE SPECIAL FISTING ISSUE OF "ON OUR BACKS."
SPARROW'S HOPING TO *EPATER* THE BEJEEZUS OUT OF *LES BOURGEOIS*.
LOOK, I JUST WANT MY PARENTS TO SEE MY REAL, UNVARNISHED LIFE.
BABE, WITH OR WITHOUT THE SHELLAC, YOUR LIFE IS MIND-NUMBINGLY UNEXCEPTIONAL.
OUR FELLOW TRAVELERS MAKE A PIT STOP.
THE THING IS, ACADEMIA IS SO MUCH MORE COMPETITIVE NOW THAN WHEN MY FATHER WAS GETTING STARTED. YOU CAN'T ACCURATELY COMPARE OUR CAREERS.
I'M **NOT** COMPARING YOUR CAREERS. JEEZ, SYDNEY. YOU JUST GOT TENURE! CAN'T YOU CALL IT A DRAW?

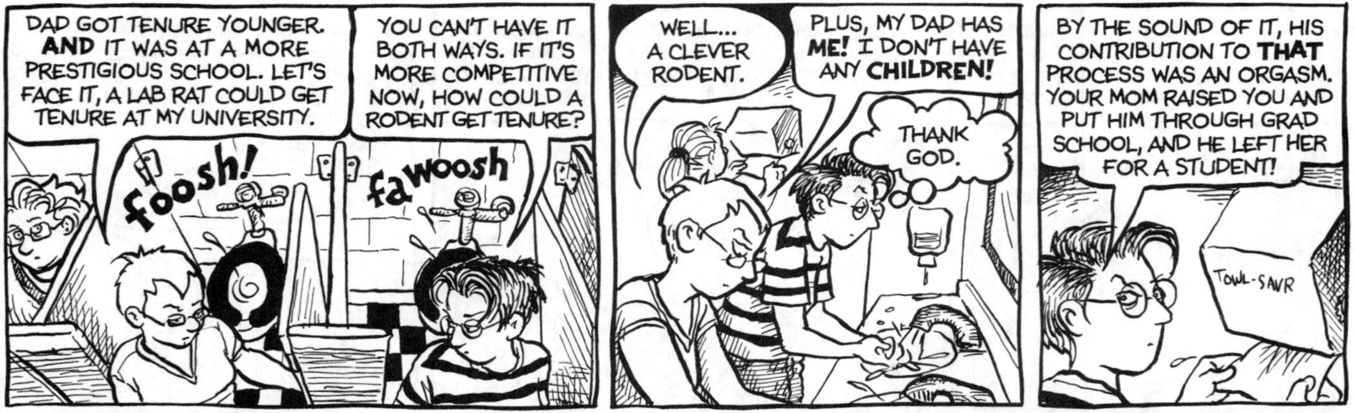
DAD GOT TENURE YOUNGER. AND IT WAS AT A MORE PRESTIGIOUS SCHOOL. LET'S FACE IT, A LAB RAT COULD GET TENURE AT MY UNIVERSITY.
foosh!
YOU CAN'T HAVE IT BOTH WAYS. IF IT'S MORE COMPETITIVE NOW, HOW COULD A RODENT GET TENURE?
fawoosh
WELL... A CLEVER RODENT.
PLUS, MY DAD HAS ME! I DON'T HAVE ANY CHILDREN!
THANK GOD.
BY THE SOUND OF IT, HIS CONTRIBUTION TO THAT PROCESS WAS AN ORGASM. YOUR MOM RAISED YOU AND PUT HIM THROUGH GRAD SCHOOL, AND HE LEFT HER FOR A STUDENT!
TOWL-SAVR

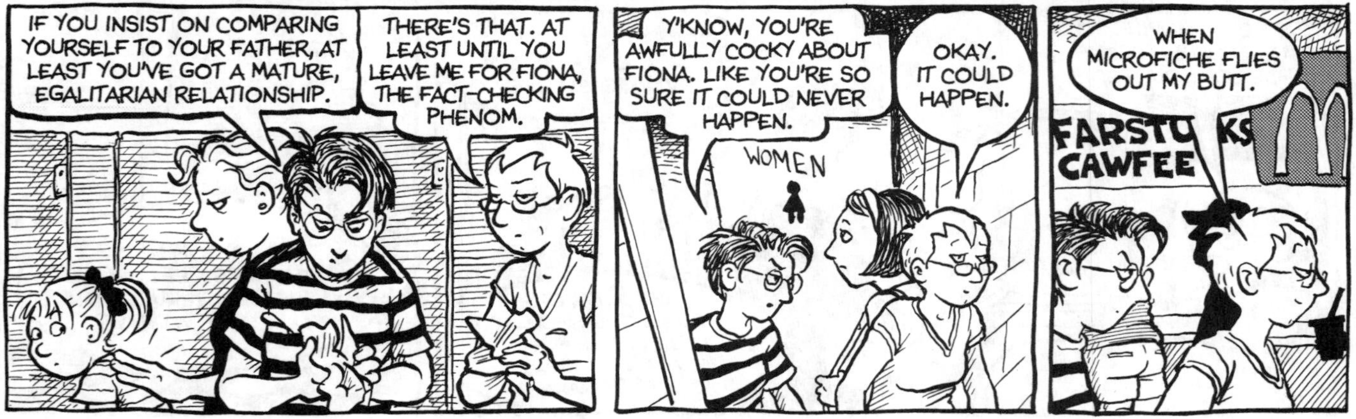
IF YOU INSIST ON COMPARING YOURSELF TO YOUR FATHER, AT LEAST YOU'VE GOT A MATURE, EGALITARIAN RELATIONSHIP.
THERE'S THAT. AT LEAST UNTIL YOU LEAVE ME FOR FIONA, THE FACT-CHECKING PHENOM.
Y'KNOW, YOU'RE AWFULLY COCKY ABOUT FIONA. LIKE YOU'RE SO SURE IT COULD NEVER HAPPEN.
OKAY. IT COULD HAPPEN.
WOMEN
WHEN MICROFICHE FLIES OUT MY BUTT.
FARSTU KS CAWFEE

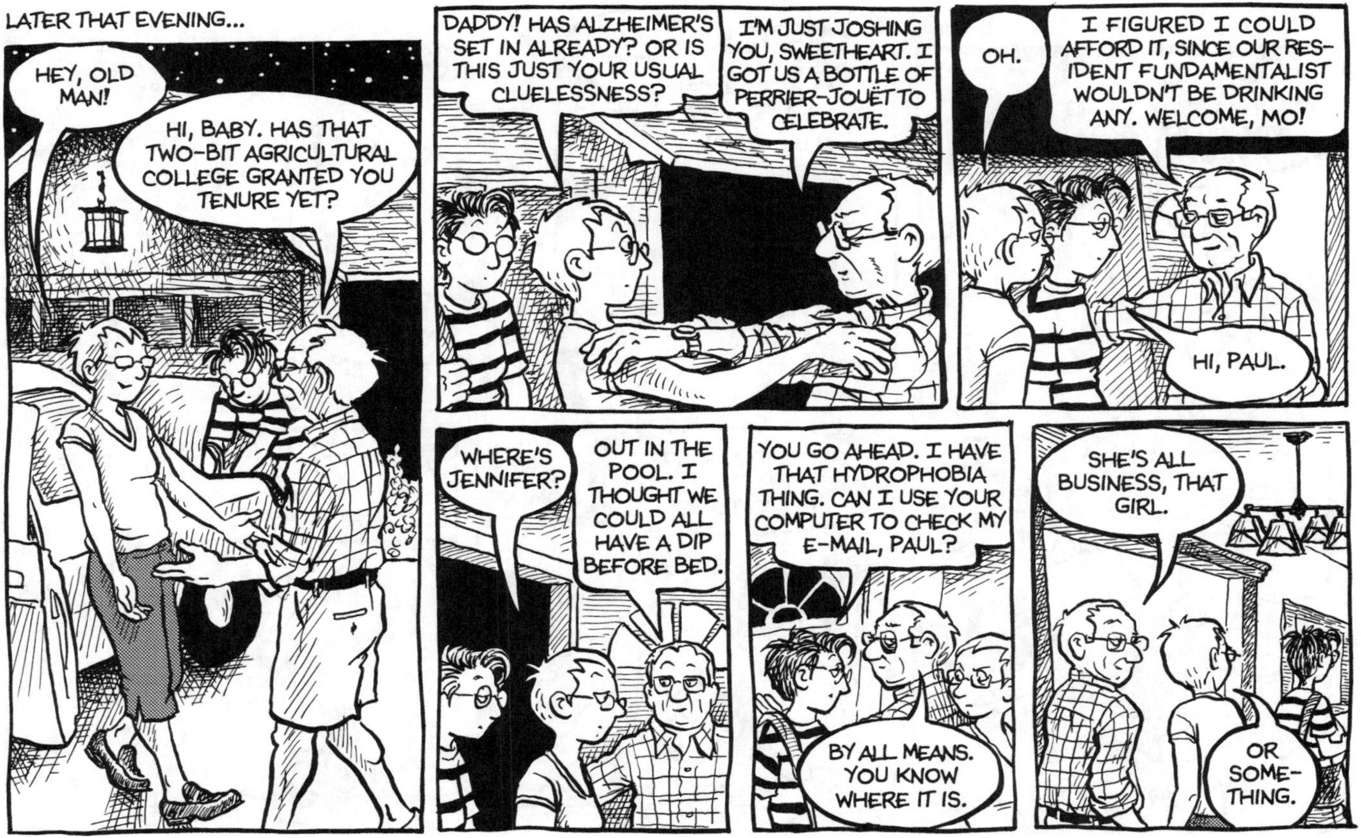
LATER THAT EVENING...
HEY, OLD MAN!
HI, BABY. HAS THAT TWO-BIT AGRICULTURAL COLLEGE GRANTED YOU TENURE YET?
DADDY! HAS ALZHEIMER'S SET IN ALREADY? OR IS THIS JUST YOUR USUAL CLUELESSNESS?
I'M JUST JOSHING YOU, SWEETHEART. I GOT US A BOTTLE OF PERRIER-JOUËT TO CELEBRATE.
OH.
I FIGURED I COULD AFFORD IT, SINCE OUR RES-IDENT FUNDAMENTALIST WOULDN'T BE DRINKING ANY. WELCOME, MO!
HI, PAUL.
WHERE'S JENNIFER?
OUT IN THE POOL. I THOUGHT WE COULD ALL HAVE A DIP BEFORE BED.
YOU GO AHEAD. I HAVE THAT HYDROPHOBIA THING. CAN I USE YOUR COMPUTER TO CHECK MY E-MAIL, PAUL?
BY ALL MEANS. YOU KNOW WHERE IT IS.
SHE'S ALL BUSINESS, THAT GIRL.
OR SOME-THING.

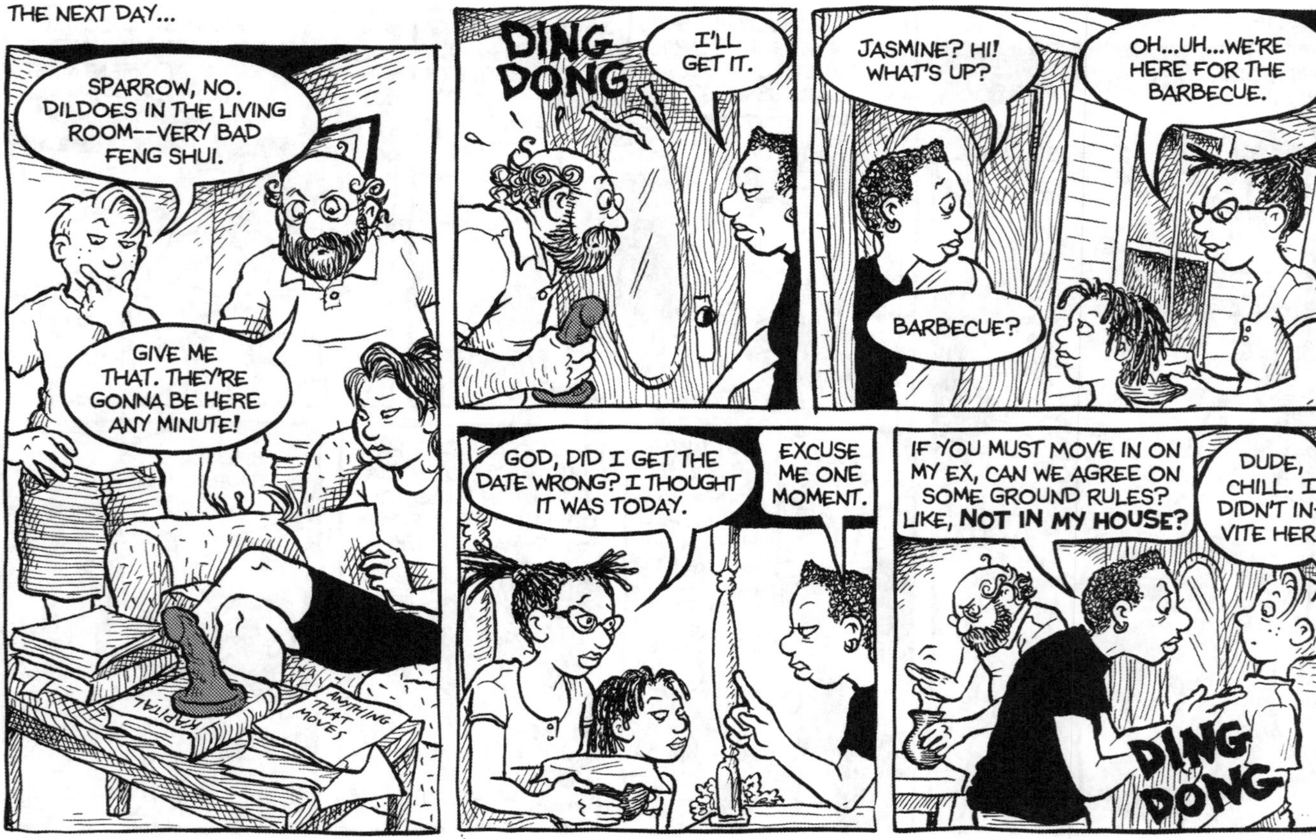
THE NEXT DAY...
SPARROW, NO. DILDOES IN THE LIVING ROOM--VERY BAD FENG SHUI.
GIVE ME THAT. THEY'RE GONNA BE HERE ANY MINUTE!
KAPITAL
ANYTHING THAT MOVES
DING DONG
I'LL GET IT.
JASMINE? HI! WHAT'S UP?
OH...UH...WE'RE HERE FOR THE BARBECUE.
BARBECUE?
GOD, DID I GET THE DATE WRONG? I THOUGHT IT WAS TODAY.
EXCUSE ME ONE MOMENT.
IF YOU MUST MOVE IN ON MY EX, CAN WE AGREE ON SOME GROUND RULES? LIKE, **NOT IN MY HOUSE?**
DUDE, CHILL. I DIDN'T IN-VITE HER.
DING DONG

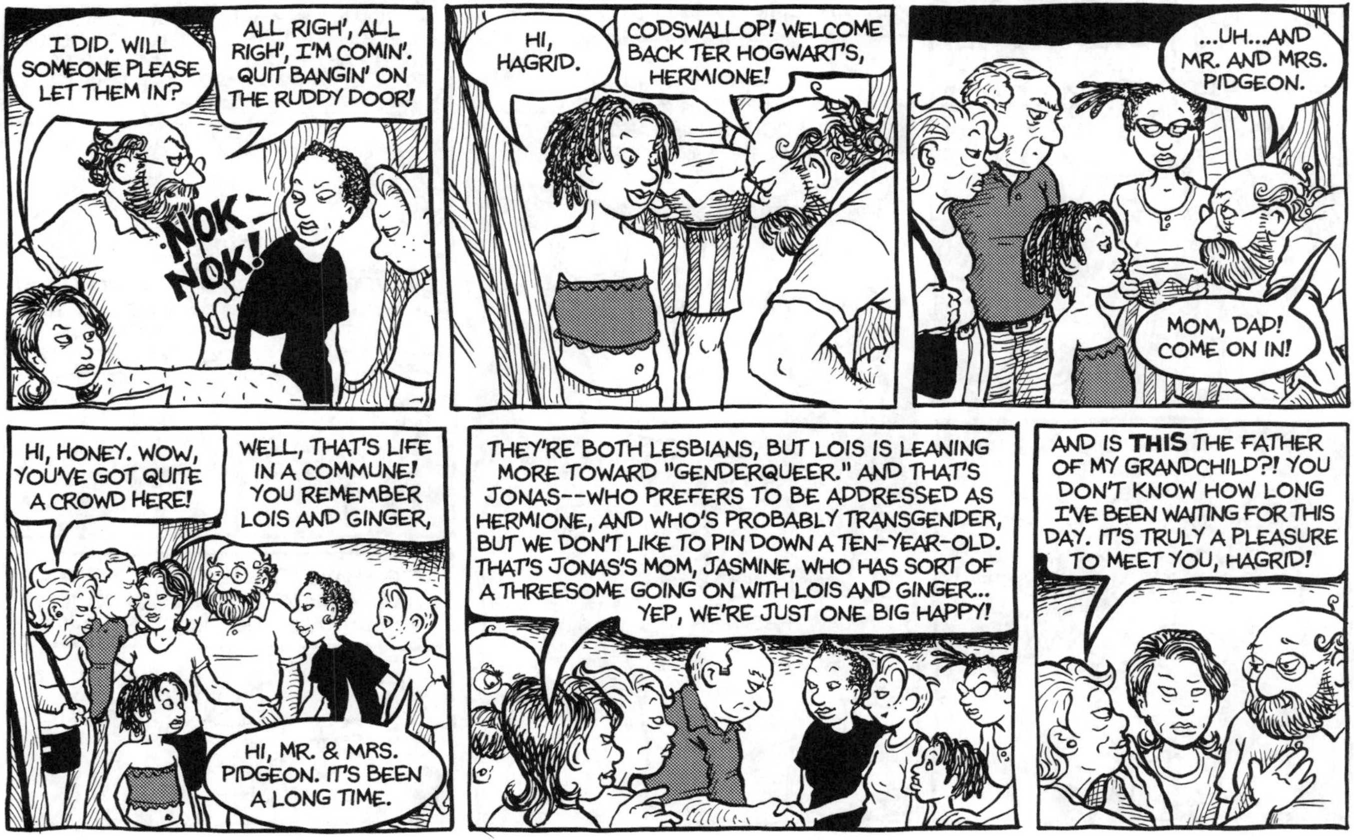

I DID. WILL SOMEONE PLEASE LET THEM IN?
ALL RIGH', ALL RIGH', I'M COMIN'. QUIT BANGIN' ON THE RUDDY DOOR!
NOK NOK!
HI, HAGRID.
CODSWALLOP! WELCOME BACK TER HOGWART'S, HERMIONE!
...UH...AND MR. AND MRS. PIDGEON.
MOM, DAD! COME ON IN!
HI, HONEY. WOW, YOU'VE GOT QUITE A CROWD HERE!
WELL, THAT'S LIFE IN A COMMUNE! YOU REMEMBER LOIS AND GINGER,
HI, MR. & MRS. PIDGEON. IT'S BEEN A LONG TIME.
THEY'RE BOTH LESBIANS, BUT LOIS IS LEANING MORE TOWARD "GENDERQUEER." AND THAT'S JONAS--WHO PREFERS TO BE ADDRESSED AS HERMIONE, AND WHO'S PROBABLY TRANSGENDER, BUT WE DON'T LIKE TO PIN DOWN A TEN-YEAR-OLD. THAT'S JONAS'S MOM, JASMINE, WHO HAS SORT OF A THREESOME GOING ON WITH LOIS AND GINGER... YEP, WE'RE JUST ONE BIG HAPPY!
AND IS **THIS** THE FATHER OF MY GRANDCHILD?! YOU DON'T KNOW HOW LONG I'VE BEEN WAITING FOR THIS DAY. IT'S TRULY A PLEASURE TO MEET YOU, HAGRID!

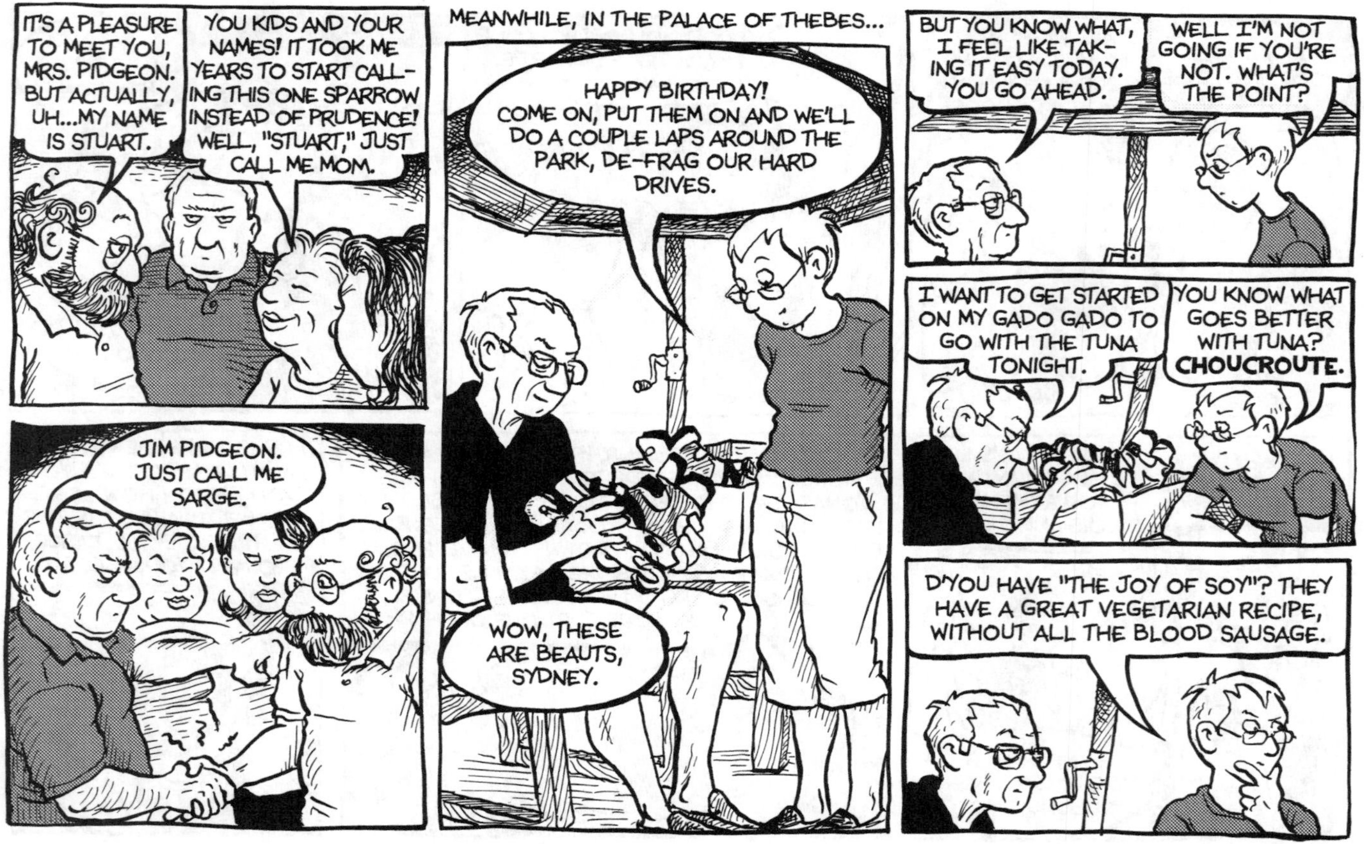

IT'S A PLEASURE TO MEET YOU, MRS. PIDGEON. BUT ACTUALLY, UH...MY NAME IS STUART.
YOU KIDS AND YOUR NAMES! IT TOOK ME YEARS TO START CALLING THIS ONE SPARROW INSTEAD OF PRUDENCE! WELL, "STUART," JUST CALL ME MOM.
JIM PIDGEON. JUST CALL ME SARGE.
MEANWHILE, IN THE PALACE OF THEBES...
HAPPY BIRTHDAY! COME ON, PUT THEM ON AND WE'LL DO A COUPLE LAPS AROUND THE PARK, DE-FRAG OUR HARD DRIVES.
WOW, THESE ARE BEAUTS, SYDNEY.
BUT YOU KNOW WHAT, I FEEL LIKE TAKING IT EASY TODAY. YOU GO AHEAD.
WELL I'M NOT GOING IF YOU'RE NOT. WHAT'S THE POINT?
I WANT TO GET STARTED ON MY GADO GADO TO GO WITH THE TUNA TONIGHT.
YOU KNOW WHAT GOES BETTER WITH TUNA? **CHOUCROUTE.**
D'YOU HAVE "THE JOY OF SOY"? THEY HAVE A GREAT VEGETARIAN RECIPE, WITHOUT ALL THE BLOOD SAUSAGE.

JENNIFER, D'YOU GUYS HAVE "THE JOY OF--" HEY, WHERE'S MO?
I THINK SHE WENT TO USE THE COMPUTER.
MARTHA BY MAIL
Re: Extramarital e-mail
Delete - Reply Reply All - Forward
From: Fiona Fingall <Ffingall@dotcom.net>
Date: Sat. Aug 17, 2002 10:19AM
To:<Mo@mindspring.com>
Subject: Re: Extramarital e-mail
Mo,
This is crazy. Marge just came in the room unexpectedly. I closed your message and clicked open the survey document in the nick of time. God, I'm slinking around like Raskolnikov. And thinking about you constantly.
I'm sorry to add fuel to our merry little fire, but the fact is, I'm completely besotted with you. The force of your intelligence, your earnestness, your awkwardness, your cowlick. Even your steadfast monogamy is appealing. But sadly, it doesn't prevent me from wanting to fling you down and
UH... HEY.
HEY. I WAS JUST LOOKING FOR YOU. UM...I HAVE TO GO GET SOME INGREDIENTS FOR MY CHOUCROUTE. WANNA COME TO THE STORE?
I THINK I'LL STAY HERE. I'M RIGHT IN THE MIDDLE OF SOMETHING.
OKAY. I'LL, UM... BRING YOU BACK A TREAT.

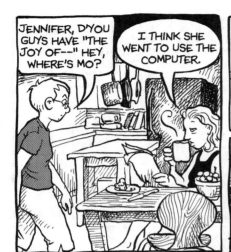

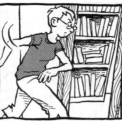

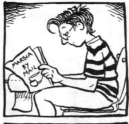

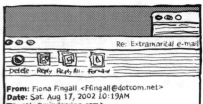

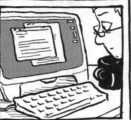

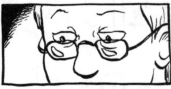

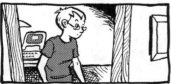

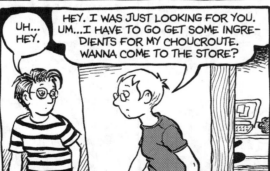

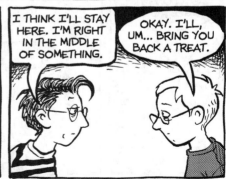

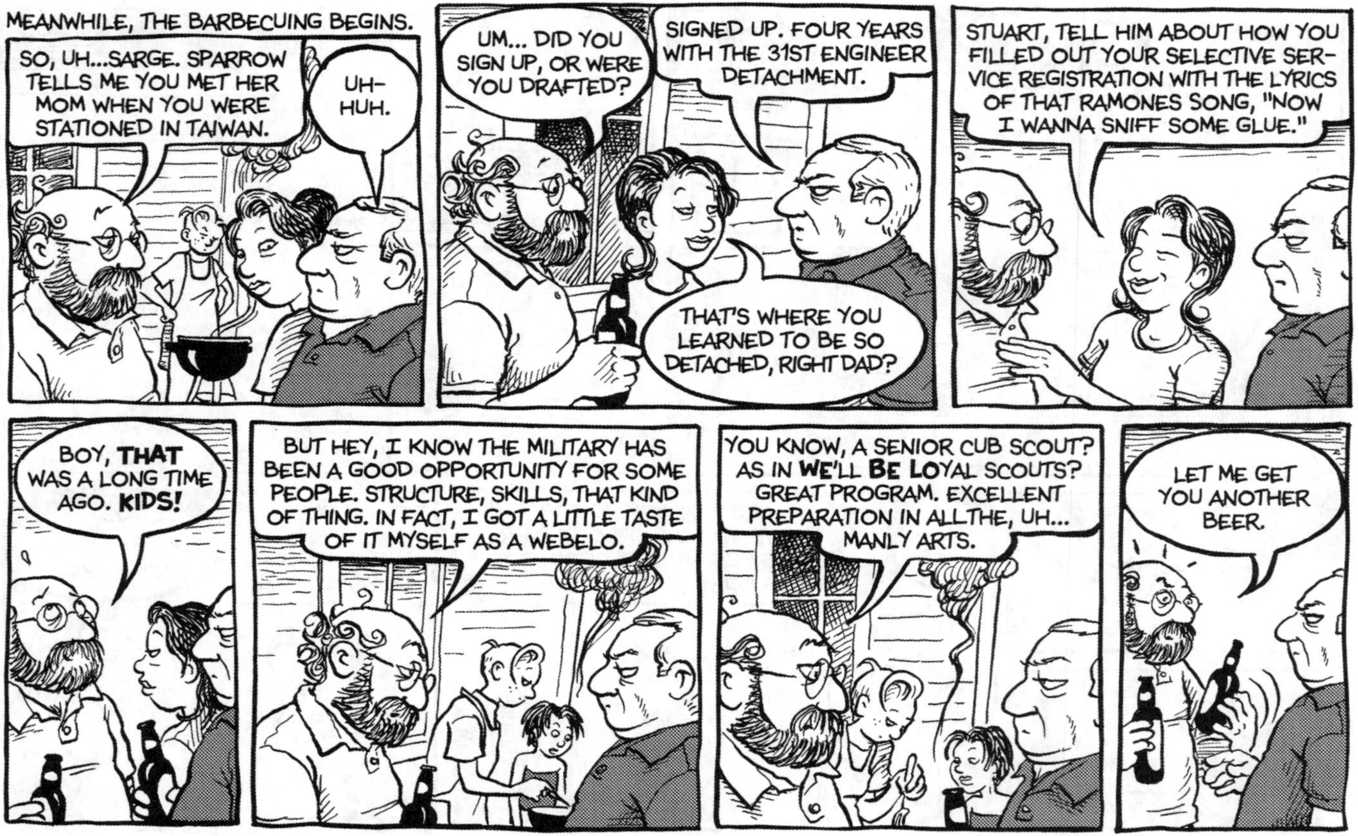
MEANWHILE, THE BARBECUING BEGINS.
SO, UH...SARGE. SPARROW TELLS ME YOU MET HER MOM WHEN YOU WERE STATIONED IN TAIWAN.
UH-HUH.
UM... DID YOU SIGN UP, OR WERE YOU DRAFTED?
SIGNED UP. FOUR YEARS WITH THE 31ST ENGINEER DETACHMENT.
THAT'S WHERE YOU LEARNED TO BE SO DETACHED, RIGHT DAD?
STUART, TELL HIM ABOUT HOW YOU FILLED OUT YOUR SELECTIVE SERVICE REGISTRATION WITH THE LYRICS OF THAT RAMONES SONG, "NOW I WANNA SNIFF SOME GLUE."
BOY, **THAT** WAS A LONG TIME AGO. **KIDS!**
BUT HEY, I KNOW THE MILITARY HAS BEEN A GOOD OPPORTUNITY FOR SOME PEOPLE. STRUCTURE, SKILLS, THAT KIND OF THING. IN FACT, I GOT A LITTLE TASTE OF IT MYSELF AS A WEBELO.
YOU KNOW, A SENIOR CUB SCOUT? AS IN **WE**'LL **BE LO**YAL SCOUTS? GREAT PROGRAM. EXCELLENT PREPARATION IN ALL THE, UH... MANLY ARTS.
LET ME GET YOU ANOTHER BEER.

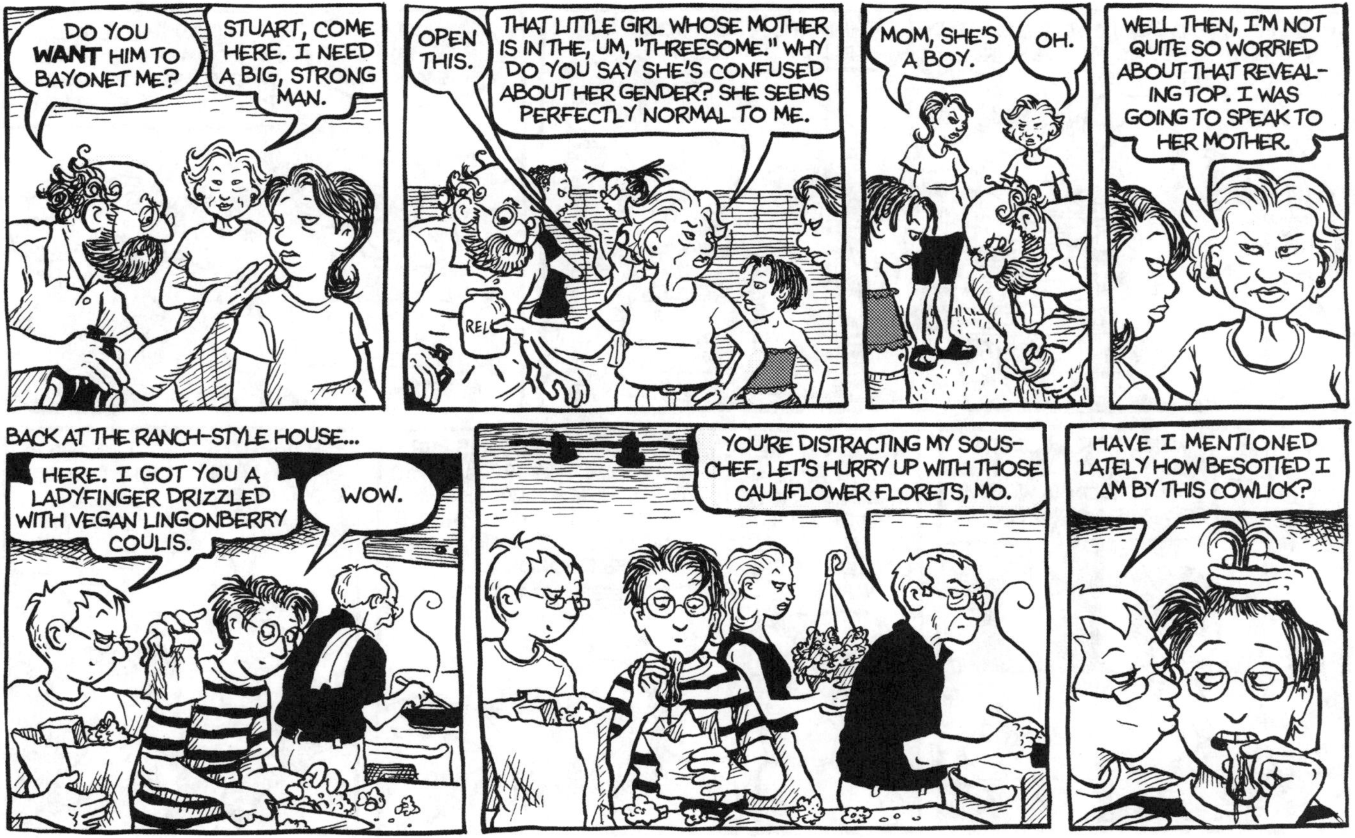
DO YOU **WANT** HIM TO BAYONET ME?
STUART, COME HERE. I NEED A BIG, STRONG MAN.
OPEN THIS.
THAT LITTLE GIRL WHOSE MOTHER IS IN THE, UM, "THREESOME." WHY DO YOU SAY SHE'S CONFUSED ABOUT HER GENDER? SHE SEEMS PERFECTLY NORMAL TO ME.
REL
MOM, SHE'S A BOY.
OH.
WELL THEN, I'M NOT QUITE SO WORRIED ABOUT THAT REVEALING TOP. I WAS GOING TO SPEAK TO HER MOTHER.
BACK AT THE RANCH-STYLE HOUSE...
HERE. I GOT YOU A LADYFINGER DRIZZLED WITH VEGAN LINGONBERRY COULIS.
WOW.
YOU'RE DISTRACTING MY SOUS-CHEF. LET'S HURRY UP WITH THOSE CAULIFLOWER FLORETS, MO.
HAVE I MENTIONED LATELY HOW BESOTTED I AM BY THIS COWLICK?

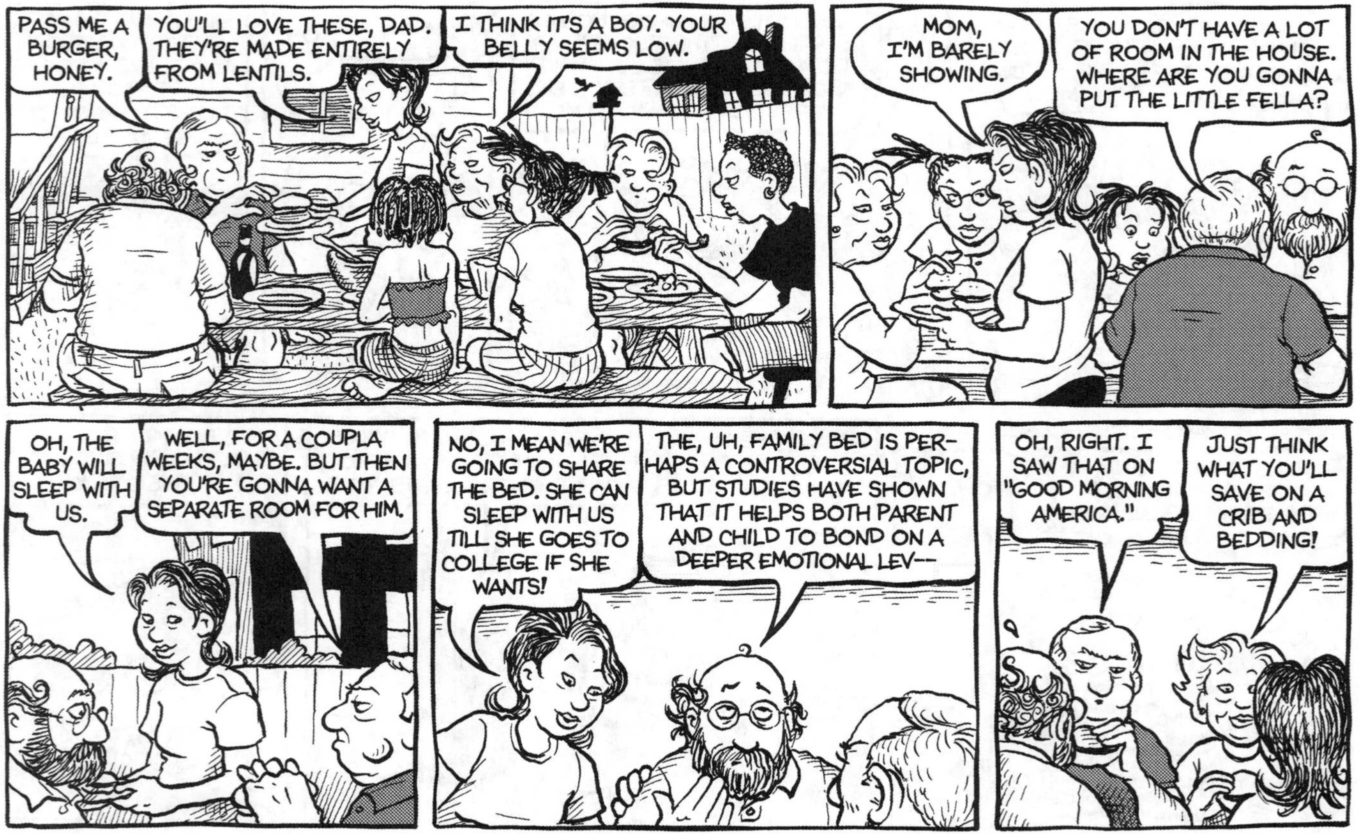
PASS ME A BURGER, HONEY.
YOU'LL LOVE THESE, DAD. THEY'RE MADE ENTIRELY FROM LENTILS.
I THINK IT'S A BOY. YOUR BELLY SEEMS LOW.
MOM, I'M BARELY SHOWING.
YOU DON'T HAVE A LOT OF ROOM IN THE HOUSE. WHERE ARE YOU GONNA PUT THE LITTLE FELLA?
OH, THE BABY WILL SLEEP WITH US.
WELL, FOR A COUPLA WEEKS, MAYBE. BUT THEN YOU'RE GONNA WANT A SEPARATE ROOM FOR HIM.
NO, I MEAN WE'RE GOING TO SHARE THE BED. SHE CAN SLEEP WITH US TILL SHE GOES TO COLLEGE IF SHE WANTS!
THE, UH, FAMILY BED IS PERHAPS A CONTROVERSIAL TOPIC, BUT STUDIES HAVE SHOWN THAT IT HELPS BOTH PARENT AND CHILD TO BOND ON A DEEPER EMOTIONAL LEV--
OH, RIGHT. I SAW THAT ON "GOOD MORNING AMERICA."
JUST THINK WHAT YOU'LL SAVE ON A CRIB AND BEDDING!

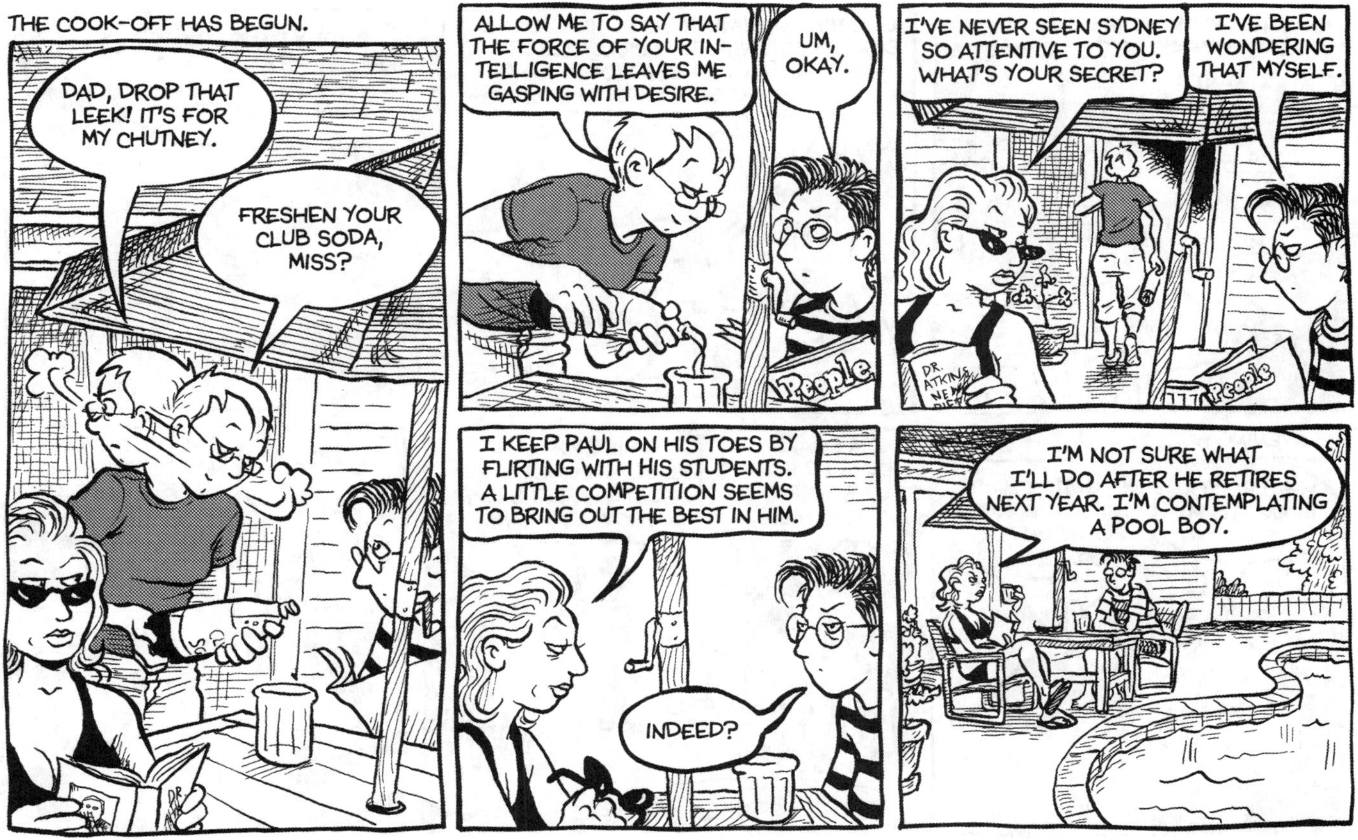
THE COOK-OFF HAS BEGUN.
DAD, DROP THAT LEEK! IT'S FOR MY CHUTNEY.
FRESHEN YOUR CLUB SODA, MISS?
ALLOW ME TO SAY THAT THE FORCE OF YOUR IN-TELLIGENCE LEAVES ME GASPING WITH DESIRE.
UM, OKAY.
People
I'VE NEVER SEEN SYDNEY SO ATTENTIVE TO YOU. WHAT'S YOUR SECRET?
I'VE BEEN WONDERING THAT MYSELF.
People
I KEEP PAUL ON HIS TOES BY FLIRTING WITH HIS STUDENTS. A LITTLE COMPETITION SEEMS TO BRING OUT THE BEST IN HIM.
INDEED?
I'M NOT SURE WHAT I'LL DO AFTER HE RETIRES NEXT YEAR. I'M CONTEMPLATING A POOL BOY.

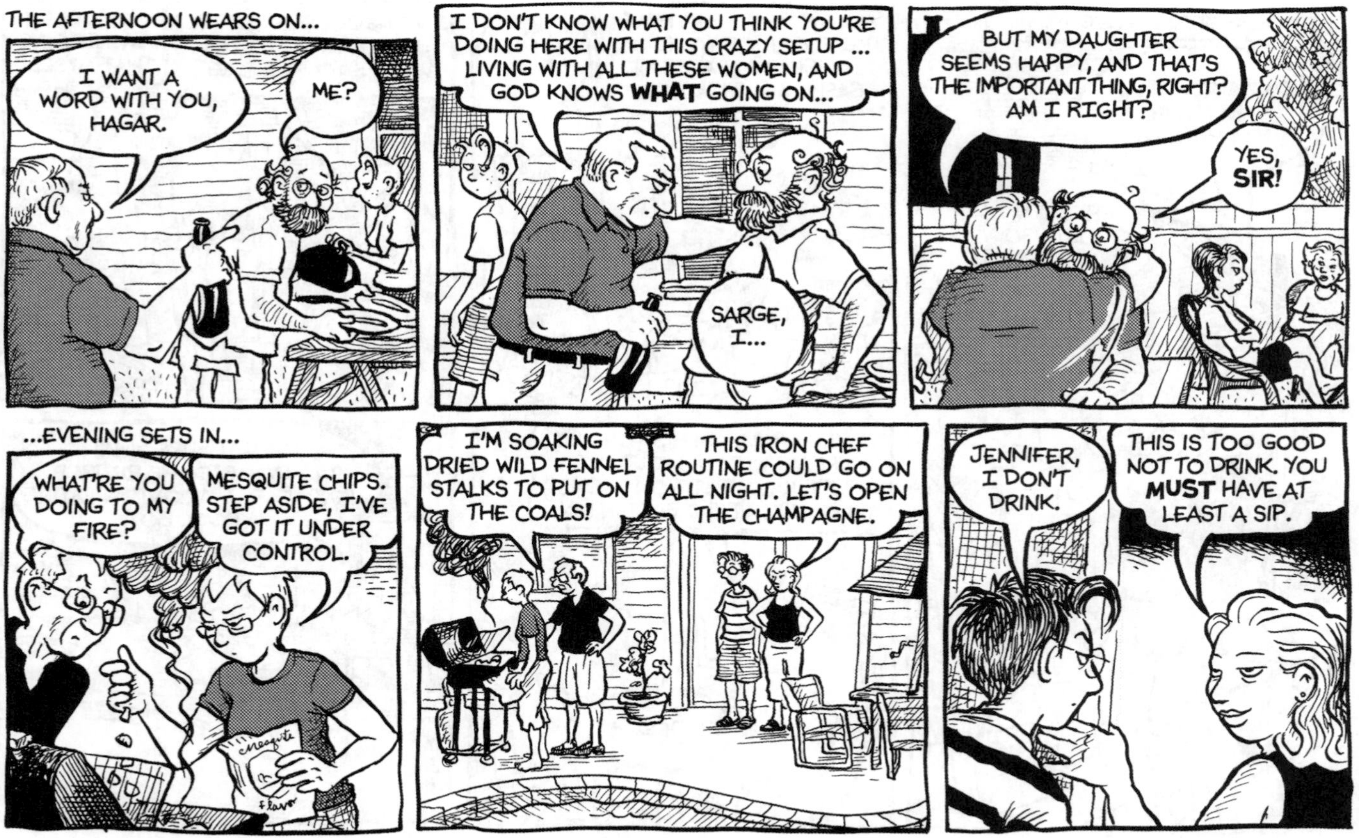
THE AFTERNOON WEARS ON...
I WANT A WORD WITH YOU, HAGAR.
ME?
I DON'T KNOW WHAT YOU THINK YOU'RE DOING HERE WITH THIS CRAZY SETUP ... LIVING WITH ALL THESE WOMEN, AND GOD KNOWS **WHAT** GOING ON...
SARGE, I...
BUT MY DAUGHTER SEEMS HAPPY, AND THAT'S THE IMPORTANT THING, RIGHT? AM I RIGHT?
YES, **SIR**!
...EVENING SETS IN...
WHAT'RE YOU DOING TO MY FIRE?
MESQUITE CHIPS. STEP ASIDE, I'VE GOT IT UNDER CONTROL.
Mesquite
I'M SOAKING DRIED WILD FENNEL STALKS TO PUT ON THE COALS!
THIS IRON CHEF ROUTINE COULD GO ON ALL NIGHT. LET'S OPEN THE CHAMPAGNE.
JENNIFER, I DON'T DRINK.
THIS IS TOO GOOD NOT TO DRINK. YOU **MUST** HAVE AT LEAST A SIP.

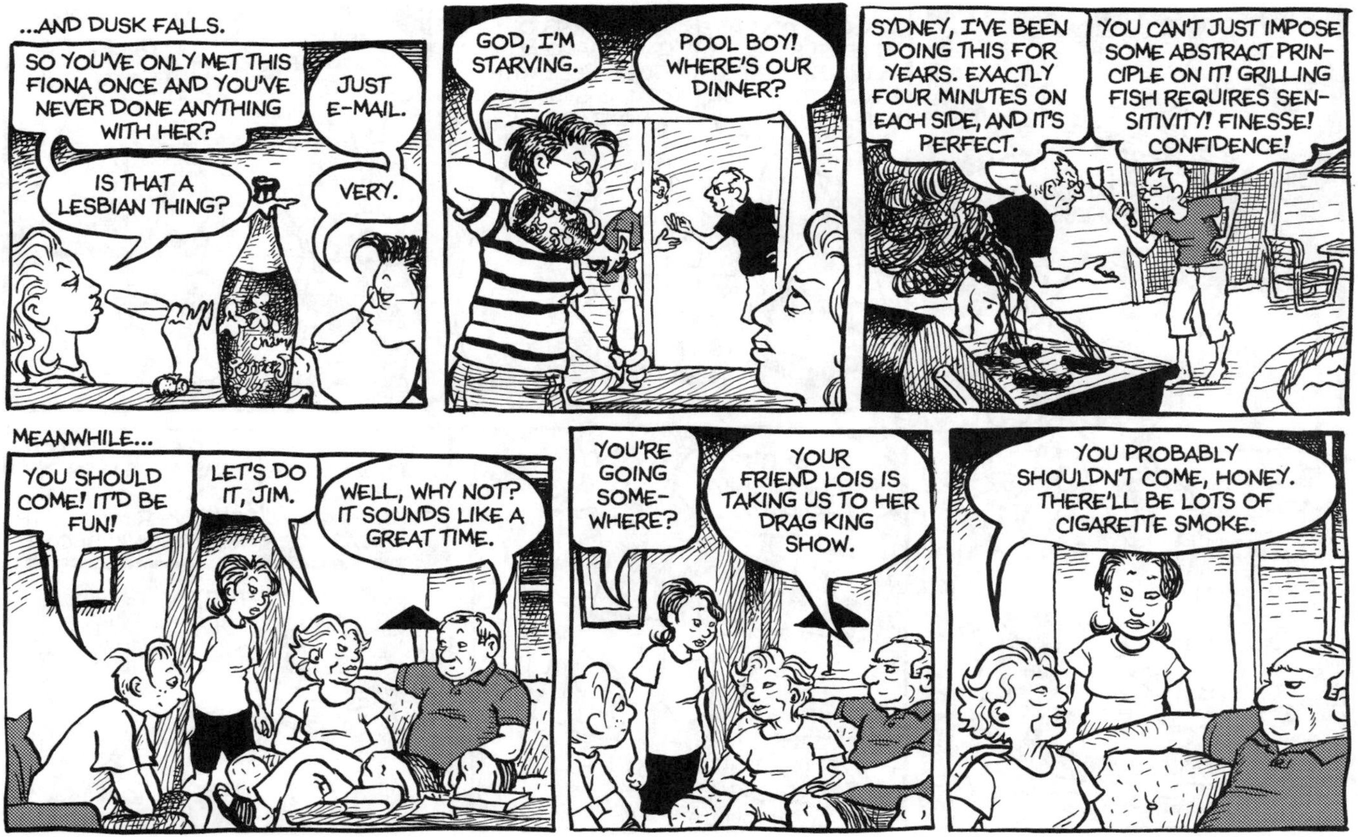
...AND DUSK FALLS.
SO YOU'VE ONLY MET THIS FIONA ONCE AND YOU'VE NEVER DONE ANYTHING WITH HER?
JUST E-MAIL.
IS THAT A LESBIAN THING?
VERY.
GOD, I'M STARVING.
POOL BOY! WHERE'S OUR DINNER?
SYDNEY, I'VE BEEN DOING THIS FOR YEARS. EXACTLY FOUR MINUTES ON EACH SIDE, AND IT'S PERFECT.
YOU CAN'T JUST IMPOSE SOME ABSTRACT PRINCIPLE ON IT! GRILLING FISH REQUIRES SENSITIVITY! FINESSE! CONFIDENCE!
MEANWHILE...
YOU SHOULD COME! IT'D BE FUN!
LET'S DO IT, JIM.
WELL, WHY NOT? IT SOUNDS LIKE A GREAT TIME.
YOU'RE GOING SOMEWHERE?
YOUR FRIEND LOIS IS TAKING US TO HER DRAG KING SHOW.
YOU PROBABLY SHOULDN'T COME, HONEY. THERE'LL BE LOTS OF CIGARETTE SMOKE.

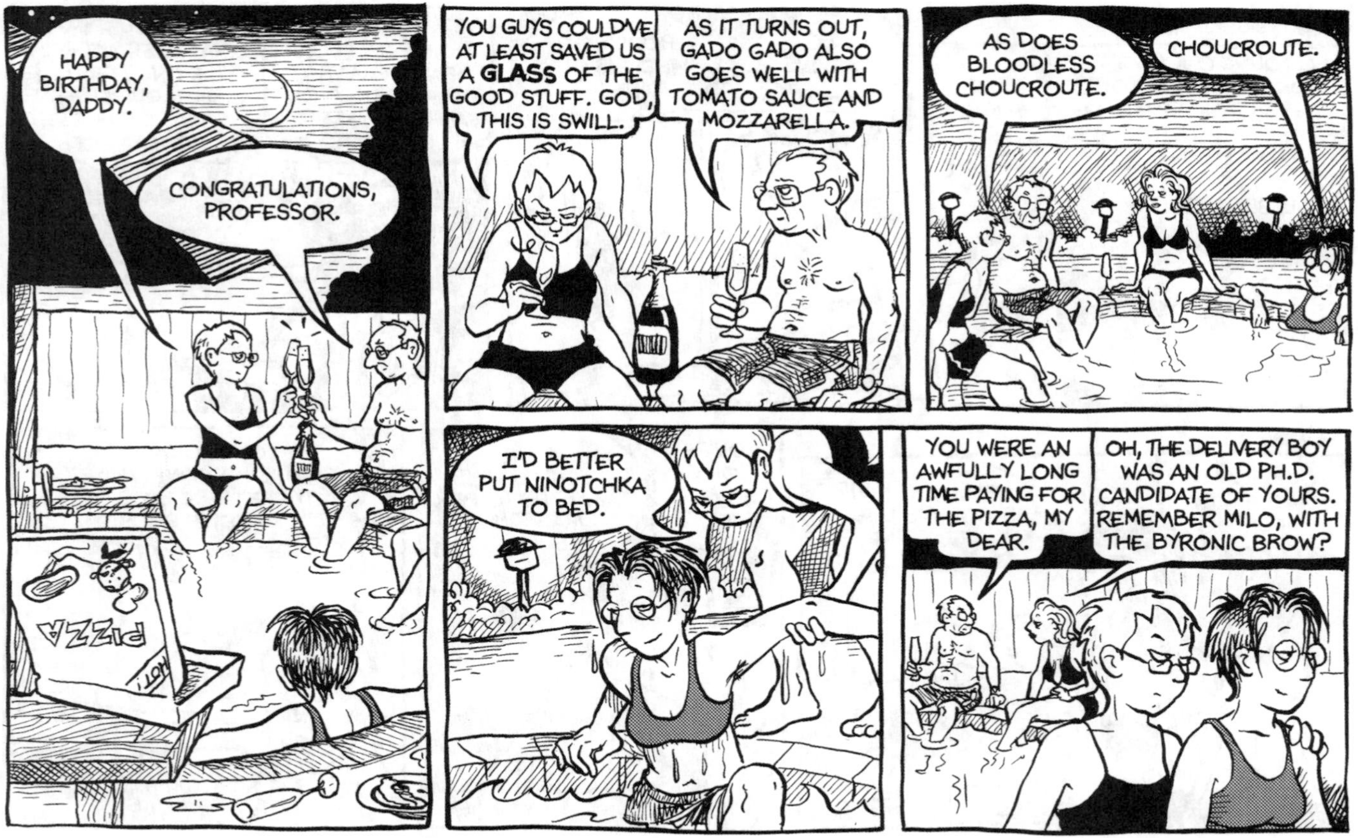
HAPPY BIRTHDAY, DADDY.
CONGRATULATIONS, PROFESSOR.
YOU GUYS COULD'VE AT LEAST SAVED US A **GLASS** OF THE GOOD STUFF. GOD, THIS IS SWILL.
AS IT TURNS OUT, GADO GADO ALSO GOES WELL WITH TOMATO SAUCE AND MOZZARELLA.
AS DOES BLOODLESS CHOUCROUTE.
CHOUCROUTE.
I'D BETTER PUT NINOTCHKA TO BED.
YOU WERE AN AWFULLY LONG TIME PAYING FOR THE PIZZA, MY DEAR.
OH, THE DELIVERY BOY WAS AN OLD PH.D. CANDIDATE OF YOURS. REMEMBER MILO, WITH THE BYRONIC BROW?

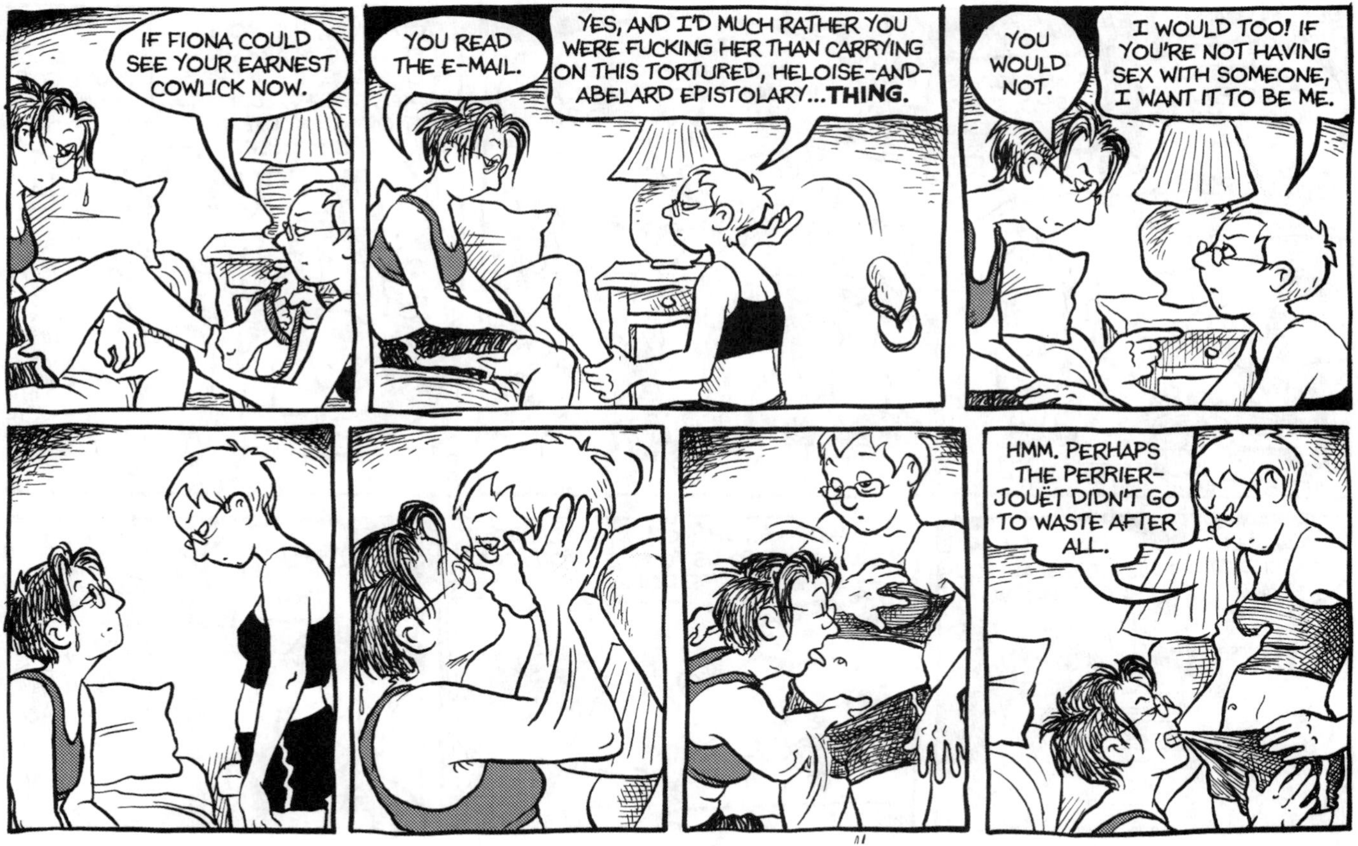
IF FIONA COULD SEE YOUR EARNEST COWLICK NOW.
YOU READ THE E-MAIL.
YES, AND I'D MUCH RATHER YOU WERE FUCKING HER THAN CARRYING ON THIS TORTURED, HELOISE-AND-ABELARD EPISTOLARY...**THING.**
YOU WOULD NOT.
I WOULD TOO! IF YOU'RE NOT HAVING SEX WITH SOMEONE, I WANT IT TO BE ME.
HMM. PERHAPS THE PERRIER-JOUËT DIDN'T GO TO WASTE AFTER ALL.

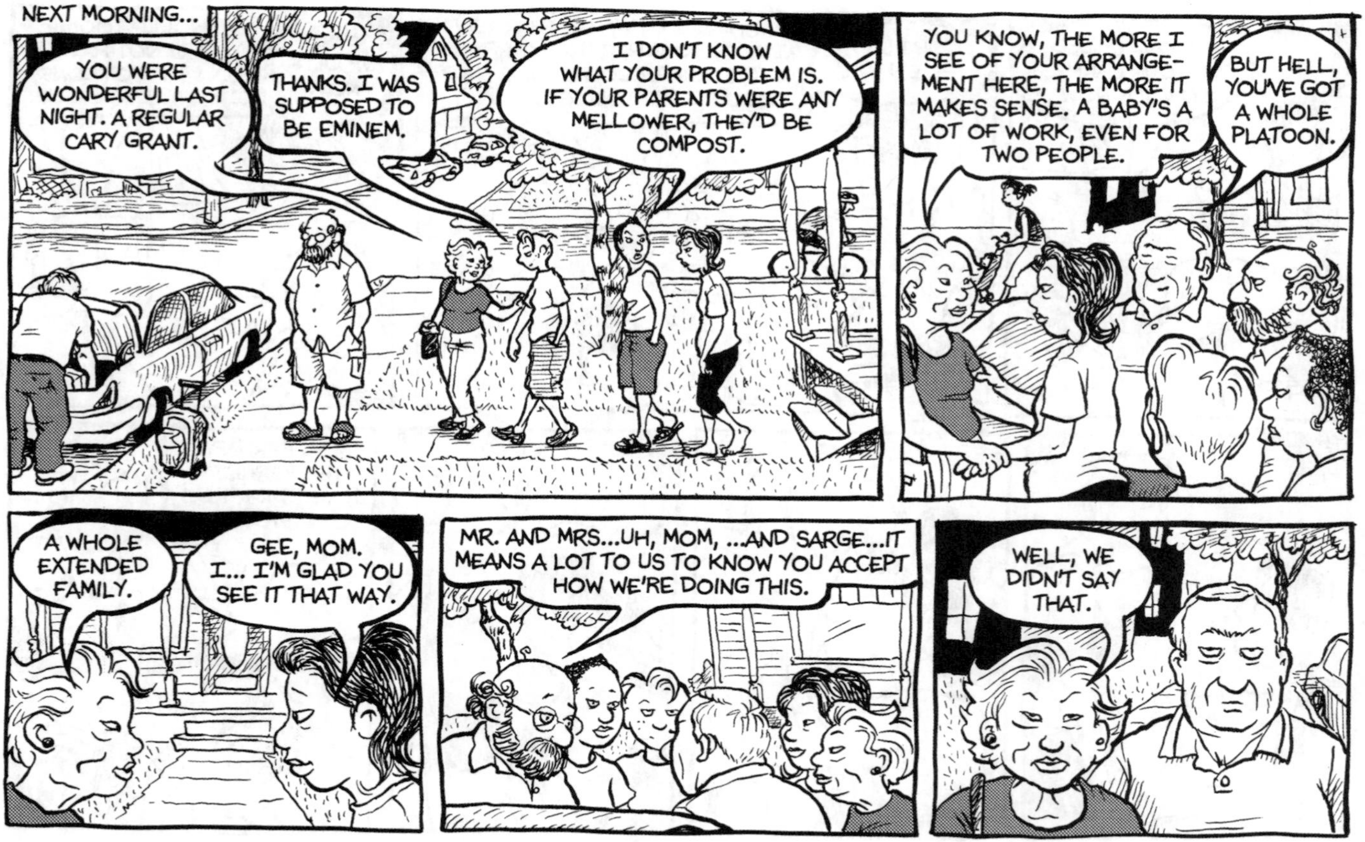
NEXT MORNING...
YOU WERE WONDERFUL LAST NIGHT. A REGULAR CARY GRANT.
THANKS. I WAS SUPPOSED TO BE EMINEM.
I DON'T KNOW WHAT YOUR PROBLEM IS. IF YOUR PARENTS WERE ANY MELLOWER, THEY'D BE COMPOST.
YOU KNOW, THE MORE I SEE OF YOUR ARRANGE-MENT HERE, THE MORE IT MAKES SENSE. A BABY'S A LOT OF WORK, EVEN FOR TWO PEOPLE.
BUT HELL, YOU'VE GOT A WHOLE PLATOON.
A WHOLE EXTENDED FAMILY.
GEE, MOM. I... I'M GLAD YOU SEE IT THAT WAY.
MR. AND MRS...UH, MOM, ...AND SARGE...IT MEANS A LOT TO US TO KNOW YOU ACCEPT HOW WE'RE DOING THIS.
WELL, WE DIDN'T SAY THAT.

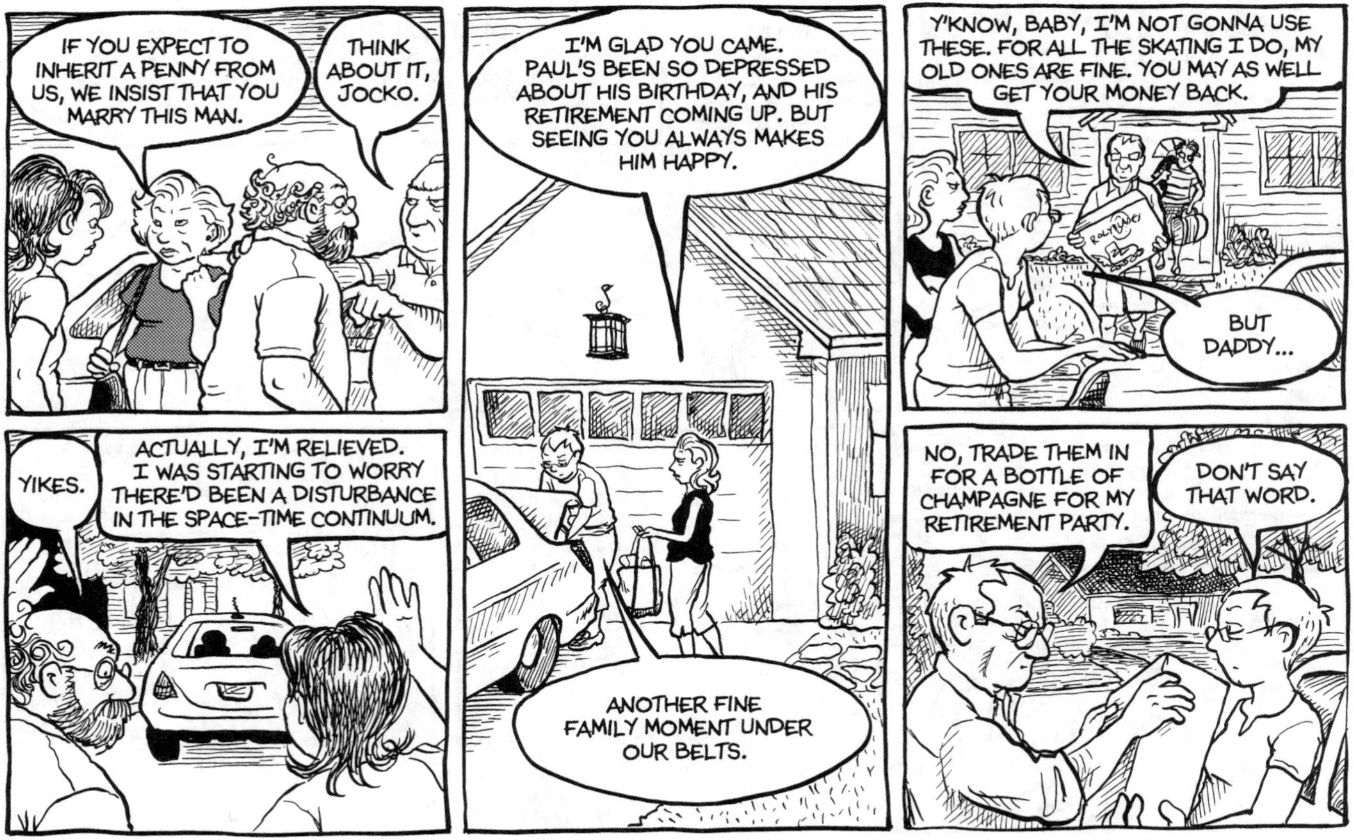
IF YOU EXPECT TO INHERIT A PENNY FROM US, WE INSIST THAT YOU MARRY THIS MAN.
THINK ABOUT IT, JOCKO.
I'M GLAD YOU CAME. PAUL'S BEEN SO DEPRESSED ABOUT HIS BIRTHDAY, AND HIS RETIREMENT COMING UP. BUT SEEING YOU ALWAYS MAKES HIM HAPPY.
ANOTHER FINE FAMILY MOMENT UNDER OUR BELTS.
Y'KNOW, BABY, I'M NOT GONNA USE THESE. FOR ALL THE SKATING I DO, MY OLD ONES ARE FINE. YOU MAY AS WELL GET YOUR MONEY BACK.
BUT DADDY...
YIKES.
ACTUALLY, I'M RELIEVED. I WAS STARTING TO WORRY THERE'D BEEN A DISTURBANCE IN THE SPACE-TIME CONTINUUM.
NO, TRADE THEM IN FOR A BOTTLE OF CHAMPAGNE FOR MY RETIREMENT PARTY.
DON'T SAY THAT WORD.

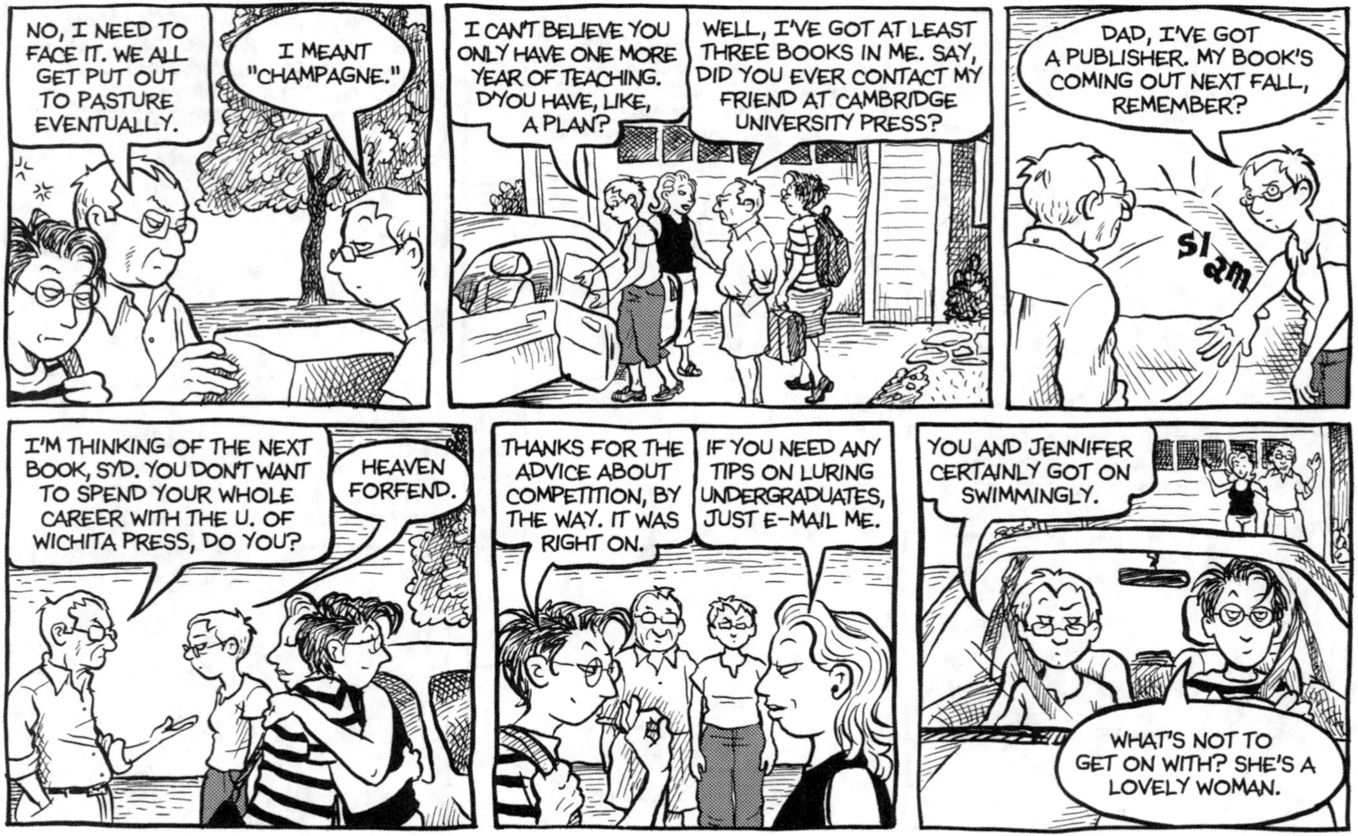
NO, I NEED TO FACE IT. WE ALL GET PUT OUT TO PASTURE EVENTUALLY.
I MEANT "CHAMPAGNE."
I CAN'T BELIEVE YOU ONLY HAVE ONE MORE YEAR OF TEACHING. D'YOU HAVE, LIKE, A PLAN?
WELL, I'VE GOT AT LEAST THREE BOOKS IN ME. SAY, DID YOU EVER CONTACT MY FRIEND AT CAMBRIDGE UNIVERSITY PRESS?
DAD, I'VE GOT A PUBLISHER. MY BOOK'S COMING OUT NEXT FALL, REMEMBER?
slam
I'M THINKING OF THE NEXT BOOK, SYD. YOU DON'T WANT TO SPEND YOUR WHOLE CAREER WITH THE U. OF WICHITA PRESS, DO YOU?
HEAVEN FORFEND.
THANKS FOR THE ADVICE ABOUT COMPETITION, BY THE WAY. IT WAS RIGHT ON.
IF YOU NEED ANY TIPS ON LURING UNDERGRADUATES, JUST E-MAIL ME.
YOU AND JENNIFER CERTAINLY GOT ON SWIMMINGLY.
WHAT'S NOT TO GET ON WITH? SHE'S A LOVELY WOMAN.